The West and the World

A History of Civilization

FROM THE ANCIENT WORLD TO 1700

KEVIN REILLY

 Markus Wiener Publishers
Princeton

To My Mother and Father

First Markus Wiener Publishers Edition, 1997

Cover Illustration: Marco Polo leaving Venice from *The Books of the GrandKhan;* c. 1400; The Bodleian Library, Oxford; ms. Bodl. 246, fd. 218r. Text Art: Fineline Illustrations, Inc.

For permission to use copyrighted material, grateful acknowledgement is made to the copyright holders on pages 356–357, which are hereby made part of this copyright page.

For information write to:
Markus Wiener Publishers
114 Jefferson Road, Princeton, NJ 08540

Library of Congress Cataloging-in-Publication Data

Reilly, Kevin, 1941-
The West and the world: a history of civilization from the ancient world to 1700/Kevin Reilly
Originally published: 2nd ed. New York: Harper & Row, © 1989.
Includes bibliographical references and index
ISBN 1-55876-152-7 (alk. paper)
1. Civilization, Western.   2. Civilization—History.
I. Title.
[CB245.R44   1997]
909'.09821—dc21   96-37674   CIP

✵ Contents ✵

MAPS

Topical Outline

WOMEN AND MEN

CITY AND CIVILIZATION

RELIGION AND SOCIETY

WAR AND PEACE

✂ Preface ✂

The West and the World has been greatly revised for this second edition. Perhaps most obviously, it is larger and more thorough. Volume I contains a new chapter on the great religious traditions and the social history of aging and the family (Chapter 4) and new material on Asian and Islamic societies in the chapters on cities, individuality, love, war, and ecology. Volume II contains three new chapters (Chapters 8, 10, and 13) on the theme of the book's title—the interaction of Western powers and the other countries of the world. It also includes new material on African history in chapters on racism and ecology (Chapters 7 and 12) and additional Asian history in the chapters on individuality (Chapters 1 and 11). The number of illustrations and maps has also been increased proportionately.

The second edition is also tighter and more sharply focused than the first. In the first volume, the more speculative chapters on gender (Chapters 1 and 2) have been entirely rewritten and refined. In both volumes, the chronological organization has been strengthened. There are now four, rather than two periods delineated between 1500 and the present, and all periods are introduced by chronological surveys.

The first edition of *The West and the World* in 1980 was intended to suggest ways in which the traditional western civilization course could become more global. Since 1980, there has been a growing recognition in American schools and colleges that knowledge of the world beyond Europe will be an essential ingredient of the education of citizens for the twenty-first century. World history and world civilization courses have been devised to meet that need. The second edition of *The West and the World* is offered as a contribution to the developing dialogue on the question of how world history and world civilization courses might be taught best in American colleges.

Some of the most common answers to that question are revised versions of the western civilization course. One such model is the encyclopedic survey, which disclaims interpretation or point of view. At its best this model is thorough and fair; at its worst it is bloodless and dull. Among more interpretive accounts, the most obvious is the attempt to tell a single story that reveals the main "turning points" in world history. This is often best accomplished by concentrating on major technological stages (e.g., agricultural, urban, industrial) but there are also versions that emphasize scientific, economic, and social changes that occurred generally, though not simultaneously, in the world. A second interpretive approach is the attempt to trace the developing intercommunication of an ever-expanding "human community." By this account world history becomes largely the story of contacts, diffusions, dispersions, migrations, and trade. It is the story of the gradual formation of a single world. Another model is "the history of civilization," usually told as a linear march up the high road. Though global versions give due account of the "contributions" of the less fortunate, these histories tend to be elitist in their concentration on the "high culture" and judgmental in their efforts to distribute credits for achievements. The "Great Books" approach is a variant of this. Less elitist is the "comparative culture," or comparative civilization approach, which attempts to characterize the essence of each great tradition, though it often loses the thread of historical context by taking each culture as a timeless whole.

The second edition of *The West and the World* incorporates elements of some of the more successful of these models of world history. Like the first two interpretive models, it attempts to tell a single coherent story of the world's major "turning points" and the story of an expanding human community. Like the high culture and "Great Books" approaches, it takes ideas and thinkers seriously. Like the great comparative cultures approach, it attempts to explore the character of individual cultures and civilizations, both to understand human diversity and to understand ourselves.

The West and the World suggests an additional model for the world history or world civilization course, however. It suggests that the value of a history course is not only in the names, dates, and even stories and interpretations remembered. It argues that the main value of a history course is in teaching students to think historically. For the ancient Greeks, I pointed out in the first edition, history was a verb. *Historia* meant inquiry. Today, in a world that changes every fifteen minutes, what could be more useful to students than to teach them to think historically? To think about the relation of the past to the present, to learn to ask questions of the past that enable us to understand the present and mold the future, to become attuned to both the limitations and the possibilities of change—these are the skills that the twenty-first century already cries out for.

The effort to teach students to think historically can be accomplished with any subject matter. But students can be approached most directly, and shown the value of historical inquiry most vividly, if we ask *their* questions and those posed by contemporary society. We do well to avoid the faddish formulations of these questions that allow only shallow historical answers because they deny the relevance of the past. We must pose questions that explain structural changes rather than ephemeral ones, questions that mine the past as process or prologue. Thus, I have chosen for *The West and the World* a series of questions that are of both present and perennial concern. These may be summarized most generally as the questions of gender, urban life, war and peace, personal identity, religion and society (which are explored in the first volume) and of autonomy, political morality, economic life, race and class, and of national and international loyalty (which are the subjects of the second volume). These issues may be studied with either topical or chronological categories as the primary focus. No one can think historically without the abstract schema of chronology and the specific dates that give that schema meaning. But neither the dates nor the chronological schema is a substitute for reasoned inquiry about the significance of the past. Students will have mastered *The West and the World* (even those who forget the specifics) if they make the spontaneous, but disciplined, inquiry of the past one of their more precious tools for understanding their present and creating their future.

ACKNOWLEDGMENTS

The first edition of this book bore the birthmarks of a very special time and place: Rutgers University in the 1960s. Eugene J. Meehan forced students to think for themselves by gleefully dismissing our most cherished prejudices. The late Warren Susman taught us that everything had a history. In a few paces on the stage, he would march back and forth through centuries. The sound of a fist smashing on the podium (and once of a broken watch) reminded us that historical interpretations mattered. Traian Stoianovich stared several millennia beyond the last row of students and whispered magical formulas that were scribbled down for later decoding and discussion. His disciples spoke of camels and dromedaries and uttered French phrases understood only by themselves and other intellectual "grandchildren" of Fernand Braudel. Donald Weinstein guided some of us through our first classes as teaching assistants, teaching us to listen as well as talk, and showing by his own example that the key to good teaching was talking *with* students, not *at* them.

The first edition of this book could not have been written without teachers like these. Rutgers in the 1960s also afforded me the opportunity to learn from faculty members like Eugene Genovese, John Lenaghan, Paul Massing, and Peter Stearns, and fellow students like Robert Rosen, Abdelwahab Elmessiri, and Steven Gosch. While it has become fashionable in some circles to criticize the student activism and progressive pedagogy of that decade, I have never known a more intellectually curious, academically serious, and socially responsible generation of students than my fellow students at Rutgers in the 1960s and my own students at Rutgers and the community college in the late 1960s and early 1970s.

Somerset County College, now Raritan Valley Community College, called me in 1969 to teach world history at a time when few such courses were offered anywhere. The natural interdisciplinary environment of a small school, with only one other historian, and the hunger of the students for useful knowledge about such matters as war and peace helped shape the course along the broadest humanistic lines. My closest friendships with a poet, Gerald Stern, a philosopher, David Massie, and a film teacher, Mark Bezanson, ensured a moveable feast of conversation about students, teaching and (as we used to say) "life," rather than departmental politics or academic specialties. Later, with the help of faculty members from many disciplines—Tom Valasek, Brock Haussamen and Myrna Smith in English; Mark Cozin and Steve Kaufman in social sciences; Jere Jones in philosophy, Paul Lorenzi in art history, among others—Bud McKinley, the other world historian, and I were able to develop a world history course as the basis of a general humanities program.

The second edition of *The West and the World* owes debts as global as its subject. It was in Cameroon, West Africa, where I first met twelve Americans, fellow participants on a study/travel tour organized by the American Historical Association (with funding from the U.S. Department of Education and the Exxon Educational Foundation), who have aided me at every turn since. Lynda Shaffer (Tufts University) has argued relentlessly with every one of my Western conceits and she has tirelessly corrected my ignorance of Chinese (and, more recently, Native American) history. John Russell-Wood (Johns Hopkins University) detailed the finest, most thorough criticism of my Latin American material that one could hope for. Marc Gilbert forced me to rethink much of my material on India. They and the other Cameroon participants, especially Dana Greene (St. Mary's College), Sarah Hughes (Hampton University), Ray Lorantas (Drexel University), Anne Barstow (SUNY, College of Old Westbury), also provided the support that one needs as much as criticism.

The American Historical Association also provided the benefit of an invitational conference on the Introductory History Course in 1980 at Anapolis in which the first edition of *The West and the World* was one of six models examined by leading scholars and teachers. As representative of the Association to another conference, on world history at the U.S. Air Force Academy in 1982, I first met William H. McNeill (The University of Chicago), Ross Dunn (San Diego State University), Jerry Bentley (University of Hawaii), Craig Lockard (University of Wisconsin at Green Bay), Martin Yanuck and Margery Ganz (Spelman College), Ernst Menze (Iona College), and many others whose assistance and criticism have been invaluable and who, along with the "Cameroonians," became the early nucleus of the World History Association.

As President of the World History Association, I enjoyed frequent contact and stimulating conversations with many of the leading scholars and world historians in the country. Philip Curtin (Johns Hopkins University) and Leften Stavrianos

(University of California at San Diego) provided specific assistance as well as rich general visions of world history. Those who read parts of the manuscript or provided specific suggestions are too numerous to name, but they include, besides those already mentioned, Gilbert Allardyce (University of New Brunswick), Jay Anglin (University of Southern Mississippi), Imre Bard (Chaminade University), George Brooks (Indiana University), Samuel D. Ehrenpreis (Bronx Community College), Charles A. Endress (San Angelo State University), Stephen Englehart (California State Polytechnic University), Robert Gardella (U.S. Maritime Academy), Joseph Gowaskie (Rider College), Joseph Grabhill (Illinois State University, Normal), James Long (Colorado State University), Bullitt Lowry (North Texas State University), David C. Lukowitz (Hamline University), John A. Mears (Southern Methodist University), David Northrup (Boston College), Jim Odom (East Tennessee State University), Richard Overfield (University of Nebraska), Robert Roeder (University of Denver), Arnold Schrier (University of Cincinnati), Stephen J. Simon (Appalachian State University), Loyd S. Swenson (University of Houston), Mary Evelyn Tucker (Iona College), Daniel Warshaw (Fairleigh Dickinson University), and Michael F. Zaremski (Iona College).

I also enjoyed special help, careful readings, and vigorous discussions from the participants in two NEH summer seminars, one on the history and literature of aging that was directed by David van Tassel (Case Western Reserve University) and the other on comparative imperialism that was directed by Robin Winks (Yale University). The Department of Higher Education of New Jersey and Rutgers University also provided the funding for my participation in a seminar on immigration, directed by Virginia Yans-McLaughlin, in which I was able to prepare the maps of major world migrations that are presented in the text (and on a large globe at Ellis Island). Two other Rutgers professors, Michael Adas and Allen Howard, gave me the benefit of their thorough readings of both editions, providing detailed criticism and suggestions. Obviously, none of these individuals are responsible for any quirks or errors that might remain.

I would like to thank those at Harper & Row, including history editor Lauren Silverman and project editor Bonnie Biller, who seemed to take a personal interest in the text, despite all of their other obligations, and ensured the usual high production standards of the house. And finally, from house to home, I would like to thank Pearl for her careful editing, but also for her loving support and her faith, often stronger than my own, that this too would someday come to pass.

Kevin Reilly

✖ Note on Chinese Spelling ✖

Two different systems are in use in the world today for the spelling of Chinese words with Roman letters. One is the Wade-Giles system, developed by missionaries and used by almost all Western scholars until fairly recently. The other is the pinyin system, used by the scholars and government of the People's Republic of China. The pinyin system is probably the most accurate, at least once one gets used to pronouncing "Q" as "Ch," and "X" as "Sh." It is also becoming the standard. The problem with using only the pinyin system is that most English library books and references are Wade-Giles transliterations.

The solution adopted here is to use the pinyin system but to add the Wade-Giles equivalent in brackets (e.g., Song [Sung]) the first time the word is used. Thus, in most cases, the first use of a Chinese term will contain the version that is most accurate for pronunciation and future recognition followed by a bracketed version that is most useful for library research.

There are only a couple of exceptions to this procedure. The Wade-Giles equivalent will not be added when it is the same as the pinyin or when the only difference is an apostrophe or hyphen (e.g., Tang, T'ang or fengshui, feng-shui). Furthermore, in some cases, the first mention of the word will be only in the pinyin or Wade-Giles format. This is in the case of an author's spelling of his or her own name and in the quotation of original sources or translations. Sources that are translated in Wade-Giles are presented in the original format with pinyin equivalents indicated in the citation note. This is to avoid changing the intent of the original author or translator and to allow the quote to read smoothly.

❧ I ❧

The
Ancient
World

To 1000 B.C.

(Head from a statue of Queen Nefertiti, queen of King Akhenaten. Plaster cast of a painted limestone original now in Berlin. The Metropolitan Museum of Art. Rogers Fund, 1925.)

Preview of the Period

To 1000 B.C.

The earth is about five billion years old. Humans are very recent inhabitants. The earliest ancestors of humans evolved from the apes about five million years ago. They stood erect, hunted, used tools, and controlled fire about one million years ago. The first humans who were "anatomically modern," or looked like us, originated in East Africa about one hundred thousand years ago. By about forty thousand years ago, they replaced the only other human competitors, the Neanderthals, and spread throughout Europe and Asia. Some time around twenty thousand years ago, during the last Ice Age, they also spread to the Western Hemisphere.

The most important change in the lives of these humans was the shift from a hunting and gathering way of life (called *paleolithic* or Old Stone Age) to the development of an agricultural *(neolithic* or New Stone Age) life-style about ten thousand years ago.

The Agricultural Revolution (to 4000 B.C.).   We speak of hunting and gathering people as Old Stone Age people because of the roughness of the stones they chipped and hacked into axes and arrowheads. Old Stone Age is Paleolithic in Greek.

The tool kit of Paleolithic hunters and gatherers included more than stone axes and arrowheads. It also included the use of fire for cooking and warmth, and the use of language, though not in written form. Cave art, mainly paintings of animals with some humans, also shows the beginnings of what we might call religion.

The agricultural revolution has been called the Neolithic, or New Stone Age, revolution because it accompanied the development of more finely polished "new stone" tools. It

3

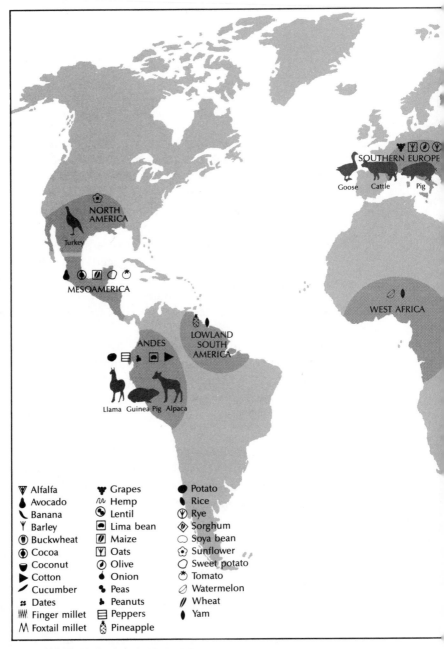

CENTERS OF DOMESTICATION
The Neolithic Revolution brought the domestication of animals as well as plants. Here we see some of the early centers of domestication.

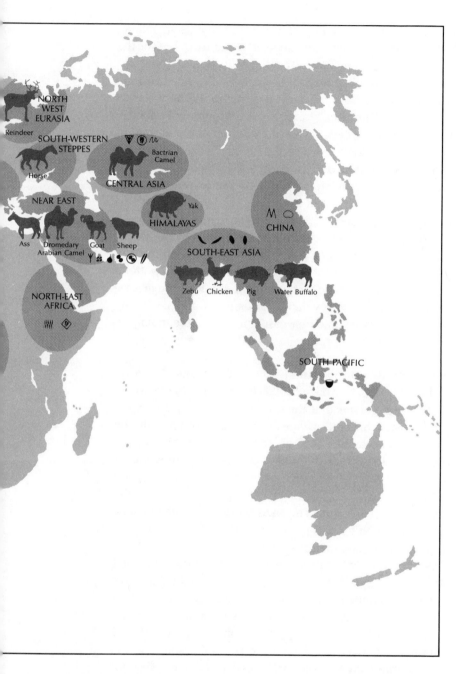

Each part of the world domesticated some of the plants and animals shared by the entire world today.

was one of the most important turning points in human history, not for the improvements in stone work but for the development of agriculture. The domestication of wheat and barley in the Middle East around 10,000 B.C., of rice in Southeast Asia about 6000 B.C., and of corn in Middle America about 8000 B.C. drastically transformed the human balance. Agriculture permitted a vast increase in the number of mouths that could be fed; a corresponding increase in population density; a settled life in villages, since people no longer needed to wander for food; and the production of storage containers, dwellings, and textiles. Agriculture also encouraged the development of earth goddesses, fertility cults, and rudimentary forms of science and government.

The development of metallurgy, especially the production of bronze, and the invention of the wheel, carts, and potter's wheels (around 4000 B.C.) may be seen as a further elaboration of the Neolithic revolution or as the first stage of the "urban revolution." In either case, the rate of technological innovation in these preliterate societies was enormous.

The Urban Revolution and Early Civilizations: The Middle East and North Africa (3000–1000 B.C.). In the broadest historical perspective, the urban revolution is one of the three most significant changes in human history. Only the agricultural revolution 5000 years before it, and the "industrial revolution" 5000 years after it, changed the world as much. The urban revolution created what we call (for good and ill) "civilization." We might attempt to enumerate the elements of civilization. The division of labor, nonfarming specialists (such as artisans, craftsworkers, priests, scribes, tax collectors, jewelers, engineers, court officials, and soldiers), and social class itself are as much products of the first cities as the irrigation canals and dams that enabled them to thrive. Governments, laws, police, citizenship, markets, and wars are the political contributions. Astronomy, calendars, writing, record keeping, temples, monuments, and the belief in immortality may be some of the cultural results.

The earliest civilizations originated in ancient Mesopotamia in the Middle East. The first cities (Sumer, Ur, Lagash,

Nippur, and Eridu) were situated on the Euphrates River near where its waters passed into the Persian Gulf, but political power gradually passed upriver along the Tigris-Euphrates Valley to envious herders who smelled the sweetness of city life. Their conquests also changed the nature of city life. Relatively independent "city-states" were replaced by empires ruled by kings like Sargon of Akkad around 2600 B.C., and then emperors, like Hammurabi of Babylon after 2000 B.C.

Civilization came to Egypt after it came to Mesopotamia. Ancient Egyptian civilization was less dynamic but more peaceful than Mesopotamian. Both were river valley civilizations, but the flooding of the Nile was predictable, and that of the Euphrates was not. Egyptian civilization was more placid, stable, and conservative, perhaps as a result. This may also account for the continuity from the Old to Middle to New Kingdom, and for the centralization of the pharaoh's realm. Egyptian confidence was perhaps best expressed in the science and engineering that led to the building of the pyramids, which are testaments to both assertions of immortality and an obsession with death. If Egyptian society became calcified by the New Kingdom, its culture became less elitist. Instead of tombs for a few, the god Osiris offered salvation for all, and the pharaoh Akhenaton (at least briefly in the middle of the fourteenth century B.C.) challenged the power of the priests with a religion of one god. Knowledge and immortality could not remain the monopoly of the ruling class. Nor could civilization remain the preserve of a single place. Diffusion was inherent in its expression.

Early Civilizations of South and East Asia (2500–1000 B.C.). The importance of rivers in the origins of civilization in India and China (as well as the Middle East and North Africa) can hardly go unnoticed. The Indus, Ganges, Brahmaputra (all in India), and Huang He [Huang Ho], or Yellow (in China), were essential. Ancient India can be seen as the gift of the Indus, sweeping down from the Himalayas to the Arabian Sea.

The earliest civilizations of the Indus were centered at the ancient cities of Harappa and Mohenjo Daro. They were planned cities. Private brick houses were two to three stories with private bathrooms. The sewer systems were superior to those of ancient Mesopotamia and Egypt, and to many in the world built since.

Around 1500 B.C. these ancient Indian civilizations were invaded by armies in horse-drawn chariots from the grasslands of eastern Europe and western Asia. The invasion by these so-called Aryans (whether or not it was the cause of the collapse of the Indus civilization) imposed a new religion (Brahmanism) and a new language (Indo-European Sanskrit) on the darker Dravidian peoples as the invaders pushed further south, into the central Indian plateau called the Deccan, and even to the island of Ceylon, or Sri Lanka, south of India.

The Aryan invaders taught their religion in poems called the Vedas, especially the Rig Veda. These prayers and poems show the importance of the caste system, based on the dominance of lighter skinned *brahman* priests and warriors *(kshatriya)* over darker skinned and subordinate farmers and serfs.

Chinese civilization was also fraught with invasions by nomadic warriors from the central grasslands of Eurasia. But Chinese history did not suffer the radical break that India experienced in the Aryan invasion. Chinese civilization originated in the northern Huang He Valley, where millet and wheat were cultivated. It then spread to the central Yangtze Valley, and only later still to the wet rice lands of the south.

The earliest Chinese civilization about which we have written evidence is the Huang He Valley civilization called the Shang dynasty (1766–1027 B.C.). Our evidence comes from oracle bones that were used in ancient Chinese religion. They provide especially valuable glimpses of everyday life.

The World in 1000 B.C. By 1000 B.C. the twin revolutions of agriculture and urban life had traveled far beyond their places of origin. Agriculture was known across the large Eurasian landmass, south of Siberia. It also extended around the Arabian Peninsula, down the Nile Valley, across North Africa, and along the west coast of Africa almost to the equator. In East Asia agriculture was spreading to the islands of

Sumatra, Java, Borneo, and the Philippines. Crops were also cultivated in the Americas after 7000 B.C., though by 1000 B.C. they were still concentrated in Mexico and Peru.

Cities dispersed over mainly agricultural areas from 4000 B.C. to 1000 B.C. In some areas, like India, society was less urbanized in 1000 B.C. than it had been a thousand years before. This was because of the conquests of pastoral nomadic tribes that (like the Aryans in India and the Hyksos in Egypt) used the new technology of the wheeled hunting chariot to challenge urban dominance. Even in their defeat, however, most urban civilizations passed on some of the institutions and ideas that made the new empires after 1000 B.C. more cosmopolitan than their predecessors. ⁊

℁ 1 ℁

Men
and
Women

Hunters and
Gatherers

WE LIVE IN A "MAN'S WORLD." World leaders are predominantly men. Families are usually run by men. Men earn more than women. Sons are preferred over daughters. Men have more options than women. In many countries women are relegated to the home. In many societies women become adults only through marriage, when they are "given away" by a father to a husband. Even in the United States, after years of feminist efforts, women are often "token" public officials.

Did men always exert power over women? Was there ever a time when women were more powerful than men, or when men and women were equal? Has male power existed throughout history? Is male domination universal, part of human nature? Has the power of men and women changed over the long course of human history? These are some of the questions asked in this chapter.

THE LONGEST VIEW OF MEN AND WOMEN

When we ask how the power of men and women has changed, we must take the longest view of human history. We must look at the most basic changes in human history to see how they affected men and women. To do this, historians require the help of archeologists. This is because historians normally study only written

11

records of human activity, and writing goes back only five thousand years, to the first cities, where writing was invented. Archeologists dig beneath these ancient cities for the silent records—the pieces of broken pottery and huts, the charred animal remains, the fragments of human bone, the painted shells, the stone axes and digging sticks. These actual pieces of the past reveal something about the earliest human societies before the invention of writing and city life.

An archeological dig resembles a trip back in a time machine. The further you dig, generally, the earlier the society you find. After a sufficient number of repetitions, archeologists discover (in reverse) general patterns of human development. In this way they have distinguished three stages of human development: hunting-gathering, followed by farming, followed by city life. Archeologists are even able to give approximate dates to these different stages of human development. Thus, they have determined that the first cities were created about five thousand years ago, and the earliest farming villages go back about ten thousand years.

We can summarize all of human history, then, in very rough terms. First, all humans were hunters of wild animals or gatherers of wild plants and insects. Then, gradually, after 8000 B.C., humans began to grow their own food and tame wild animals. A third stage of human history began around 3000 B.C., when the first cities appeared, generally in areas that had begun the agricultural revolution five thousand years before. The urban revolution was based on improved agricultural practices, including the use of a plow drawn by animals. The efficiency of the plow allowed society to become more specialized. Not everyone had to farm to eat. A larger population was also possible. Cities were both larger and more specialized than agricultural villages. We might even add a recent fourth stage to this outline of history. In the last two hundred years the world has experienced an industrial revolution that has increased productivity and changed human life every bit as much as the agricultural revolution did ten thousand years ago and the urban revolution did five thousand years ago.

It is safe to say that no changes in human history have been as important as these. Obviously, not all hunters, or all farmers, are alike. But the differences between hunters and farmers are much greater than the differences between any two groups of either. And while there are still farmers in city societies (since people have to eat), the lives of these farmers have been transformed by city markets, governments, tools, culture, and communications. Farmers today are very different people from those who lived before the development of the first cities five thousand years ago. If the power of men is universal, then, we should expect it to have remained relatively constant from hunting to farming to city society.

HUNTERS AND GATHERERS: SEXUAL DIVISION OF LABOR

It is a common practice among hunting-gathering societies to assign different tasks to men and women. These separate assignments go far beyond what is required by the differences in size or strength between men and women or the need of women to carry and nurse infants. In fact, some jobs are thought of as "masculine" in one society and "feminine" in another. There are certain generalizations, however, that are almost universal among hunters and gatherers.

> Everywhere men hunt large land and water fauna, trap small animals and birds, hunt birds, build boats, and work with wood, stone, bone, horn and shell. Everywhere women gather fuel and food, fetch water, prepare drinks and vegetable foods, and cook. Most of women's activities are performed close to the home and involve monotonous tasks that require no concentration and can easily be interrupted and resumed. Male activities may require long absences from home and travel over great distances, not possible for women burdened with children. Male tasks may be dangerous, because men do not bear or rear children, and may be more highly valued in order to motivate the expendable male to perform them. Men do women's jobs more than women do men's jobs.[1]

While small bands of men followed the larger wild animals, women gathered grains, seeds, nuts, fruits, roots, eggs, grubs, small animals, and insects. Women's work was steady and regular. Men's work was more spectacular, but less reliable. In a society that lacked the means for preserving food, gathering was more reliable than hunting.

Every generalization has its exceptions. The Agta of the Philippines are a hunting-gathering society in which the women hunt game animals, fish in the streams, and exchange goods with the lowland Filipinos. Especially among the more remote Agta in the mountains of northeastern Luzon, women use bows and arrows or machetes to hunt wild pigs and deer. They go out in small groups, sisters together or with their brothers, sharing the work of stalking, killing, and dragging the carcass home. Some Agta men laugh at the idea of women hunting. They say it is done only by the older generation or those in the more remote mountains. Their attitude might be an indication that the practice is ancient, or that it is unusual. In any case, Agta men also hunt, and there are many societies in which men also participate in the gathering.

The one thing that women alone do is produce life from their own bodies. Childbirth must have seemed like magic to early men. The oldest human art testifies to the importance of female fertility in the minds of these hunters and gathers. The oldest statues that archeologists have found are statues of women, or, more accurately, of womankind, since they emphasize sexual features. Typical of these is the Venus of Willendorf, with full breasts, pregnant belly, and large buttocks and thighs. This statue, made fifteen thousand years ago, and the many others like it seem to have been objects of worship. Many such statues have been found near what appear to be altars next to charred bones, suggesting animal sacrifice. Their emphasis on fertility must have had religious meaning for hunters and gatherers.

It seems very likely, then, that in the oldest human societies the gods were not

Paleolithic Venuses like these are the oldest sculptural representations of the human form. They testify to the religious importance of female fertility in the Old Stone Age when the deities may have been goddesses. The Venus of Willendorf (bottom) is the one with the braided head. The rough, squatting figure (top left) is one of many found in excavations at Jarmo (Iraq). The Venus of Lespugue (top, right) was found in France. (Naturhistorisches Museum, Wien; Oriental Institute, University of Chicago; Musée de l'homme, Scala, EPA)

gods at all, but goddesses. The most magical and mysterious of human experiences was the giving of life, and that was woman's work. The fertility goddess enshrined woman's magical "labor" and her regular daily work: producing life and sustaining it.

GODDESSES ON EARTH?

A hundred years ago some European thinkers imagined that the first human society was a "matriarchy" (literally, a world of female power, or "mother-power"). They reasoned that if goddesses were worshiped, women must have been treated as goddesses.

Now there is little evidence about the ways of life of these hunters and gatherers thousands of years ago. Words like "matriarchy" for societies where women are in control and "patriarchy" for societies dominated by men are also very fuzzy. No society is ruled entirely by either men or women. Certainly, both mothers and fathers have some influence in any society. Neither sex can exclude half the population (the other sex) from all power, position, or influence. Even in societies where women are not allowed to have jobs outside the home, their influence on the children, the family, and home life is bound to be considerable.

We cannot assume that a society that worships female fertility gives real power to women. The evidence of a few fertility goddesses, even without signs of gods, is not enough. Imagine a fortieth-century archeologist trying to understand twentieth-century society with only the remains from a pornographic newsstand. While the archeologist might be right in concluding that twentieth-century men "worshiped" women (in some sense), an inference that women ruled twentieth-century society would not be correct. Therefore we should be careful about assuming that women were goddesses in hunting-gathering society simply because the few bits of evidence that we have indicate that the gods were women. We should be aware of the way in which women are sometimes put on a pedestal in order to be kept out of the real world.

EQUALITY RATHER THAN ANY "ARCHY": THE LESSONS OF ANTHROPOLOGY

On balance, the study of hunting-gathering peoples in the world today suggests that there probably was no ancient matriarchy because there was no "archy" (power concentration) at all. We are not likely to find a mirror image of the modern patriarchy in the Paleolithic world because hunting-gathering society was fairly egalitarian. There was little private property, and thus no one was richer than anyone else. Food was distributed to all because everyone was related, mutual support was expected, and to refuse support was unthinkable. There was relatively little variation in wealth or power, because everyone did much the same work,

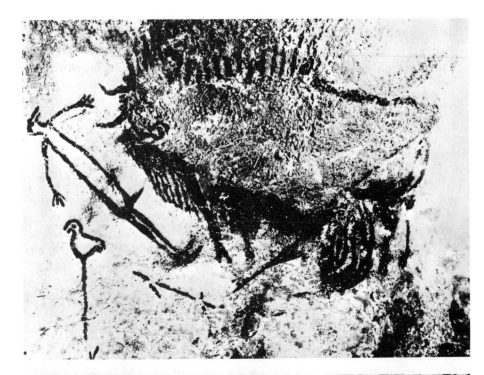

hunting and gathering, and all worked together. This general level of equality carried over into the relations between men and women as well.

Thus, instead of looking for Amazons or women tyrants in Paleolithic society, we might more usefully examine the ways in which women exercised autonomy, exerted power, or generally expressed themselves. The question is not whether women were ever rulers. The question is what the quality of women's lives in Paleolithic society was. One way of attempting to answer this question is to observe how the relative equality of Paleolithic society prevented certain kinds of behavior that developed later in less-egalitarian societies. This is the approach of the anthropologist Kathleen Gough:

> In general in hunting societies, . . . women are less subordinated in certain crucial respects than they are in most, if not all, of the archaic states, or even in some capitalist nations. These respects include men's ability to deny women sexuality or to force it upon them; to command or exploit their labor to control their produce; to control or rob them of their children; to confine them physically and prevent their movement; to use them as objects in male transactions; to cramp their creativeness; or to withhold from them large areas of the society's knowledge and cultural attainments.
>
> Especially lacking in hunting societies is the kind of male possessiveness and exclusiveness regarding women that leads to such institutions as savage punishments or deaths for female adultery, the jealous guarding of female chastity and virginity, the denial of divorce to women, or the ban on a woman's remarriage after her husband's death.[2]

Anthropologists are divided on the question of whether women had greater status or freedom in hunting-gathering society than they do today. While "anthropology" literally means the study of humankind, most anthropologists have specialized knowledge of only a few societies. Their specialized knowledge of particular societies living in the world today is enormously useful in supplementing the finds of archeologists. But one of the strongest points of agreement among anthropologists is that human experience is immensely varied. Almost every anthropological example has an opposite.

A further difficulty with anthropological accounts is that virtually all hunting-gathering societies in the world today have had contact with agricultural and urban societies. There are no "pure" hunter-gatherers left. There were some such societies in the early years of anthropology (approximately 1870–1950). The reports of travelers and early anthropologists are thus valuable for their closeness to "uncorrupted sources." But these older accounts often have other weaknesses; they frequently reflect the expectations of their own society, dominated by white men. We

---

The violence and beauty of the male, Paleolithic hunt is captured in these cave paintings from Lascaux, France (Wide World; Granger)

will, therefore, look at a few examples of hunting-gathering societies of the recent past as interpreted by modern anthropology.

NISA AND THE !KUNG

An example of woman's freedom from male possessiveness is demonstrated in a recent anthropolgical study of the !Kung of southern Africa. (The exclamation mark is used to indicate a "click" sound in the language.) The study, *Nisa,* by Marjorie Shostak, is particularly revealing because the author allows the !Kung woman Nisa to speak for herself. Nisa describes her struggle to separate from her husband, Besa, because he abandoned her when she was pregnant. Besa later returned and wanted Nisa to take him back, but she had already become involved with Twi. Nisa told Besa that she no longer wanted to have anything to do with him. "That's when Besa brought us to the Tswana headman to ask for a tribal hearing," Nisa told the anthropologist:

> Once it started the headman looked at everything. He asked me, "Among all the women who live here, among all those you see sitting around, do you see one who lives with two men?" I said, "No, the women who sit here . . . not one lives with two men; not one among them would I be able to find. I, alone, have two. But it was because this man, Besa, mistreated and hurt me. That's why I took this other man, Twi, who treats me well, who does things for me and gives me things to eat." Then I said, "He is also the man I want to marry; I want to drop the other one. Because Besa has no sense. He left me while I was pregnant and the pregnancy almost killed me. This other one is the one I want to marry."
>
> We talked a long time. Finally the headman told Besa, "I have questioned Nisa about what happened and she has tied you up with her talk; her talk has defeated you, without doubt. Because what she has said about her pregnancy is serious. Therefore, today she and Twi will continue to stay together.[3]

There are many things one might emphasize about this encounter. But here and in later meetings with the headman, Nisa's case clearly won out, and she was granted her wish to divorce Besa and marry Twi.

!Kung women have greater freedom and autonomy than the women of some other hunting-gathering societies. This may be because the !Kung women's gathering accounts for more than half of the food supply. They gather from among 105 species of plants, including nuts, berries, bulbs, roots, beans, leafy greens, and other fruits and vegetables. They also gather honey, birds' eggs, small mammals, tortoises, reptiles, and insects. The large animals that men hunt, including the occasional giraffe, account for 20–40 percent of !Kung subsistence. The !Kung live in a harsh environment. As is true of many Paleolithic peoples today, they have been pressed into the land that no one else wants. For the !Kung that is the semiarid area of the Kalahari Desert in southern Africa. As do many other Paleolithic peoples, the !Kung have an understanding of their environment that allows them to live comfortably on two or three days of work a week, and much of their time is engaged in leisure. But the environments of these peoples are clearly not as abundant as they once were. One wonders if the more barren natural environments of today's hunters and gatherers have increased or decreased the freedom of women.

NORTH ALASKAN ESKIMO

One of the least-hospitable environments in the world is surely the Arctic. The Eskimo peoples who live in Arctic areas like North Alaska suffer periods of extreme deprivation, even famine. Among contemporary hunting-gathering societies, the Eskimo show the greatest degree of male domination and female subservience. This is probably because hunting provides almost the entire food supply of the Eskimo, and the men are the only hunters. Coastal Eskimo hunt seals and whales. Inland Eskimo hunt caribou. In both cases, the terrain offers little for women to gather. Instead, women spend their time preparing the food and making the clothing from the animal hides the men give them.

Some anthropologists speak of the compatibility of the two different lives of Eskimo men and women. But while well-made clothing is important for the men in a climate where winter temperatures go below 30 degrees below zero, women cannot live without men's food. Perhaps as a result of this need, men act as if they own the women. They demonstrate their prowess by seducing and controlling women. For them, women are pawns in their negotiations with other men. Friendships are sealed by lending or sharing wives, and the women are rarely consulted.

A glaring exception to this exclusion of women is the role that women sometimes play as shamans. Women as well as men can become shamans, the spiritual and healing specialists who keep the balance between the community and the forces of nature and the supernatural. Eskimo society assigns the job of religious specialist to those least useful for the hunt and those who seem least balanced for the normal world. In this way even Eskimo women sometimes exert considerable power in their society.

THE PYGMIES OF ZAIRE

Not all contemporary hunters and gatherers live in sparse environments. The Pygmies of the central African rain forest live in a Garden of Eden that is abundant in plant and animal life. Today most of these short forest people have been absorbed by the agricultural villages of the Bantus who have infiltrated the forest. Some hunters and gatherers remain, however, in the less-accessible areas of the tropical rain forest. One of these groups, the Mbuti Pygmies, is revealed in an engaging anthropological study by Colin Turnbull called *The Forest People*.

The first time I ever visited a hunting camp I heard its many sounds some fifteen minutes before I finally walked into the clearing. First I heard a sharp, hollow tapping sound. Then the whole orchestra of children's voices, loudly gossiping women and chattering men blended with the hammering and occasional shouting and snatches of song. In the camp there was only a handful of people; but they were all busy, and when Pygmies are busy they are noisy.[4]

The Pygmy men have a religious festival called the *molimo,* from which the women are excluded, but there is a legend that the *molimo* was once "owned" by the women, and women still sometimes take over the singing from the men. "The woman is not discriminated against in Mbuti society," according to the anthropologist.

She has a full and important role to play. There is relatively little specialization according to sex. Even the hunt is a joint effort. A man is not ashamed to pick mushrooms and nuts if he finds them, or to wash and clean a baby. A woman is free to take part in the discussions of men, if she has something relevant to say.[5]

Womanhood among the Mbuti is the same as motherhood. The Mbuti do not refer to gender when they refer to children. All children are *miki.* Grandparents are all *tata* (elders). The words do not distinguish between male and female children or elders. Similarly, adults refer to others of their own age without referring to gender. The only time the Mbuti distinguish between male and female is when speaking of parents. The identity of a woman is different from that of a man because a woman is a mother.

Both men and women see themselves as equal in all respects except the supremely vital one that, whereas the woman can (and on occasion does) do almost everything the male does, she can do one thing no male can do: give birth to life.[6]

This fact is reflected in Mbuti rituals. More important even than the *molimo* is the *elima,* the puberty ritual that initiates womanhood. Women conduct the *elima.* They choose a young man, signify their choice by whipping him with a sapling, and then invite him through an obstacle course of ritually protective older women. Among the Mbuti, the women choose the men. The home and dwelling of the family is also more the property of the woman than of the man.

Among the many vignettes of daily life that Turnbull recounts, there is one story of the interaction of a husband and wife that suggests much about the relationship of men and women and of both to the larger society. It begins as an account of how women repair or change the family dwelling.

These changes are usually made by the women, since the hut is considered the woman's property. This is one of the strongest points a woman has in arguments with her husband. I have seen a woman turn around and start methodically pulling all the leaves off the hut. Usually the husband stops her halfway. In this case, however, the husband was particularly stubborn. He waited until she had taken all the leaves off, then remarked to the camp at large that his wife was going to be dreadfully cold that night. There was nothing for her to do, without losing face, but to continue; so reluctantly, and very slowly, she started to pull out the sticks that formed the framework of the home.

By this time the camp was agog, because it had been a long time since anyone had seen a domestic argument carried quite this far. The poor woman was in tears, for she was very much in love with her husband, and the final step, if he did not stop her, was for her to pack her few belongings and walk off, having completely demolished their home first. Then she would return to the home of her parents. It is the nature of a Pygmy never to admit he is wrong, and the husband was beginning to feel anxious. Things had gone too far for either of them to patch up the quarrel without being shamed in the eyes of all those who were watching to see what would happen next. He sat silent, hugging his knees, looking as miserable as his wife. Then he brightened up suddenly and turned around to see how far the demolition had gone. Only a few sticks had been pulled out. He called to his wife not to bother with the sticks, it was only the leaves that were dirty. She looked at him with a puzzled *"Ayiiiiii?"*—and then, understanding, asked him to help her carry the leaves down to the stream. This they did, and together they gravely washed every single leaf and brought them back. While she joyfully put the leaves back on the hut he stoked up the fire and then went off with his bow and arrows to see if he could find some game for a special dinner.

The pretense was that she had been taking the leaves off not because she was angry, but because they were dirty and attracted ants and spiders. Nobody believed this, but everyone was glad the quarrel was over. For several days women talked politely about the insects in the leaves of their huts, and took a few leaves down to the stream to wash, as if this was a perfectly normal procedure. I have never seen it done before or since.[7]

Turnbull's account of a domestic squabble sounds almost too familiar. But it reminds us that this is a world in which men and women have to get along. Perhaps even more among the Mbuti, where the issue concerns a few sticks and leaves, than among ourselves, in a world layered with things, domestic and social peace depends on relative equality.

FOR FURTHER READING

While the theories of an ancient matriarchy have been generally discredited by modern anthropology, the classic works are still worth reading. If one does not go all the way back to J. J. Bachofen's *Mutterrecht (Mother Right)* of 1861, it might be interesting to look at Henry Lewis Morgan's *Ancient Society* (1877), which was adapted by Friedrich Engels in *The Origin of the Family, Private Property, and the State* (1884) and generations of Marxists ever since.

Among recent considerations of this issue by anthropologists, there is a good collection of essays in *Woman, Culture, & Society,* edited by Michelle Zimbalist Rosaldo and Louise Lamphere. Ernestine Friedl's *Women and Men: An Anthropologist's View* is perhaps the best recent presentation of the problem. Other valuable recent studies include *Sexual Meanings: The Cultural Construction of Gender and Sexuality,* edited by Sherry B. Ortner and Harriet Whitehead; *Toward an Anthropology of Women,* by Rayna Rapp Reiter; *Female Power and Male Dominance: On the Origins of Sexual Inequality,* by Peggy Reeves Sanday; and *Matrilineal Kinship,* edited by David M. Schneider and Kathleen Gough. Perhaps the most sweeping testament to male domination by an anthropologist is still Lionel Tiger's *Men in Groups* (1969).

Historians can only borrow from the work of anthropologists and archeologists when they discuss primitive society, but sometimes historians contribute a useful overview that connects prehistory and history. One such stimulating effort is Gerda Lerner's *The Creation of the Patriarchy* (1986), which updates the vision of Morgan and Engels. Another is Elise Boulding's *The Underside of History* (1976). Evelyn Reed's *Woman's Evolution: From Matriarchal Clan to Patriarchal Family* (1975) remains very loyal to Engels. Some of the most interesting writing on Paleolithic and Neolithic society is that of Jacquetta Hawkes, especially her *Prehistory* and *Man and the Sun.*

Specialists in art and mythology have also produced some interesting, if speculative, works about Paleolithic society. One is Joseph Campbell's *The Masks of God: Primitive Mythology.* Another is Erich Neuman's *The Great Mother: An Analysis of the Archetype.* From a very different perspective is S. Gideon's *The Eternal Present: The Beginnings of Art.*

There are a few books that have had a popular, but not an academic, following. Often they have engendered controversy. One thinks of Merlin Stone's *When God Was a Woman,* Elaine Morgan's *The Descent of Women,* Elizabeth Gould Davis's *The First Sex,* and Elizabeth Fisher's *Woman's Creation.*

Finally, to remind students that our concentration on the issue of gender is certainly not the only way of studying Paleolithic society, we mention two good general texts, Brian M. Fagan's *People of the Earth* and John E. Pfeiffer's *The Emergence of Man,* and the beautifully written firsthand account of one hunting society, Colin M. Turnbull's *The Forest People.*

NOTES

1. Frances Dahlberg's introduction to *Woman the Gatherer* (New Haven: Yale University Press, 1981), p. 13.
2. Kathleen Gough, "The Origin of the Family," *Journal of Marriage and the Family,* no. 33 (November 1971). Reprinted in *Toward an Anthropology of Women,* ed. Rayna R. Reiter (New York: Monthly Review Press, 1975), pp. 69–70.

3. Marjorie Shostak, *Nisa: The Life and World of a !Kung Woman* (New York: Vintage, 1981), pp. 255–256.
4. Colin M. Turnbull, *The Forest People* (New York: Simon and Schuster, 1961), p. 130.
5. *Ibid.,* p. 154.
6. Colin M. Turnbull, "Mbuti Womanhood," in Dahlberg, *op. cit.,* p. 206.
7. Turnbull, *op. cit.,* pp. 132–133.

✖ 2 ✖

Mothers
and
Fathers

Agricultural and
Urban Revolutions

WE HAVE SEEN THAT MEN AND WOMEN were relatively equal in hunting and gathering societies. There was, in general, neither matriarchy nor patriarchy. We must therefore ask where and how patriarchy originated, because clearly male domination has been a characteristic of society for some time. To answer this question we must examine the next two stages of human society: agricultural and urban. The agricultural revolution occurred ten thousand years ago, first in the Middle East and India, and then in China and the Americas. The shift to city life, the urban revolution, normally followed the agricultural revolution in these same areas beginning about five thousand years ago.

How were women affected by the agricultural revolution? How were they affected by the urban revolution? Did the patriarchy begin with the shift from gathering to agriculture? Did it begin with the urban revolution? These are the questions we will ask in this chapter.

What do we mean by "patriarchy"? A patriarchy is a society in which men have most of the important powers, at home as well as in the larger society. Patriarchal families are run by fathers, societies by kings or male officials. In patriarchal societies daughters are less valued than sons. Sons, rather than daughters, inherit their father's property. Daughters are controlled by fathers and husbands. In extreme patriarchies women have no legal rights. Often the symbols of the society reflect male dominion: gods, priests, officials, authorities are men.

Our own society is currently challenging some of these patriarchal ideas and institutions. Some would say we have a patriarchy no longer. But the fact that the patriarchy is under attack does not mean that it has disappeared. Some of its ideas and institutions are very deeply embedded. Perhaps the strength of patriarchal institutions can be measured by the extent to which they are attacked. As deep as the patriarchy goes, it is not eternal. By understanding its origins, we can better evaluate its legacy. By understanding its past, we are better able to change it.

THE ORIGIN OF THE FAMILY, PRIVATE PROPERTY, AND THE STATE

One of the first attempts to deal with this question appeared in a little book by Friedrich Engels a hundred years ago called *The Origin of the Family, Private Property, and the State.* In it Engels reshaped some of the findings of an American anthropologist, Lewis Henry Morgan, to form a general theory of historical development. Engels argued that women became subject to men when private property developed. His reasoning was that the existence of private property (by which he meant productive resources, like potter's wheels, oxen, or looms) allowed some men to control the labor of others. This "exploitation" of other men's labor made some men richer than others. Rich men desired to pass their property to their sons, so they had to control their wives.

Much of Engels's argument has been challenged by later anthropology. He follows Morgan in arguing, for instance, that before private property there existed a "primitive stage when unrestricted sexual freedom prevailed within the tribe, every woman belonging equally to every man and every man to every woman."[1] This fantasy is no longer supportable. But Engels might have been correct in suggesting that the patriarchal family developed along with private property. We have already seen how hunting-gathering society provided relative equality to women because property was minimal. The growth of private property was gradual over human history, and we cannot date it from a particular period. But there may well have been a connection between the desire of fathers to build estates that could be passed on to legitimate heirs and the rise of laws and institutions that restricted women's rights and mobility.

WOMEN'S WORK

Women were probably the discoverers of agriculture. As the gatherers, they were more familiar with the world of plants. They knew which plants were edible, which were poisonous, which grew most easily, and which provided the most food. They were also equipped with an important tool, the gatherer's digging stick, which could be used to plant seeds as well as to uproot the harvest. Also, the work routine of agriculture was very much like that of gathering. It was steady, regular, and tedious; it lacked excitement, but usually provided a reliable food supply.

Agriculture created the first economy of abundance: the first economy where people could have more food than they needed to eat immediately. But this could come about only through saving and planning. In the early stages, women probably had to keep some of the grains and other seeds that they gathered away from the men. The invention of planting may have required the first systematic saving and planning for the future. It was eventually so successful that the density of agricultural populations multiplied to hundreds of times that of gathering populations.

The agricultural revolution was more than the invention of planting, though. It was a whole set of interrelated inventions that made farming efficient and increased the uses of the harvest. Most of this work was women's work. One archeologist, V. Gordon Childe, has summarized women's achievement this way:

> To accomplish the neolithic [agricultural] revolution mankind, or rather womankind, had not only to discover suitable plants and appropriate methods for their cultivation, but . . . also [to] devise special implements for tilling the soil, reaping and storing the crop, and converting it into foods. . . .
>
> It is an essential element in the neolithic economy that sufficient food shall be gathered at each harvest and stored to last till the next crop is ripe, normally in a year's time. Granaries or storehouses were accordingly a prominent feature. . . . Wheat and barley need to be separated from the husk by threshing and winnowing, and then ground into flour. The grinding could be done by pounding in a mortar, but the standard procedure was to rub the grains on a saucer-shaped or saddle-shaped stone with a bun-shaped or sausage-shaped rubbing-stone. . . .
>
> The flour can be easily converted into porridge or into flat cakes, but to make it into bread requires a knowledge of some biochemistry—the use of the microorganism yeast—and also a specially constructed oven. Moreover, the same biochemical process as was used to make bread rise opened to mankind a new world of enchantment.[2]

The source of the enchantment that Childe refers to is woman's invention of beer, wine, and liquor. These were made by adding yeast to liquefied grains or grapes. Alcoholic drinks must have been an especially convincing demonstration of the magical power of woman's agricultural efforts. The earliest priests and priestesses in ancient Mesopotamia and Egypt drank and offered these intoxicants to their gods and goddesses to increase their power over the crops.

The invention of fermented liquors meant the invention of permanent, often elaborate, containers. Childe continues:

By 3000 B.C., indeed, intoxicants had become necessities to most societies in Europe and Hither [Near] Asia, and a whole service of jars, jugs, beakers, strainers, and drinking-tubes had come into fashion for their ceremonial consumption.

All the foregoing inventions and discoveries were . . . the work of the women. To that sex, too, may by the same token be credited the chemistry of pot-making, the physics of spinning, the mechanics of the loom, and the botany of flax and cotton.[3]

SEXUALITY OF TOOLS?

The challenging, sometimes infuriating, psychoanalytic historian Lewis Mumford has suggested in *The City in History* that the very sexuality of woman is evident in women's inventions throughout the Neolithic or agricultural village.

> Woman's presence made itself felt in every part of the village: not least in its physical structures, with their protective enclosures, whose further symbolic meanings psychoanalysis has now tardily brought to light. Security, receptivity, enclosure, nurture—these functions belong to woman; and they take structural expression in every part of the village, in the house and the oven, the byre and the bin, the cistern, the storage pit, the granary, and from there pass on to the city, in the wall and the moat, and all inner spaces, from the atrium to the cloister. House and village, eventually the town itself, are woman writ large. If this seems a wild psychoanalytic conjecture, the ancient Egyptians stand ready to vouch for the identification. In Egyptian hieroglyphics, "house" or "town" may stand for symbols for "mother," as if to confirm the similarity of the individual and collective nurturing function. In line with this, the more primitive structures—houses, rooms, tombs—are usually round ones: like the original bowl described in Greek myth, which was modelled on Aphrodite's breast.[4]

ÇATAL HÜYÜK: THE GODDESS RETURNS

Among the earliest Neolithic villages unearthed by archeologists are Hacilar (7040–7000 B.C.) and the nearby successor Çatal Hüyük (6250–5720 B.C.) in present-day Turkey. Çatal Hüyük (pronounced CHAY-tal HOO-yook) might actually be called a town. It sheltered between six and eight thousand inhabitants at its height. Excavations of Hacilar reveal no pictures of humans, male or female. There are pictures only of animals. However, at the 6200 B.C. layer of Çatal Hüyük the first representations of humans appear. Like the Paleolithic Venuses, they are pictures of women with grossly exaggerated sexual characteristics: breasts, buttocks, and hips. Pictures of a woman giving birth and another holding a child are surrounded by sculptured breasts on the wall. The archeologist responsible for the excavation of Çatal Hüyük, James Mellaart, calls these women goddesses, noting their association with flower, grain, and plant patterns on the walls and with other symbols of fertility.[5]

How typical were these figurines of Neolithic art generally? We cannot be certain. Most Neolithic settlements have not provided us with such a treasure of art objects. However, one specialist, E. O. James, says that fertility cults "became firmly established in the religion of the Ancient Near East with the rise of agriculture in the Neolithic civilization in and after the fifth millennium B.C. [5000–4000 B.C.]."[6] Statues of goddesses have been found throughout the Middle East and Europe at Neolithic sites. One scholar, Marija Gimbutas, reports that thirty thousand figurines have been found at three thousand sites in southeastern Europe alone, and that these figurines show the continuation of mother goddess worship into the third millennium (3000–2000 B.C.) in the area surrounding the Aegean Sea and into the second millennium (after 2000 B.C.) in Crete.[7]

EARTH MOTHERS AND FERTILITY GODDESSES

In the Neolithic Age women were unquestionably the source of life. Not only did they possess magical properties of the moon that enabled them to give birth to human beings, but they also gained control of the earth and the sun in order to feed the life they gave. Neolithic women seemed to be the source of all fertility, all life. The major divinities of agricultural peoples were Earth Mothers, goddesses who caused the earth to flower and bear fruit. The ancient Mesopotamians worshiped the mother goddesses Tiamat, Ninhursag, and Ishtar; the Egyptians, Isis. While these fertility goddesses were not the only deities worshiped in agricultural societies, they had considerable powers. Here is a typical Mesopotamian prayer to the goddess Ishtar:

> *Gracious Ishtar, who rules over the universe,*
> *Heroic Ishtar, who creates humankind,*
> *who walks before the cattle, who loves the shepherd . . .*
> *You give justice to the distressed, the suffering you give them justice.*
> *Without you the river will not open,*
> *the river which brings us life will not be closed,*
> *without you the canal will not open,*
> *the canal from which the scattered drink,*
> *will not be closed . . . Ishtar, merciful lady . . .*
> *hear me and grant me mercy.*[8]

To create humankind was to rule the universe, including the cattle and shepherds, the rivers and canals. Other prayers address Ishtar as "mistress of the battle field, who pulls down the mountains; . . . strongest among rulers, who leads kings by the lead; you who open the wombs of women."[9] The power to bring life was also the power to heal, the power of life over death.

Isis, the Egyptian goddess, stretches out her winged arms to protect all creatures. Worship of this Neolithic Earth Mother survived well into the age of male-dominated civilizations, when birds had become words, as this tomb painting of 1292 B.C. attests. (Granger)

NEOLITHIC INDIA AND THE GODDESS

Was the cult of the fertility goddess common beyond Europe and the Middle East? Most statues have been found in the area from the Tigris-Euphrates to the western Mediterranean, but this may be because more archeological excavation has been done there. Agriculture developed in India at about the same time. Is there any evidence of goddess worship there as well?

Indian history before 1500 B.C. was the story of the rise of complex agricultural villages, and then cities, in the Indus Valley, and of smaller, nonurbanized peoples in the south. Then in the centuries around 1500 B.C. an invasion of nomadic pastoral people from the grasslands of Eurasia, north of India—people later called Aryans— led to the imposition of a very different culture on the Indians. These Aryan invaders were very similar to another group of Eurasian invaders in Greece and the Mediterranean. (Their family resemblance accounts for the similarity of Indo-European languages from the Atlantic to India today.)

Before the Aryan invasion "the earliest civilized inhabitants of India worshipped a Mother Goddess and a horned fertility god," according to A. L. Basham,[10] a leading historian of India. By contrast, "the early gods of the Aryans . . . were chiefly connected with the sky and were predominantly male."[11] Excavations of Harappa have revealed sculptures of animals, men, and women. The statues of these nearly naked women, according to Basham, "are certainly icons of the Mother Goddess, and are so numerous that they seem to have been kept in nearly every home."[12]

We have no written records from ancient Harappa or its sister city, Mohenjo Daro, since both were destroyed before or during the Aryan invasion. We know even less of the agricultural tribes in central and southern India before the Aryan invasion. Today the peoples of southern and southeastern Asia demonstrate a high proportion of matrilineal descent, and women play an important economic role. Polyandry (taking more than one husband) is practiced in Assam and Bhutan. It is not unusual for Indian historians to see women-centered customs as vestiges of an ancient Indian matriarchy. D. D. Kosambi, for instance, writes of the *holi* festival, a ceremony of fire and dance, in this way:

> Some features of the *holi* festival seem to go back to a prehistoric matriarchal stage. In some places one man (called the *kolima*) had to wear woman's clothing and join the dancers around the *holi* fire. . . . These rites and festivals have been taken over by men though originally [they were] women's monopoly.[13]

Here and elsewhere, however, a matriarchal stage is assumed rather than established. The evidence is too limited. We can be more certain, however, in describing as masculine the religion of the Aryan invaders who overran both the Harappan cities and Indian tribal society. In that regard Aryan religion was like that of other pastoral peoples. Some historians have argued that the migration of these Indo-Europeans from the grasslands of central Eurasia brought Sky Father religion and patriarchal society to Europe as well as India in the second millennium B.C. (2000–1000 B.C.).

WOMEN IN NEOLITHIC CHINA AND JAPAN

Some historians have also suggested that Neolithic China was matriarchal.

> Society in the late neolithic age was probably matriarchal. Women were responsible for carrying out the sacred family ritual offerings, and often the eldest daughter remained single in order to maintain the necessary purity. Descent was considered to pass through the mother; and even today the normal Chinese word for "surname" is composed of two parts, meaning "woman" and "birth." Legends of the birth of the earliest kings speak only of the mother; the legendary king Yao, for example, was said to be born of his mother Ch'ing Tu and a red dragon. It is possible that women practiced polyandry, taking

several husbands, and may have been the owners of the houses and villages. This status was to be changed during the second and first millennia, with the establishment, completed during the Eastern Chou period, of a patriarchal clan society.[14]

Chinese culture distinguished between the *yang* masculine principle and the *yin* feminine principle, but illustrated these as two sides of the same circle, divided by a wavering *S* that gave each side equal space. The blend of *yang* and *yin* suggested the need for hot and cold, outside and inside, heaven and earth, respectively. Some philosophical schools, like the Daoists of the sixth century B.C., even saw themselves as part of a *yin* tradition that preferred the feminine and passive to the masculine and active. But for others, masculine *yang* stood for good, and feminine *yin* for evil, perhaps especially in the Eastern Chou period (770–256 B.C.), referred to above. The Daoists were one group of philosophers from that period. The Confucians were another. In speaking of the importance of "the gentleman ideal" in Confucian thought, Max Weber wrote:

> Confucius viewed woman as a thoroughly irrational creature often as difficult to deal with as servants. . . . The Buddhist horror of women, which was determined by flight from the world, thus found its counterpart in Confucianism's lack of esteem for women, determined by rational sobriety.[15]

The future of Chinese civilization after 500 B.C. belonged more to Confucianism and Buddhism than to Daoism, as we shall see. Chinese civilization in the last two thousand years has been distinctly patriarchal. It is interesting, however, to speculate about an earlier age that may have been very different.

Neolithic Japan suggests a similar transition. Female figurines were used in fertility cults during the Neolithic Jomon period from about 8000 B.C. to the third century. During the later "tomb period" (A.D. 250–552) figurines of female shamans were common. The earliest Chinese account of Japan describes an unmarried queen Pimiko who was said to be a sorceress. The earliest Japanese accounts of their origins, the *Kojiki* and *Nihon,* relate the myth that Japanese emperors were descended from the Sun Goddess. This belief might account in part for the large number of empresses who ruled Japan until the eighth century A.D., when a Buddhist priest caused a reaction by gaining too many political favors from the ex-empress Koken (r. 749–758), who returned to the throne as Empress Shotoku (r. 764–770).

WOMEN AND THE AGRICULTURAL REVOLUTION

Was women's power enhanced by the agricultural revolution? How did women's religious and symbolic significance translate into actual power? The combination of women doing the most important work and goddesses worshiped as the most important deities must have contributed significantly to women's power and prestige in a number of societies. This was especially true among some Native American societies. The argument of Lewis Henry Morgan and Friedrich Engels was based on a study of the American Iroquois.

The Iroquois was a confederation of five nations (Mohawk, Oneida, Onondaga, Cayuga, and Seneca), in what is now New York State, that was organized in the middle of the fifteenth century. The constitution of this confederation, which was passed on orally until being written down at the end of the nineteenth century, declared the following:

> The lineal descent of the peoples of the Five Nations shall run in the female line. Women shall be considered the progenitors of the Nation. They shall own the land and the soil. Men and women shall follow the status of the mother.[16]

One contemporary anthropologist, Peggy Reeves Sanday, has agreed with Morgan and Engels on the matriarchal character of Iroquois society:

> In the symbolic, economic, and familial spheres, the Iroquois were matriarchal, that is, female dominated. Iroquois women headed the family longhouse and much of the economic and ceremonial life centered on the agricultural activities of women.[17]

Women appointed men to the positions of authority in the league, but they retained the right to veto the men's decisions. Men were important in intertribal affairs. Sanday sees a connection between men's responsibility for the hunt, warfare, and intertribal matters. Men took over, Sanday argues, when these "outside" concerns of men took precedence. This occurred in periods of crisis, often brought on by invasion or prompted by the need to migrate.

Navaho society was similar. It was also matrilineal (figuring inheritance from the mother) and matrilocal (husbands lived with their wives' families). While Navaho men did some of the farming, Navaho women were engaged in the more profitable pottery making and rug and blanket weaving. The most important Navaho deity was called Changing Woman, the benevolent giver of corn and mother of the Twin Heroes.

While matrilineal descent probably increased with the agricultural revolution, a majority of agricultural societies may have remained patrilineal. Studies of twentieth-century societies show matrilineal traditions among 10 percent of hunters and gatherers and among 25 percent of agriculturalists. Matrilineality does not guarantee female dominance, however. Often, in fact, authority is exercised by the mother's brother. Matrilineality is more often an indication of sexual equality.

Perhaps we should distinguish between early Neolithic hoe-farming societies and later Neolithic plow agriculture. One of the leading historians of the period, Jacquetta Hawkes, makes this distinction when she says that "the earliest Neolithic societies throughout their range in time and space gave woman the highest status she has ever known."[18] The inventiveness of women's work, the prestige of women's deities, the awe of women's magic must have given women status and respect considerably beyond what they had known in the Paleolithic Age. In any case, the origin of the patriarchy was not likely in the world of hoe farming or horticulture. We must look for it in the replacement of horticulture by large-scale plow agriculture, a transition, accomplished largely by men, that made possible the urban revolution.

MEN'S PLACE

We have said very little so far of the male contribution to the Neolithic Age. Men domesticated wild animals. This achievement was probably less important than women's cultivation of plants because agriculture was the more basic source of the food supply and its cultivation led to many other inventions and social changes.

While women developed the art of hoe farming after 8000 B.C., men were increasing their knowledge of wild animals. Gradually men learned to keep animals in controlled herds so that they would reproduce in the captivity of the range. In this way, sheep, goats, horses, and oxen were most successfully domesticated. By 3000 B.C. these herds could supply enough food to sustain much denser populations than the earliest Neolithic villages. Even more significantly, however, men learned to use some of these animals (especially oxen) to plow large fields, whereas previously, women had cultivated small plots by hand.

As men invented the plow and harnessed their world of animals to women's world of farming, the increased agricultural surplus was able to support human settlements that were much more dense and complex than the Neolithic village. These settlements, with their high specialization of labor and leisure class, were the first great cities. In virtually every case these cities were more patriarchal than their predecessors.

THE ORIGINS OF THE PATRIARCHY: PLOWS AND CITIES

The first Neolithic villages included men and women, of course. But since the main business of these farming communities was women's work, men's role was often subordinate. On the other hand, in the pasture land around these villages, herders led a very different style of life. They moved around more frequently than the villagers; they had fewer permanent possessions; and their lives were usually harder and more violent. Women also lived with the herders, but in these nomadic bands it was the women who were subordinate. (Two-thirds of the modern pastoral tribes are patrilineal; fewer than 10 percent are matrilineal.)

Cities were the children of the marriage of these two different Neolithic cultures:

farm and pasture. The farm culture was more inventive and more complex than the pastoral culture. Indeed, the herders often raided agricultural settlements for food and women. When the two cultures achieved a union, peacefully or by force, the men usually took over.

The marriage of these two cultures took thousands of years to occur. American Westerns remind us that the conflict between farmers and cattle ranchers was one of the main themes of our own history just a hundred years ago. The process may not have been too different in ancient Mesopotamia, Egypt, China, or India. In some cases, bands of herders probably took over scattered farming communities and stumbled upon a system of using animals to plow fields more efficiently. In some cases, nomadic, pastoral people, propelled by population pressure or the need for new grasslands, conquered earlier Neolithic cultures, as the Aryan invaders conquered India, in a migration that took many generations, and possibly as much as a thousand years. Individual husbands may have aided their wives in farming: first, just clearing the land; later, using animals to pull a heavier plow than their wives could manage. Whether we look at the level of the individual family or that of the mass migration, the rise of cities was often preceded by the shift from women's hoe horticulture to men's plow-field agriculture.

FATHERS AND SONS

Many early Neolithic societies were organized around matrilineal clans. As men took over women's work, increasing the yield of garden horticulture with their animals and plowed fields, they were in a position to demand greater control over how the agricultural surplus was distributed. In matrilineal clans, a husband was a stranger. Power was exercised by his wife's clan: her mother and uncle especially. Increasingly in plow-agricultural society, the patriarchal family replaced the matrilineal clan. In the patriarchal family, husbands exchanged daughters, who moved in as strangers. Property was passed on to sons. So that fathers could be sure that their sons were their own, a woman's virginity at marriage and loyalty during marriage became important concerns. Often the more property there was, the more elaborate the concerns. Complex law codes developed that established a double standard for men and women.

This can be seen much later in elaborate institutional form in Hammurabi's code, created in Mesopotamia around 1750 B.C. The code devoted more attention to property and women than to any other issues. And frequently women were treated as if they were simply additions to men's property.

> #141. If a man's wife, living in her husband's house, has persisted in going out, has acted the fool, has wasted her house, has belittled her husband, he shall prosecute her. If her husband has said, "I divorce her," she shall go her way; he shall give her nothing as her price of divorce. If her husband has said, "I

will not divorce her," he may take another woman to wife; the first wife shall live as a slave in her husband's house.[19]

In some ways women were the first slaves. A daughter was sold for a bride-price by her father to the future husband or his father. Marriage was a financial arrangement between these men. The law intervened to protect their financial arrangement, not the well-being of the daughter. And always there was the double standard.

> #151. If a man had a debt before he married a woman, his creditors can take his wife for payment. If a woman had a debt before she married a man, her creditor shall not take her husband for it.[20]

Much the same transition seems to have taken place in other ancient civilizations. In India restrictions on women combined with restrictions on sexuality increased with the Aryan conquest. "The wild fertility cults of the early Tamils"[21] were replaced by the Laws of Manu by the end of the first millennium B.C. The duties of a wife, they declared, were to wait on her husband.

> *She should do nothing independently*
> *   even in her own house.*
> *In childhood subject to her father,*
> *   in youth to her husband,*
> *and when her husband is dead to her sons,*
> *   she should never enjoy independence. . . .*
>
> *In season and out of season*
> *   her lord, who wed her with sacred rites,*
> *ever gives happiness to his wife,*
> *   both here and in the other world.*
>
> *Though he be uncouth and prone to pleasure,*
> *   though he have no good points at all,*
> *the virtuous wife should ever*
> *   worship her lord as a god.*[22]

The depth of a patriarchy can sometimes be measured by its attitude toward widows. Indo-European nomadic tribes had little use for widows, and they were sometimes expected to die with their husbands. This was institutionalized later in Indian *sati* with the expectation that a widow would jump on her husband's funeral pyre. But that was not a common practice in ancient Neolithic India. Like the

---

The top of the pillar of Hammurabi's code reveals the symbols of the urban patriarchy: the Sky Father, male kingship, and written law. Even the phallic tower is symbolic of a male age, with Hammurabi at the head—above the law. (Louvre, Paris)

prohibition on widow remarriage, it became increasingly prevalent with the spread of the patriarchy in the last two thousand years.

SKY FATHERS AND SONS

As men took over the most important work in the new field agriculture and the patrilineal family replaced the matrilineal clan, men shaped the culture in their own image as well. Goddesses were replaced by gods. One historian finds a distinct pattern to this change:

> The observable pattern is: first, the demotion of the Mother-Goddess figure and the ascendance and later dominance of her male consort/son; then his merging with a storm-god into a male Creator-God, who heads the pantheon of gods and goddesses. Wherever such changes occur, the power of creation and of fertility is transferred from the Goddess to the God.[23]

The "demotion" of the mother goddess may be suggested in the numerous myths of a "sacred marriage" that were celebrated widely in the fourth and third millennia B.C.

> Not until the Goddess had mated with the young god and his death and rebirth had taken place, could the annual cycle of the seasons begin. The sexuality of the Goddess is sacred and confers the blessings of fertility to earth and to the people who through their ritual observances please her. The ritual of the Sacred Marriage took many forms and was widely practiced in Mesopotamia, Syria, Canaan, and the Aegean. Among its many complex meanings is that it transformed the all-encompassing fertility of the Mother-Goddess into the more domesticated fertility of the "goddess of cultivated grain."[24]

Myths about the goddess's young virgin daughter who had to be awakened by the god of the underworld may have served a similar function. Thus, according to ancient Greek legend, the Earth Mother Demeter retires to a cave

> to mourn the disappearance of her daughter Persephone. The fruits of the earth perish and famine threatens. But a miracle occurs. The god of the underworld restores Persephone to her earthly abode in exchange for her promise to rejoin him annually. Upon her return the earth dons a garment of green, fruits grow again, life is joy.[25]

While mother goddesses were demoted to sisters, daughters, and specific vegetation goddesses, who needed the help of male gods, they were also sometimes ignored by the new class of male priests who administered the city temples. Samuel Noah Kramer suggests this may have been the reason why Namu, the Sumerian mother goddess who was creator of the universe and mother of the gods in the third millennium B.C., was omitted in a list from the second millennium B.C. Her powers were transferred to her son Enki "to justify this bit of priestly piracy," he says.[26]

Thus, even agriculture became the province of male gods: Enki in Mesopotamia, Osiris in Egypt, and Bacchus in Greece, among many. Gods even replaced Mother Earth deities as the source of life and procreation. The Sky Father became as important as the Earth Mother. Rain was now often imagined to be the fertilizing sperm of the Sky Father. One Egyptian myth even denied the female role in conception completely, imagining that the god Atum created the universe out of his own body, by masturbation.

CITY SKYLINES

Lewis Mumford summarizes the new shape of things suggestively (if not too metaphorically):

> Male symbolisms and abstractions now become manifest: they show themselves in the insistent straight line, the firmly bounded geometric plan, the phallic tower and the obelisk, finally, in the beginnings of mathematics and astronomy.... It is perhaps significant that while the early cities seem largely circular in form, the ruler's citadel and the sacred precinct are more usually enclosed by a rectangle.[27]

Even today when one travels from the agricultural countryside of much of Africa to the large cities, one often moves from a world of round dwellings in circular enclosures to one of rectangular blocks, straight streets, and jagged skylines. The Neolithic world sought meaning in the earth. Cities reach to the sky.

FOR FURTHER READING

One of the best introductions to the topic is an anthropological study by Peggy Reeves Sanday, *Female Power and Male Dominance: On the Origins of Sexual Inequality.* A less-feminist introduction is provided by Martin King Whyte in *The Status of Women in Preindustrial Societies.* A more radical (Marxist and feminist) argument is offered in Karen Sacks's *Sisters and Wives.*

There are a number of good general studies of goddess worship in Neolithic society and the development of the patriarchy. Most recent titles are the essays in *The Book of the Goddess,* edited by Carl Olson, and Gerda Lerner's *The Creation of Patriarchy,* a radical history. More popular is Merlin Stone's *When God Was a Woman. The Book of Goddesses and Heroines* by Patricia Monaghan lists over a thousand names (worldwide) with brief summaries. There are a number of books on some of the most popular ancient goddesses— Isis and Inanna/Ishtar, for instance. One particularly evocative re-creation of the ancient stories is in *Inanna: Queen of Heaven and Earth* by Diane Wolkstein and Samuel Noah Kramer.

In the scholarly *The Female Experience and the Nature of the Divine*, Judith Ochshorn argues that gender was not important in the polytheistic religions of the Middle East before the rise of Judaism, which was much more patriarchal. In *And They Took Themselves Wives: The Emergence of the Patriarchy in Western Civilization*, David Bakan argues that the patriarchy came late to Judaism.

The literature on women's role in Neolithic and early urban society is much richer than that on Paleolithic (hunting-gathering) society. Lewis Mumford's *The City in History* is still a fascinating interpretive beginning. Joseph Campbell's *The Masks of God* is an enormously valuable four-volume set. Jacquetta Hawkes's *Prehistory* is a thorough study of the Neolithic period. The work of Georges Dumezil, a historian of Indo-European myth, is also helpful.

Among archeological studies, Marija Gimbutas's richly illustrated *The Gods and Goddesses of Old Europe* is thorough and revealing. On Çatal Hüyük, see the work of James Mellaart, *Çatal Hüyük: A Neolithic Town in Anatolia*. For more general introductions, see Mellaart's *The Archeology of Ancient Turkey* and *The Neolithic of the Near East*. For archeological interpretations of ancient India, the standard older work is Mortimer Wheeler's *The Indus Civilization*. The work of Gregory L. Possehl is more recent. A. L. Basham's *The Wonder That Was India* is a classic that is still well worth reading.

There are a number of more general studies of ancient religion that relate to the topic. The work of Mircea Eliade is rich and informative. His *History of Religious Beliefs and Ideas* and *Gods, Goddesses, and Myths of Creation* make excellent introductions. There are a number of excellent studies in religion in ancient Greece, beyond this time period, by Jane Harrison, J. N. Coldstream, and W. K. C. Guthrie. Closer to our period is the work on the ancient Middle East by Henri Frankfort, like *Kingship and the Gods,* and the work of Samuel Noah Kramer.

Another approach to the topic can be taken through the anthropological literature on women in different agricultural societies. On Africa, start with *African Women*, edited by Margaret Jean Hay and Sharon Stichter. A more general collection of essays is offered in *Toward an Anthropology of Women*, edited by Rayna R. Reiter.

NOTES

1. Friedrich Engels, *The Origin of the Family, Private Property and the State* (New York: International Publishers, 1942), p. 27.
2. V. Gordon Childe, *What Happened in History* (Baltimore: Penguin, 1942), p. 65.
3. *Ibid.,* p. 66.
4. Lewis Mumford, *The City in History* (New York: Harcourt Brace Jovanovich, 1961), pp. 12–13.
5. James Mellaart, *Çatal Hüyük: A Neolithic Town in Anatolia* (New York: McGraw-Hill, 1967), is the authority. I am also indebted to Gerda Lerner's *The Creation of Patriarchy* (Oxford: Oxford University Press, 1986), to Anne L. Barstow's "The Prehistoric Goddess," in *The Book of the Goddess Past and Present,* ed. Carl Olson (New York: Crossroad, 1985), and to Professor Barstow for her kind clarifications.
6. E. O. James, *The Ancient Gods: The History and Diffusion of Religion in the Ancient Near East and the Eastern Mediterranean* (London: Weidenfeld and Nicolson, 1960), p. 47.

See also E. O. James, *The Cult of the Mother Goddess: An Archaeological and Documentary Study* (London: Thames & Hudson, 1959).

7. Marija Gimbutas, *Goddesses and Gods of Old Europe* (Berkeley: University of California Press, 1982), p. 18.
8. Cited in Lerner, *op. cit.,* p. 142.
9. *Ibid.*
10. A. L. Basham, *The Wonder That Was India* (New York: Grove Press, 1954), p. 232.
11. *Ibid.,* p. 233.
12. *Ibid.,* p. 21.
13. D. D. Kosambi, *The Culture and Civilization of Ancient India* (Delhi: Vikas Publishers, 1970), p. 47.
14. F. Roy Willis, *World Civilizations,* vol. 1, 2nd ed. (Lexington, Mass.: D.C. Heath, 1986), pp. 79–80.
15. Max Weber, *The Religion of China,* trans. Hans H. Gerth (New York: Free Press, 1951), pp. 161–162.
16. Arthur C. Parker, "The Constitution of the Five Nations," *New York State Museum Bulletin,* no. 184, 1916.
17. Peggy Reeves Sanday, *Female Power and Male Dominance: On the Origins of Sexual Inequality* (Cambridge: Cambridge University Press, 1981), p. 177.
18. Jacquetta Hawkes, *Prehistory* (New York: New American Library, 1963), pp. 356–357.
19. Hammurabi's Code, in C. H. W. Johns, *Babylonian and Assyrian Laws, Contracts and Letters* [Library of Ancient Inscriptions] (New York: Charles Scribner's Sons, 1904), pp. 44–67.
20. *Ibid.*
21. Basham, *op. cit.,* p. 185.
22. Manu, v. 147ff. Quoted in Basham, *op. cit.,* pp. 180–181.
23. Lerner, *op. cit.,* p. 145.
24. *Ibid.,* p. 150.
25. Traian Stoianovich, *A Study in Balkan Civilization* (New York: Knopf, 1967), pp. 7–8.
26. Samuel Noah Kramer, "Poets and Psalmists; Goddesses and Theologians: Literary, Religious and Anthropological Aspects of the Legacy of Sumer," in *The Legacy of Sumer: Invited Lectures on the Middle East at the University of Texas at Austin,* ed. Denise Schmandt-Besserat (Malibu, Calif., 1976), p. 14. Quoted in Lerner, *op. cit.,* p. 153.
27. Mumford, *op. cit.,* p. 27.

❧ 3 ❧

Cities
and
Civilization

Civility
and Class

THE WORDS "CITY" AND "CIVILIZATION" do not ring well in the modern ear. Cities seem to be impossible places to live for all but the very wealthy. Urban ghettos have become prisons for the poor. The middle class works for a home in the suburbs. The young seek salvation in the country. Civilization is no longer an ideal. The word conjures up images of technological narrowness or upper-class snobbery.

This chapter confronts some of these ideas. It argues on behalf of both cities and civilization, accepting the common origins that the words imply. It argues that city life has been largely responsible for the achievements of civilization, and that those achievements have enhanced human life enormously. The chapter does not deny that cities are ridden by class differences. Nor does it deny that civilization has been largely the product of upper-class interests. It argues, in fact, that class differences were at the root of the urbanizing and civilizing process.

Our examination of the origins of ancient civilization suggests, however, that one of the achievements of ruling classes was to make themselves superfluous and create new possibilities for us all.

BEFORE THERE WERE CITIES

The "urban revolution" began only about five thousand years ago, and it has spread considerably only within the last few hundred years. For thousands of years before the development of cities, most of the world's people lived in small village settlements. Some people even continued a pre-Neolithic (before herding and farming) life of hunting and food gathering.

We have already accepted Lewis Mumford's suggestion that the first cities were the fruits of a "marriage" between the rough, male-dominated pastoral society and the settled, female-centered village society of the farmers. At times it must have been a marriage of convenience. Most frequently, however, it must have been a forceful abduction.

Only force can explain why some self-sufficient farming villages turned over enough of their crops to support new classes of specialists—chiefs, kings, priests, soldiers, administrators, and craftsworkers—who grew no food themselves. It is difficult to imagine the conservative farming villagers, attuned as they were to the eternal, natural rhythms of planting and harvesting, suddenly deciding that their lives should become more complicated.

Even if village life were not the golden age that later city poets imagined, it was certainly more peaceful and egalitarian than city life was to become. One Sumerian poet wrote that in the village even the wolf and lion were not dangerous. That seems too unlikely to be taken literally, but it does appear that institutionalized warfare was absent from village life. Ancient dramatists often put their peace speeches in the mouths of the villagers:

> *I fix my eyes upon my fields and lust for Peace.*
> *I loathe the stingy, greedy city. I long*
> *for my own ungrudging countryside, my generous*
>   *village,*
> *my openhearted home sweet home. It never barked,*
> *"Buy Coal! Buy Oil! Buy Vinegar!" Gratis it gave me*
> *everything, unstintingly supplied my wants, and that*
>   *blasted*
> *city byword "BUY"—*
> *Goodbye to that!*[1]

The village raised no armies and drafted no soldiers. Nor did the village make people buy things. Money, buying and selling, and the market were inventions of the city. The village supplied the wants of its members gratis (free of charge) because each of the villagers contributed to the communal storage. The average villagers did not try to avoid work because everyone gained equally from the advantages of work. Work was life—everyone's life. Villagers could not afford to allow any of their members to monopolize the communal resources. There were no leisure classes or families who lived on the work of others. Even a taste for idle luxury, special privilege, private property, or greater power seems to have been absent. Village crops were varied and ample. There was rarely enough of a surplus to allow the development of a special class of nonfarming administrators—but there often was enough of a surplus to tempt the nomadic herders. Perhaps the very success of village life proved to be its undoing.

It is unlikely that villagers would have freely chosen to create the class of specialists, rulers, tax collectors, and armies that made the first cities possible. It is also unlikely that the force for such a change would have been raised in the stable, nurturing village itself. The drives for acquisition and power and conquest were much more typical of the herders than of the villagers.

It is also unlikely that all villages would have eventually grown large enough to be cities. We make a mistake when we think of a city as only an overgrown or especially populated village. There were some very large villages in the ancient world that never became cities. In some places with particularly fertile soil, a village might support a couple of thousand inhabitants, most of whom were farmers.

Villages did not gradually evolve into cities. A few villages were forged into the first cities, probably by conquering herders from the surrounding grasslands. This explains the suddenness of the change and the character of the first cities. In many ways the city still bears the stamp of that forge.

VILLAGE TO CITY

The earliest cities were, of course, towns that retained much of village life. They were still small in size and population, had a limited variety of nonsubsistence occupations, and were still pretty classless and democratic. (At least the graves are all equal.) One of the oldest of these that archeologists have discovered is the biblical Jericho. If a wall marks the difference between a village and a city, then Jericho was a city almost ten thousand years ago—at the beginning of the Neolithic period. Possibly the first city wall ever constructed, Jericho's wall of 8000 B.C. was constructed of stones dragged from a riverbed half a mile away to protect the desert oasis of about ten acres and possibly a couple of thousand inhabitants. Five thousand years before the construction of the Sumerian temples and the Egyptian pyramids (and six and a half thousand years before Joshua's Israelite army destroyed a later wall at Jericho) the urban revolution may have begun. If we prefer Lewis Mum-

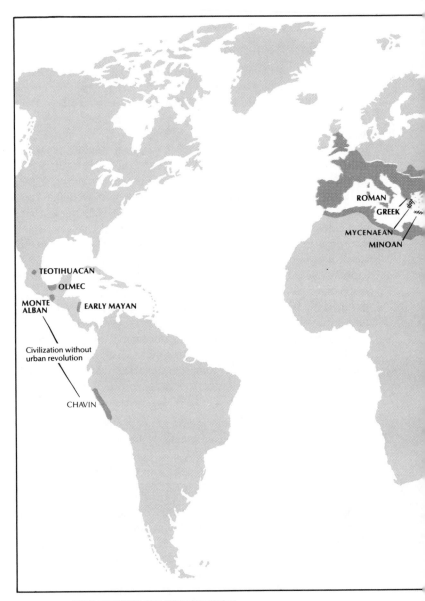

ROMAN
GREEK
MYCENAEAN
MINOAN

TEOTIHUACAN
OLMEC
MONTE
ALBAN   EARLY MAYAN

Civilization without
urban revolution

CHAVIN

THE SPREAD OF CIVILIZATION

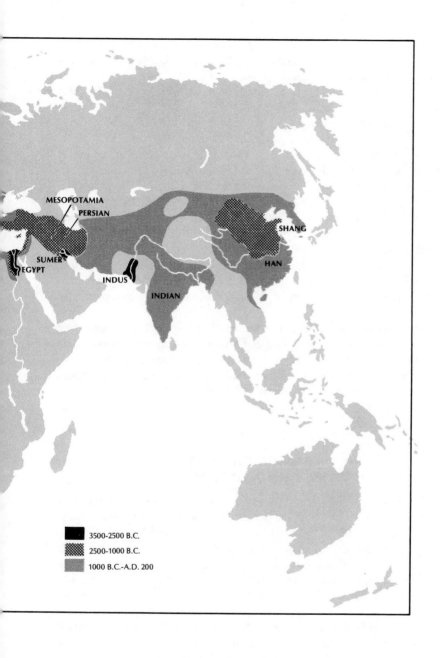

MESOPOTAMIA

PERSIAN

SHANG

SUMER

EGYPT

INDUS

HAN

INDIAN

3500-2500 B.C.

2500-1000 B.C.

1000 B.C.-A.D. 200

ford's distinction between the round cottages of villages and the rectangular buildings of cities, then Jericho was a city after 7000 B.C. Suddenly after that date the houses of Jericho showed the shape of things to come.

Jericho is probably not unique. It has received more extensive archeological work because of the biblical story. Other mounds in ancient Palestine, Turkey, Syria, Iraq, and Iran have already, or no doubt will, yield the remains of fairly permanent, defended settlements from the period between 8000 and 3000 B.C.

It may be preferable, however, to limit the word "city" to some of the settlements that achieved maturity closer to 3000 B.C. The Sumerian settlements from this period show a much more developed Neolithic technology. (The Jericho of 8000 B.C. did not even know pottery.) And more significantly, the settlements of Sumer had by the period of 4000–3000 B.C. begun the process of an urban technological revolution that far surpassed the Neolithic. The perfection of Neolithic technology between 6000 and 4000 B.C. involved such inventions as the ox-drawn plow, the wheeled cart, the sailboat, metallurgy, irrigation, and the domestication of new plants, all of which made agriculture productive enough to support settlements of tens of thousands of inhabitants in a particular area.

"True" cities were possible when these advanced Neolithic settlements used their increased agricultural productivity to create specialized artists, metalworkers, architects, writers, accountants, bureaucrats, physicians, and scientists, and to institutionalize their skills and achievements. This is what happened along the Euphrates River at a number of places shortly before 3000 B.C.

THE URBAN REVOLUTION: CIVILIZATION AND CLASS

The full-scale urban revolution occurred not in the rain-watered lands that first turned some villages into cities, but in the potentially more productive river valleys of Mesopotamia around 3500 B.C. Situated along the Tigris and Euphrates rivers, large villages like Eridu, Erech, Lagash, Kish, and later Ur and Babylon built irrigation systems that increased farm production enormously. Settlements like these were able to support five thousand, even ten thousand people, and still allow something like 10 percent of the inhabitants to work full-time at nonfarming occupations.

A change of this scale was a revolution, certainly the most important revolution in human living since the invention of agriculture five thousand years earlier. The urban revolution was prepared by a whole series of technological inventions in agricultural society. Between 6000 and 3000 B.C. people not only learned how to harness the power of oxen and the wind with the plow, the wheeled cart, and the sailboat; they also discovered the physical properties of metals, learned how to smelt copper and bronze, and began to work out a calendar based on the movements of the sun. River valleys like those of the Tigris and Euphrates were muddy swamps that had to be drained and irrigated to take advantage of the rich soil deposits. The dry land had literally to be built by teams of organized workers.

Therefore, cities required an organizational revolution that was every bit as important as the technological one. This was accomplished under the direction of the new class of rulers and managers—probably from the grasslands—who often treated the emerging cities as a conquered province. The work of irrigation itself allowed the rulers ample opportunity to coerce the inhabitants of these new cities. Rain knows no social distinctions. Irrigated water must be controlled and channeled.

It is no wonder then that the first cities gave us our first kings and our first class societies. Almost everywhere that cities spread (or were again invented) after 3000 B.C.—along the Nile of Egypt, on the Indus River in Pakistan, or in Turkey and China, and later in Middle America—the king is usually described as the founder of cities. Almost everywhere these kings were able to endow their control with religious sanction. In Egypt and America the king was god. In Mesopotamia a new class of priests carried out the needs of the king's religion of control.

In some cities the new priesthood would appoint the king. In others, the priests were merely his lieutenants. When they were most loyal, their religion served to deify the king. The teachings of the new class of Mesopotamian priests, for instance, were that their god had created the people solely to work for the king and make his life easier. But even when the priesthood attempted to wrest some of the king's power from him, the priests taught the people to accept the divided society, which benefited king and priesthood as providers of a natural god-given order. The priesthood, after all, was responsible for measuring time, bounding space, and predicting seasonal events. The mastery of people was easy for those who controlled time and space.

The priesthood was only one of the new classes that insured the respectability of the warrior-chieftain turned king. Other palace intellectuals—scribes (or writers), doctors, magicians, and diviners—also struggled to maintain the king's prestige and manage his kingdom. This new class was rewarded, as were the priests, with leisure, status, and magnificent buildings, all of which further exalted the majesty of the king and his city.

Beneath the king, the priesthood, and the new class of intellectuals-managers was another new class charged with maintaining the king's law and order. Soldiers and police were also inventions of the first cities. Like the surrounding city wall, the king's military guard served a double function: they provided defense from outside attack and an obstacle to internal rebellion.

This reconstruction shows how the pyramids were built. Stone blocks were pulled over slippery, milky surfaces and rollers to be prodded into place at ever higher levels of the inclined plane that became the pyramid. The pharaoh's dream of a monumental tomb was realized by architects and court officials directing the forced labor of peasants and craftspeople. (Museum of Science, Boston)

That these were the most important classes of city society can be seen from the physical remains of the first cities. The archeologist's spade has uncovered the monumental buildings of these classes in virtually all of the first cities. The palace, the temple, and the citadel (or fort) are, indeed, the monuments that distinguish cities from villages. Further, the size of these buildings and the permanency of their construction (compared with the small, cheaply built homes of the farmers) attest to the fundamental class divisions of city society.

CIVILIZATION: SECURITY AND VARIETY

The most obvious achievements of the first civilizations are the monuments—the pyramids, temples, palaces, statues, and treasures—that were created for the new ruling class of kings, nobles, priests, and their officials. But civilized life is much more than the capacity to create monuments.

Civilized life is secure life. At the most basic level this means security from the sudden destruction that village communities might suffer. Civilized life gives the feeling of permanence. It offers regularity, stability, order, even routine. Plans can be made. Expectations can be realized. People can be expected to act predictably, according to the rules.

The first cities were able to attain stability with walls that shielded the inhabitants from nomads and armies, with the first codes of law that defined human relationships, with police and officials that enforced the laws, and with institutions that functioned beyond the lives of their particular members. City life offered considerably more permanence and security than village life.

Civilization involves more than security, however. A city that provided only order would be more like a prison than a civilization. The first cities provided something that the best-ordered villages lacked. They provided far greater variety: more races and ethnic groups were speaking more languages, engaged in more occupations, and living a greater variety of life-styles. The abundance of choice, the opportunities for new sensations, new experiences, knowledge—these have always been the appeals of city life. The opportunities for growth and enrichment were far greater than the possibilities of plow and pasture life.

Security plus variety equals creativity. At least the possibility of a more creative, expressive life was available in the protected, semipermanent city enclosures that drew, like magnets, foreign traders and diplomats, new ideas about gods and nature, strange foods and customs, and the magicians, ministers, and mercenaries of the king's court. Civilization is the enriched life that this dynamic urban setting permitted and the human creativity and opportunity that it encouraged. At the very least, cities made even the most common slave think and feel a greater range of things than the tightly knit, clanish agricultural village allowed. That was (and still is) the root of innovation and creativity—of civilization itself.

The variety of people and the complexity of city life required new and more general means of communication. The villager knew everyone personally. Cities brought together people who often did not even speak the same language. Not only law codes but written language itself became a way to bridge the many gaps of human variety. Cities invented writing so that strangers could communicate, and so that those communications could become permanent—remembered publicly, officially recorded. Emerson was right when he said that the city lives by memory, but it was the official memory that enabled the city to carry on its business or religion beyond the lifetime of the village elders. Written symbols that everyone could recognize became the basis of laws, invention, education, taxes, accounting, contracts, and obligations. In short, writing and records made it possible for each generation to begin on the shoulders of its ancestors. Village life and knowledge often seemed to start from scratch. Thus, cities cultivated not only memory and the past, but hope and the future as well. City civilizations invented not only history and record keeping but also prophecy and social planning.

Writing was one city invention that made more general communication possible. Money was another. Money made it possible to deal with anyone just as an agreed-upon public language did. Unnecessary in the village climate of mutual obligations, money was essential in the city society of strangers. Such general media of communication as writing and money vastly increased the number of things that could be said and thought, bought and sold. As a consequence, city life was more impersonal than village life, but also more dynamic and more exciting.

THE "EYE" AND "I"

Marshall McLuhan has written that "civilization gave the barbarian an eye for an ear." We might add that civilization also gave an "I" for an "us." City life made the "eye" and the "I" more important than they had been in the village. The invention of writing made knowledge more visual. The eye had to be trained to recognize the minute differences in letters and words. Eyes took in a greater abundance of detail: laws, prices, the strange cloak of the foreigner, the odd type of shoes made by the new craftsworker from who-knows-where, the colors of the fruit and vegetable market, elaborate painting in the temple, as well as the written word. In the village one learned by listening. In the city seeing was believing. In the new city courts of law an "eyewitness account" was believed to be more reliable than "hearsay evidence." In some villages even today, the heard and the spoken are thought more reliable than the written and the seen. In the city, even spoken language took on the uniformity and absence of emotion that is unavoidable in the written word. Perhaps emotions themselves became less violent. "Civilized" is always used to mean emotional restraint, control of the more violent passions, and a greater understanding, even tolerance, of the different and foreign.

Perhaps empathy (the capacity to put yourself in someone else's shoes) increased in cities—so full of so many different others that had to be understood. When a Turkish villager was recently asked, "What would you do if you were president of your country?" he stammered: "My God! How can you ask such a thing? How can I . . . I cannot . . . president of Turkey . . . master of the whole world?" He was completely unable to imagine himself as president. It was as removed from his experience as if he were master of the world. Similarly, a Lebanese villager who was asked what he would do if he were editor of a newspaper accused the interviewer of ridiculing him, and frantically waved the interviewer on to another question. Such a life was beyond his comprehension. It was too foreign to imagine. The very variety of city life must have increased the capacity of the lowest commoner to imagine, empathize, sympathize, and criticize.

The oral culture of the village reinforced the accepted by saying and singing it almost monotonously. The elders, the storytellers, and the minstrels must have had prodigious memories. But their stories changed only gradually and slightly. The spoken word was sacred. To say it differently was to change the truth. The written culture of cities taught "point of *view*." An urban individual did not have to remember everything. That was done permanently on paper. Knowledge became a recognition of different interpretations and the capacity to look up things. The awareness of variety meant the possibility of criticism, analysis, and an ever-newer synthesis. It is no wonder that the technical and scientific knowledge of cities increased at a geometric rate compared with the knowledge of villages. The multiplication of knowledge was implicit in the city's demand to recognize difference and variety. Civilization has come to mean that ever-expanding body of knowledge and skill. Its finest achievements have been that knowledge, its writing, and its visual art. The city and civilization (like the child) are to be seen and not heard.

It may seem strange to say that the impersonal life of cities contributed greatly to the development of personality—the "I" as well as the "eye." Village life was in a sense much more personal. Everything was taken personally. Villagers deal with each other not as "the blacksmith," "the baker," "that guy who owes me a goat," or "that no-good bum." They do not even "deal" with each other. They know each other by name and family. They love, hate, support, and murder each other because of who they are, because of personal feelings, because of personal and family responsibility. They have full, varied relationships with each member of the village. They do not merely buy salt from this person, talk about the weather with this other person, and discuss personal matters with only this other person. They share too much with each other to divide up their relationships in that way.

City life is a life of separated, partial relationships. In a city you do not know about the butcher's life, wife, kids, and problems. You do not care. You are in a hurry. You have too many other things to do. You might discuss the weather—but while he's cutting. You came to buy meat. Many urban relationships are like that. There are many business, trading, or "dealing" relationships because there are simply too many people to know them all as relatives.

The impersonality of city life is a shame in a way. (It makes it easier to get mugged by someone who does not even hate you.) But the luxurious variety of impersonal relationships (at least some of the time) provide the freedom for the individual personality to emerge. Maybe that is why people have often dreamed of leaving family and friends (usually for a city) in the hope of "finding themselves." Certainly, the camaraderie and community of village life had a darker side of surveillance and conformity. When everything was known about everyone, it was difficult for the individual to find his or her individuality. Family ties and village custom were often obstacles to asserting self-identity. The city offered its inhabitants a huge variety of possible relationships and personal identities. The urban inhabitant was freer than his village cousin to choose friends, lovers, associates, occupation, housing, and life-style. The city was full of choices that the village could not afford or condone. The village probably provided more security in being like everyone else and doing what was expected. But the city provided the variety of possibilities that could allow the individual to follow the "inner self" and cultivate inner gardens.

The class divisions of city society made it difficult for commoners to achieve an effective or creative individuality. But the wealthy and powerful—especially the king—were able to develop models of individuality and personality that were revolutionary. No one before had ever achieved such a sense of the self, and the model of the king's power and freedom became a goal for the rest of the society. The luxury, leisure, and opportunity of the king was a revolutionary force. In contrast to a village elder, the king could do whatever he wanted. Recognizing that, more and more city inhabitants asked, "Why can't we?" City revolutions have continually extended class privilege and opportunities ever since.

Once a society has achieved a level of abundance, once it can offer the technological means, the educational opportunities, the creative outlets necessary for everyone to lead meaningful, happy, healthy lives, then classes may be a hindrance. Class divisions were, however, a definite stimulus to productivity and creativity in the early city civilizations. The democratic villagers preferred stability to improvement. As a result, their horizons were severely limited. They died early, lived precipitously, and suffered without much hope. The rulers of the first cities discovered the possibilities of leisure, creation, and the good life. They invented heaven and utopia—first for themselves. Only very gradually has the invention of civilization, of human potential, sifted down to those beneath the ruling class. In many cases, luxury, leisure, freedom, and opportunity are still the monopolies of the elite. But once the powerful have exploited the poor enough to establish their own paradise on earth and their own immortality after death, the poor also have broader horizons and plans.

MESOPOTAMIAN AND EGYPTIAN CIVILIZATIONS: A TALE OF TWO RIVERS

Experts disagree as to whether Mesopotamian or Egyptian civilization is older. Mesopotamian influence in Egypt was considerable enough to suggest slightly

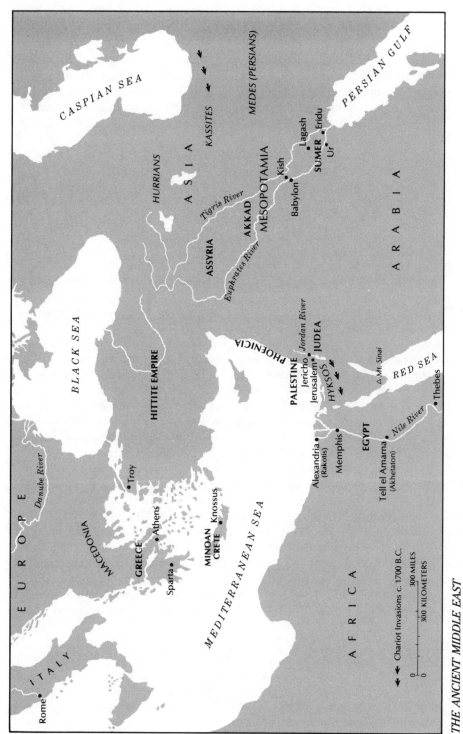

THE ANCIENT MIDDLE EAST
Mesopotamian, Egyptian, and Greek civilizations.

earlier origins, but both had evolved distinct civilizations by 3000 B.C. Indeed, the difference between the two civilizations attests to the existence of multiple routes to civilized life. In both cases, river valleys provided the necessary water and silt for an agricultural surplus large enough to support classes of specialists who did not have to farm. But the differing nature of the rivers had much to do with the different types of civilization that evolved.

The Egyptians were blessed with the easier and more reliable of the two rivers. The Nile overflowed its banks predictably every year on the parched ground in the summer after August 15, well after the harvest had been gathered, depositing its rich sediment, and withdrawing by early October, leaving little salt or marsh, in time for the sowing of winter crops. Later sowings for summer crops required only simple canals that tapped the river upstream and the natural drainage of the Nile Valley. Further, transportation on the Nile was simplified by the fact that the prevailing winds blew from the north, while the river flowed from the south, making navigation a matter of using sails upstream and dispensing with them coming downstream.

The Euphrates offered none of these advantages as it cut its way through Mesopotamia. The Euphrates flowed high above the flood plain (unlike the neighboring Tigris) so that its waters could be used, but it flooded suddenly and without warning in the late spring, after the summer crops had been sown and before the winter crops could be harvested. Thus, the flooding of the Euphrates offered no natural irrigation. Its waters were needed at other times, and its flooding was destructive. Canals were necessary to drain off water for irrigation when the river was low, and these canals had to be adequately blocked, and the banks reinforced, when the river flooded. Further, since the Euphrates was not as easily navigable as the Nile, the main canals had to serve as major transportation arteries as well.

In Mesopotamia the flood was the enemy. The Mesopotamian deities who ruled the waters, Nin-Girsu and Tiamat, were feared. The forces of nature were often evil. Life was a struggle. In Egypt, on the other hand, life was viewed as a cooperation with nature. Even the Egyptian god of the flood, Hapi, was a helpful deity, who provided the people's daily bread. Egyptian priests and philosophers were much more at ease with their world than were their Mesopotamian counterparts. And, partly because of their different experiences with their rivers, the Mesopotamians developed a civilization based on cities, while the Egyptians did not. From the first Sumerian city-states on the lower Euphrates to the later northern Mesopotamian capital of Babylon, civilization was the product and expression of

---

SUMERIAN UR: THE WALLED CITY AND OPENED LIFE
A walled city like Ur (shown in the top portion of the map) could
open the possibilities of life by requiring public participation in its
crowded neighborhoods (shown in detail in the bottom portion of the
map).

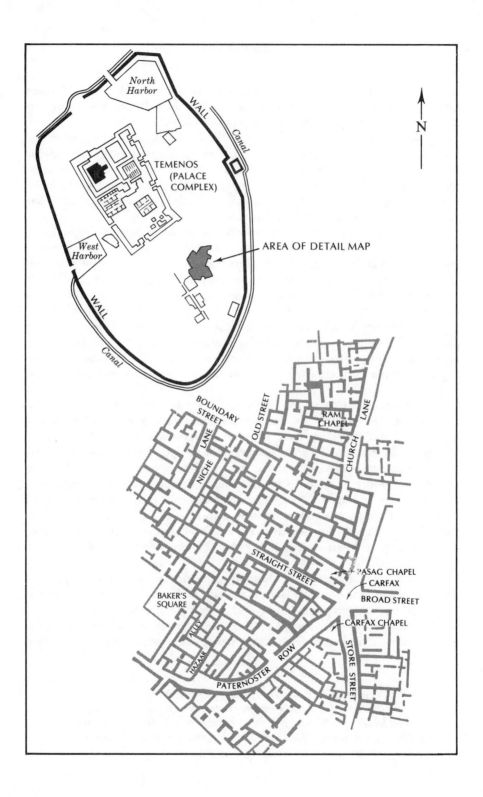

city life. Egyptian civilization, in contrast, was the creation of the pharaoh's court rather than of cities. Beyond the court, which was moved from one location to another, Egypt remained a country of peasant villages.

A prime reason for Egypt's lack of urbanization was the ease of farming on the banks of the Nile. Canal irrigation was a relatively simple process that did not demand much organization. Small market towns were sufficient for the needs of the countryside. They housed artisans, shopkeepers, the priests of the local temple, and the agents of the pharaoh, but they never swelled with a large middle class and never developed large-scale industry or commerce.

In Sumer, and later in Mesopotamia, the enormous task of fighting the Euphrates required a complex social organization with immediate local needs. Only communal labor could build and maintain the network of subsidiary canals for irrigation and drainage. Constant supervision was necessary to keep the canals free of silt, to remove salt deposits, to maintain the riverbanks at flood-time, and to prevent any farmer from monopolizing the water in periods of drought. Life on the Euphrates required cooperative work and responsibility that never ceased. It encouraged absolute, administrative control over an area larger than the village, and it fostered participation and loyalty to an irrigated area smaller than the imperial state. The city-state was the political answer to the economic problems of Sumer and Mesopotamia.

The religious practices in the Euphrates Valley reflected and supported city organization. Residents of each local area worshiped the local god while recognizing the existence of other local gods in a larger Sumerian, and eventually Mesopotamian, pantheon of gods. The priests of the local temple supervised canal work, the collection of taxes, and the storage of written records, as well as the proper maintenance of religious rituals. Thus, religious loyalty reinforced civic loyalty. Peasant and middle-class Sumerians thought of themselves as citizens of their particular city, worshipers of their particular city god, subjects of their particular god's earthly representative, but not as Sumerian nationals. By contrast, the Egyptian peasant was always an Egyptian, a subject of the pharaoh, but never a citizen.

The local, civic orientation of Mesopotamian cities can be seen in the physical structure of the capital city of Sumer, the city of Ur. Like other cities on the Euphrates, Ur was surrounded by a wall. It was dominated by the temple of Nannar, the moon-god who owned the city, and the palace complex beneath the temple. The residential areas were situated outside of the sacred Temenos, or temple

---

EGYPTIAN AKHETATON: OPEN SPACES AND IMPERIAL ORDER
A city without walls could be rigidly controlled. The pharaoh's city,
surrounded by desert, was safe from outside attack. But it also lacked
any internal dynamic. The housing area (shown in detail at bottom)
looks more like a military barracks than a neighborhood.

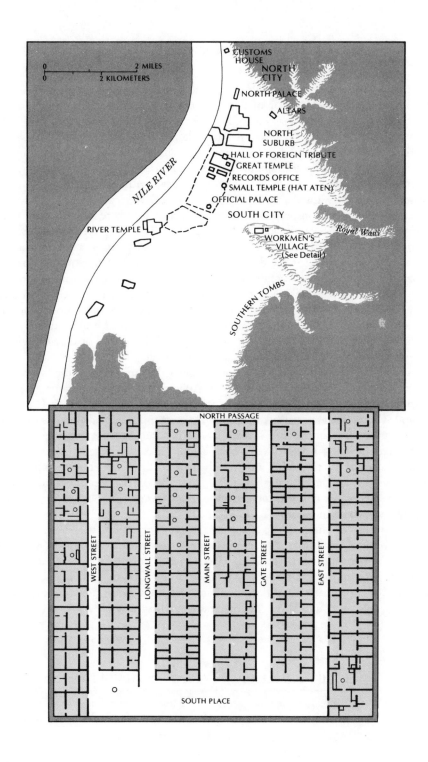

compound, but within the walls, between the river and the main canal. The well-excavated remains of Ur of the seventeenth century B.C. show a residential street plan that looks like many Middle Eastern cities of today. A highly congested area of winding alleys and broad streets sheltered one- and two-story houses of merchants, shopkeepers, tradespeople, and occasional priests and scribes that suggest a large, relatively prosperous middle class. Most houses were built around a central courtyard that offered shade throughout the day, with mud-brick, often even plastered, outside walls that protected a number of interior rooms from the sun and the eyes of the tax inspector. The remains of seventeenth-century Ur show both the variety and the density of modern city life. There are specialized districts throughout the city. Certain trades have their special quarters: a bakers' square, probably special areas for the dyers, tanners, potters, and metalworkers. But life is mixed together as well. Subsidiary gods have temples outside the Temenos. Small and large houses are jumbled next to each other. There seems to be a slum area near the Temenos, but there are small houses for workers, tenant farmers, and the poor throughout the city. And no shop or urban professional is more than a short walking distance away. The entire size of the walled city was an oval that extended three-quarters of a mile long and a half a mile wide.

A well-excavated Egyptian city from roughly the same period (the fourteenth century B.C.) offers some striking contrasts. Akhetaton, or Tell el Amarna, Pharaoh Akhenaton's capital on the Nile, was not enclosed by walls or canals. It merely straggled down the eastern bank of the Nile for five miles and faded into the desert. Without the need for extensive irrigation or protection, Tell el Amarna shows little of the crowded, vital density of Ur. Its layout lacks any sense of urgency. The North Palace of the pharaoh is a mile and a half north of the temple complex and offices, which are three and a half miles from the official pleasure garden. The palaces of the court nobility and the large residences of the court's officials front one of the two main roads that parallel the river, or they are situated at random. There is plenty of physical space (and social space) between these and the bunched villages of workers' houses. The remains suggest very little in the way of a middle class or a merchant or professional class beyond the pharaoh's specialists and retainers. Life for the wealthy was, judging from the housing, more luxurious than at Ur, but for the majority of the population city life was less rich. In many ways, the pharaoh's court at Tell el Amarna was not a city at all.

CASTE AND CLASS IN ASIAN CIVILIZATION

Within a short time after the establishment of Mesopotamian and Egyptian civilizations, other civilizations developed in the Middle East, on the Indus River in

India, and on the Yellow River in China. We know relatively little of the earliest Indian and Chinese civilizations. The Indian cities of Harappa and Mohenjo Daro flourished from about 2500 B.C. to 1500 B.C., when they were burned, destroyed, and left in rubble by invading Aryan-speaking tribes from the north. The ruins suggest a highly organized, class-divided society run by priests: the streets follow a strict grid plan, most of the housing is quite small, and the remains of a temple quarter and large temple residences stood above the rest of the city.

It is not clear to what extent the ancient Indus civilization had already developed the Indian caste system. It is most likely that it had not. Important elements of the system were probably introduced by the Aryan invaders as ways of legitimating their control over the Indian people they conquered. One of these elements is the idea of *varna* (an Indian Sanskrit word for "color" that far predates the Portuguese word "caste"). The Aryan Vedas spoke of the four *varnas,* placing the *brahmans,* priests, at the top. Second were the *kshatriyas,* the aristocrats and warriors. A third *varna,* called the *vaishyas,* was made up of farmers, artisans, and merchants. The fourth *varna,* the *shudras,* was made up largely of workers. In the age of the Vedas (after about 1000 B.C.) the first three *varnas* considered themselves as the especially holy "twice-born" (born a second time when they were initiated into Vedic teachings). The *shudras* were denied access to the secrets of the Vedas. Later, all four *varnas* distinguished themselves from a still lower outcaste group of darker, non-Aryan indigenous peoples called "untouchables," who were required to do the work that all other groups considered "polluting" (such as garbage removal and burial of the dead).

Increasingly, these *varnas* were theoretical distinctions that were less important in daily life than specific occupations were. As these occupations became largely hereditary among communities of people who ate and married only among themselves, they became the *jatis,* literally "births," that we have called (since the Portuguese) castes. There are hundreds, if not thousands, in India today.

Given China's lack of castes, it is tempting to speculate as to whether early Chinese civilization may have been less socially divided than Indian civilization. Modern Chinese Marxists like Guo Moruo [Kuo-Mo-jo] called early Chinese history (before 1000 B.C.) "primitive communism." This Marxist term corresponded with a traditional pre-Marxist Chinese view that saw the Neolithic Age and earliest civilization as a golden age of equality. Unfortunately, there is little evidence to judge either way. One factor to consider, however, is the absence of the plow from Chinese agriculture until as late as the fourth century B.C. The rich loess (nutritive dust) soil of the Yellow River could be easily worked with hoe and spade. Draft animals were not needed without plows. (Even today, the Chinese diet has virtually no dairy products and little meat.) The plow, we have seen, was an important factor in the development of the patriarchy because it caused a shift from women's horticulture to men's field agriculture with draft animals. Plow agriculture was also instrumental in drastically increasing the yield of farming, thus allowing an economic surplus that could be used for increased population, greater nonagricultural specialization, or luxury production to distinguish and satisfy a ruling minority.

The Shang dynasty (1766–1027 B.C.), on the other hand, was founded by Eurasian pastoral peoples very much like the Aryans in their origins and technology, including the use of horses, cattle, and wheeled chariots. Their civilization had many of the marks of other Eurasian class-divided civilizations. It was a military society that engaged in wars for tribute, the enslavement of captives, and human sacrifice. It developed writing, advanced metallurgy, currency, and monument building in part to enhance the power of the rulers. Further, graves show considerable differences of status (if not as much as in Egypt or later under the Qin [Ch'in] dynasty). Shang China did not have castes, but it very definitely had classes.

DIVERSITY, DIFFUSION, AND DEVELOPMENT OF CIVILIZATION

As civilization spread, it continued to serve the interests of ruling classes. A pleasant style of life must have developed in those like the courtly, sea-borne civilization of Minoan Crete. The paintings found in the palace of Minos (first built about 1900 B.C.) show an exhilarating spontaneity, elaborate dress, and fondness for nature and life that reminds us of the courtly Egyptian society that the Cretans knew through trade. In some ways, however, Minoan Crete reminds us more of a Neolithic society. The chief deity seems to have been a Great Mother goddess. Women, in their ornate, open-breasted gowns appear to play prominent roles, and there appears to be a gaiety, charm, and peacefulness (neither city walls nor military imagery) that is far removed from the struggles of other Middle Eastern civilizations.

The civilization of Sumer passed upriver as the delta soil became salted or merely as less-civilized armies upstream conquered by controlling the water supply. Akkad dominated Sumer after 2250 B.C., and both were controlled by Hammurabi's Babylon further north by the eighteenth century B.C. Their northern Semitic languages replaced Sumerian, but they retained enough of Sumerian culture to be called Mesopotamian.

By 2000 B.C. Mesopotamian civilization was circled by various satellite civilizations—Kassites, Hittites, Canaanites, Hurrians, and Assyrians—whose pastoral-military organization made conquest and imitation easier than permanent rule,

---

The "Snake Goddess" of Minoan Crete wears the traditional dress of Minoan civilization, but the snake recalls an older Neolithic cult of fear and fertility, birth and rebirth. (Alinari, EPA)

but who became civilized in the process. The periodic invasions of these protoci-vilized tribes (especially around 1700, 1500, and 1200 B.C.) probably resulted more in the diffusion of civilization to the new conquerors, and the development of civilized life in the rain-watered lands from which they came, than in the destruction of civilized ways of life. Even when the native inhabitants regained their lands, as the Egyptians did from the Hyksos in the sixteenth century B.C., the resulting native dynasties (like those of the New Kingdom or Empire in Egypt, 1600–1200 B.C.) often displayed the same militarism and lack of inventiveness shown by their former conquerors. By the advent of the first Iron Age invasions after 1200 B.C., the civilization of cities—bronze, plows, and writing—was no longer the monopoly of a few vulnerable river valleys. Its diffusion meant its ultimate survival, even after particular cities, peoples, or writing systems had long been forgotten.

If the first millennium of civilization building (about 3500 to 2500 B.C.) had produced in rapid succession most of the technological and organizational achievements of the Bronze Age, the second millennium insured the continuance of that accomplishment through diffusion. Bureaucratization, militarization, and war may have slowed the pace of technological development between 2500 and 1200 B.C., or it may have been that the potentialities and limits of the Bronze Age were reached rather early. Whatever the case, the Egyptian Middle Kingdom (2050–1750 B.C.) did little more than imitate the pyramid building and institutions of kingship of the Old Kingdom (3000–2250 B.C.), and the Semitic empires of northern Mesopotamia (like Babylon) mainly enlarged and militarized the achievements of the earlier Sumerians.

Culturally, however, the period between 2500 B.C. and the development of Iron Age technology around 1200 B.C. was more innovative. One thinks, for instance, of developments in law, religion, and writing that opened the possibilities of cultural achievement even within the boundaries of Mesopotamian and Egyptian civilization. The law codes of Hammurabi (1750 B.C.) enshrined patriarchal power and class rule, but even in doing so provided a measure of certainty and justice lacking in more traditional tribal societies. Further, the efficiency of a bureaucratic empire required a responsible as well as powerful ruling class. Thus, Hammurabi's code stipulated heavier punishment of nobles convicted of certain crimes, as well as heavier punishment for crimes committed against nobles. The nobility were expected to conduct themselves better than subjects.

In Egypt, the concrete (or stone) expression of personal immortality during the main period of pyramid building (2700–2500 B.C.) filtered down to the rest of the

---

Akhenaton, his wife Queen Nefertiti, and one of their daughters stand with offerings to the sun god Aton at the pharaoh's new city of Aton, Akhetaton (Tell el Amarna today). (Metropolitan Museum of Art)

society in cults of the god Osiris by 2000 B.C. Osiris, who himself had been restored to life by his loving wife Isis, after being dismembered by his wicked brother Seth, was pictured as a god of the underworld who weighed the souls of all deceased Egyptians against the feather symbol of justice. Immortality was opened to those beyond the family of the pharaoh, and a person's worth could no longer be measured by wealth and social position. Osiris worship became so common in the New Kingdom (1600–1200 B.C.) that the priests attempted to counteract its democratic implications by devising fees and duties that would insure a light heart (or a heavy feather). That was one of the corruptions that Akhenaton (c. 1375–1358 B.C.) attempted to reform by his espousal of one god, Aton, who demanded moral goodness of his worshipers. Akhenaton's monotheism may have even been a source of the Judeo-Christian idea of a single almighty deity, since this was the period of the Hebrew presence in Egypt. If so, it departed with the Hebrew exodus. Akhenaton's young successor, Tutankhamen, allowed the priests to abandon the revolutionary doctrine and its capital at Tell el Amarna.

Like law and religion, the art of writing also achieved greater flexibility after 2000 B.C. The pictorial Egyptian hieroglyphic and Mesopotamian cuneiform writing were still the standards for international trade and the models of classic style. The Hittites and Minoans actually copied the pictorial style so that their inscriptions could look as impressive as those of the Egyptians. But increasingly after 1600 B.C., pictorial writing was replaced in everyday work by phonetic (sound) systems instead of pictures. Phonetic systems are much simpler because the human voice makes fewer sounds than the human imagination makes pictures. That means a smaller set of symbols. Pictorial writing can be cumbersome if everything is drawn, or it can be confusing if detail is omitted. What is the meaning, for example, of a stick-figure man leaning on a stick? Does it mean "leaning" or "walking" or "soldier" or "old age"? The transition from pictorial to phonetic writing was very gradual. At first the pictorial images were used to do double duty as sounds as well as pictures. This led to an elaborate system of visual puns. An English equivalent would be writing the word "belief" with a picture of a bee and a picture of a leaf. Gradually, certain symbols became standard for certain sounds, first symbols for syllables, then symbols for consonants, and finally the alphabet of separate symbols for consonants and vowels.

The development of phonetic writing was not complete by 1000 B.C. It is not used in China today. By 1000 B.C. in the Middle East, symbols for syllables instead of pictures and puns were increasingly used. But even that much of a transition opened the mastery of writing to a broader population than the priests and scribes. As with the idea of legal justice and the idea of individual moral responsibility, the ruling class of the ancient world had devised more efficient tools for ruling subjects and empires. But like any tools, once devised they could not remain the property of a dynasty, a civilization, or a class.

FOR FURTHER READING

There are a number of interesting books on the development of the first city societies or civilizations by archeologists and historians. V. Gordon Childe's *Man Makes Himself* first outlined the importance of the Neolithic and urban revolutions, and although dated, it is still absorbing. Dora Jane Hamblin and the editors of Time-Life books update the older interpretation in a beautifully illustrated collection of essays on specific cities entitled *The First Cities*. Another well-illustrated, readable introduction is Glyn Daniel's *The First Civilizations: The Archaeology of Their Origins*. For a short, well-argued, comparative history with a cyclical perspective, the student might try Rushton Coulborn's *The Origin of Civilized Societies*. A much fuller comparative treatment can be found in Jacquetta Hawkes's *The First Great Civilizations* and in Sir Leonard Woolley's *The Beginnings of Civilization*, also published as Hawkes and Woolley, *Prehistory and the Beginnings of Civilization*. For vivid histories of archeological discovery that are also studies of ancient civilizations, Leonard Cottrell's volumes on Egypt *(The Lost Pharaohs)* and Crete *(The Bull of Minos)* and his *Lost Cities* make exciting reading. A catchy series of urban "firsts" is recorded in Samuel Noah Kramer's *History Begins at Sumer*. A more sophisticated analysis of the philosophy and mythology of the ancient civilizations of the Middle East can be found in the volume by Henri Frankfort and others called *Before Philosophy* and in S. H. Hooke's *Middle Eastern Mythology*.

For students who wish to explore the history of a particular ancient civilization, there are a wide range of possibilities. For ancient Mesopotamia, besides some of the titles already mentioned, there are James Mellaart's *Earliest Civilizations in the Near East*, W. W. Hallo and W. K. Simpson's *The Ancient Near East*, Milton Covensky's *The Ancient Near Eastern Tradition*, Cyrus H. Gordon's *The Ancient Near East*, C. Leonard Woolley's *Ur of the Chaldees*, Samuel Noah Kramer's *The Sumerians: Their History, Culture, and Character*, A. Leo Oppenheim's *Ancient Mesopotamia: A Portrait of a Dead Civilization*, Henri Frankfort's *The Birth of Civilization in the Near East*, and H. W. F. Sagg's *The Greatness That Was Babylon*.

On ancient Egyptian civilization, besides sections of some of the books already mentioned, there are C. Aldred's *The Egyptians, Ancient Peoples and Places*, Elizabeth Riefstahl's *Thebes in the Time of Amunhotep III*, Sir Alan Gardiner's *Egypt of the Pharaohs*, Barbara Mertz's *Temples, Tombs and Hieroglyphs: The Story of Egyptology*, Torgny Save-Soderbergh's *Pharaohs and Mortals*, and John A. Wilson's *The Burden of Egypt* and *The Culture of Ancient Egypt*. The classic works of James Henry Breasted, *The Development of Religion and Thought in Ancient Egypt* and the enormous *A History of Egypt*, are still superb after fifty years. A good collection of primary sources can be found in *The Literature of Ancient Egypt, An Anthology of Stories, Instructions, and Poetry*, edited by W. K. Simpson. Pyramid buffs would enjoy Ahmed Fakhry's *The Pyramids*.

Other ancient Middle Eastern civilizations are treated in O. R. Gurney's *The Hittites*, D. B. Harden's *The Phoenicians*, R. W. Hutchinson's *Prehistoric Crete*, W. A. McDonald's *Progress into the Past: The Rediscovery of Mycenaean Civilization*, and A. T. Olmstead's *History of the Persian Empire*.

On India there are Stuart Piggott's *Prehistoric India*, Sir Mortimer Wheeler's *The Indus*

Civilization, William Theodore DeBary's *Sources of Indian Tradition*, Romila Thapar's *A History of India*, and O. I. Chavarria-Aguilar's *Traditional India*.

On China there are W. A. Fairservis, Jr.'s *Origins of Oriental Civilization*, C. P. Fitzgerald's *China: A Short Cultural History*, W. Eichhorn's *Chinese Civilization: An Introduction*, James T. C. Liu and Wei-ming Tu's *Traditional China*, W. Watson's *China Before the Han Dynasty*, *The Making of China*, edited by Chun-shu Chang, and Hefflee G. Creel's *The Birth of China*.

NOTE

1. Aristophanes, *The Archarnians*, trans. Douglass Parker (New York: New American Library, 1961), pp. 16–17.

Chronological Table of
The Ancient World

to 1000 B.C.

Before 8000 B.C.	Paleolithic (Old Stone) Age: hunting and gathering.
8000 B.C.	Beginning of Neolithic (New Stone) Age: farming and herding.
8000–1500 B.C.	Diffusion of Neolithic revolution through 99 percent of world population. Neolithic inventions: polished stone tools, planting, seed use, hoe, containers, pottery, yeast for bread, alcoholic drinks, plant knowledge, spinning and weaving, settled life, villages, Earth Mother goddesses, domestication of animals.
6000–4000 B.C.	Perfection of Neolithic technology. Early metallurgy, wheeled carts, sailboats, irrigation, plows, small cities.
3500–3000 B.C.	Urban revolution in Sumer. Beginnings of Mesopotamian and Egyptian civilizations. Development of irrigation, calendars, writing, kingship, priests, classes, urban occupations, mathematics, rudimentary astronomy, bureaucracies, royal culture, patriarchal institutions, and religion.
3000 B.C.	Unification of Egypt. Old Kingdom, 3000–2250 B.C.
2700–2500 B.C.	Pyramid building in Egypt. Beginning of Minoan and Indus civilizations, Neolithic farming in China.
2250 B.C.	Beginning of empire of Sargon of Akkad in Mesopotamia.
2000 B.C.	Emergence of satellite civilizations on rain-watered land in Middle East. Egyptian Middle Kingdom 2050–1750 B.C.
1750 B.C.	Hammurabi's Mesopotamian Empire and law code.
1700–1500 B.C.	Nomadic tribes in chariots invade civilizations. Minoan and Indus civilizations destroyed. Egyptian New Kingdom (1600–1200 B.C.) after defeat of Hyksos. Shang dynasty in China (c. 1766–1122 B.C.).
1600–1300 B.C.	Early development of alphabetic writing. Osiris worship in Egypt spreads idea of personal immortality.
1375–1358 B.C.	Akhenaton's monotheistic reforms. Capital at Tell el Amarna.
1200–1000 B.C.	Iron Age invasions. Dorians in Greece. Zhou dynasty in China (c. 1027–256 B.C.). Further Aryan conquest of India and spread of Vedic religion.

II

The
Classical
World

1000 B.C. – A.D. 500

(Atalanta, antique Greek marble statue. Granger.)

Preview of the Period

1000 B.C.–A.D. 500

This period is called "classical" because it saw the rise of many of the world's great cultural traditions that later generations thought "classical," or authoritative models. Greek civilization (especially from 500 to 31 B.C.) was one such tradition. It was followed in the Mediterranean world by the Roman civilization, which lasted almost to A.D. 500.

Classical civilizations also emerged in India and China during this period. India developed at least two major religious traditions, Buddhism and Hinduism, which have since transformed much of the world. Chinese civilization in this period took a shape and a set of values, modeled largely on the works of Confucius and his followers, that it has retained until the present.

The terms "ancient" and "classical" are sometimes used interchangeably. These "classical" civilizations were also "ancient" in a broad sense. What distinguishes them from those of the earlier period is not only the revolutions in religion and thought that occurred but also an increased technological productivity, largely a result of the shaping of iron (casting in China; shaping wrought iron in the West) for more efficient plows, tools, and weapons. Just as the period from 3000 to 1000 B.C. can be called the Bronze Age, the period from 1000 B.C. to A.D. 500 can be called the Iron Age.

Persian and Greek Civilizations (1000–300 B.C.).   Classical Greek civilization followed the flowering and decline of ancient Minoan civilization (2900–1150 B.C.) on the Mediterranean island of Crete and the mainland Mycenaean civilization (1600–1150 B.C.). The destruction of both of these centers, including the city of Troy around 1250 B.C., led to a Greek Dark Age (1100–750 B.C.).

Greece emerged in a period of colonization and tyranny

(700–500 B.C.) that produced the poetry of Homer (c. 725 B.C.) and Hesiod (c. 700 B.C.) and the legal reforms of Solon in Athens (c. 600 B.C.).

By 500 B.C. Greek city-states confronted the much larger Persian Empire that had been fashioned by Croesus (c. 560–546 B.C.), Cyrus the Great (c. 550–530 B.C.), and Darius I (c. 521–486 B.C.). Persian supremacy in the Middle East had been aided by the spread of Zoroastrianism, a religion that saw a cosmic struggle between the forces of goodness and evil. A series of wars between the Greek and Persian empires (between 560 and 467 B.C.) resulted in the victory of the Greeks in the eastern Mediterranean, and of the Athenians in Greece.

The golden age of Athens spanned a brief period in the middle of the fifth century B.C. Athenian political supremacy and cultural flowering came with the victory over the Persians in the first third of the fifth century, but it dissipated in the squabbling between city-states, especially Athens and Sparta, in the last third of the century. This conflict, called the Peloponnesian War (432–404 B.C.), ended in the surrender of Athens to Sparta. Greek classical thought ended in the fourth century B.C. The classical world of independent Greek city-states surrendered to the Greek Empire under Alexander the Great (356–323 B.C.). His larger world of conquest ushered in what has been called the Hellenistic Age. It spread through Persia as far as the Indus Valley in the east, the Euphrates and Persian Gulf in the south, and the coast of Africa, where his followers built one of the many cities called Alexandria to immortalize his conquests.

Roman Civilization (500 B.C.–A.D. 500). Classical Roman civilization is important to Western civilization as a source of law and language, a transmitter of Greek and Christian culture, and an innovator in architecture and engineering. From a global perspective, however, the Roman Empire is a break in the long nomadic tribal rule of the Eurasian steppe. It also represents the first conquest of tribal Europe and the beginning of the imposition of a band of civilization or city life that facilitated orderly trade from the Atlantic to Han China.

The struggle with barbarian incursions is one of the central themes of Roman history. It marks the limits of Rome's rise and fall, the expansion of a small city-state into a Mediterranean empire, the assumption of the Hellenistic legacy, and the development of much of the political-military character of Roman politics and society. The defense of the borders, the creation of the empire, and the militarization of society are all parts of the same story. Roman expansion, especially the Punic wars (264–146 B.C.), changed Roman society from a small republic, governed largely by the citizen army's centuriate assembly, to a large empire of huge landed estates inside and tributary states outside. It had become an empire in fact by the time of Julius Caesar (104–44 B.C.), and the declaration of Caesar's nephew and successor, Octavian, as revered "Augustus" in 27 B.C.

The emergence of Christianity from a persecuted Jewish sect was not assured until the conversion of the emperor Constantine in A.D. 312. The fate of Christianity, however, was due as much to the increasing invasions by the Huns of the Eurasian grasslands and the tribes they pushed toward Rome as it was to internal developments of a creed and papacy. The religion survived better at Constantinople than at Rome, and in monasteries as well as in cities. In many ways the success of Christianity paralleled that of Buddhism in Asia.

India (1000 B.C.–A.D. 500). Buddhism originated in India around 500 B.C. The rise of Buddhism owed something to the flowering of small urban kingdoms in northern India (like Magadha) in the sixth century. The Buddha was said to be a son of a *kshatriya* (or aristocratic family). But Buddhism, even more than Christianity, preached an inward salvation that was virtually the opposite of Greco-Roman state religion.

The rise of Buddhism is perhaps best understood in the context of Indian religious development and reform, stretching back to the consequences of the Aryan invasion. As were the reforms of Mahavira, the Buddha's contemporary, Buddhism was a response to perceived limitations of Brahmanism: the caste system, the burden of continual reincarnations, *brahman* arrogance and sacrifice, and the quest for deeper emotional and philosophical satisfaction evidenced by the Upanishads.

The eventual fate of Buddhism in India was to stimulate the reform of Brahmanism. Buddhism enjoyed a brief period of official acceptance in India during the reign of Ashoka (273–232 B.C.), but it was soon thereafter replaced by a revived Hinduism. Buddhist monks were more successful at winning followers in Tibet, Ceylon, southern Asia, and China, especially after the first century A.D.

The Gupta Empire (A.D. 320–550) reunited northern India for the first time since Ashoka. It was a much more sophisticated empire than Ashoka's had been, however. In many ways the Gupta Empire was the most economically and culturally advanced in the world of its day. It was the hub of trade routes linking Asia, Africa, and Europe. The visiting Chinese Buddhist monk Fa Xian [Fa Hsien] tells of the wealth of Pataliputra (current Patna), where free hospital care attracted "the poor of all countries." The university at Nalanda, with its libraries, astronomers, and mathematicians (more advanced than those anywhere else in the world), gave us the zero, place-value notation, negative quantities, quadratics, and square roots. Textile, steel, and iron manufacturers were impressive, and there was a considerable private sector of merchant and artisan guilds. Some historians have suggested that the economic transformation of modern society had its roots in Gupta India, from where it passed to Song dynasty China and the Islamic world to Europe.

The Chinese World (1000 B.C.–A.D. 500)   The Zhou [Chou] dynasty (1027–256 B.C.), the longest, was the classical age of Chinese philosophy. It included the writings attributed to Confucius (551–479 B.C.) and Lao Zi [Lao Tzu] (c. 600 B.C.).

Chinese classical thought concentrated on such subjects as the importance of the family and ancestor worship, the idea of the emperor as father of the entire Chinese family, and the emperor's "mandate of heaven" to govern as long as he observes *ren* (humanity), wisdom, and courage.

Chinese history after the Zhou dynasty shows remarkable

parallels to Roman history. It too begins and ends in disorder and invasion. The Chinese, like the Romans, created a unified empire in this period, under the Han dynasty (202 B.C.–A.D. 220). Then the Han Empire was broken up by the same nomadic forces that overran the Roman Empire (except for the eastern half). Like the Roman Empire, the Han originated in the need for a unified defense against barbarian invasions.

Chinese and Roman history intersected in two other important ways. Not only did they both originate and end in the same battles against the invading tribes of the Eurasian grasslands, they also combined to serve as a bridge of civilization against the nomads. The first regular trade developed between the Atlantic and the Pacific across the Silk Road, which joined the Han and Roman empires, and as Christianity spread throughout the Roman Empire, Buddhism spread throughout China. In fact, the monastic movements of both religions played important roles in maintaining the cultural traditions of both civilizations long after the barbarian conquests ended the empires.

If the administration of the Roman Empire owed much to the spread of Roman law and magistrates, the governance of the Han Empire was similarly stabilized by the creation of a bureaucracy chosen by the world's first civil service exams, based on Confucian principles and learning. And as the Roman jurists were eventually eclipsed by emperors who styled themselves "Augustus," so did the Chinese emperor rule according to the "mandate of heaven." Neither the Roman "middle class" of magistrates or entrepreneurs *(equites)* nor the Chinese "middle class" of "scholar-bureaucrats" managed to wrest power from older landed aristocracies until well after this period.

In at least one important respect the Chinese imperial system was different from the Roman. Confucian social structure, at least its ideal, was markedly different from Roman ideal or reality. Confucian thought divided society into four classes. At the top were the scholars. They were followed in turn by the peasants, the craftsworkers, and the merchants. Soldiers were despised as outsiders, garrisoned at a safe distance on the frontier.

Chinese culture during the Han dynasty reflected the rule of scholars. Paper was invented in A.D. 105 (a thousand years before its development in the West) and used in the writing of tens of thousands of volumes by thousands of authors. Scientists charted the moon's movement around the earth, predicted solar eclipses, and invented magnetic compasses.

The World in the Year 500. By the year 500 the Eurasian landmass had achieved its first integration. Cultural and trading contacts were maintained across the Silk Road and Southern Seas, thereby making events in Mediterranean, Indian, and Chinese civilizations interdependent. Each area had experienced a cultural flowering that would shape its culture for over a thousand years. Christianity, Greco-Roman classicism, Buddhism, Hinduism, and Confucianism all originated within the middle 500 years of this period, and served to integrate large populations, often speaking different languages, in the expression of common ideals. Indeed, the commonality of the human experience was one of the most frequently voiced ideals of all of these traditions. At a time when village, tribal, and clan identities were being replaced by those of large cosmopolitan empires that embraced much of the known world, new religions and philosophies were recognizing that new common human identity.

These great civilizations of Eurasia experienced a more ominous unity as well. They were all prey to the nomads of the Eurasian steppe frontier. The eruption that destroyed Rome also destroyed the Han Empire. By the year 500 the ashes of that eruption covered most of Eurasia. Only the Eastern Roman Empire at Constantinople and Gupta India thrived.

New areas of civilized life beyond the domain of the nomads also began to thrive around A.D. 500. The most vibrant civilization, the Maya in Mexico, was already near its prime. More recent kingdoms in western Africa were beginning a consolidation that would continue another thousand years. ↯

❈ 4 ❈

Age
and
Family

Religion and
Cultural Change

MODERN SOCIETY HAS A GREATER PROPORTION of elderly people than any other society in world history. In 1800 only two out of every hundred Americans were over the age of sixty-five. Today twelve out of a hundred are, and by the year 2030 about 20 percent of the population will be sixty-five or older.

As the proportion of the elderly in the population increases dramatically, society's need for them seems to lessen. In a rapidly changing environment, the "wisdom of age" offers less guidance. Modern technology puts a premium on the skills of the young rather than the old, on adaptability and dexterity rather than experience and seasoning. Two hundred years ago almost no one retired. Today retirement is the norm, often encouraged before sixty-five and mandatory after seventy.

The elderly are losing their place in the home as well as their role in the economy. Children leave earlier, travel further, and provide less financial support for their parents. More of the elderly are placed in nursing homes, institutions that barely existed a hundred years ago.

The plight of the elderly is aggravated by changes in the American family. The modern American family is a much weaker institution than the family of earlier times. It cannot demand the loyalty and obedience, or offer the security and support, that was commonplace a few hundred years ago. The modern American family has seen many of its responsibilities taken over by the government, media, and business. The care of the elderly is only one of these traditional responsibilities.

This chapter is an investigation into some of the problems confronting modern society regarding the elderly and the family. We will attempt to understand some of the forces that are transforming the elderly and the family in modern society by taking the broadest view of the historical process. We will look at societies very different from our own in the ancient world to see whether and why their treatment of the elderly was different. And we will look at the roots of Western attitudes regarding the elderly and the family. In this way we may gain insight into a number of issues: What is new? What is unique to Western society and culture? What can be done?

ARE PEOPLE LIVING LONGER?

First, we must have some basic numbers. We began by pointing out the enormous increase (from 2 percent to 20 percent) of people over sixty-five between 1800 and what is expected by 2030. That is unique. In no historical society were there ever over 10 percent above the age of sixty-five. In fact, for most of human history before 1800, 2 percent or fewer were over sixty-five. Thus, the study of history is not going to provide us with any example of a society as full of older people as the one we are entering.

The reasons for the "graying" of modern American society are partly general and partly specific. The specific reason is that the people born in the post–World War II "baby boom" will be entering old age after 2010. (If they are your parents, you are part of what is sometimes called the "echo" of that 1945–1960 "boom.") After 2030 or so, the percentage of elderly will decline again. But it will never again naturally fall below 10 percent, which brings us to our general reason.

More people live longer in modern society. The human life span has changed only slightly if at all. The maximum human life span has always been about 110 years. Very few people ever have attained that maximum, in the ancient world or today. It may increase to 115 or even 120, but few scientists expect it to go much beyond that, and very few people will live that long. Most people in most of human history have died far short of the maximum possible life span. The general increase in the elderly in modern society is only partly due to greater numbers of the very old. The unique thing about modern society is that more people survive childhood and more women survive childbirth. Childhood diseases and childbirth, not old age, were the real killers of the ancient world.

Imagine taking a completely representative sample of people from modern American society, say a hundred in all. Imagine sitting them on ten steps according to their ages, those from birth to age nine on the first step, those from ten to nineteen on the second step, those in their twenties on the third step, up to those in their nineties on the tenth step. What would it look like? There would be people on each step, though very few on the top step and only slightly more on the next. From the sixth step down to the first, there would be about the same number of people on each step.

If you were to do the same thing in any society before about 1800, you would have a strikingly different picture. There would still be people on the top steps. Some of the great dramatists and philosophers of ancient Greece lived into their eighties and nineties. They would be fewer, but still there. The main difference would be the large numbers on the first step (the infants and children) and the drastic decline going up to the second (because of childhood mortality), and another sharp decrease from the second to the third step (because of the deaths of young women in childbirth).

These imagined steps are the models for what sociologists call age pyramids. The pyramid shape, however, describes ancient society; modern society looks more like the boxes of modern architecture. Only their height is roughly the same.

This is what it means to say that life expectancy has doubled in the last two hundred years. The average life expectancy at birth for most of the period before 1800 (that is, before modern sanitation and medicine) was thirty to forty because half the children died young. Modern life expectancy is seventy to eighty because children survive childhood and mothers survive childbirth. There are more old people in modern society, but the elderly have always been around.

The answer to the question "Do we live longer?" is yes, but it is not as simple a yes as might at first be imagined. Most of us will not live as long as some ancients did, but most of us will live longer than most of them. The real difference between modern and earlier societies is that we have a higher proportion at all ages over thirty. In ancient Rome 60–70 percent of the population died before the age of thirty, 70–75 percent before fifty, and 80–85 percent before seventy. Colonial America was not very different. The world before the last hundred years was a world of many young people and a few middle-aged and old people.

AGE AND PRESTIGE

The earliest human societies placed a great premium on age. Especially in "oral societies" (before writing) the elderly were venerated as unique sources of knowledge and wisdom. Their experience and memories often provided the edge necessary for success or survival.

The anthropological evidence is, as always, subject to the "Bongo Bongo principle": any generalization is sure to be countered by the discovery of some group, the "Bongo Bongo," who do not fit the generalization. But most Paleolithic and Neolithic peoples create a special place for the useful elderly. Elders often govern. Religious leaders (shaman and priests) are often elderly. Families, clans, villages, and tribes are led by the oldest members. Some Paleolithic and Neolithic peoples distinguish between the useful elderly and those who are senile or infirm. In some of these the latter are discarded, left to die, expected to commit suicide, or otherwise treated brutally. This is especially true in societies bordering on the edge of starvation. In such desperately poor conditions, the expertise of the still vital elderly is as valuable as the extra mouths of the unproductive elderly are not. In other societies even the senile are thought useful. In China an old person in the household is a sign of well-being, a badge of prestige—the equivalent of a Mercedes in the driveway.

The great urban civilizations of the ancient world could substitute written records for the memories of old people, but this was a gradual process. Even after writing became widespread, not everything got into the books. There were powerful "secrets" that could not be passed on lightly. Books were not safe; anyone could read them. Urban civilizations instituted orders, ranks, hierarchies, customs, and laws that protected older people and encouraged respect for them, especially older men. This was, perhaps, part of the general conservatism of these complex urban civilizations. "If there were no old men," the Roman lawyer Cicero wrote, "there would be no civilized states at all."

What was true of civilization generally was especially true in ancient Chinese civilization. There the respect for the elderly, living and dead, reached a point unequaled elsewhere.

CHINESE ANCESTOR WORSHIP

Ancestor worship in China is a reflection of the importance given by the Chinese to the family. The Chinese use the terms "inside" (meaning "family") and "outside" much more than other peoples. The old Chinese word for wife was "inside person." Every peasant home traditionally had two sources of gods: the "inside" ancestor gods and the "outside" hearth, stove, or kitchen gods. Even the kitchen gods were special protective spirits for each family, however. No two families, not even two married brothers, would share the same hearth. When a son left his parents to set up his own household, he would take some coals from his parent's fire to invite his own stove god. The stove god and ancestral gods were both synonymous with the family. The stove god was the representative spirit from the political world at large, a representative of the village god, who was seen as a delegate of the provincial god and ultimately the god of the emperor himself. The ancestral gods were the ancestors themselves, the progenitors of the current family, their "blood" rather than their spiritual representative to the outside world.

Chinese ancestor worship and family cohesiveness are reflected in another distinctly Chinese tradition: filial piety, the loyalty and obedience that the son owes to his parents in life as well as in death. The Chinese son is expected to honor his father and mother when they are alive and worship them when they are dead. This is so important that "if a man dies as a young adult, his father will usually beat the coffin to punish his son for being so unfilial as to die before his parents."[1]

ORIGINS OF ANCESTOR WORSHIP
IN CHINESE FEUDALISM

Ancestor worship was practiced in some form at least as early as the Shang dynasty (1766–1122 B.C.) in China.

> After a man died, his spirit presumably left the body and was wafted into the air, but it would extend protection to the family if properly humored and worshipped. By means of sacrifices and by magic incantations the spirits could be summoned before a priest and could be persuaded to reveal what the future held for the family. The Shangs would not do anything important without consulting the spirits, whether it be making a trip or fighting a war.[2]

Shang worship, however, seemed to focus on the sacrifice and the prophecy more than on the actual ancestors. Kings, especially, were known for sacrificing hundreds of sheep or cattle, sometimes even captured prisoners, possibly to show their power or out of a sense of desperation.

Prophecies were pronounced with the aid of turtle shells or animal bones that were placed on a flame by the priests until they cracked, forming various patterns. The priests would read the patterns of the cracks to tell the future. These "oracle bones," incidentally, unearthed only after A.D. 1899, gave us our first clues to the origins of the Chinese language. This is because the priests would write their questions and answers on the bones.

It was not, however, until after the Shang dynasty that ancestor worship became central to Chinese religion. The period of the Zhou dynasty (1122–222 B.C.), especially the second half, was probably crucial.

The Zhou (pronounced Joe) dynasty began as a strong, prosperous, and aggressive state. Two of its founders, King Wu and Duke Zhou, were among China's greatest statesmen. They are credited with suppressing the rebellions of smaller states and integrating these local powers into a central state. Their creation held together for four hundred years (1122–722 B.C.). During the next five hundred years (722–222 B.C.) the idea of a central state remained strong even though China was divided into several warring kingdoms from the sixth to third century B.C. The unification of China was accomplished in 221 B.C. by the founder of the Qin dynasty, and the imperial system has continued to the present.

One of the methods the Zhou used successfully to administer their vast realm was feudalism. Rather than govern the conquered tribes through their own leaders, the Zhou distributed large areas of land to selected individuals (former rulers, relatives, generals, and statesmen) and appointed them "lords." The land was still controlled by the king, but these lords were allowed to use it in return for military service to the king.

The Zhou instituted this feudal system of military allegiances (between king and nobility, lords and vassals) as a way of increasing the king's control over rebellious tribes. Initially this was successful. Feudalism began as a means of gaining central control of diverse peoples and warring armies. After about 722 B.C., however, it unraveled. Local lords became more powerful than the king. They deprived the central administration of its control over armies in the provinces. Periodic civil war returned.

Ultimately, then, feudalism came to mean (after 722 B.C.) decentralization (as it later did in Europe in the Middle Ages), even though it had begun as an effective centralization of Chinese administration. In one other important respect Chinese feudalism was different from the feudalism that later developed in Europe. Whereas European feudalism led to a focus on territorial allegiance and alliance, Chinese feudalism increased family identities, family loyalty, and even ancestor worship. New rules of succession, for instance, changed the Shang practice that allowed younger brothers to succeed older brothers and sons born of a concubine to succeed their fathers. Under the Zhou, only the sons of legal wives—and first sons at that—could succeed. Zhou feudalism was especially familial in other ways as well. Family relationships between king and lord, or lord and duke, were expressed even when the two were not related. Dukes who had the same name as the king were addressed as paternal uncles. Chinese feudalism thus developed a presumed set of family relationships that gave it extra force. One of the reasons for this was no doubt the importance of ancestor worship before Zhou times. An additional element, however, was brought about by the need to govern rebellious "foreign" tribes by lords who were not related to their subjects. In these cases, the lord's relation to the king, to the king's ancestors, or even to his own ancestors reinforced his justification to rule.

A complex code of ancestor worship took form. The higher the official, the more ancestors he could worship. Only a king could erect a temple for worshiping ancestors; a noble was allowed to worship fewer generations of ancestors than a king was, but more than his own inferiors were. Feudal rank also determined how much of an ancestral blessing could be expected. Eventually, however, even a soldier could expect something from his ancestors.

> The living were completely in the shadow of their ancestor. . . . In time of war the expeditionary troops were given their orders in the ancestral temple; the ancestral tablets were sometimes taken along when the ruler led the troops in person. . . . A warrior's ancestors might be asked to help him win the battle.[3]

Thus, Chinese feudalism under the Zhou had the effect of strengthening family ties and ancestor worship. This was the background for the development in the late Zhou period of a great philosophical outpouring. Among these classics were the anonymous *Book of Rites,* the *Analects,* or "sayings," of Confucius, and later, *The Classic of Filial Piety.*

CONFUCIANISM: XIAO, REN, AND LI

Chinese thought sometimes strikes a Westerner as very concrete. The words seem to have a reality that they generally lack in Indo-European languages. If this is so, it may be because Chinese developed (as we see from the Shang oracle bones) as a set of shorthand pictures of actual things. Each "letter" or "character" is a word because originally it was a picture of something or a representation of an idea. The character for a horse has four legs. The character for a house has a roof with a pig underneath. The two words do not look at all similar, as they do in English, because a horse does not look like a house. Some characters have phonetic elements (symbols for sounds), so a single Chinese character may contain both a picture word (pictograph) or idea word (ideograph) and a sound symbol (like an alphabet letter).

One very important character was *xiao* (pronounced she-ow), the word for filial piety. It is drawn with a kind of abstraction for "old" on the top and a child on the bottom. The combination suggests the relationship of the older generation to their children. Thus, it means being dutiful to one who is older.

The history of the character *xiao* is interesting. In the early Zhou period it meant only "ancestor worship." But in the later Zhou period it came to mean "filial piety" as well. Both concepts stem from the image of training the generations. Both are distinctly Chinese and almost completely absent from modern Western culture.

One of the great teachers of late Zhou times, indeed of all Chinese history, was Confucius, who lived between about 550 and 479 B.C. Confucius was an eminently practical man for a philosopher. He would dismiss questions about the gods and spirits, saying it was difficult enough to understand human beings. He traveled throughout China teaching students and looking for a prince who would give him a good job. He hoped to reform public morality by teaching people proper personal behavior. *Xiao,* especially in the emerging sense of filial piety, was one of the most important moral needs, according to Confucius. People spoke of *xiao,* he said, but they did not go far enough.

> Nowadays for a man to be filial means no more than that he is able to provide his parents with food. But even hounds and horses are provided with food. If a man shows no reverence, what is the difference?[4]

Xiao must be more than going through the motions, Confucius was saying. It must be done with reverence, with deep feeling.

> The real sign is the expression on one's face. Taking on extra work and giving the old extra wine and food hardly deserves to be called filial.[5]

Confucius (c. 551–479 B.C.). This conservative image of the philosopher was made in 1734. (Granger)

Some of the followers of Confucius went even further in expanding the meaning and importance of *xiao*. One of these was the philosopher Mencius (372–298 B.C.). Mencius suggested an idea that much later (in the Song dynasty) became a core doctrine of Confucianism. That was the idea that filial piety was the root of all benevolence, all humanity. Mencius believed that by showing reverence toward one's parents, one learned reverence for all human life.

Confucius had suggested this idea when he said "being good as a son and obedient as a young man is, perhaps, the root of a man's character."[6] He even spoke of the importance of "loving humanity." But by "humanity," he more frequently meant gentlemen, not everyone. Mencius meant everyone.

The word for humanity (and for benevolence) was *ren* (pronounced run). It is drawn as a person on the left and the number two on the right. Thus, it suggests a person in relationship, a key element of Confucian thought.

Confucius used *ren* sometimes to mean "other gentlemen" (or aristocrats), and sometimes to mean "humanity." Mencius used it only in the sense of all humanity. Mencius argued that *ren* was not just a virtue of the gentlemen. Rather, it was natural to all mankind. Everyone has fellow feeling for humanity, he said. Imagine the most wicked man you can. Imagine him suddenly seeing a child about to fall into a well. This most wicked of men would at least be startled or frightened at the sight of the child about to fall. This is because all human beings have an instinctive identity with each other, Mencius concluded.

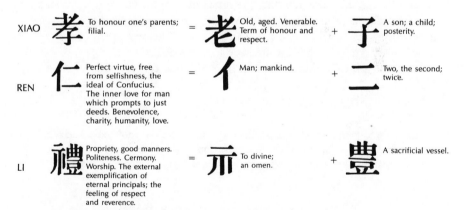

THREE KEY WORDS
The word for filial piety, or the duty of the child to the parents (xiao), *was made from the roots for "old" at the top and "child" on the bottom. The word for humanity, or benevolence,* (ren), *was made from the signs for "person" on the left and "two" on the right. The word for rituals, rules, rights, or good behavior* (li), *consisted of the characters for "to divine" on the left and "sacrificial vessel" on the right.*

The idea that only *xiao* can lead to *ren* is still an axiom of Confucian thought. A modern Confucian scholar puts it this way:

> Western philosophers generally appeal to reason, to conscience, to sympathy, or to the idealism of universal love of mankind in order to discover or expound the source of morality. All these are important, of course, in the exploration of the ethical domain. And yet, without filial piety as their mainstay, all go adrift in confusion or are limited in their development and application. In other words, if one's love toward his parents withers away due to negligence of cultivation, where can he find better soil for developing reason, conscience, sympathy, and fraternal love? In this case, his conscience or sympathy may go astray or even die. His moral sense, then, is liable to become twisted into an abnormal state.[7]

The body of Confucianism that shaped Chinese thought in the last twenty-five hundred years emphasized filial piety and humanity, *xiao* and *ren*. It also set great store in *li* (pronounced lee), the rituals, rules, or rites of social behavior. And the most important *li* were those that regulated the behavior of children toward parents, younger brother toward older brother, everyone toward ancestors.

The character for *li* is drawn with an abstract symbol for gods or spirits on the left and a sacrificial vessel on the right. This suggests an original meaning of ancestor worship—pouring offerings to the dead. By Zhou times, *li* too had a much broader meaning, including not only the rituals of ancestor worship and filial piety but many others as well. Confucius used *li* to mean proper behavior in general. "He who can submit himself to ritual [*li*] is good," he said in the *Analects*.[8] "A man who is not good, what can he have to do with *li?*"[9]

One of the great Confucian classics, from the first century B.C., was the *Li Ji* [*Li Chi*] *(Book of Rites)*. The *Li Ji* is full of rules as specific as how a young person should behave when asking advice of an elder:

> In going to take counsel with an elder, one must carry a stool and a staff for the elder's use. When the elder asks a question, it would be improper to blurt out an answer too quickly without first pleading ignorance.[10]

FAMILY AND STATE IN CHINA

China changed considerably from the decentralized feudalism of the late Zhou period to a unified state after 221 B.C. The Han dynasty (206 B.C.–A.D. 220) was a highly centralized, bureaucratic state, much more dominated by the emperor and his court than was possible under the Zhou. At least one modern historian has argued that China changed from a society dominated by the family to one dominated by the state in the Han period:

We shall use the term "familialistic" to describe the [late Zhou] period of 722–464 B.C. The familialistic relationship was manifest in the familial concept of the state, the strong clan organization, and the system of self-sufficient estates or "manors." Kinship ties maintained social stratification in terms of heredity; hence social mobility was restricted. However, when the familialistic relationship broke down, family ties disintegrated and a social vacuum appeared in which men moved upward or downward as a result of their own actions. Before the end of the [Warring States] period of 463–222 B.C. a system of contractual relationships started to emerge: bureaucracy, employer-employee relations, and commercial exchange all came into existence.[11]

It is interesting that during the same period in which China was changing from a family-dominated feudal society to a government-dominated empire, the importance of filial piety, the family, the elderly, and the ancestors increased. The insistence of Mencius and the Confucians that filial piety was the root of benevolence and the numerous books on the rituals of filial piety attest to the importance of the family in imperial China.

This is an important issue because Western society is going through a similar transition today. In a similar period of a few hundred years we have changed from a family-dominated society to one dominated by the state. Many aspects of life that used to be performed by the family (education, social welfare, morals, employment) are increasingly becoming the responsibility of the state. There is also considerable concern that family solidarity, respect for parents and the elderly, and knowledge of one's ancestors has declined in the last few hundred years. The example of China over two thousand years ago suggests that the transition can be made without losing respect for family.

INDIA AND THE BUDDHA

At almost exactly the same time that Confucius was teaching in China, Siddhartha Gautama, the Buddha, was born in India. "Buddha," which means "the enlightened one," was a title he received from his followers, who founded a religion, Buddhism, which spread throughout Southeast Asia and China. In doing so, Buddhism spread religious attitudes that showed less concern with the elderly, ancestors, the family, and the rituals of this world than Confucianism.

The Buddha was born around 566 B.C. into a noble family (of the *kshatriya,* or warrior caste) in which the traditional religious rites of Brahmanism (or Hinduism[12]) were observed. According to the legends told about his early life, the issues of old age, family life, and religion were uppermost in his mind. The traditional legend says that Siddhartha was expected to rule after his father. When he was a young boy, however, certain Hindu holy men predicted that the youth would leave his father's kingdom and become a hermit. In order to ensure that this would never happen, Siddhartha's father provided everything Siddhartha needed on the palace grounds so he would never have to leave. Even a wife was brought for him, and she bore a son. All of his needs were satisfied. The world seemed perfect. This led Siddhartha, according to the legend, to think that if the world inside the palace grounds was so comfortable, it must be similar outside, and he asked his father if he might go outside. His father was beside himself. But not wanting to deny his son any request, he sent his painters and carpenters and gardeners into the town so that they could make it look perfect for Siddhartha's arrival. The day came.

Siddhartha set out in his father's best coach to see the town. The houses glistened as if they had just been painted. All of the gardens were in flower. The people looked as if they had put on new clothes for the occasion. Siddhartha was remarking to his coachman about how perfect everything was when suddenly out of nowhere stumbled an old man who had not gotten the message that he was to remain inside. "What is that?" Siddhartha asked his coachman. "Why is that man's hair so white? Why is he so bent over?" The coachman, not knowing what to say, chose the truth. "That is what is called old age, my Lord." Siddhartha did not understand. "What is old age?" he asked. "Does it come to everyone, or only a few people?" Having already committed himself to the truth, the coachman replied: "I'm afraid it comes to everyone, my Lord." Siddhartha was shocked and asked the coachman to return to the palace.

In the manner of dreams and fairy tales, this story is told four times. The second time, after Siddhartha gets the courage to go out again, his coach accidentally runs by a sick person, and he discovers illness. The third time there is a corpse, and Siddhartha discovers death. The fourth time he discovers a wandering ascetic. These discoveries of old age, sickness, death, and poverty are so overwhelming for Siddhartha that he decides to devote his life to finding out why they occur.

Then he does something that the Confucian Chinese would find incomprehensible. He leaves his wife and son as well as his father and family and goes off into the forest, as Indian holy men did before and have done since. To understand why there is suffering in the world, he becomes a hermit. He realizes that one cause of suffering is expecting too much, and so he decides to reduce his life to bare subsistence.

> To such a pitch of asceticism have I gone that naked was I, flouting life's decencies, licking my hands after meals, never heeding when folk called to me to come or to stop, never accepting food brought to me before my rounds or cooked expressly for me, never accepting an invitation. . . . I have visited only one house a day and there taken only one morsel. . . . I have lived on a single saucer of food a day, or on two. . . . I have lived on wild roots and fruit, or on windfalls only. . . . I lived to torment and to torture my body—to such a length in asceticism have I gone.[13]

The Buddha, Siddhartha Gautama (c. 566–483 B.C.), as imagined by an Indian sculptor of the Gupta period, 1,000 years later. (Granger)

Extreme asceticism did not work, however. It did not lead to true wisdom or enlightenment. He reflected: "It is no easy matter to attain that bliss with a body so emaciated. Come, let me take some solid food, rice and vegetables; and this I ate accordingly."[14]

Better fed, but not overfed, Siddhartha sat under a tree to meditate. He entered into a deep state of meditative concentration in which he saw his entire life pass before him. After some time and despite various temptations, he attained enlightenment. He began to understand that the cause of suffering was desire. To conquer suffering, one must conquer desire. But extreme asceticism was not the way to conquer desire, any more than the luxury of his father's palace had been the fulfillment of desire. One must find a "middle path" between the two extremes, he said, in what is called his first sermon.

> The two extremes should not be practiced by those who seek the truth. There is the extreme devotion to sensual pleasure which is the indulgence of most ordinary people. There is also the extreme devotion to self-denial which is the indulgence of the hermit. One should avoid both these extremes and follow the middle path. It is simply the Noble Eightfold Path, namely right view, right thought, right speech, right action, right livelihood, right effort, right mindfulness, and right concentration. This Middle Path gives vision, knowledge and leads to calm, insight, enlightenment, and nirvana.[15]

After considerable reflection on whether or not to teach, the Buddha decided to speak about the "four noble truths": all life is suffering; the cause of suffering is desire; suffering can be conquered by conquering desire; desire can be conquered by following the "noble eightfold path." Finally around 486 B.C. the Buddha passed on to that state of bliss called nirvana (usually translated as "extinguishing" or "without wind").

CHINESE VERSUS INDIAN CULTURE

Almost any Chinese would have had a difficult time with a philosopher who left his family. A Chinese person would be sympathetic to the effort to understand suffering, especially the burdens of old age, illness, and death. But for the Chinese, the discovery of mortality could lead only to the family, the morality of *xiao,* and the practice of *li.* Abandoning family and society would be incomprehensible and unforgivable.

Perhaps the differences between Chinese and Indian cultures can best be seen in the differences between Chinese ancestor worship and Indian ideas of reincarnation. In China ancestor veneration provided the ancestors with immortality. The ancestors were literally and figuratively kept alive by the prayer and nurturing of their descendants. By having children and continuing the family line, these descendants ensured their own immortality in their turn.

A martian might think Chinese immortality less satisfying than Indian. Chinese ancestors were imagined as ghosts, more spiritually than materially nourished by their descendants. Indians, on the other hand, believed each spirit was reincarnated in another body after death. Thus, immortality was more personal, more individual, and perhaps more "real" for Indians. In any case, the belief that one never really died, that all life was a recycling of past life, that one could be (as an old American song had it) one's own grandpa, did not lead to ancestor worship. The living family was important in India (as it was in China), but the ancestors were not. Immortality was not gained in the family. Indeed, it was not thought a gain in India. Immortality was thought inevitable. You couldn't escape it. *Samsara* was the wheel of eternal birth and rebirth, again and again, in one form after another. The best an Indian might hope for was the cessation of this eternal cycle of life. The Buddhist idea of "nirvana," like the *brahman* idea of *moksha,* was a different kind of immortality from that envisioned by other religious traditions: it offered eternal peace rather than a life after death.

OLD AGE IN INDIA

The Indian society in which Siddhartha was raised had a tradition of forest withdrawal for the elderly. According to the Indian scriptures there were four stages of life. In the first stage the duty of a young man was to study the scriptures and observe celibacy. In the second stage of life—"householding"—a man and woman marry and raise children. The husband is expected to follow the career of his particular caste and to serve the larger community. The third stage of life for a man is called "dwelling as a forest hermit." It begins when he "sees his skin wrinkled and his hair white, and the sons of his sons." Then he is expected to turn over the administration of the household to his sons and, with or without his wife, retire to the forest. He is expected to spend his time in contemplation and worship of the gods. Finally, the last stage of a man's life is a period of asceticism and renunciation of the world. He is expected to live alone, discard attachments to others, and strive for spiritual perfection. Thus, two of the four stages of life (often combined in Indian thought today) are stages of withdrawal from the world, including the family.

The Buddha drew on this Indian tradition of withdrawal. But in Buddhism, the householding stage became secondary to the quest for individual enlightenment. To a certain extent the forest retreat replaced the village and the monastery replaced the family as the center of life, at least as the Buddhist ideal.

Such a break with Indian values may have been a reason why Buddhism eventually almost disappeared in India. Even today, India remains enormously family-centered. One observer has written:

The normal social expectation in India is that elderly persons will be cared for by their grown children, preferably their sons, and it is not surprising that in the absence of other forms of provision for old-age security, a high value is placed on having children, particularly males. Couples childless by design are almost nonexistent. . . . There is furthermore in India a broader conception of family solidarity than we are accustomed to in the United States, which recognizes the responsibility of nephews, grandsons, and others of the extended kinship network to take care of older persons in the absence of direct descendants. The ideal family system is one in which young men remain in the household of their parents after marriage, their wives joining this household and taking on the tasks of caring for their aged in-laws when this becomes necessary. . . . Consequently, old parents are rarely expected to live on their own if they have living sons, and old persons without living children are expected to be taken in by whichever close junior relative may be available.[16]

If the family was almost as important in India as it was in China, age was not. At least there were religious values in India that emphasized other things, such as "purity," more than age. The Laws of Manu, a *brahman* moral code from about the time of the Buddha, contained injunctions like the following:

Neither through years, nor through white hairs, nor through wealth, nor through kinsmen comes greatness. He who has learned the Veda is considered great by us.

The seniority of *brahmans* is from sacred knowledge, that of *kshatriyas* from valour, that of *vaishyas* from wealth in grain, but that of *shudras* alone from age.[17]

Knowledge of the holy Vedas and adherence to the occupations of one's caste are more important than age. It is interesting that age is given precedence only in the last caste, the *shudras*, or laborers. That is like saying that age is all they can acquire. Even the elderly *shudras* must be guided by the children of the three higher, holier, "twice-born" castes, according to the Laws of Manu.

We should not push the argument too far, however. Even the phrase "the seniority of *brahmans* comes from sacred knowledge" admits to the importance of seniority. It might be better to say that there are two sides to Indian religion (and probably to most others as well): that side which emphasizes the importance of age, tradition, and the past; and that which prefers personal enlightenment even when it leads in radically new directions.

Ultimately in Hindu India, caste was more important than age. But both caste and age were part of the religion based on the past, the religion of the *brahman* priests, the Vedas, and the Laws of Manu. The other side of Indian religion was that of the holy men, the forests, and enlightenment. The Buddha, of course, was one of these holy men. He was not a *brahman* priest; he was a seeker. He was not interested in Brahmanic ritual and law; he wanted to understand, and to be. He did not believe that caste was eternal; he saw the obligations of caste as obstacles to genuine enlightenment.

Perhaps there had always been these divisions in India, at least since the Aryan invaders had imposed Brahmanism on earlier inhabitants around 1500 B.C. The early Vedas concentrated on ritual sacrifice, but the later Upanishads sought union with the divine. Priests presided over ritual, while holy men sought wisdom.

The Buddha around 500 B.C. was only another of a long line of wandering hermits who looked for wisdom rather than worship, who cast off the trivia of the world for the experience of something beyond. Age and family had less meaning to them because the world had less meaning to them. The Hindu holy men, the hermits, the Buddha, and the later followers of Buddhism were seeking salvation.

SALVATION RELIGION

By what appears at first glance to be a remarkable coincidence, a number of the world's great traditions turned to the goal of salvation or escape from the world at about the same time. The most notable examples are Christianity and Buddhism. What they left behind is not always clear to those who have been raised in salvation traditions (which today include Islam as well as Christianity, Buddhism, and other religions). To put it simply, Buddhists and Christians started looking for salvation from the world as we know it. Our study of Chinese culture shows how unusual that was. The Confucians sought social justice, but they accepted the world; they did not see life as basically sinful or painful. Nor did they ask about the meaning of life, the cause of death, and the way to salvation. On the whole, Chinese philosophy, like that of Confucius, was fairly practical before the Buddhists came to China. Chinese religion was full of spirits, gods, and ghosts, but its concerns were about life in this world. Rituals were devised and practiced to bring fertility, cure disease, maintain health, and keep the ancestors happy. Philosophical questions about attaining another world were rarely part of this.

Similarly, Brahmanism in India prescribed many sacrifices and rituals for health and well-being, but offered little vision of salvation from the rigors and sufferings of the world. According to the *brahman* priests, life was a series of duties, for them as well as others. *Kshatriyas* (warriors), *vaishyas* (farmers), and *shudras* (laborers) all had their own rituals and obligations, and they also had to accept the priestly function of the *brahmans*. There was hope of reincarnation (or rebirth) in a higher caste, but only if the duties of this life's caste were strictly observed. Only an obedient *vaishya* might become a *kshatriya* in the next life; only a *kshatriya* who had fulfilled all of the obligations of caste might be reborn as a *brahman*. While there was some idea of possible release *(moksha)* from the wheel of life, it would be somewhat misleading to see this as an idea of salvation from this world, as later developed in Buddhism and devotional Hinduism.

Buddhism, in the tradition of the Upanishads and forest hermits, challenged the permanence of caste, and thus the wheel of life.[18] The Buddhists offered salvation from this world. They imagined a victory over life itself, an end to the eternal return. Nirvana was open to all, regardless of caste. This was a revolutionary message two thousand years ago.

It developed in one other place, about the same time. It became the message of Christianity as well as of Buddhism.

ANCIENT JUDAISM

Ancient Judaism, like Brahmanism, was a very practical and worldly religion. Abraham and his descendants promised loyalty to their God in return for prosperity in this world. Abraham and his tribe agreed to show their loyalty by circumcising their sons and obeying dietary and other laws. In return they were promised many descendants and good land. That was the essence of the "covenant," or contract, that the Bible describes. There is no mention of "life after death" or "heaven" or "hell" here. Rather, there is a practical agreement between a people and its God for mutual aid in this world.

The absence of an idea of a life after death can be inferred in another way. There is much celebration of long life. The long lives mentioned in the Bible (930 years for Adam, 950 years for Noah, 175 years for Abraham, 120 years for Moses) are to be understood as divine rewards for their loyalty. There is no suggestion of another reward beyond life in this world. The point of these stories is simple:

> The fear of the Lord brings length of days; the years of the wicked are few.
> (Proverbs 10: 27)

Respect for the elderly was an important element in the ancient Hebrew society that lived according to the Bible.

> Honor your father and your mother, that you may live long in the land which the Lord your God is giving you.
> (Exodus 20: 1)

This commandment ranks second in importance to those that enshrined monotheism (the belief in one god). The law book, Deuteronomy (21: 21), adds a severe punishment for the rebellious son. His parents shall bring him to the elders of the city, who will stone him to death.

Not just parents, but all "gray hairs" deserve respect.

> You shall rise in the presence of gray hairs, give honor to the aged, and fear your God.
> (Leviticus 19: 32)

Gray hair is a crown of glory, and it is won by a virtuous life.

(Proverbs 16: 31)

These sentiments of the ancient Hebrews suggest almost a gerontocracy (rule by the elders). The political power of the elders is enshrined in the Book of Numbers (11: 16–18), where the Lord tells Moses: "Assemble seventy elders from Israel, men known to you as elders and officers in the community . . . and they will share with you the burden of taking care for the people; then you will not have to bear it alone."

There was another strain in ancient Judaism, however, just as there was in ancient Indian religion. Just as some Indian hermits and holy men withdrew from *brahman*-administered ritualized religion, some Hebrew prophets challenged what they saw as the easy complacency of the elders. The Hebrew prophets, like the early Buddhists, began to look for salvation from the world rather than prosperity in it. This was especially true after the ancient Jews had seen their "promised land" occupied and desecrated by numerous invaders from 600 to 200 B.C.

We know very little of the early history of ancient Judaism. Most historians now think that there probably was an Abraham. Perhaps he did leave the city of Ur around 2000 B.C. and wander with his nomadic tribes on the arid rim of the Fertile Crescent. These shepherds might have settled in Egypt around 1400 B.C., been driven out around 1300 B.C., and organized themselves in Palestine shortly thereafter. After 1000 B.C. we know in much greater detail of their kingdom in Palestine. In some ways the kingdoms of Solomon and David after 1000 B.C. were a Hebrew golden age that never returned. One after another wave of invaders from the surrounding empires destroyed the small Hebrew kingdom, divided after 800 B.C. into Judah and Israel. First the Assyrians conquered the northern kingdom of Israel around 700 B.C. Then the Babylonian Empire conquered Judah and brought the cream of Judean youth as captives to Babylon. This "Babylonian captivity" was recounted by the prophet Daniel in a book that took form during the continuing assaults by the Persians (around 500 B.C.) and the Greeks (around 300 B.C.) and their successors until 165 B.C.

The Book of Daniel was written after this long history of oppression, when Jerusalem was ruled by the Syrian successors of Alexander the Great. In 168 B.C. Syrian King Antiochus Epiphanes (r. 175–163 B.C.) desecrated the Jewish Temple. The shock was so profound, not even the traditional promise of worldly prosperity made sense to the author of Daniel. He cast the book as prophecy foretold by the young Daniel who had been taken to Babylon around 600 B.C. He told how Daniel had seen all of this oppression in a dream—oppression by the Persians, the Greeks, and then these Syrian Greeks. The message was that all of this was part of God's plan. The suffering had a purpose. It was preparing the faithful for a final resolution, nothing less than the end of the world. God would descend in a fiery chariot and judge the living and the dead. The end of suffering would occur for all alike in a final conflagration soon after the Temple had been desecrated. When would all this occur? Daniel's first answer was after "a time, times, and a half." When pressed further he said the end would come 1290 days after the desecration of the Temple—in 165 B.C. (later adding a blessing for those who waited 1335 days).

In 165 B.C. the forces of Antiochus Epiphanes were defeated by Judas the Maccabee. The world had not ended. The Temple was cleansed and rededicated. Ever since, however, the vision of the end of the world has been central to the Judeo-Christian tradition. After Daniel there were two strains in Judaism, one that continued to hope for a renewal of the promised land and one that sought salvation from this world.

CHRISTIANITY

Christianity was a continuation of the strain of Judaism that, beginning with Daniel, prepared for the expected end of the world. It looked to the future rather than the past. It was impatient and expectant. It depended on the young rather than the old.

Like the Essenes (whose lives have been revealed in the last forty years with the discovery of the Dead Sea Scrolls) the followers of Jesus looked for salvation from the latest phase of foreign rule, the Roman. Some looked to a political Messiah, a new king, who would lead a successful political rebellion, much as the Maccabees had in the time of Daniel. Others could only hope for an end of all political oppression in a fiery finale, last judgment, and heavenly "kingdom of God." While some of the followers of Jesus thought he was the political Messiah, Jesus seems to have expected the final salvation of a kingdom of God, the end of the world. That is what accounts for the moral urgency in the gospels: let the dead bury the dead; if thy right eye offend thee, pluck it out [Matthew, 8:22, 5:29]. These were critical times. The end was at hand. As John the Baptist had said, the axe had already been laid to the root of the tree.

But Jesus died before the world ended. His followers must have been confused at first. Some suggested he would return, that there would be a "second coming." There were accounts of a resurrection.

It was the apostle Paul who gave meaning to the death of Jesus. He determined that the death of Jesus, followed by a resurrection, was (instead of an embarrassment) part of God's plan to redeem mankind from sin. It was not just an episode in Jewish history; it was the most important event in human history. Nothing less.

Paul was a Hellenized Jew. That meant he had contacts among the early Jewish followers of Jesus, but he also thought like a Greek. The idea of a "son of God" was a Greek, not a Hebrew, idea. Similarly, the idea of a god's dying and being reborn was common throughout the Greco-Roman world—except among the Jews. Paul was an inveterate traveler and convincing communicator. While engaged in persecuting the followers of Jesus for the Roman authorities, he fell from his horse on the road to Damascus and experienced what he later called a command from God to stop persecuting the followers of Jesus. In the remaining years of his life he traveled throughout the Mediterranean, trying to persuade other followers of his Greek interpretation. Jesus was not just a Jewish prophet, he said. He was the son of God and the savior of all mankind. One need not be Jewish. One need not be circumcised. One need not observe Jewish law. One need only accept the sacrifice of Jesus for the sins of humanity, and one would be saved. Eternal salvation was available to anyone with faith.

It was an easy message, one accessible to second, third, and later generations. Faith did not require experience. It was also a message that appealed to a troubled world, and one that could travel swiftly through an empire like the Roman.

Further, it was a message that undermined the traditional role of elders and the family. In that regard, the life of Jesus seemed to set an early example. He died not at 120 or 950 years old, but at thirty-three. He left his family early, never to return. His message that the kingdom of God was at hand demanded a commitment far more important than the commitment to family.

> For I am come to set a man at variance against his father, and the daughter against her mother, and the daughter-in-law against her mother-in-law.
> (Matthew 10: 35)

Jesus seemed to suggest that the end of the world was too close at hand to accept family peace over moral regeneration.

Paul and the second generation of followers retained some of this original sense of urgency. A preference for celibacy over family was part of that. But they could not build a church if they expected the world to end soon. The second generation took a longer view of the world's future than the first had taken. Converts, missions, churches, and families were part of that longer view.

In one important sense, however, the Christians undermined the role that elders and families had enjoyed in traditional Judaism. The Hebrew "family" was a tribal entity that consisted of far more members than a modern family, but it was held together by "blood." When Paul called together the "elders" and "brothers," he conferred new meaning to the words. The "elders" were not the older members of a tribal family; they were the leaders of a community that cut across tribal, family, and ethnic bounds. The "brothers" of the Christian community were related in a new family, a family in Christ, that included Jews and gentiles, Greeks and Africans, Romans and Persians. It was an international family with a universal mission. There could be only one Father and one family for Paul:

> For this cause I bow my knees unto the Father of our Lord Jesus Christ, of whom the whole family in heaven and earth is named.
> (Ephesians 3: 14)

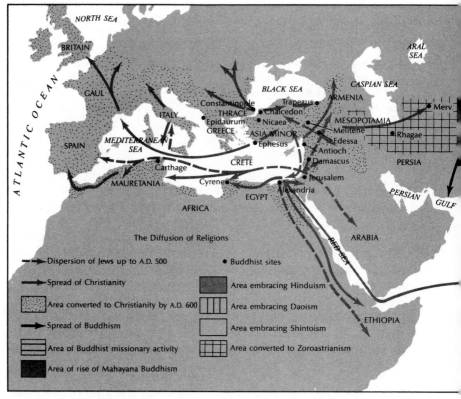

NORTH SEA
BRITAIN
ATLANTIC OCEAN
GAUL
ITALY
SPAIN
MEDITERRANEAN SEA
MAURETANIA
Carthage
Cyrene
CRETE
AFRICA
BLACK SEA
Constantinople
THRACE
Epidaurum
GREECE
ASIA MINOR
Ephesus
Chalcedon
Nicaea
Trapezus
ARMENIA
CASPIAN SEA
ARAL SEA
Merv
MESOPOTAMIA
Melitene
Edessa
Antioch
Damascus
Jerusalem
Alexandria
EGYPT
Rhagae
PERSIA
PERSIAN GULF
ARABIA
RED SEA
ETHIOPIA

The Diffusion of Religions

- - - ▶ Dispersion of Jews up to A.D. 500   ● Buddhist sites

▶ Spread of Christianity

Area converted to Christianity by A.D. 600   Area embracing Hinduism

▶ Spread of Buddhism   Area embracing Daoism

Area of Buddhist missionary activity   Area embracing Shintoism

Area of rise of Mahayana Buddhism   Area converted to Zoroastrianism

THE SPREAD OF RELIGIONS

Christianity and Buddhism were the great missionary religions between
A.D. 100–600. They took root in soil prepared by Judaism, Hinduism,
Daoism and Zoroastrianism, all of which continued to thrive.

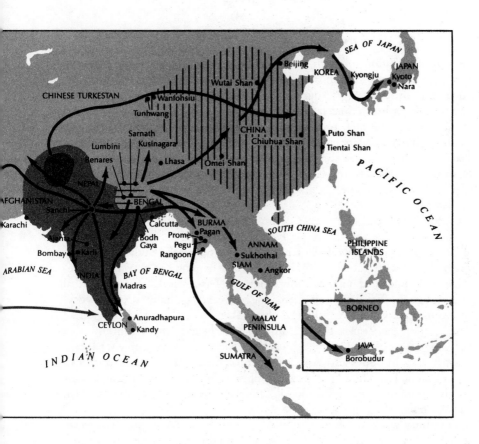

CHINESE TURKESTAN

Wanfohsiu
Tunhwang

Beijing
Wutai Shan
KOREA
Kyongju
SEA OF JAPAN
JAPAN
Kyoto
Nara

Sarnath
Lumbini
Kusinagara
Benares
Lhasa
NEPAL
CHINA
Chiuhua Shan
Puto Shan
Tientai Shan
Omei Shan
AFGHANISTAN
Sanchi
Karachi
BENGAL

PACIFIC OCEAN

Ajanta
Calcutta
Bombay
Karli
Bodh
Gaya
Prome
Pegu
Rangoon
BURMA
Pagan
ANNAM
Sukhothai
SIAM
Angkor
SOUTH CHINA SEA
PHILIPPINE
ISLANDS

ARABIAN SEA
INDIA
Madras
BAY OF BENGAL
GULF OF SIAM

CEYLON
Anuradhapura
Kandy
MALAY
PENINSULA

INDIAN OCEAN

SUMATRA

BORNEO

JAVA
Borobudur

MISSIONARIES AND MONASTERIES

The two great salvation religions of two thousand years ago, Christianity and Buddhism, gave us our first missionaries and our first monasteries. This is not coincidental. Both religions sent out missionaries because both believed they held the keys to universal salvation. It is very likely that neither Jesus nor Siddhartha claimed such a role, but their followers did for them. Mahayana Buddhists, much like Pauline Christians, taught of a person who was also a savior. "Amitaba Buddha" and "Christ" were seen as saviors of all humanity, regardless of caste, family, or tribe. Christ died for the sins of mankind; one need only believe in him. Amitaba held back from entering nirvana in order to bring others along; one had only to say his name.

What accounts for this similarity? Certainly one of the factors was the existence of the extensive empires, especially the Roman and the Indian: initially the Mauryan (322–185 B.C.), especially under King Ashoka, and later the Kushan, especially under King Kanishka (r. A.D. 90–110). Huge political empires had universal pretensions that accommodated universalistic religions. Their very scale made tribal religions inconsequential. They also offered the roads and communication networks that made missionary work possible. Without Roman roads and Mediterranean shipping, without the Roman peace, Paul could not have carried out his mission. Similarly, the developed and pacified Asian trade routes made it possible for Indian Buddhists to travel to Southeast Asia and then for the Southeast Asian Buddhists to return to India. From Southeast Asia, Buddhism spread to China, taking advantage of the communication networks of Southeast Asian empires and the Han Empire of China.

The monastery was also a contribution of Christians and Buddhists. Even today Buddhist monks can be seen throughout Asia. It might be a bit extreme, but not too far off the mark, to think of the monastery as salvation religion's alternative to the family. It was, after all, the place where all of the universal brotherhood could come together. Monasteries were the families for the full-time devotees.

In this light it is interesting to look at Buddhist missionaries and monasteries in China, where the family was such a revered institution.

BUDDHISM IN CHINA

Buddhism first entered China during the Han dynasty in the first century A.D. The Chinese were initially interested in whether Buddhism could add to their store of potions and practices for improved health and increased longevity. The first translations of Buddhist texts into Chinese were made for this purpose.

Interest in Buddhist thought developed later. After the invasions of the fourth century (which also reduced the Roman Empire), Chinese political centers prospered only in the South. Confucians were prepared for the idea of life as suffering by the invasions of the "barbarians." As if in a state of shock, the Chinese courts turned their backs on the invasions and instead cultivated increasingly abstract philosophical discussions with the new Buddhist monks.

The difficulty that the Chinese had with Buddhism can be seen in a Buddhist document from the fifth century that attempts to answer their questions.

> "Why do monks not marry?" a questioner asked. . . . "Now of pleasures there is none greater than the continuation of one's ancestral line; of unfilial conduct there is none worse than childlessness. The monks forsake wife and children, reject property and wealth. Some do not marry all their lives. How opposed this conduct is to happiness and filial piety!"[19']

The Buddhist answer could hardly have satisfied the Chinese concern for *xiao* and *li*. "Wives, children, and property are the luxuries of the world, but simple living and inaction are the wonders of the Way," the monk replied.

BUDDHISM AND DAOISM IN CHINA

There was a tradition in China that Buddhism could use to clear the way. It was Daoism [Taoism], a philosophy of spiritual naturalism that was associated in Chinese minds with the legendary Lao Zi [Lao Tzu], who was said to have lived in the time of Confucius. The writings attributed to Lao Zi and his disciple Zhuang Zi [Chuang Tzu] represented a radical alternative to the worldly practicality of Confucianism. The Han dynasty had enshrined Confucianism as the official philosophy, and relegated Daoism to a minor sect.

The rise of Buddhism in China in the period between A.D. 300 and 500 was accompanied by a revival of Daoism. Buddhist monks emphasized the similarity of the two doctrines. Was it not Lao Zi who said "Only he that rids himself of desire can see the secret essences; He that has never rid himself of desire can see only the surfaces"? That was exactly the message of the Buddha. A famous pamphlet of the third century by Wang Fo represented Buddhism as "the conversion of the barbarians by Lao Zi."

The revival of Daoism is not a sufficient explanation for the rise of Buddhism, however. We would have to ask why Daoism became so popular. Perhaps a better question is why both Daoism and Buddhism appealed to so many Chinese in this period.

The answer must lie in the pessimism of the period after the fall of the Han dynasty in A.D. 220. Between A.D. 220 and 589 (often called the Six Dynasties period) Confucianism fell into disrepute. After all, it had not saved the Han dynasty. Further, new warrior rulers of northern China, mainly barbarian in origin, could not be given the loyalty and *xiao* prescribed by Confucius.

SALVATION FROM BARBARIANS

The success of Buddhism and Christianity as salvation religions depended as much on the barbarian invasions from the grasslands of the Eurasian steppe as it did on the prior strengths of the Indian, Han, and Roman empires. There were two steps to the process. The empires were necessary to sow the seeds that blossomed during the invasions because they were fundamentally seeds of despair.

One of the more popular Buddhist stories in China after its translation in A.D. 188 was of Vimalakirti, a white-robed layman who took the sins of the world on himself. The sins of the world, and the sufferings of humanity, seemed particularly burdensome in the centuries of the barbarian invasions. The invasions marked a watershed in Eurasian history. Their legacy was not only the destruction of the roads, cities, laws, and stability of the Han and Roman empires. It was also terror and suffering. The spread of Buddhism and Christianity may have accelerated in local situations of hardship and conquest. Both had pessimistic visions of the world and its institutions. That pessimism, and the quest for salvation, became generalized in the period of the barbarian invasions. Christian saints and the equivalent Buddhist *bodhisattvas* (who refrained from their own nirvana in order to aid others) appeared as special agents of salvation. People prayed to them to gain heaven or nirvana in the same way that prior Chinese peasants had honored their ancestors and stove gods for worldly success.

FAMILY, SELF, AND SALVATION

We live in a world shaped largely by these ancient salvation religions. If, as a result, the ancestors, the elders, and the family are no longer honored, we should not be surprised. "The erosion of parental authority and the delegation of discipline to other agencies have created in the American family a growing gap between discipline and affection,"[20] one contemporary historian, Christopher Lasch, has written.

> In America the family still supervises the child's early development, but new modes of child care have lowered the temperature of family life and reduced overt tensions. Parents accept their obsolescence with the best grace they can muster, voluntarily relegating themselves to the background of their children's lives.[21]

If the family in the United States has been undermined by corporations, government agencies, peers, and mass media, this is certainly not the case in China. Perhaps both Christian and Buddhist cultures had a tendency to undermine the role of the family. But Chinese Buddhists eventually had to speak Chinese. The missionaries were converted. A "neo-Confucianism" regained control of Chinese culture about a thousand years ago and modified even the salvationists.

The victory of Christianity in Europe was more complete. That might have been a result of the strength of Byzantium. There was no equivalent to the Chinese revival of Confucianism in Europe. The early Christians converted Greek thought, as Paul did, to Christian purposes. Perhaps, the equivalent of neo-Confucianism would have been a revival of Judaism, but the Jews were dispersed throughout the Roman Empire after A.D. 70, and they often assimilated into Christian culture and never attempted to reconvert it.

There was, of course, an important revival of pre-Christian Greek and Roman thought in the European Renaissance after the twelfth century, but that may have further encouraged a European tendency toward individuality, small families, and greater tolerance of celibacy, chastity, late marriage, and bachelorhood than was common in other cultures. Further, the Renaissance was accompanied by the Protestant Reformation, with its revival of Pauline Christianity. While Protestantism provided greater sanction to the family, marriage, and the elders, it probably helped clear the ground for the enlarged role of commerce and the state in modern society.

Ultimately, perhaps, the impact of Christianity was more the result of what it ignored than of what it said. The church was not opposed to the family as much as it was concerned with other matters. Thus, the family was not encouraged to remain the alternative to the state as the latter developed. Rather, Western culture in all its versions, Protestant and Greco-Roman as well, allowed the family to atrophy in order that it might preserve the individual against, and within, the emerging state.

FOR FURTHER READING

The history of aging and the elderly is still a fairly new field. Simone de Beauvoir's *The Coming of Age* (1972) is quirky and dated, but still a good place to start. Most recent academic studies concentrate on modern Europe or the United States. They include Peter Stearns's *Old Age in European Society* (since 1500), Jill Quadagno's *Aging in Early Industrial Society* (nineteenth-century England), Andrew Achenbaum's *Old Age in the New Land* (the United States), and David Hackett Fisher's *Growing Old in America*. A good anthropological study can be found in Nancy Foner's *Ages in Conflict*.

On ancestors, the elderly, and the family in China, there is Thomas W. Ganschow's "The Aged in a Revolutionary Milieu: China" in *Aging and the Elderly*, edited by Stuart F. Spicker, Kathleen M. Woodward, and David D. Van Tassel, Francis L. K. Hsu's *Under the Ancestor's Shadow*, William L. Parish and Martin King Whyte's *Village and Family in Contemporary China*, and Ada Elizabeth Sher's *Aging in Post-Mao China*.

Among the better general introductions to Chinese history are K. C. Wu's *The Chinese Heritage*, Leon E. Stover's *The Cultural Ecology of Chinese Civilization*, and Dun J. Li's *The Ageless Chinese*. Two excellent collections of primary sources are *Sources of Chinese Tradition*, edited by William Theodore de Bary, and *Classical China*, edited by William H. McNeill and Jean W. Sedlar.

Still one of the best introductions to Chinese philosophy is Arthur Waley's *Three Ways of Thought in Ancient China.* Frederick W. Mote's *Intellectual Foundation of China* is also useful. On Confucius, one can hardly do better than to read the *Analects,* which, like the *Mencius* and Lao Zi's *Tao Te Ching,* is available in an inexpensive edition. Arthur F. Wright's *Buddhism in Chinese History* is very valuable.

Our favorite introduction to India is A. L. Basham's *The Wonder That Was India.* Francis Watson's *A Concise History of India* and Stanley Wolpert's *A New History of India* also are good. For a challenging anthropological approach, students might try Richard Lannoy's *The Speaking Tree.* Romila Thapar's *A History of India,* volume 1, is a rich account of pre-1500 India.

There are numerous translations of ancient Indian literature. The collections edited by William Theodore de Bary, *Sources of Indian Tradition,* and by William H. McNeill and Jean W. Sedlar, *Classical India,* are as good as the companion volumes on China. Professor de Bary also edited a collection called *The Buddhist Tradition in India, China, and Japan* and served as the general editor for a volume called *The Hindu Tradition,* edited by Ainslie T. Embree. There are also inexpensive editions of the *Vedas,* the *Upanishads,* the *Mahabharata,* the *Bhagavad Gita, Buddhist Scriptures,* and a volume called *The Teachings of the Compassionate Buddha.* Hermann Hesse's *Siddhartha* is a modern novel that offers a good introduction to the temper of early Buddhism. K. M. Sen's *Hinduism* is a brief history of the tradition.

The best introduction to the Judeo-Christian tradition is, of course, the *Bible.* The Revised Standard Version is considered the most accurate. *The Penguin Shorter Atlas of the Bible* is a useful aid, as are the various commentaries, perhaps *Adam to Daniel* and *Daniel to Paul,* edited by Gaalyahu Cornfeld, or *The Israelites,* by the editors of Time-Life books, or *Asimov's Guide to the Bible* by Isaac Asimov. For background on the origins of Christianity, one might see A. Powell Davies, *The Meaning of the Dead Sea Scrolls,* and Henri Daniel-Rops, *Daily Life in the Time of Jesus.* Among studies of Jesus, Gunther Bornkamm's *Jesus of Nazareth* is persuasive. Humphrey Carpenter's *Jesus* is short and accessible.

Most histories of the family focus on modern Europe. One that does not is Stuart A. Queen and Robert W. Habenstein's *The Family in Various Cultures.* One that does is Edward Shorter's *The Making of the Modern Family.* We recommend both, as well as Christopher Lasch's intriguing study of modern American social thought about the family, *Haven in a Heartless World.*

NOTES

1. Arthur P. Wolf, "Gods, Ghosts, and Ancestors," in *Religion and Ritual in Chinese Society,* ed. Arthur P. Wolf (Stanford: Stanford University Press, 1974), p. 148.

2. Dun J. Li, *The Ageless Chinese,* 3rd ed. (New York: Scribners, 1978), p. 40.

3. Cho-yun Hsu, *Ancient China in Transition: An Analysis of Social Mobility, 722–222 B.C.* (Stanford: Stanford University Press, 1965), pp. 19–21.

4. *The Analects of Confucius,* bk. II, no. 7. Adapted from translation by D. C. Lau (Penguin, 1979).

5. *Ibid.* Adapted from bk. II, no. 8.

6. *Ibid.,* bk. II, no. 2.

7. Hsieh Yu-Wei, "Filial Piety and Chinese Society" in *The Chinese Mind,* ed. Charles A. Moore (Honolulu: University Press of Hawaii, 1967), p. 172.

8. *The Analects of Confucius,* bk. XII, no. 1.

9. *Ibid.,* bk. III, no. 3.

10. Adapted from *Li Chi: The Book of Rites,* trans. James Legge, ed. Ch'u Chai and Winberg Chai (New Hyde Park, N.Y.: University Books, 1967), book I, part II, 1.

11. Hsu, *op. cit.,* p. 2.

12. While "Hinduism" has designated Indian religion after the Aryan invasion, it has recently become more accepted to distinguish between Aryan "Brahmanism" and the later Indian devotional religion that emerged around the first century A.D. as "Hinduism." See, for instance, Romila Thapar, *A History of India,* vol. 1 (Harmondsworth, England: Penguin, 1966), p. 132.

13. Lord Chalmers, trans., *Further Dialogues of the Buddha, I* (London: Oxford University Press, 1926), pp. 53–54. Quoted in Mircea Eliade, ed., *From Medicine Men to Muhammad* (New York: Harper & Row, 1974), pp. 38–39.

14. Chalmers, *op. cit.,* p. 177; also in Eliade, *op. cit.,* p. 43.

15. Adapted from *Dhammacakkapavattana-sutta,* trans. in Walpola Rahula, *What the Buddha Taught* (New York: Grove Press, 1974), p. 92.

16. Sylvia Vatuk, "Cultural Response to Aging in India," in Christine L. Fry, *Aging in Culture and Society* (New York: Bergin, 1980), pp. 132–33. See also Sylvia Vatuk, "Old Age in India," in *Old Age in Pre-Industrial Society,* ed. Peter N. Stearns (New York: Holmes and Meier, 1983), pp. 70–103.

17. The Laws of Manu, trans. George Buehler in *The Sacred Books of the East,* vol. 25 (Oxford: Clarendon Press, 1886), chapter 2, numbers 153–155. Recent scholarship questions the significance of the Laws of Manu for Indian society. The "laws" may have been little more than wishful fantasies of a small *brahman* elite.

18. Hinduism was beginning to emerge from Brahmanism around the first century A.D. with a similar emphasis. Hindu salvation was nurtured in the *bhakti,* or devotional, cults that became very popular.

19. *The Disposition of Error* (Li-huo lun), author and date unknown. Adapted from William Theodore de Bary, *The Buddhist Tradition in India, China, and Japan* (New York: Vintage Books, 1969), p. 134.

20. Christopher Lasch, *Haven in a Heartless World: The Family Besieged* (New York: Basic Books, 1977), p. 174.

21. *Ibid.,* p. 175.

✖ 5 ✖

Self and Society

Communal and Individual Identity

WHAT DOES IT MEAN TO BE AN INDIVIDUAL? Are people more, or less, individualistic than they used to be? Do some societies encourage individuality more than others? Can a society or a person be too individualistic? Are there different kinds of individuality? These are some of the questions raised in this chapter.

We are not used to thinking of the development of individuality as a historical process. But we have only to recall the stick figures of Paleolithic cave art to realize how little attention Stone Age people paid to individual differences.

In this chapter, we are going to argue that there is a definite connection between a people's attention to individual differences and their encouragement of individuality. We are going to argue that both attention to and encouragement of individuality have increased in historical time. We see this as a result of increasing specialization and technological complexity. People make themselves by making new tools, and they make newer models all the time. This process of "individualization," however, can take many forms. Different cultures have developed different kinds of individuality. And all have come at the cost of social tensions and the loss of other identities.

As you read this, you might consider not only what individuality has meant and how it has developed in different forms, but also to what extent it was worth it.

TRIBE AND INDIVIDUAL

In the broadest terms, human history has seen the replacement of tribes by states. Tribal organization was the most common form of social organization before the rise of cities and states. In the last few thousand years, tribes have become secondary not only to cities and states but also to families, castes, and, in some cases, individuals.

Every civilization balanced the claims of city, state, caste, family, and individual differently. China, we have seen, gave considerable authority to the state and family. India accorded a greater role to caste. Regardless of the particular balance, however, all societies must balance the competing interests of different social groups. The individual is often the weakest of these.

In general, the role of the individual has probably increased with the decline of tribal society. This is because tribal societies were relatively uniform, were able to afford only a modest division of labor, and thus allowed only minor differences in people's lives. Jamake Highwater, a contemporary Native American, explains the difference this way:

> The idiosyncratic characteristics that gradually arose in Europe during the Renaissance and became known as *individuality* and *originality* are virtually unknown among Indians and other aboriginal craftsmen, whose work is considered no more rarefied or conceptually discrete than that of the farmer, shaman, hunter, or any other person of the tribe.[1]

Tribal religions usually demonstrated the same lack of concern for individuality. "In tribal religions there is no salvation apart from the continuance of the tribe itself because the existence of the individual presupposes the existence of the community," according to Highwater.[2] Some Native American languages have no word for "I" or "myself," while they have rich vocabularies to designate relationships among tribal members.

There are enormous differences among tribal societies, even Native Americans, and some tribes did encourage personal developments that might be considered individualistic. In eastern North America and among the Plains peoples of the West, for example, it was common for a young boy (and sometimes a girl) to seek a vision of a guardian spirit that would help establish a personal identity.

> Typically, the vision of the guardian spirit is individual, sought and obtained in solitude and isolation out in the wilderness—for example, on secluded mountains and hills. Having prepared himself with purifying baths, sacred smoking, nightly vigil, and meditation, the supplicant is visited by the spirit.

This spirit often appears in animal form but in some visions his shape changes
from animal to human. The spirit endows his protégé with that supernatural
skill which is his special characteristic or one which it pleases him to communicate, perhaps because his client has asked for this particular "medicine."[3]

The vision quest, found most frequently among hunting tribes, may actually be
an older religious practice than the more communal and ceremonial rites of
agricultural societies. Some scholars think that totemism (a collective identification
of the tribe with a particular animal) might have evolved from the earlier practice
of vision quests.[4] Another possible legacy is the custom among Native Americans
to name children with attention to their "personal qualities, heroic exploits, un-
common abilities, unique physical characteristics, visionary experiences, and other
designations that point specifically to the singularity of the person being named."[5]
This suggests greater concern for the person's individuality, Highwater suggests,
than the European custom of naming a child with a common "George" and a
family "Washington." In fact, he says, while Western names are fixed and public,
tribal names are often changed by the tribe over a person's life, and they are
sometimes private. Examples like these caution against stereotyping and urge
careful consideration of what we mean when we use terms like "individuality,"
but they may not change our generalization. "Regardless of this 'individuality,'"
Highwater concludes, "there is nothing in Indian tribal life that even begins to
approximate the Western conception of individuality and free will."[6]

Tribal life is public, not private. All of the activities in the village are public
and ceremonial. The hunt, the feast, the marriage, the war are all carried out
publicly and according to traditions of ancestors. Tribal peoples simply cannot
afford the luxury of letting individuals "do their own thing," and thus no one ever
dreams of it. Even the housing is usually public. A person who wants to be alone
might sit facing the wall. This is the extent of privacy that is possible.

The idea of "the self" or the individual "personality," then, depends on the
breakdown of this tribal life. In the last five thousand years, the tribe has been
replaced gradually by the family, the caste, the state, and the individual. This has
occurred only with the rise of cities, which are really societies of specialists. In other
words, only as people have led increasingly specialized lives have they thought of
themselves as special, unique individuals.

METALS AND MEDALS: HEROIC BRONZE
AND DEMOCRATIC IRON

Just as stone grinding was the hallmark of the agricultural New Stone Age, the
smelting of bronze (from tin and copper) was the hallmark of the Bronze Age that
brought our first cities. Metallurgy required an investment in labor and specialization of life that villages could not afford, but it created weapons of war that won

for cities a permanent claim on the fruits of the countryside. Bronze encouraged the tendency of the first cities to create classes and armies, but since the new technology was available only to the few, the Bronze Age army was upper class. The Bronze Age (after 3000 B.C.) has in fact often been called the age of heroic individualism. Aristocratic warfare was largely an individualistic conflict, like a series of duels. Homer, the father of Greek poetry, told in his *Iliad* of the exploits of Bronze Age warriors of ancient Greece. The climax of the story is the slaying of Hector, the Trojan champion, by Achilles, the Greek hero.

> And when they were come nigh in onset on one another, to Achilles first spake great Hector of the glancing helm: "No longer, son of Peleus, will I fly thee, as before I thrice ran round the great town of Priam, and endured not to await thy onset. Now my heart biddeth me stand up against thee; I will either slay or be slain. . . .
>
> Thus saying he drew his sharp sword that by his flank hung great and strong, and gathered himself and swooped like a soaring eagle that darteth to the plain through the dark clouds to seize a tender lamb or crouching hare. So Hector swooped, brandishing his sharp sword. And Achilles made at him, for his heart was filled with wild fierceness, and before his breast he made a covering with his fair graven shield, and tossed his bright four-plated helm; and round it waved fair golden plumes. As a star goeth among stars in the darkness of night, Hesperos, fairest of all stars set in heaven, so flashed there forth a light from the keen spear Achilles poised in his right hand, devising mischief against noble Hector, eyeing his fair flesh to find the fittest place. Now for the rest of him his flesh was covered by the fair bronze armour he stripped from strong Patroklos when he slew him, but there was an opening where the collar bones coming from the shoulders clasp the neck, even at the gullet, where destruction of life cometh quickliest; there, as he came on, noble Achilles drave at him with his spear, and right through the tender neck went the point. Yet the bronze-weighted ashen spear clave not the windpipe, so that he might yet speak words of answer to his foe. . . .
>
> Then with faint breath spake unto him Hector of the glancing helm: "I pray thee by thy life and knees and parents, leave me not for dogs of the Achaians to devour by the ships, but take good store of bronze and gold, gifts that my father and lady mother shall give to thee, and give them home my body back again, that the Trojans and Trojans' wives give me my due of fire after my death.[7]

Bronze Age warrior-heroes like Achilles and Hector are among history's first individuals. They are proud of their individual strength and prowess. They face battle, and possible death, alone; they succeed or fail on the basis of their own powers or their influence with the gods. But they are still very public heroes, and public heroism is a weak basis for popular beliefs in individualism. In Bronze Age society just a few aristocrats could be genuine individuals.

The Chigi Vase depicts the Greek phalanx. Each man's shield covers the next, and the unbroken line charges to a single beat. (Hirmer Fotoarchiv)

Iron was more plentiful than bronze. Once its smelting was known after 1200 B.C., the Iron Age spread throughout the world until the development of steel and industry around A.D. 1800. Iron could afford to make common peasants, as well as aristocrats, individuals. Iron tools were efficient enough to free the average farmer to cultivate personality as well as land. Iron plows made farming less work; fewer people were needed to provide society's food. Iron Age societies were more specialized than Bronze Age societies: there were more individual differences in the jobs people performed and the lives they led.

In general, then, the Iron Age extended individuality in two ways: people became more differentiated from one another and more conscious of themselves—their own personalities, thoughts, and feelings. Iron democratized individuality by giving many of the common people a sense of their own identity. But this process took three thousand years.

The short-range effect of iron technology was just the opposite. Initially, iron destroyed the heroic individualism of aristocrats like Hector and Achilles and left nothing in its place. In fact, for almost a thousand years after the introduction of iron, almost all traces of individuality were reduced. The reasons for this lie in the fact that most of the first Iron Age armies were infantries. The common farmer became important as a soldier when armies adopted iron weapons. But he was important as part of a mass formation, not as an individual. A modern historian describes the Greek version of Iron Age infantry—the phalanx—and he dramatizes how limited Greek individualism actually was:

About 650 B.C. a momentous change in military tactics gave a secure basis to the common farmer's participation in political life. This was the invention of the phalanx—a densely massed infantry formation eight ranks deep whose members were trained to run and charge in unison. A skillful charge delivered by several thousand armored men moving as a single man proved capable of sweeping cavalry or any other kind of opposing force off the field. As this became obvious, every city had to organize and train as big a phalanx as possible from among the citizenry. Anything that interfered with strengthening the phalanx endangered the city. . . .

Every young man who could possibly afford to buy the necessary armor and weapons spent long hours with his fellow youths practicing the rhythms and skills needed to fight effectively in the phalanx. Speed, strength, and courage were only part of what was required. In addition every man had to learn to keep time to the beat set up by the war chant, so that the wall of shields would not break when the phalanx charged across the field of battle. Every man's safety depended upon his neighbor keeping his place in the ranks, for each man's shield helped to cover the right side of the man next to him. Conspicuous personal feats of arms were as much out of place in such a situation as cowardice or inability to keep pace with the rhythm of the charge, for anything that broke the line threatened immediate disaster. . . .

Every Greek citizen soldier who endured the long hours of training needed for skillful service in the phalanx and had then undergone the fatigues and dangers of a campaign and known the fierce joys and sudden exertions of battle emerged from such adventures marked for life by a deep sense of solidarity with all those who had shared these experiences with him. This intense sentiment became the basis for a fiercely collective pride in the greatness and glory of the city to whom all equally belonged, and in whose service all might find personal fulfillment and an unusually vivid sense of personal freedom by submitting to a common rhythm and demanding regimen.

It is not therefore surprising that with the introduction of the phalanx the Greeks altered their ideal of personal behavior. In the earlier aristocratic age, individual self-assertion and conspicuous consumption had been generally admired. Feats of individual prowess, such as those celebrated by Homer, and personal display of luxury went hand in hand. The phalanx, however, made close conformity to a norm absolutely mandatory in military matters. This principle was soon carried over into civil life as well, so that it became ill-mannered, un-Greek, improper to live luxuriously or, indeed, to differ in any conspicuous way from one's fellows. Competitive self-assertion was instead transferred to the collective concerns of the polis.[8]

SOCRATES AND THE SELF

Whether we are digging through ruins or looking through an art history, when we reach the statues of the ancient Greeks (about twenty-five hundred years ago), for the first time we see a large number of real individuals. The change is startling. Here are people that we feel we know: real individuals with personal feelings, recognizable "personalities." And we see not only kings, gods, and goddesses, but also fishmongers, widows, soldiers, drunkards, and ordinary peasant farmers.

Some people have said that the Greeks "invented" the individual. At least their artists, poets, and philosophers celebrated individuality and human personality to a much greater degree than anyone ever had before. Between 450 and 400 B.C., the Greek philosopher Socrates taught the children of Athens, including Plato, that wisdom begins with an understanding of one's own self. Socrates was sharply critical of what most people considered common knowledge. He continually challenged traditional ideas with searching questions, asking how such ideas were known and what they meant. Socrates called himself the "midwife" of knowledge because he would force people by continual questioning to realize that they did not know as much as they thought they knew; and this doubt was at least the beginning of real knowledge, or wisdom. Similarly, Socrates believed that all genuine knowledge was inborn in people, and that it had only to be brought out through questioning. When Socrates urged his students, "know thyself," he was telling them to dig deep into their own minds, where all truths ultimately lay.

The teaching of Socrates was pretty radical medicine for most respectable Athenians. He was telling their children not only to doubt traditional opinions, but also that the truth was "in" them, if only they would try to pull it out. This meant that even the most uneducated slave had as much potential for wisdom as a philosopher or king.

Though classical Athens could produce a philosopher like Socrates who preached that we should follow the "little god" (or conscience) within us, Athenian society was unable to tolerate such individualism. The Athenian respectables brought Socrates to trial on charges of atheism and "corrupting the youth." Socrates' response to his conviction tells us much about the limits to individualism twenty-four hundred years ago. Offered the choice between death and exile, Socrates chose death. For him, living away from his beloved Athens, outside of the reach of Athenian law and custom, was a fate worse than death.

No Greek, including Socrates, could imagine individual freedom outside of society, tradition, or the community. Freedom meant the quality of life that was possible only in political society, especially in the Greek polis (city-state). The community was thought to be the source of all virtue; there could be no morality outside of that community. The Greek word that meant "to take part in community life" was also the word that meant "to live." Human life outside of the community was unthinkable. The philosopher Aristotle, Plato's most famous pupil, makes this assumption clear when he defines man as the political animal. The difference between human beings and the animals, according to Aristotle, is that humans live in a society.

The Greeks of Aristotle's time (the fourth century B.C.) were so interested in individuality that they invented a new type of literature, which they called "biography." But, because they were much more concerned with the public society, they wrote biographies about public figures: statesmen, lawgivers, generals, and rulers. Individuality, then, was a virtue for some in ancient Athens, but it was a public virtue.

Some of the other Greek city-states never developed any individualistic culture at all. The Spartans, for instance, built a police state that depended on spies and the total militarization of the ruling aristocracy. Spartan law, according to the Greek historian Plutarch, "made the citizens accustomed to have neither the will nor the ability to lead a private life; but, like the bees, always to be organic parts of their community, to cling together around the leader, and, in an ecstasy of enthusiasm and selfless ambition, to belong wholly to their country."⁹

When the Spartans conquered their neighbors, they made them slaves of the Spartan state. The Spartans could control this subject population, which outnumbered them twenty to one, only by turning their own society into an armed camp, and making every citizen a professional soldier. Spartan law required all male citizens between the ages of twenty and thirty to live and eat in army barracks. From the age of seven, Spartan boys were educated for strict military discipline and an absolute devotion to the state. They were removed from family life and taught by the state to steal, spy on the slaves, and accept strenuous exercise, miserable food, and brutal beatings.

THE ROMAN SELF POSSESSED: TRIMALCHIO

The Romans allowed slightly more individuality and privacy than the Greeks. The Roman (Latin) word for private, *privatus* (from which our English word comes), meant a lack or absence of the advantages of public life. The Romans felt that the private citizen "deprived" himself of the values of society. Privacy was an error; people who were deprived could not lead a full life. But the Greeks had been much more critical of the private life than the Romans were. The Greek word for privacy had been *idiotes,* which meant unskilled or uneducated or even "idiotic." The Greeks believed that the private person not only deprived himself of society but became an idiot, since all knowledge and intelligence came from society. The private Roman lacked something; the private Greek lacked everything.

There were individuals in ancient Rome who were much more self-centered and selfish than any Greek would have allowed himself to become. The Roman writer Petronius described this kind of socially irresponsible individual in his book *The Satyricon.* He satirized a type of Roman self-made man, called Trimalchio, who

The bust or portrait, which captured individual facial expressions, became, like the biography, an important art in Roman culture. Clearly, individuality was of greater interest to these Romans than it had been before. (top left and bottom: Musei Vaticani; top right: Alinari, EPA)

was born a foreign slave but rose to become a millionaire through his own shrewdness and ambition. Petronius has Trimalchio describe his rise from rags to riches:

> Friends, make yourselves comfortable. Once I used to be like you, but I rose to the top by my ability. Guts are what make the man; the rest is garbage. I buy well, I sell well. . . . It's through my business sense that I shot up. Why, when I came here from Asia I stood no taller than that candlestick there. . . . For fourteen years I was my master's pet. . . . So he made me joint heir with the emperor to everything he had, and I came out of it with a senator's fortune. But we never have enough, and I wanted to try my hand at business. To cut short, I had five ships built. Then I stocked them with wine—worth its weight in gold at the time—and shipped them off to Rome. I might as well have told them to go sink themselves since that's what they did. Yup, all five of them wrecked. No kidding. In one day the sea swallowed down a cool million. Was I licked? Hell, no. That loss just whetted my appetite as though nothing had happened at all. So I built some more ships, bigger and better and a damn sight luckier. No one could say I didn't have guts. But big ships make a man feel big himself. I shipped a cargo of wine, bacon, beans, perfume, and slaves. And then Fortune came through nicely in the nick of time. . . . On that one voyage alone, I cleared about five hundred thousand. Right away I bought up all my old master's property. I built a house, I went into slave-trading and cattle-buying. Everything I touched just grew and grew like a honeycomb. Once I was worth more than all the people in my home town put together, I picked up my winnings and pulled out. I retired from trade and started lending money to ex-slaves. . . .
>
> I built this house. As you know, it used to be a shack; now it's a shrine. It has four dining rooms, twenty bedrooms, two marble porticoes, an upstairs dining room, the master bedroom where I sleep, a fine porter's lodge, and guestrooms enough for all my guests. . . . Take my word for it: money makes the man. No money and you're nobody. But big money, big man. That's how it was with yours truly: from mouse to millionaire.[10]

There had never been any Trimalchios in ancient Greece. No Greek would have been so materialistic, and no Greek would have ranted this way about how "I" did this and "I" did that. No character in Greek fiction thinks so much of himself as Trimalchio does. The Romans tolerated brash, egotistical individuals like Trimalchio because they lived in a different world than the Greeks. Roman society was much more fluid and dynamic than Greek society had been. Rome was also much more money-conscious and business-oriented. An aggressive Roman could easily rise from "mouse to millionaire" because Roman society was always changing so rapidly. Also, Roman society offered the ambitious individual more opportunity to "make it" on his own because it was a much larger society than the Greek city-state. The Romans ruled a vast empire that presented innumerable opportunities for exploitation and personal fame as a businessman, soldier, or government official. There was more room in which the aggressive Roman could maneuver. He not only had the whole Mediterranean world at his disposal, but he also could take advantage of the wide gap that separated him from government. While the Greek had always felt the influence of the city-state, the Roman had only to obey the laws of a distant emperor.

The kind of aggressive, selfish individualism that Trimalchio practiced and preached seems very modern to us. This is because ancient Rome was beginning to develop the expansive, materialistic mentality and the money-oriented, business society that has formed much of our own way of life. But the early development of this business society was cut short in ancient Rome, and it has been revived to reach its fullest possibilities only in the last few hundred years. Of all the ancient peoples, the Romans probably came closest to developing modern business's aggressive individualism. But ancient Rome never fully became a business civilization, and Trimalchio was never more than a writer's exaggeration.

THE CHRISTIAN SOUL CONFESSED: AUGUSTINE

Another kind of individual was created by ancient Rome, one very different from the kind of individual that Trimalchio represents. Rome gave us the spiritualistic individual as well as the materialistic. There are some hints of the individual in spirit, feeling, and thought in ancient Greece. Socrates suggests such an idea of the self when he speaks of his conscience, or the "little god" inside him. But it was not really until the Roman Empire that large numbers of people took such an ideal seriously.

There are many types of this spiritual individuality in the Roman Empire. The philosophers of the Roman Empire (Stoics and Epicureans) taught their students to achieve "inner calm," "self-control," and a "mind at peace," and sometimes they argued (as Socrates had) that there was a spark of the divine in everyone. At the same time, many less-educated Romans turned from the formal, official state religious ceremonies to new religions that promised personal experience and an individual life after death. The most successful of these new religions of personal salvation was, of course, Christianity. Its appeal (like that of many religions and philosophies of the empire) was that it offered personal security in a confusing and increasingly impersonal world.

Christianity grew out of the Old Testament religion of the ancient Jews—but with at least one important difference. The ancient Jews had hoped for a social salvation for the whole tribe. They dreamed of the day when they, the "chosen people," would return to "the promised land," their ancestral home. Some Jews, like Jesus, had (at least by the time of Roman occupation) begun to think that their salvation might be personal, not social, and that the future kingdom might be "not of this world." The followers of Jesus traveled throughout the Roman Empire and taught that every individual was born with his own divine "soul," and that he was personally responsible to God for the care of that soul. These Christians insisted that a person might live after dying, but that such a future life depended on what the individual did himself, not on what others did for him.

The idea that God was interested in the behavior and beliefs of every individual must have been very appealing to those who felt lost in the bigness of the empire. But the immense responsibility to God that this idea implied must have been an awesome burden to those Romans who took it seriously. As a result, the Christians were usually very introspective. They asked questions about themselves, their faith, and their behavior that most ordinary people had never cared to raise. They sought to know themselves in order to know God. They examined all of their past experiences in their search for personal experiences of the divine.

Self-knowledge was the goal of Augustine, the church father, when he wrote his *Confessions* around A.D. 400. This spiritual autobiography was an extreme example of the typical Christian attempt to arrive at a detailed understanding of the inner life, especially sin. Probably no one before Augustine had tried to understand himself so fully.

> I wish to bring back to mind my past foulness and the carnal corruptions of my soul. This is not because I love them, but that I may love you, my God. Out of love for your love I do this. In the bitterness of my remembrance, I tread again my most evil ways, so that you may grow sweet to me. . . .[11]

He confessed his private thoughts (the "sickness of the soul") as well as his acts. In one instance, he asked God's forgiveness for pretending to be as sexually experienced as his companions when he was sixteen.

> I was ashamed to be remiss in vice in the midst of my comrades. For I heard them boast of their disgraceful acts, and glory in them all the more, the more debased they were.
>
> There was pleasure in doing this, not only for the pleasure of the act, but also for the praise it brought. . . . So they wouldn't make fun of me, I made myself more depraved than I was.[12]

Augustine searched his memory to recall everything, even the most minor acts—such as stealing pears from a neighbor's tree.

> I willed to commit theft, and I did so, not because I was driven to it by any need, unless it was a need of justice and goodness. For I stole a thing of which I had plenty of my own and of much better quality. Nor did I wish to enjoy that thing which I desired to gain by theft, but rather to enjoy the actual theft and the sin of theft.
>
> In a garden nearby to our vineyard there was a pear tree, loaded with fruit that was desirable neither in appearance nor in taste. Late one night . . . we had kept up our street games, and a group of very bad youths set out to shake

down and rob this tree. We took great loads of fruit from it, not for our own eating, but rather to throw it to the pigs; even if we did eat a little of it, we did this to do what pleased us because it was forbidden.[13]

A man in his mid-forties, a bishop in the Roman Catholic church, forced himself to remember a typical sixteen-year-old's prank. Why? The Christians felt that they were as responsible for childhood sins as they were for sins committed the day before. They believed that the individual would be judged as a total person, for everything he or she had been in the past as well as in the present. Most religions before Christianity saw human sins as particular mistakes or errors that could be "corrected" by the appropriate sacrifice. The Christians, however, believed that sin was a sign of a corrupt personality that had to be converted to Christ before sinning would cease.

Certainly, not everyone in ancient Rome was as intensely self-conscious or individualistic as Augustine or Trimalchio. Probably no more than 10 percent of the inhabitants of the Roman Empire were Christians before Christianity became the state religion (during Augustine's lifetime). As soon as Christianity was established as the official religion of the empire, many people became Christians for political reasons, not necessarily because they were seeking individual salvation.

Nevertheless, there were many Romans who were much more aware of their own individuality than any group of people ever had been before. Roman society was probably more specialized than any previous society. This means that there actually were more individual differences among Romans than previously: there was a greater variety of jobs, living conditions, life-styles, and ways of thinking. Thus, in a real sense, there was a greater degree of individuality in Rome than there had been in Greece or before.

THE SELF IN INDIA

There is a Buddhist story about the meeting of the Greek king Milinda, or Menander, who ruled in northwestern India in the middle of the second century B.C., with the Buddhist monk Nāgasena. The story highlights the difference between Greek and Indian ideas of individuality. According to the story:

King Menander went up to the venerable Nāgasena, greeted him respectfully, and sat down. Nāgasena replied to the greeting, and the King was pleased at heart. Then King Menander asked: "How is your reverence known, and what is your name?"

"I'm known as Nāgasena, your Majesty, that's what my fellow monks call me. But though my parents may have given me such a name . . . it's only a generally understood term, a practical designation. There is no question of a permanent individual implied in the use of the word."

"Listen, you five hundred Greeks and eighty thousand monks!" said King

Menander. "This Nāgasena has just declared that there's no permanent individuality implied in his name!" Then, turning to Nāgasena, "If, Reverend
Nāgasena, there is no permanent individuality, who gives you monks your
robes and food, lodging and medicines? And who makes use of them? Who
lives a life of righteousness, meditates, and reaches Nirvana? Who destroys
living beings, steals, fornicates, tells lies, or drinks spirits? . . . If what you say
is true there's neither merit nor demerit, and no fruit or result of good and
evil deeds. If someone were to kill you there would be no question of murder.
And there would be no masters or teachers in the [Buddhist] Order and no
ordinations. If your fellow monks call you Nāgasena, what then is Nāgasena?[14]

King Menander, according to the story, then asked Nāgasena if his nails, his teeth,
his skin, or his entire body were Nāgasena, to which the monk said no. Then
Menander asked if his body, sensations, perceptions, ideas, and consciousness (the
five parts of individuality according to the Buddha) constituted Nāgasena, and the
monk still said no.

When asked to explain himself, Nāgasena pointed out that his name, just like
the word for King Menander's chariot, was a practical term for something that was
more than the sum of its parts; further, it was always changing. "When a man is
born, . . . he neither remains the same nor becomes another," Nāgasena remarked.
It is "through the continuity of the body [that] all stages of life are included in
a pragmatic unity."[15]

REINCARNATION AND *ATMAN*

The problem with the Greek idea of individuality, from the Indian standpoint, was
that it was too fixed, too permanent. For Nāgasena, Western individuality was like
a prison: it was limited to one body and one life. The Indian idea of the individual
was much broader than that. It spanned not only the changes from childhood
through the stages of adulthood, but also the changes from one body to the next.
The great Indian poem the *Bhagavad Gita* (from the epic *Mahabharata*) shows the
way in which the Indian idea of reincarnation leads to a different notion of the
individual. In it, Lord Krishna explains to the young Arjuna, about to engage in
battle against people he knows well, that their lives continue after death.

> *Arjuna, when a man knows the self*
> *to be indestructible, enduring, unborn,*
> *unchanging, how does he kill*
> *or cause anyone to kill?*
>
> *As a man discards*
> *worn-out clothes*
> *to put on new ones,*
> *so the embodied self*

discards
its worn-out bodies
to take on new ones.

Weapons do not cut it,
fire does not burn it,
waters do not wet it,
wind does not wither it.[16]

The indestructible self in Indian thought was called the *atman*, often translated as "soul." Unlike the Christian "soul," however, the *atman* was not associated with a particular personality. The *atman* was the essence of the individual, which continued from one reincarnation to the next. The *atman* changed in each life, becoming purer or more polluted, gaining good or bad *karma* from the experiences of the world, but these changes were moral rather than physical. Christians usually imagined the dead in heaven or hell having the same physical appearance as they did in life. Indians did not imagine that a reincarnated person would look the way he or she did in a previous life. Rather, they believed that the moral effects, the *karma,* of a previous life would be evident. In general, one's good *karma* from a previous life would improve one in the current life, just as good deeds in this life improved one.

Thus, Indian culture taught the improvement of self rather than the improvement of the world. The Indian self was to be engaged not in a struggle with the world, but in a struggle to overcome its own bad actions (bad *karma*). In general, this was a struggle to detach the *atman* from the daily involvements and "static" of the world, seen as *maya,* or illusion, in order to reunite it with the larger divinity, *Brahman,* which was the universe. To make *atman* into *Brahman,* self into universal divinity, was the goal of Indian culture. "Who sees all beings in his own self, and his own self in all beings, loses all fear," the Isa Upanishad counseled. That is why Indian religious thinkers sought to relinquish the ties that bind the self to the world. "When all ties that bind the heart are unloosened, then a mortal becomes immortal," the Katha Upanishad declared.

Always dwelling within all beings is the Atman, the Purusha, the Self, a little flame in the heart. Let one with steadiness withdraw him from the body even as an inner stem is withdrawn from its sheath. Know this pure immortal light; know in truth this pure immortal light.[17]

ATMAN VERSUS EGO

The difference between Western and Indian ideas of individuality stem from different ideas of the self. Both materialist and spiritualist ideas of the self in Greco-Roman culture, both Augustine and Trimalchio, envisioned a "self" that was separate from God. "In the beginning, this universe was nothing but the Self in the form of man," the Brihadaranyaka Upanishad declared around 700 B.C., a few hundred years before the Hebrews declared, "In the beginning, God created the Heavens and the Earth." According to one tradition, God and the Self were one. According to the other, God created each self. The individual in the Judeo-Christian tradition was imperfect and had to work: obey, pray, worship, be saved. The Christian soul was "immortal," but Augustine and other Christians had to shape, cultivate, and improve that soul. It would not become perfect without religious effort, certainly not by being relinquished.

In some ways, Indian thought was psychologically more subtle than Western thought. While both the Greco-Roman and the Judeo-Christian traditions concentrated on the actions of an objective self, Indian thought explored the levels of self and self-consciousness. We might say that Indian culture concentrated on the psychology of consciousness rather than on the self. "Develop the state of mind of consciousness . . . for thus the pride of selfhood will grow less," the Buddha is thought to have said.[18] A man should breathe his last breath in "full consciousness, and not unconsciously." From the Indian standpoint, the active self interferes with consciousness. To be fully conscious, according to this view, one must conquer the self.

There is a tendency to assume that since Indians cultivated the deeper "dreamless self" instead of the superficial worldly self, they did not *do* anything. In fact, they did quite a lot. The cultivation of techniques of yoga and meditation (as many people have learned since) often made material accomplishments effortless. The habit of listening to the "real" self rather than the superficial self enhanced the ability to distinguish the important from the trivial. A peaceful consciousness could be far more effective than a preoccupied ego. By "relinquishing attachment," the *Bhagavad Gita* taught, "men of discipline perform action . . . for the purification of the self."

> Men who master the worldly world
> have equanimity—
> they exist in the infinite spirit,
> in its flawless equilibrium.[19]

FOR FURTHER READING

We have chosen to discuss Native American society as our example of tribal society, and have found some of the following quite useful: Jamake Highwater's *The Primal Mind,* Ake Hultkrantz's *The Religions of the American Indians,* Dorothy Lee's *Freedom and Culture,* and Paul Radin's *Primitive Man as Philosopher.*

On the "heroic" individuality of the Bronze Age, the student is invited to read Homer's *Iliad* and *Odyssey* (many editions) firsthand. M. I. Finley's *The World of Odysseus* is an excellent companion. William H. McNeill's *Rise of the West* and *A World History* offer suggestive interpretations of the meaning of Bronze Age and Iron Age warfare for individuality in ancient Greece and worldwide.

The story of classical Greece as a golden age of individuality is told in almost every text and history of the age. Those students who would like to explore the subject are alerted to Werner Jaeger's difficult but rewarding *Paideia,* E. R. Dodds's *The Greeks and the Irrational,* M. I. Finley's *The Ancient Greeks: An Introduction to Their Life and Thought,* and Bruno Snell's *The Discovery of the Mind.* But no understanding of Greek individuality is possible without some sampling of the individuals of the classical age. There are enough editions of Plato, Aristotle, Herodotus, Thucydides, Euripides, Sophocles, Aeschylus, and Aristophanes (to name only a few) to please any tastes.

We have entered the Roman world of individuality through Petronius' *Satyricon* and Augustine's *Confessions* (many editions); both are worth reading in full. For an understanding of the classical Roman individual, the student might also read Cicero, Caesar, Tacitus, Suetonius, Livy, Horace, Juvenal, or Ovid (among so many others). Many secondary sources have already been mentioned, but perhaps Jérôme Carcopino's *Daily Life in Ancient Rome* stands out. For Roman Christianity, the letters of Paul or Jerome say as much as Augustine. Harold Mattingly's *Christianity in the Roman Empire* and A. D. Nock's *Conversion* add (in different ways) to our understanding of the Christian stress on the individual.

Among the general histories of India, the most useful for this topic are A. L. Basham's *The Wonder That Was India* and Romila Thapar's *A History of India.* Joseph Campbell's *The Masks of God: Oriental Mythology* is full of interesting discussions of myth and literature. Students should be encouraged to read some of the classics discussed here as well. The *Bhagavad Gita* is available in an excellent translation by Barbara Stoler Miller. The *Upanishads* are available in a number of good editions. A demanding, but highly rewarding, study by a specialist on Indian culture that touches on this topic is Richard Lannoy's *The Speaking Tree.* Sudhir Kakar's *The Inner World: A Psychoanalytic Study of Childhood and Society in India* is a study of individuality in modern India by an Indian psychologist.

NOTES

1. Jamake Highwater, *The Primal Mind: Vision and Reality in Indian America* (New York: Harper & Row, 1981), p. 56.
2. *Ibid.,* pp. 171–172.
3. Ake Hultkrantz, *The Religions of the American Indians,* trans. Monica Setterwall (Berkeley: University of California Press, 1979), p. 77.
4. Hultkrantz, *op. cit.,* p. 83.
5. Highwater, *op. cit.,* p. 173.
6. *Ibid.,* pp. 179–180.
7. Homer, *Iliad,* bk. XXII, trans. Andrew Lang, Walter Leaf, and Ernest Myers (New York: Grolier, 1969), pp. 337–340.
8. William H. McNeill, *A World History* (New York: Oxford University Press, 1979), pp. 90–91.
9. *Lycurgus,* 25, trans. Werner Jaeger in *Paideia* (New York: Oxford University Press, 1965), pp. 83–84. For a complete translation of *Lycurgus,* see one of the many editions of *Plutarch's Lives.* The problem of conveying Spartan public identity can be seen in

the ambiguity of classical translation of John and William Langhorne (1819): Lycurgus "taught his citizens to think nothing more disagreeable than to live by, or for, themselves. Like bees, they acted with one impulse for the public good. . . ." (New York: Mentor Books, 1950), p. 31.

10. Petronius, *The Satyricon,* trans. William Arrowsmith (New York: New American Library, 1959), pp. 81–83.

11. Augustine, *The Confessions of St. Augustine,* trans. John K. Ryan (Garden City, N.Y.: Doubleday, 1960), bk. 2, ch. 1, p. 65.

12. *Ibid.,* bk. 2, ch. 3, p. 68.

13. *Ibid.,* bk. 2, ch. 4, pp. 69–70.

14. *Sources of Indian Tradition,* vol. 1, ed. William Theodore de Bary (New York: Columbia University Press, 1958), pp. 103–104.

15. *Ibid.*

16. *Bhagavad Gita,* trans. Barbara Stoler Miller (New York: Bantam, 1986), II: 21–23.

17. "The Katha Upanishad," in *The Upanishads,* trans. Juan Mascaro (Harmondsworth, England: Penguin, 1965), p. 66.

18. de Bary, *op. cit.,* p. 109.

19. *Bhagavad Gita,* V: 19.

✖6✖

City
and
State

The Indo-European
Tradition

WE ARE USED TO THINKING OF CITIES in terms of numbers. We define a city as an area with so many people. We identify the problems of cities with overcrowding, congestion, and vertical living. Cities seem to have too much of everything: too many people, too much traffic, too much pollution. The sheer weight of numbers seems to make city life too fast and frantic.

Sometimes we have to be reminded that it is not population size, but population density that defines a city and contributes to its problems. Density is more of a problem than simple size or numbers of people. But decreasing population density does not by itself make a city more habitable, any more than decreasing the number of people. Modern cities like New York and Tokyo, for instance, have about one-fifth the density of population as the ancient, compact, walled cities.

Cities may have become larger in population and smaller in density, but if their problems have increased we may have to look elsewhere for the reasons. This chapter will look at the history of ancient cities to explore a different kind of distinction—that of *function* rather than numbers.

The classical world distinguished between city-states and imperial capital cities, and this may be a useful distinction for us even today. The city-state was different from the capital city in the functions it performed. It served the needs of the inhabitants in town and country, and it often functioned quite autonomously and even democratically (at least for its citizens). The function of the capital city, on the other hand, was usually to magnify the power of the ruler, rather than to serve the interests of the inhabitants. The two types of cities were often different in size and density, but their differences in function said a lot more for the possibilities of life that they offered.

Most cities in the classical world also served a commercial function. While all cities engaged in some degree of economic activity, however, most had political, religious, or social functions that were thought more important. Nevertheless, some cities were primarily commercial centers, engaged in trade or manufacturing, or both. In modern society, commercial cities outnumber city-states and capital cities. Thus, in order to understand how different cities function, we will examine all three types.

To understand the city-state, we will examine the most famous, the Athens of classical Greece. To understand the functioning of the capital city, we will study two, Alexandria and Rome. Finally, to understand the commercial city, we will look at Pataliputra in India.

As you read, you might ask yourself about the appeals and drawbacks of life in these cities. What were the attractions of urban life in the classical world? Would life in some cities be preferable to life in others? How would life in a city-state be different from life in a large capital? How would life in a commercial city be different from life in a city that had mainly political functions? Where would you like to live, and why?

You might also consider what the politics of city life in the classical world tell us about city life today. Were these cities more, or less, "democratic" than our own cities today? Can we learn anything from the way they were governed or run? Do you see any ideas or institutions in these classical cities that we might do well to borrow? Has urban life improved?

ATHENS: THE CITY-STATE AND THE GOOD LIFE

Aristotle said that "men come together in the city to live; they remain there in order to live the good life." He was writing about the city in general, but he must have been thinking of his native Athens. By "the good life" Aristotle most certainly did not mean physical comforts and material possessions. One Greek visitor remarked:

> The road to Athens is a pleasant one, running between cultivated fields the whole way. The city is dry and ill supplied with water. The streets are nothing but miserable old lanes, the houses mean, with a few better ones among them. On his first arrival a stranger would hardly believe this is the Athens of which he has heard so much.[1]

The sanitary facilities that ancient Sumerian Ur or Indian Harappa had enjoyed two thousand years before were virtually unknown in Athens. The houses of the city were made of unbaked brick with tile roofs or even of mud and straw. There was no paving to prevent the narrow streets from turning into mud in the spring and dust in the summer. The charcoal fires never seemed to take the chill out of the winter, and the small, closely built one-story houses worked like ovens in the summer.

Athens lacked the amenities of big city life. Like earlier city-states it was really something of a small town. It was only a fifteen-minute walk from the center to the outskirts. It was a city of peasant farmers, many of whom still walked to the

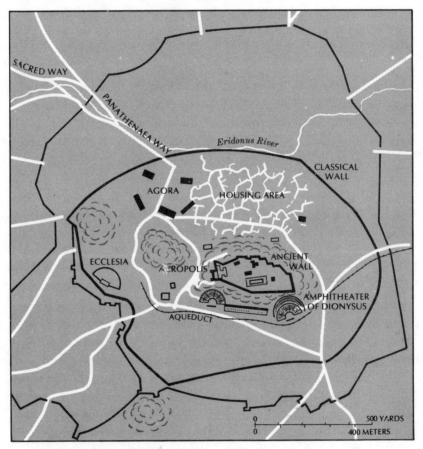

ATHENS, C. FIFTH CENTURY B.C.
Classical Athens was a city of public meeting places and narrow, winding streets.

surrounding fields to tend their plots. In terms of technology, comforts, physical layout, and the lives of the inhabitants, Athens was not very far removed from the peasant village. That, in fact, may have been its great strength.

The democratic ways of the village continued in most of the early city-states, but in Athens they were taken especially seriously. Power was exercised by a far larger proportion of the population than in any other city. At its largest in the fifth century B.C. the city contained seventy-five thousand people, and the entire city-state around three hundred thousand. There were probably about forty thousand male citizens, another hundred and fifty thousand free women, children, and foreigners, and another hundred thousand slaves. The exclusion of women from citizenship and the creation of a slave class were less democratic than village life, of course. But all cities excluded women and captured slaves. The uniquely democratic character of Athens lay in the rough equality of its male citizens and the degree of their participation in political life.

If we concentrate on that unusually large one-seventh of the population that consisted of the citizens, the Athenian political system seems extremely demo-cratic—perhaps even more than our own. These citizens were chosen by lot (like a lottery) to serve on virtually all of the governing bodies of the city. This avoided some of the pitfalls of elections: it minimized the importance of the "big names" of the traditional aristocracy, slowed the growth of political machines, and gave many more citizens the opportunity and experience of public service than an election system; it allowed greater flexibility in changing government policy without confronting entrenched deadwood bureaucrats or damaging the egos of the authors of the old policy; and it forced citizens to keep in touch with public affairs, since they might suddenly find themselves on the town council. More than a representative democracy, the Athenian system of lot selection made public service the education and creation of the citizens.

When special knowledge or skill was necessary (managing finances or building docks), special boards of "professionals" were appointed. But the Athenians under-stood (perhaps better than we do) that governing does not require expertise as much as an active, informed citizenry.

The big choices (laws, decisions of war and peace, determination of how much money to collect and what to spend it on) were made by the Ecclesia, or mass assembly. Unlike our Congress, this legislative body consisted of all of the citizens. Anyone could speak. Everyone had a vote. The town council prepared most of the issues for this assembly, but the assembled citizens were the final judges of what was to be done.

It is appropriate that the Greek word for city-state, *polis,* is the root of our word for politics. Athens showed the potential of the democratic city, but more funda-mentally it taught the possibility of the participatory city and the creative city. That is what Pericles, the great Athenian statesman who was *elected* general from 443 to 430 B.C., meant when he said that Athens was "an education to Greece." We would add: "and to the world."

ATHENS: ACROPOLIS, AGORA, AND AMPHITHEATER

The Ecclesia was only one center of Athenian social life. There were also the acropolis, the agora, and the amphitheater to enrich public life. The acropolis, the home of the gods, presides over Athens today on a high bluff in the center of the city, just as it did in the time of Pericles, when the present temples were built. The contrast must have been even more striking then: the new majestic, colored buildings and the rubble of houses beneath. Before it became the museum of marble art (and the most beautiful in the world), it was the Athenian's source of life, identity, and meaning. In the most important city festival, the Panathenaea, the Athenians marched in a winding processional up the slopes to the acropolis, where they gathered to present their gifts to the goddess Athena. This festival, like many others, was a kind of celebration that occurred often in the ancient city-state. Special times for collective rejoicing, gaiety, and festivity served to rededicate the people to their city and to each other—just as the Ecclesia sharpened their sense of political participation.

The female goddess, the sacred mountain, caves, springs, and shrines connected the acropolis with the magic and rituals of a Neolithic past. Similarly, the agora, the market and meeting place, affirmed the continuity of the "village square" or, more appropriately, the central, circular open space where all the villagers gathered and some spread out their wares. The market was secondary to the meeting place. Homer's *Iliad* first describes the agora as a "place of assembly" where "town folk gathered around" as the elders "seated on polished stones in the midst of the hallowed circle" rendered their judgment of an accused villager. In the city the meeting place became more of a marketplace, but the exchange of ideas and gossip must have kept pace with the exchange of goods. The agora was the most vital element of the city. The large square swarmed with activity: between the fountain and the ceramic stalls the sausage seller and the silversmith compete for space; on the steps between the fish market and the temple Socrates has buttonholed Alcibiades to talk about "the different types of virtue"—and to escape from his wife; the argument of a group of men about freedom in Sparta grows louder with the approach of two young boys who are playing flutes; a peasant and his donkey jostle Plato, who pauses to watch the intricate work of a carpenter in his open shop.

The Athenian amphitheater, a huge semicircle of steps carved out of a sloping hill, is another outlet for sociability that connects the public concerns of the city with the ritual of ancient religion. In the century before Sophocles died in 406 B.C., twelve hundred plays were written and produced, one hundred by Sophocles himself. Like many of those of Euripides, Aeschylus, and Aristophanes (to name a few), they are enthralling even today. Under the open sky the Greek tragedies and comedies put human foibles, political policy, and the eternal dramas of human life on stage for all to see. The performance was both an opportunity for social intercourse and a stimulus to self-examination. The amphitheater, like the acropolis and the agora, involved an enormous expense of public energy. Many Athenians

played a part at some time or another. There was little distinction between performer and audience. Often the playwright expressed public sentiment in parts designed for a "chorus." Contests were held. Prizes were awarded. Some plays were booed off the stage. But despite the public expense and enthusiasm, the drama was still close enough to its primitive sacred origins to be prized at its most controversial. During the Peloponnesian War, while Athens was being conquered by Sparta, Aristophanes was able to perform *The Archarnians,* a play in which the hero makes his "private peace" with the enemy. Athenians found public space and time in order to deepen private consciousness and free expression.

Popular participation on such a high level naturally required a certain amount of leisure time. The city, Aristotle said, "should be such as may enable the inhabitants to live at once temperately and liberally in the enjoyment of leisure." Much of the citizen's leisure was no doubt provided by the slaves who worked in the mines and ships, or who served in the city police or the homes of the wealthy. But the average peasant or craftsman owned no slaves, the moderately wealthy owned only a dozen, even the very rich owned no more than fifty. Leisure was due not only to slavery. It was also the result of the acceptance of a temperate technological standard of living that enabled the citizens to live "the good life" of public participation, reflective conversation, and artistic expression more "liberally." Leisure was after all a village value. Farmers have always probably had more free time than city people. The Athenians insisted on using that leisure to expand the possibilities of human life. They did so at the expense of slaves, but before we criticize them in terms of modern morality we might notice that we usually use our much more productive machines to increase work and hurry time. And we use our cities for private exploitation. At least for the Athenian citizens, the enrichment of human life was the goal. And the polis made it possible.

THE GREEK IMPERIAL CITY: ALEXANDRIAN CAPITALS OF CULTURE

In his discussion of ideal cities, Aristotle was more appreciative of variety, plurality, and particular local needs than his teacher, Plato. Plato's ideal city would have been a geometric absolute: exactly 5040 citizens and 5040 lots; three classes of people, educated and living separately; twelve sections to the city, each with a separate god and temple; each of the houses lined up like a wall, "the form of the city being like a single dwelling." In short, everything was to be regular and uniform. Plato admired the discipline and military organization of Sparta. Aristotle was less taken by ideal forms, and more concerned (possibly because of his extensive study of

The ruins of the Athenian Acropolis as it still presides over Athens. (Hirmer Fotoarchiv)

biological organisms) with process, purpose, function, growth, and potential—in short, the kinds of living produced by certain cities rather than the "ideal" shell.

The future was designed by Aristotle's most famous student, Alexander the Great. However, Alexander's design was closer to Plato's. By the time the thirty-three-year-old Alexander died in 323 B.C., he had founded seventy cities, most of which he named Alexandria. Many have not survived. The Alexandria that served as the capital of Alexander's North African empire has. Now it shows us what the other cities of this Hellenistic Age must have looked like, and then it performed a more valuable service than the rest: it preserved much of the learning of the earlier Hellenic culture of the Greek city-states. Its design was the model of future city planning even for the next rulers of the Mediterranean, the Romans. And at the same time, it recaptured the design and style of the ancient imperial cities of the Middle East—of Babylonia, Assyria, Crete, and Egypt.

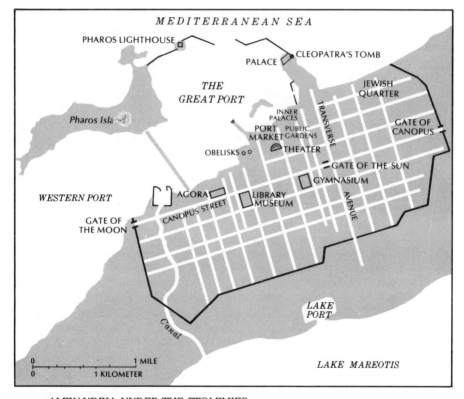

ALEXANDRIA UNDER THE PTOLEMIES
Alexandria was an emperor's city, laid out for easy access and control.
The monuments were for the enjoyment of the court and the
admiration of the multitude.

It was an ideal site. Maybe Alexander remembered Homer's mention in the *Odyssey* of "an island in the surging sea in front of Egypt, and men call it Pharos. . . . Therein is a harbour with good anchorage, whence men launch the shapely ships into the sea." The island (whose name probably was a corruption of the Egyptian word for pharaoh) protected a narrow strip of land between the Mediterranean and a large Egyptian lake. Alexander decided to build his city on that strip. A canal joined the Mediterranean to the lake. Another canal gave access to the Nile. Broad streets were laid out in a rectangular grid pattern, the long ones running east and west along the strip and the shorter ones running north and south from the sea to the lake. Most of the streets were eighteen to nineteen feet wide, but the main east-west street, Canopus Street, was probably a hundred feet wide. Thus, everything was designed for easy, direct movement. Alexandria was to be a model of efficiency and clarity. It was the dream of a city founder who could not take time to learn the lay of the land. It was the ideal of a world ruler who desired to show the extent and evenness of his control. It was the model of the foreign general who feared the potential threat of tight native quarters protected by narrow winding streets. And it was the envy of the foreign merchants and visitors who could do their business, see the sights, and never get lost.

ALEXANDRIA: SIGHTS, SEEING, AND SPECTACLES

And what sights there were! One visitor, the Greek novelist Achilles Tatius, reminds us that the spectacular city could be a feast for the eyes:

> After a voyage lasting for three days, we arrived at Alexandria. I entered it by the Sun Gate, as it is called, and was instantly struck by the splendid beauty of the city, which filled my eyes with delight. From the Sun Gate to the Moon Gate—these are the guardian divinities of the entrances—led a straight double row of columns, about the middle of which lies the open part of the town, and in it so many streets that walking in them you would fancy yourself abroad while still at home. Going a few hundred yards further, I came to the quarter called after Alexander, where I saw a second town; the splendour of this was cut into squares, for there was a row of columns intersected by another as long at right angles. I tried to cast my eyes down every street, but my gaze was still unsatisfied, and I could not grasp all the beauty of the spot at once; some parts I saw, some I was on the point of seeing, some I earnestly desired to see, some I could not pass by; that which I actually saw kept my gaze fixed, while that which I expected to see would drag it on to the next. I explored therefore every street, and at last, my vision unsatisfied, exclaimed in weariness, "Ah, my eyes, we are beaten." Two things struck me as especially strange and extraordinary—it was impossible to decide which was the greatest, the size

A reconstruction of ancient Alexandria as it is believed to have appeared when viewed from the harbor. (From Cities of Destiny, *edited by Arnold Toynbee. © 1967 Thames and Hudson Limited)*

of the place or its beauty, the city itself, or its inhabitants; for the former was larger than a continent, the latter outnumbered a whole nation. Looking at the city, I doubted whether any race of men would ever fill it; looking at the inhabitants, I wondered whether any city could ever be found large enough to hold them all. The balance seemed exactly even.[2]

Exaggeration probably came easy to visitors of Alexandria. Within a hundred years of its founding by Alexander in 331 B.C., it was the largest city in the world. By the second century B.C., it was the first city in human history to number between a hundred and a hundred and fifty thousand people within its walls. Its inhabitants came from India and the Iberian Peninsula. They included Arabians, Babylonians, Assyrians, Medes, Persians, Carthaginians, Italians, and Gauls. But besides the cosmopolitan population of three continents, there were distinct native quarters—the Greek royal quarter on the harbor, the native Egyptian quarter on the west, and the Jewish quarter on the east—that were separate cities in themselves. A visit to Alexandria was a visit to three foreign countries and to "the city of the world."

Architecturally, it was unique. Even the ordinary dwellings were built, like the finer residences, of stone, with foundations of masonry, vaulted arches, and cisterns connected to the Nile. The absence of wood (even for floors and timbers) made Alexandria more fireproof than both other ancient cities and many modern ones. But it was probably the monumental buildings that attracted the eye of the visitor.

Alexander and each of the successive rulers (called the Ptolemies) built their own palaces as a way of continually enhancing the city's magnificence. The palaces alone occupied one-quarter to one-third of the entire city. There was also a giant stadium, an amphitheater, beautiful public gardens, two obelisks (called Cleopatra's Needles—after the last of the Ptolemies—now in London and New York), a lighthouse that the ancients considered one of the seven wonders of the world, and many elaborate gates and temples. The Greek geographer Strabo had seen much of the

Mediterranean world when he visited Alexandria in 24 B.C., but he was still impressed:

> The city is full of public and sacred buildings, but the most beautiful of them is the Gymnasium, which has porticoes more than a stadium [two hundred yards] in length. And in the middle [of the city] there are both the court of justice and the groves. Here, too, is the Paneum, a man-made eminence; it has the shape of a fir-cone, resembles a rocky hill, and is ascended by a spiral road; and from the summit one can see the whole of the city lying below it on all sides.[3]

Alexandria's greatest contributions to civilization took place in another monument—the palace museum, which was actually a kind of research university with the largest library of antiquity (over seven hundred thousand volumes). It was there that seventy-two scholars from Jerusalem, invited by Ptolemy, translated the Old Testament into the Greek edition that was spread by Christianity. The library catalogued and collected the most accurate editions of classical literature, preserving much of what remains today:

> It was there that Eratosthenes, assembling the information brought back by the explorers sent into Africa and Arabia, prepared his map of the world. This served as a basis for Ptolemy's map. It was there also that Euclid codified geometry and that Aristarchus of Samos ventured on the conjecture that the Earth moves around the Sun. . . . Herophilus and Erasistratus gained accurate knowledge of the anatomy of the brain, of the heart, and of the eye, and this opened-up possibilities of more efficient surgery.[4]

ALEXANDRIA: SPECTACLES AND SPECTATORS

Under the Ptolemies, even (after Cleopatra) under the Romans, Alexandria was the cultural capital of the Mediterranean world. It preserved the ancient heritage and, especially in science, increased human knowledge far beyond the capacity of the city-state. In many ways Alexandria achieved a level of intellectual sophistication that was unmatched for another thousand years.

Alexandria points to what the Hellenistic city, or the capital city, could do toward the embellishment of life as monument, art, intellect, and power. But it shares with other cities built by Alexander (or other founders, for that matter) and other monumental cities of the Hellenistic Age (or any age, for that matter) in causing a deadening effect on the human spirit.

All rectangular cities lost something in human interaction and spontaneity in order to achieve artificial regularity and order. No capital city could allow self-government to the extent that it might threaten the rule of the palace or the vested interests of wider dominion. All monumental cities substituted (to some degree) monuments for men, museums for muses, and palaces for poets. When the city itself became a work of art, the people became the spectators. Lewis Mumford observes:

> Consider the kind of urban "arena" necessary for the coronation of Ptolemy Philadelphus, a not untypical monarch of the period at its best. To mount that spectacle there were 57,000 infantrymen, 23,000 cavalry, innumerable chariots, of which 400 bore vessels of silver, 800 were filled with perfumes; a gigantic chariot of Silenus, drawn by 300 men, was followed by chariots drawn by antelopes, buffaloes, ostriches, and zebras. What later circus could compare with this prototype? Such a parade could not have found its way through the streets of fifth-century Athens even in broken order.[5]

But the Athenians would not have held such a brash display of power. That is Mumford's point. "Democracies are often too stingy in spending money for public purposes, for [the] citizens feel that the money is theirs. Monarchies and tyrannies can be generous because they dip their hands freely into other people's pockets."[6]

Further, it was not only the coronation but all of life that was a spectacle in the spectacular city. And we have been living in such places since the decline of the city-state. To quote Mumford again:

> The city thus ceased to be a stage for a significant drama in which everyone had a role, with lines to speak: it became, rather, a pompous show place for power; and its streets properly presented only two-dimensional facades that served as a mask for a pervasive system of regimentation and exploitation. What paraded as town planning in the Hellenistic Age was not unrelated to the kind of smooth lies and insidious perversions that go under the name of public relations and advertising in the American economy today.[7]

THE ROMAN IMPERIAL CITY: CAESARIAN
CAPITAL OF POWER

If Alexandria shows the capital city or the city of the Hellenistic Age at its best, Rome shows it at its worst. Rome, even more than the other regimented Hellenistic cities, was a "show place for power." And unlike Alexandria, Rome cannot apologize that it was born that way. The earliest Rome was an Etruscan village and then a city-state. Even in the early days of the Roman Republic, before the imperial expansion of the second century B.C., Rome retained many of the features of the city-state. The empire itself changed all of that. Let us look at the Rome of the Caesars, the capital city of a Mediterranean empire.

We do not have time to examine in very much detail imperial Rome over its course of four or five hundred years beginning after Julius Caesar. We will have to be satisfied with a few telltale signs. Strabo, as perceptive as ever, noted that the Greeks planned their cities with attention to the quality of harbors and the fertility of the soil and occupied themselves with beauty and fortification, while the Romans concentrated on providing their cities with adequate water, streets, and sewers. Indeed, the oldest monument of Roman engineering is the Great Sewer (the Cloaca Maxima). It was constructed in the sixth century B.C. "on a scale so gigantic that either its builders must have clairvoyantly seen, at the earliest moment, that this heap of villages would become a metropolis of a million inhabitants, or else they must have taken for granted that the chief business and ultimate end of life is the physiological process of evacuation."[8] The Great Sewer was built so well that it has been used for over twenty-five hundred years, and is still in use today. Monumental scale and engineering efficiency, however, had little to do with the needs of the urban masses. The sewer line ended at the first floor of the better Roman buildings and was not connected to the crowded tenements of the poor at all. As a result, despite the technological mastery of sewerage, the average Roman was forced to dodge excrement emptied from (in some cases) nine floors above and live with the stench of collected excrement, garbage, and corpses in open cesspools and trenches. The large number of city shrines to the Goddess of Fever attest to the sanitary calamity that ensued. When plagues (as in 23 B.C. and A.D. 65 and 79) added thousands of dead in a single day and the gladiatorial contests made it necessary to dispose of five thousand animals and men in a day, breathing must have been an occupational hazard of living.

Water aqueducts and pavement were equally monumental and equally socially unconscious, if not equally disastrous. There was more than enough water for mammoth public baths, but only the rich enjoyed private baths, and (again) there is no sign of water above the first floor. All roads led to Rome, but once they got there they became parking lots. The congestion was so intense that Julius Caesar banned wheeled vehicles from the middle of the city during the day. Then the racket at night kept everyone awake.

ROME: STREETS, SLEEP, AND SOCIAL INSOMNIA

"It takes a lot of money to get a night's sleep in Rome," the poet Juvenal wrote. Many of the wealthy lived in estates surrounded by gardens on one of the hills above the city. When they ventured to walk through the unlit streets at night, they could afford a retinue of slaves to light their way with torches and bodyguards for protection. For the poor, nightfall meant locking themselves behind bolts and bars until dawn. Outside, "the poor man's freedom, after being punched and pounded to pieces," Juvenal tells us, was "to beg and implore that he be allowed to go home with a few teeth left."

During the day (and with the introduction of street lighting in the fourth century A.D. even at night) the streets were safer, but impossibly crowded. The population had grown from a hundred thousand in the second century B.C. to over

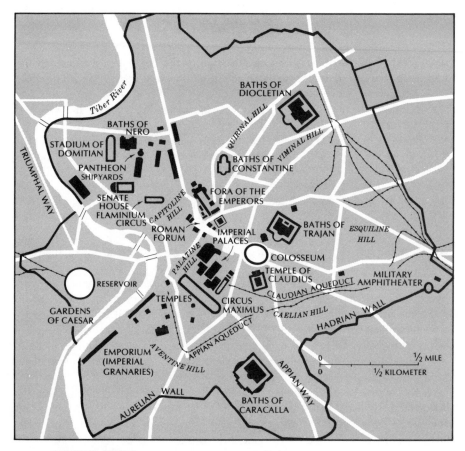

IMPERIAL ROME
Imperial Rome was a city of large public spaces that offered relief
from squalid tenements. Note the size and number of public baths and
gladiatorial circuses.

half a million by the second century A.D. The vast majority of inhabitants (who could not afford the hills or suburbs) were crowded into six square miles, most of which was occupied by public buildings and thoroughfares. Only one building in twenty-six was a private home. Most of the people lived in crowded tenements, five to seven stories high. Generally an entire family lived in a single dingy room off a common balcony and steep staircase. The wooden construction and crowding made fire a regular disaster, despite the fire department of seven thousand freedmen (former slaves) established by Augustus. Fire fighting, police work, and ordinary business was further complicated by the absence of street names (other than those named for their activities, like the "Street of the Money Changers") and the total lack of street signs or building numbers.

Traffic congestion went from bad to worse because nothing was done about the root problem—the overcrowding of the center. The speculators, the contractors, and the landlords were allowed a free hand in buying, building, and renting where profits were highest—in the center of the city:

> [It] was a speculative enterprise in which the greatest profits were made by both the dishonest contractors, putting together flimsy structures that would barely hold up, and profiteering landlords, who learned how to subdivide old quarters into even narrower cells to accommodate even poorer artisans at a higher return of rent per unit. (One notes, not without a cynical smile, that the one kind of wheeled traffic permitted by day in Rome was that of the building contractors.)
>
> Crassus, who made a fabulous fortune in tenement house properties, boasted that he never spent money in building: it was more profitable to buy partly damaged old properties at fire sales and rent them with meager repairs. . . .
>
> The houses of the patricians, spacious, airy, sanitary, equipped with bathrooms and water closets, heated in winter by hypocausts, which carried hot air through chambers in the floors, were perhaps the most commodious and comfortable houses built for a temperate climate anywhere until the twentieth century: a triumph of domestic architecture. But the tenements of Rome easily take the prize for being the most crowded and unsanitary buildings produced in Western Europe until the sixteenth century, when site over-filling and room over-crowding became common, from Naples to Edinburgh.[9]

If the houses of Athens had been no better constructed, at least they were not piled one on top of another to the point of spontaneous combustion or epidemic infestation. More significantly, the houses of Athens were all rude, those of rich and poor alike. Class divisions between rich and poor, powerful and weak, were radically accelerated in the capital city, especially Rome. Housing construction was just another vehicle for widening that gap: builders could afford palaces *because* they packed the poor into cheap tenements and reduced the quality of their lives. Brutalization paid.

Imperial Rome could not offer its urban masses an opportunity to participate meaningfully in community affairs, as Athens could for its citizens. Nor could Rome give its inhabitants the Athenian citizen's sense of autonomy nourished by assembly, agora, acropolis, and amphitheater. In Rome the monumental public structures—like the public baths and the arena—provided diversion rather than participation.

ROME: MONUMENTAL ENGINEERING AND MASS DIVERSION

Mumford has written that the whole history of Rome can be seen in the development of the "bath." In the days of the early Republic the bath "was a pool of water in a sheltered place where the sweaty farmer made himself clean." By 33 B.C. the

A reconstruction of the imperial city of Rome as it must have
appeared in the reign of Emperor Aurelian (270–275). (Granger)

first free public bath set the style of the later empire: huge halls, eating areas, lounging areas, gymnasiums, playing fields, separate temples for hot, warm, and cool baths—everything in short that would serve the new religion of the body and take people's minds away from the world outside. The scale of these buildings boggles the imagination. Today (during the summer months) the Roman Opera performs with hundreds of participants and thousands of spectators in a small niche at the ruins of the Baths of Caracalla.

To the Roman engineer, size was everything. Masses of people kept their mass identity in the mammoth baths, markets, amphitheaters, racecourses, and arenas. The special Roman contribution to handling masses, according to Mumford, was the "vomitorium." The word was originally used for a room next to the dining room (in the mansions of the rich). Here the stuffed diner could vomit in order to return to the table or couch for more of the host's rich and exotic food. Then the Romans used the word for the massive exits that they created from public arenas. Like the sewer, the Roman vomitorium was a superb symbol for a civilization that was "poorly digested but splendidly evacuated."

When a city's inhabitants no longer have any control over the life of the city, they must be entertained. The baths and arenas did the job for the Romans in much the same way as spectator sports and television do the job today. The arena, particularly its gladiatorial extravaganzas, combined the contest of sports with the thrill of vicarious violence even more effectively than modern TV. But both the arena and TV perverted the original urban contribution of empathy and mutual understanding into a deadening inability to live except through the lives of others. And where life had been most brutalized, the most exciting vicarious thrill was imagining oneself as the mutilator or murderer of others. The brutalized could only hope to brutalize others. The gladiatorial arena satisfied that dream.

In the first gladiatorial "games" in 264 B.C., prisoners were publicly executed.

> Too soon, unfortunately, the ordeal of the prisoner became the welcome amusement of the spectator, and even the emptying of the jails did not provide a sufficient number of victims to meet the popular demand. As with the religious sacrifices of the Aztecs, military expeditions were directed toward supplying a sufficient number of victims, human and animal. Here in the arena both degraded professionals, thoroughly trained for their occupation, and wholly innocent men and women were tortured with every imaginable body-maiming and fear-producing device for public delight. And here wild animals were butchered, without being eaten, as if they were only men.[10]

During the reign of the emperor Claudius (A.D. 41–54) there were 93 days of games a year at public expense. By A.D. 354 there were 175 such days. By then there were enough arenas and theaters to hold almost half the population of Rome simultaneously. Almost a quarter of a million people, unable to find ample work, were supported by the daily dole of bread, and free to dream their revenge, or try to forget at the Circus Maximus. By then the city had become, in Mumford's telling phrase, a necropolis, a city of the dead:

> From the standpoint of both politics and urbanism, Rome remains a significant lesson of what to avoid: its history presents a series of classic danger signals to warn one when life is moving in the wrong direction. Wherever crowds gather in suffocating numbers, wherever rents rise steeply and housing conditions deteriorate, wherever a one-sided exploitation of distant territories removes the pressure to achieve balance and harmony nearer at hand, there the precedents of Roman building almost automatically revive, as they have come back today: the arena, the tall tenement, the mass contests and exhibitions, the football matches, the international beauty contests, the strip-tease made ubiquitous by advertisement, the constant titillation of the senses by sex, liquor, and violence—all in true Roman style. So, too, the multiplication of bathrooms and the over-expenditure on broadly paved motor roads, and above all, the massive collective concentration on glib ephemeralities of all kinds, performed with supreme technical audacity. These are symptoms of the end: magnifications of demoralized power, minifications of life. When these signs multiply, Necropolis is near, though not a stone has yet crumbled. For the barbarian has already captured the city from within. Come, hangman! Come, vulture![11]

THE ORIGINS OF THE COMMERCIAL CITY IN INDIA

There is another type of city besides the city-state and the capital city. It is the commercial city, perhaps the most common in our own world, and its roots go back to classical India. It might seem strange to say that the commercial city originated in India. For one thing, we have already seen the importance of economic and commercial activity in Athens, Alexandria, and Rome. The Indian cities that first developed along the Ganges River in the sixth century B.C., however, became the first cities that were primarily trading centers. Their main function was economic. The successors of those early cities on the Ganges, the cities of the Gupta Empire (A.D. 320–550) like Pataliputra, developed the earliest form of a commercial capitalism that has since transformed the world. But we are getting a bit ahead of our story. The Pataliputra of Gupta India rose on the site of a much earlier Pataliputra of the Mauryan dynasty (321–181 B.C.), which was itself a reincarnation of Rajagriha, the capital of the state of Magadha that the Buddha knew in the sixth century B.C.

There is another reason why our suggestion that India was the home of the first purely commercial cities might seem strange. We are used to thinking of both the caste system and Indian religion as hindrances to commercial activity. Not so long ago, people would explain away India's limited economic development by referring to the caste system. Even today, it is sometimes said that the caste system discourages initiative or limits social mobility, both of which are necessary for economic growth. It is also said that Indian religion is excessively spiritualistic, while a commercial culture must be materialistic.

In response to these objections, we will argue here that in some ways the caste system turned out to be a spur to commerce and that some Indian religious traditions were quite materialistic.

CASTE AND COMMERCE

The Aryan tribes who conquered India from the northwest had cleared most of the forests along the Ganges River plain by about the sixth century B.C. The agriculture that developed along the Ganges and its tributaries supported monarchial states in the fertile river valleys and independent republics in the Himalayan foothills. Both types of new political states supported towns and cities along the river. They were useful sources of luxury goods for the monarchs and economic opportunities for the republics.

Towns grew around villages that specialized in particular crafts, such as pottery, carpentry, and textiles. Specialists in a particular craft would often congregate in order to take advantage of a particular local resource (a potter's clay, for instance) or the benefit of market or mutual aid. Thus, as one historian has written, artisans and craftspeople developed occupational identities in guilds, which became like subcastes.

> The expansion of towns brought about an increase in the number of artisans who were organized in guilds *(shreni)*. Each guild inhabited a particular section of the town, so that members of a guild lived and worked together and generally had such a close-knit relationship that they came to be regarded as a sub-caste.[12]

A society organized by *varnas* could be quite compatible with commercial activity. Most *brahmans* might prefer to be priests, doctors, teachers, or intellectuals. Most *kshatriyas* might feel more comfortable as soldiers, administrators, officials, or aristocrats. By the sixth century B.C., *vaishyas,* who initially were farmers, were thought of as artisans, merchants, and traders. (By then *shudras* were raised to farmers, and outcasts took the former servile role of the *shudras.*) Further, as we have seen, these broad categories were less important than the smaller *jatis* of people who actually shared their lives together. They not only ate together and intermarried; they also shared the same work, jobs, and ambitions. Their productivity was often enhanced by their close contact.

RELIGIOUS REFORM, COMMERCE, AND CITIES

The economic and social changes of the sixth century B.C. were reinforced by the religious reforms that led to the rise of Buddhism and Jainism. Both of these were philosophically materialistic religions. They believed that humans were made of dust and would return to dust. They objected to what they saw as the senseless rituals of the priests. They concerned themselves instead with problems of knowledge and everyday life. Philosophically, they were atheistic, since a belief in god was irrelevant to their doctrines.

Jainism was founded by Mahavira (c. 510 B.C.). He taught that all matter in the universe had a soul, that the purpose of living is to purify one's own soul so that it can be released from the body. For Mahavira and his followers, the life of the ascetic or monk offered the clearest path to self-purification. The regime was strenuous. It required a complete commitment to nonviolence. Even the killing of insects was to be avoided. Jains wore muslin masks covering their mouths and noses in order to prevent the involuntary inhalation of the smallest of insects. Before sitting in a chair, a Jain would sweep off any possible insects.

Trade and commerce were among the few possible occupations open to Jains. Agriculture required killing insects. Some crafts endangered the lives of other creatures. The encouragement of discipline and frugality in Jainism (as in Protestantism later in Europe) allowed the Jains to channel their energies into future productivity instead of present consumption. They were savers. Since they were not able to use agricultural land, they specialized in the exchange of manufactured goods, served as middlemen, provided financing, and developed a trading network that stretched far beyond India. In so doing, they became associated with the spread of urban culture and trade.

Buddhism, we have seen, challenged Brahmanism in many of the same ways as Jainism did.

> There was much in common between Buddhism and Jainism. Both were started by members of the *kshatriya* caste and were opposed to brahmanical orthodoxy, denying the authority of the Vedas, and antagonistic to the practice of animal sacrifices, which had by now become a keystone of brahmanical power. Both appealed to the socially down-trodden, the *vaishyas* who were economically powerful, but were not granted corresponding social status, and the *shudras* who were obviously oppressed. . . . [The] Buddhist following was drawn mainly from the mercantile community, the artisans, and the cultivators.[13]

According to a Buddhist tradition, when the Buddha was about to die, one of his disciples, Ananda, said that he regretted that the Buddha had to die in such a small town as Kusinagara. There were, he added, six cities that were important enough for the Buddha to die in.

This emphasis on the importance of cities might surprise us. We are used to thinking of Buddhism in terms of the retreat to the forest. But the town and the city were always important to Buddhism. The expansion of Buddhism was due in part to the support of King Bimbisara of Magadha (r. c. 540–490 B.C.). The king was able to make Magadha the dominant state on the Ganges plain because of the wealth of its towns. Towns gave support to new ideas. The lower classes in the towns were responsive to anticaste ideas of equality that challenged the power of the *brahman* priests. The *kshatriya* landowners, who lived in the towns and governed most republics as well as kingdoms, had their own conflicts with arrogant and expensive *brahmans*.

THE MAURYAN EMPIRE

The first Pataliputra, the Mauryan, could have been another Alexandria. Alexander the Great's armies penetrated India in 323 B.C., but they did not reach as far as the Ganges plain. Alexander's withdrawal provided the opportunity for a young adventurer and heir to the Nanda throne in 321 B.C. to fill the vacuum. Chandragupta Maurya took his first step in acquiring an empire by conquering Magadha and planting his capital near the old site of the Magadha capital. He called it Pataliputra. It became the center of a vast empire, stretching from Alexander's conquests in Afghanistan to the Ganges plain. In the course of the Mauryan dynasty that Chandragupta founded, the empire was extended across the middle of the Indian subcontinent by his son, Bindusara (r. 297–272 B.C.), and to southeast India by his grandson, Ashoka (r. 272–232 B.C.).

The agrarian economy of the Ganges plain built the Mauryan Empire, but, as one historian has written, the empire made possible other kinds of economic activity.

> One of the more notable results of the political unification of the subcontinent, and the security provided by a stable, centralized government, was the possibility of expansion in the various craft guilds and consequently in trade. Efficiency in administration rendered the organization of trade easier, and crafts were gradually converted into small-scale industries.[14]

The sources of economic strength in the Mauryan Empire were the government and the guilds. "Government is the science of punishment," Chandragupta's *brahman* mentor Kautilya wrote in his *Arthashastra*. Kautilya provided detailed instructions on the use of spies, the need for poison tasters at the king's table, and the way to prepare for war while tricking enemies with talk of peace. Kautilya's strategic advice must have been valuable to the young Chandragupta, age twenty-five when he took the throne, inexperienced, and from a lower-caste, apparently *vaishya*, family.

But with or without the advice of Kautilya, Chandragupta was able to create a centralized government that did more than punish. Vast areas were cleared for agriculture, roads and dams were built, and an extensive taxation system was devised. The state employed large numbers of people in these and other activities. Armorers and shipbuilders were employed directly by the state, exempt from taxation. State spinning and weaving workshops as well as state mines employed many workers, who paid taxes. Products were taxed one-fifth of their value when completed and an additional one-fifth at the time of sale. These high levies supported an army estimated by the Roman Pliny to include nine thousand elephants, thirty thousand cavalry soldiers, and six hundred thousand infantrymen.

Those who did not work for the state or farm (their own land or the king's) worked individually or in guilds.

> The guilds were large and complex in structure and artisans found it advantageous to join them, since this eliminated the expense of working alone and having to compete with the guilds. From the point of view of the state, guilds facilitated the collection of taxes and the general running of the industry. Localization of occupation and the hereditary nature of occupations strengthened the guilds.[15]

Chandragupta was said to have converted to Jainism, retired to the forest, and (in keeping with Jain tradition) slowly starved himself to death. His grandson, Ashoka, converted to Buddhism and renounced war (and the eating of meat) after a particularly bloody conquest of Kalinga on the east coast. Pataliputra was the site of an important meeting of Buddhists, the Third Buddhist Council, around 250 B.C. The council decided to send out missionaries to win converts to Buddhism. While Ashoka may have refrained from active participation in the council because of a sense that as emperor it was his duty to be tolerant of all religions, his own attitude was also that of the missionary. He registered his presence in his empire by placing rocks and pillars engraved with his edicts everywhere from the Himalayas to the southern frontiers of the empire. He also kept himself informed about activities in his vast empire by sending out *dharma* (righteousness) ministers who were to ensure that "compassion, liberality, truth, purity, gentleness, and saintliness will thus grow among mankind."[16]

MAURYAN PATALIPUTRA

What was Pataliputra like in the age of the Mauryans? Pataliputra stretched nine miles along the bank of the Son River at its juncture with the Ganges. It was a narrow city, only one and a half miles wide. Built as a rectangle, its streets were laid out on the grid plan recommended by Kautilya. It was surrounded by a wooden wall, with 64 gates and 560 towers. The Son River surrounded the city like a moat.

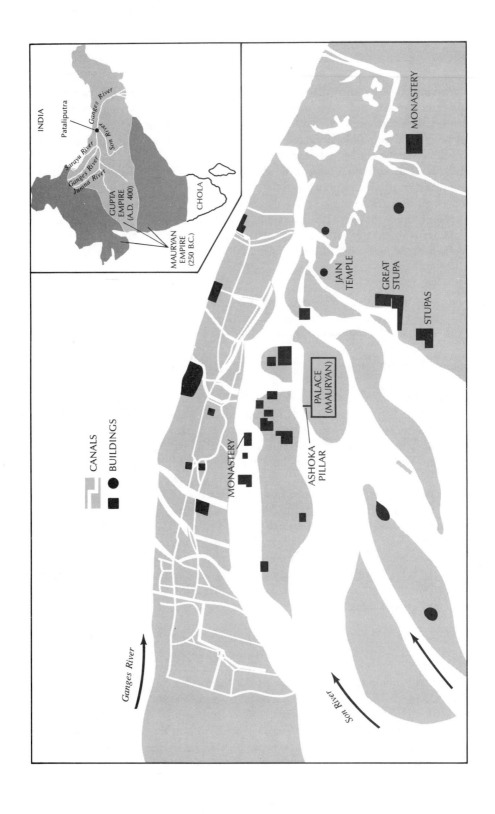

The city had two focal points: the palace and the temple. Megasthenes, the Greek Seleucid ambassador to the court of Chandragupta at Pataliputra in 302 B.C., said that the city was governed by a committee of thirty members. This committee was divided into six subcommittees of five members each to supervise the following functions: industry, trade and commerce, public sale of manufactures, collecting of taxes on all articles sold, welfare of foreigners, and registering of births and deaths. If Megasthenes is correct (and we have no other sources), the preponderance of economic matters (four of the six subcommittees) is striking, as is the attention to foreigners (also necessary for successful trade).

THE GUPTA AGE

The decline of the Mauryan Empire did not mean the end of trade. The series of Indo-Greek and Scythian kingdoms between 180 B.C. and A.D. 320 actually increased Indian trade with the Mediterranean region and opened land trade with China by way of the northwest passage to Afghanistan.

Thus, while the Gupta dynasty had to begin afresh in establishing an empire after five hundred years of disunity, the trade of Gupta towns and merchants continued on the base established by successive smaller kingdoms: Bactria in the second century B.C., and the Kushans (A.D. 48–250), whose King Kanishka converted to Buddhism and spread the religion to China at the end of the first century A.D.

The Gupta dynasty was founded by Chandra Gupta I (unrelated to Chandragupta Maurya). His son Samudra Gupta doubled the size of the empire, and his grandson Chandra Gupta II (r. A.D. 375–415) extended control west to the Arabian Sea. Throughout the Gupta Age (A.D. 320–449), neither its size nor its degree of centralization was as great at that of the Mauryan Empire. Economically and culturally, however, it was far richer.

If the Mauryan government and the guilds had been the source of the economic strength of the Mauryan dynasty, in the Gupta Age it was principally the guilds. Each city was governed by a council that consisted of the president of the city corporation (representing all guilds), the chief representative of the guild of merchants, a representative of the artisans, and the chief scribe. In Mauryan times the members of the governing committee were appointed by the ruler. In the Gupta city the members of the council were chosen by the guilds.

PATALIPUTRA
The political and economic importance of Pataliputra can be seen from its location at the junction of the four rivers that formed the Ganges. The many canals and excavated buildings give a hint of its appearance. Most of the wooden Mauryan city, and much of the stone Gupta city, however, lie hidden under modern Patna.

One is forced to conclude that the guilds were more important than the government. They performed many of the functions that were carried out by the citizens of a city-state or the rulers of cities like Rome or Alexandria.

> Apart from their role in the economy, the guilds provided education as well, though not "formal" education, which remained in the hands of the brahmans and the monks. The guilds, by restricting membership to artisans of a particular craft, were centers for technical education. Knowledge of mining, metallurgy, weaving, dyeing, carpentry, etc., was maintained and improved upon by the relevant guild.[17]

The guilds were the only major institutions involved in manufacture and commerce; state activity was minimal. They were self-governing. Their laws were drafted by a larger corporation of guilds and were honored by the government. If one were to look for a second force in Gupta society, perhaps it would not be the government but the Buddhist church, or *sangha,* now grown rich and powerful, able to act as banker, lend money on interest, and underwrite some of the large-scale projects of the corporation of guilds.

The vitality of the Gupta economy was a culmination of a centuries-long process, it was confined in Gupta times to northern India, and it did not withstand the onslaught of the Huns. But its material, technological, and scientific achievements were permanent. Its textiles—silk, muslin, calico, linen, wool, and cotton—were a major source of foreign currency and gold. Along with Indian jewels, imported spices, and other luxury goods, they were enough, according to Pliny, to cause a serious drain on the Roman treasury—550 million sesterces a year.

In Indian agriculture, waterwheels were used for irrigation. A Chinese Buddhist pilgrim was struck by the wide variety of grains, fruits, and other crops that were grown. Metalwork was highly specialized: an iron column from the period shows little sign of rust even today. Indian merchant ships brought silk from China, ivory from Ethiopia, and horses from Arabia.

Indian science followed Indian merchants into uncharted seas. The Indian astronomer Aryabhata in A.D. 499 first posed some of the questions of modern astronomy. He believed the earth was a sphere that rotated on its axis, and that the shadow of the earth on the moon was the cause of eclipses. He also calculated pi and the length of the solar year with remarkably modern precision. Indian mathematics benefited from the use of the numerals we call Arabic (because the Arabs learned them in India), the decimal system, and zero, which made multiplication and division much easier than they were with Roman numerals.

There were limits to Indian science and technology, which should also be observed because they help us understand both the strength of its innovations and the cultural obstacles. Aryabhata was opposed by later astronomers. One of his contemporaries, Varahamihira, gave equal weight in his work to astrology, horoscopy, astronomy, and mathematics, an emphasis Aryabhata would have found appalling. At the same time that Indian merchants were sailing from eastern Africa to the South China Sea, some *brahman* lawmakers were declaring it a great sin to travel because Hindus would be forced to mix with the impure in foreign lands.

PATALIPUTRA IN THE GUPTA AGE

It is a testament to the success of Indian trade that Pataliputra was not the only important city at the end of the Gupta dynasty. But it was still a well-constructed city and an important destination for pilgrims. By the Gupta period, its wooden buildings in the wealthy sections had been replaced by brick. Larger town houses were typically three stories. (We might accept a literary reference to a building of seven stories, but another reference to an eleven-story building seems an exaggeration.)

According to the Chinese Buddhist pilgrim Fa Xian [Fa-hsien], who traveled throughout India for six years around A.D. 400, Pataliputra was a city of palaces. It was so affluent, he said, that hospitals were provided free of charge for "the poor of all countries, the destitute, crippled, and diseased. . . ."[18]

Buddhist pilgrims commented on the safety and peace of Indian cities. Fa Xian pointed out that he traveled all over India without concern. Buddhists were also impressed with the widespread vegetarianism in India. Fa Xian, probably exaggerating, said that he saw no respectable person who ate meat. The Buddhist pilgrims came from China and elsewhere to worship at the holy sites of the Buddha's life, to collect the sacred texts of Buddhism, and to study at the monastery of Nalanda near Pataliputra. Like the universities in other Indian cities, especially those at Banaras and Taksasila, Nalanda taught the Vedas, Hindu philosophy, logic, grammar, and medicine as well as Buddhist scripture.

The Gupta Empire was destroyed by the invasion of the White Huns (A.D. 480–500). They in turn were followed by the Rajputs, a warrior aristocracy that ruled northern India for the next five hundred years, until the arrival of the Muslims. Indian trade continued, especially in the south. Many of the commercial skills and institutions that had flourished in Gupta India were passed on from southern India to Muslim and Chinese traders, and the technological and commercial development of India spurred the economies of Islam and China for the next thousand years.

THE INDO-EUROPEAN CITY

We have examined four Indo-European cities: Athens, Alexandria, Rome, and Pataliputra. They represent three types of cities: the city-state, the capital city, and the commercial city. As a group they remind us that not all cities are alike. Different

A reconstruction of an ancient Indian city like Pataliputra. (The New York Public Library)

cities serve different functions. The function of Athens was to satisfy the citizens. Alexandria and Rome were responsible to the larger goals of an emperor and an empire.

Pataliputra was at times the capital of an empire, but increasingly its purpose was determined by its commercial guilds. In that regard perhaps Gupta Pataliputra was more like Athens than like Alexandria or Rome. But the citizens of Athens always viewed their city as more than a place to do business. At least in moments like the funeral oration of Pericles in the midst of the war with Sparta, the Athenian citizens spoke of their city-state as something to die for. We hear none of this from Pataliputra. If the Athenians invented patriotism, the guilds of Pataliputra invented the "corporate community," as we use that phrase today to mean the interests of business. These interests are sometimes synonymous with the interests of the people, and sometimes not.

Perhaps the questions to ask as we survey the problems of modern urban life are these: In what kind of city do we want to live? What functions do we want our cities to perform? Whose interests do we want our cities to serve? When we are able to answer these questions, we have a standard by which to judge the successes and failures of our own cities. The past is rich with models for setting that standard. Even those who choose democracy over spectacle are faced with two alternative visions of democracy. Athens and Pataliputra might suggest to us the difference between the political democracy of the citizens and the economic democracy of the producers. Further, Athens and Pataliputra might suggest the relative value of two very different loyalties in Indo-European culture: political loyalty to our city, state, or place and social loyalty to our class, profession, or peers.

FOR FURTHER READING

Lewis Mumford's *The City in History* is a masterpiece of interpretive integration, telling detail, and stunning style. It is also eccentric, almost perversely pessimistic, and controversial. To make Mumford more accessible we have followed his argument closely in the text. But this is meant as suggestive stimulation rather than definitive answer.

For a more traditional textbook on world urban history, the student would do well to read *World Civilizations* by F. Roy Willis. For a magnificently illustrated book of thoughtful essays on assorted cultural and political capital cities, the student could do little better than *Cities of Destiny*, edited by Arnold Toynbee.

A short, but encyclopedic, study of Greek cities can be found in R. E. Wycherley's *How the Greeks Built Cities*. It is an archeological classic, which examines the agora, shrines, gymnasiums, theaters, fortifications, and Greek urban planning in some detail. For a broader view of the society of the Greek polis there are many good books available. Among the best are Frank J. Frost's *Greek Society*, H. D. F. Kitto's *The Greeks*, Moses I. Finley's *The Ancient Greeks*, and the evocatively photographed *Horizon Book of Ancient Greece*.

Among the best of the numerous separate studies of Athens are Angelou Procopiou's beautifully illustrated *Athens, City of the Gods,* Charles A. Robinson, Jr.'s *Athens in the Age of Pericles,* and Robert Flaceliere's *Daily Life in the Athens of Pericles.*

Alexandria is studied in E. M. Forster's *Alexandria: A History and a Guide* and in Kenneth Heuer's readable introduction to Alexandrian astronomy, *City of the Stargazers,* as well as the chapter in Toynbee's *Cities of Destiny* that is cited in the text. The ambitious student might want to go further with A. H. M. Jones's *The Greek City from Alexander to Justinian.*

Further study of the Roman city might well begin with the influence of Greece. Kathleen Freeman's *Greek City-States* examines Greek cities in Italy, and Lidia Storoni Massolani in *The Idea of the City in Roman Thought* studies the appeal of the Greek idea of the city for the Romans. The physical appearance of the Roman city is described in some detail in Henry T. Rowell's *Rome in the Augustan Age,* and the streets come alive in Jérôme Carcopino's *Daily Life in Ancient Rome,* Harold Mattingly's *The Man in the Roman Street,* and J. P. V. D. Balsdon's *The Romans.* Besides the many recent Roman histories (most of which place the city in the background), the student might also wish to consult the nineteenth-century classic on the role of religion in almost "primitive" Greece and Rome—*The Ancient City* by Fustel de Coulanges.

Primary sources that touch on the character of the ancient Greek and Roman cities are almost too numerous to mention. It will have to suffice to suggest the histories of Herodotus and Thucydides, the *Republic* and *Laws* of Plato, the *Politics* of Aristotle, a play of Aristophanes like *The Archarnians* (especially the Douglass Parker translation), and the Roman histories of Livy, Tacitus, and Suetonius.

The best introduction to city life in Indian history is A. L. Basham's *The Wonder That Was India.* Among the better general introductions to Indian history are Francis Watson's well-illustrated *A Concise History of India,* Stanley Wolpert's more thorough *A New History of India,* and Romila Thapar's standard *A History of India.* A good collection of literary sources can be found in *Classical India,* edited by William H. McNeill and Jean W. Sedlar. For an excellent study of trade in world history, one could hardly do better than with Philip D. Curtin's *Cross-cultural Trade in World History.*

NOTES

1. Dicaearchus, quoted by Mumford, *The City in History* (New York: Harcourt Brace Jovanovich, 1961), p. 163.
2. Achilles, Tatius, *Clitophon and Leucippe,* trans. S. Gaselee (London: L.C.I., 1917), bk. V-1-2. Quoted in Edward Alexander Parsons, *The Alexandrian Library* (New York: American Elsevier, 1952), p. 61.
3. Strabo, cited in Claire Preaux, "Alexandria Under the Ptolemies," in *Cities of Destiny,* ed. Arnold Toynbee (New York: McGraw-Hill, 1967), pp. 112–113.
4. Toynbee, *op. cit.,* p. 114.
5. Mumford, *op. cit.,* p. 201.
6. *Ibid.,* p. 197.
7. *Ibid.,* p. 196.
8. *Ibid.,* p. 214.
9. *Ibid.,* pp. 219–221.
10. *Ibid.,* p. 232.
11. *Ibid.,* p. 242.

12. Romila Thapar, *A History of India,* vol. 1, (New York: Penguin, 1966), p. 62.
13. *Ibid.,* pp. 67–68.
14. *Ibid.,* p. 78.
15. *Ibid.*
16. Pillar Edict VII, trans. in Vincent A. Smith, *Ashoka, the Buddhist Emperor of India,* 3rd ed., rev. and enl. (Oxford: Clarendon Press, 1920). Quoted in William H. McNeill and Jean W. Sedlar, *Classical India,* (New York: Oxford University Press, 1969), p. 111.
17. Thapar, *op. cit.,* p. 122.
18. Quoted in Stanley Wolpert, *A New History of India* (New York: Oxford University Press, 1977), p. 90.

❧ 7 ❧

Love
and
Sex

Passion and Conquest
in Greece, Rome, and India

PEOPLE WHO HAVE REACHED ADULTHOOD in America since World War II have a problem that would have been an undreamed luxury for the mass of people throughout most of human history. Only some small ruling classes in past history have been able to afford such a problem. The problem is difficult to define. In general, it is that love, sex, and marriage have become problematic for us. A simple way of putting it is that we do not have to get married. The increasing divorce rate is just a symptom of the much greater freedom we have to choose love, sex, or marriage. It is a "problem" of vastly expanded experience, consciousness, and ability to choose. The problem is that since we can enjoy sex without love, and either or both without marriage, we have to figure out what we want. Perhaps no problem is more difficult than self-understanding and self-realization.

Most ordinary people in traditional society never had to ask themselves if they wanted to get married. There were some respectable, especially religious, alternatives, but aside from these, people simply married because they were expected to. People in traditional society had a lot more opportunity for sexual satisfaction outside of marriage than we usually think, but such activities were rarely translated into feelings of love, and even more rarely threatened the basic social institution of marriage. Marriages were arranged by parents and normally were permanent because they formed the only social cement (for those without status and money) that protected people from periodic disaster. Marriage was simply too important to be left to individual feelings.

Modern governments, middle-class mobility, the money economy, and the independent nuclear family have all created a contraceptive technology and a pleasure ethic that make marriage an entirely different arrangement. Instead of a liaison between families, it has become a possible life-style to choose for love, sex, children, friendship, or whatever else one desires. We have made it one of many options because we have had the option to do so. We have the luxury to experiment, but that inevitably leads us to ask ourselves what we want.

We will examine some of the first societies in which people in fairly large numbers began to have these experiences and ask these questions. These elite members of a leisure class developed much of the self-conscious understanding of sex and love that both burdens us and frees us today. When we think of sex and love, we use ideas and feelings that they developed and passed on.

GREEK LOVES

The ancient Greeks spoke of love as if they had invented the word. Actually, they invented two words for love: *eros,* meaning physical or sexual love, and *agape,* meaning spiritual love. They also spoke of *philia* when they meant affection or friendship. They spoke of love often, symbolized it as the heart pierced by Cupid's arrow, diagnosed it as a newly discovered disease, and talked endlessly about its meaning and effects.

It is interesting that in so much of their talk about love, they rarely mentioned marriage. The purpose of marriage had much more to do with housekeeping and insurance against old age. The Athenian aristocrat, soldier, and statesman Xenophon put it this way:

> Did you ever stop to consider, dear wife, what led me to choose you, and your parents to intrust you to me? It was surely not because either of us would have any trouble in finding another consort. No! it was with deliberate intent, I for myself, and your parents for you, to discover the best partners of house and children we could find. . . . If at some future time God grants us children, we will take counsel together how best to bring them up, for that, too, will be a common interest, and a common blessing if happily they live to fight our battles and we find in them hereafter support and succor for ourselves.[1]

For the Greeks married life was not expected to yield either *eros* or *agape.* In this respect Greece was no different from other societies. One Greek summed up the situation this way: "Mistresses we keep for pleasure, concubines for daily attendance upon our persons, and wives to bear us legitimate children and be our housekeepers."[2]

Greek men entered marriage out of a sense of duty rather than of love. They felt a duty to their ancestors, the city, and their religion to have children. And if they were to lead lives in the city, they needed someone to take care of the children and the household. Wives served this function amply. But a wife was hardly a person to spend time with. Women were not educated, and their lives were occupied with dull trivia.

Marriage was so unpopular that the government of Athens, the leading Greek city, considered making bachelorhood illegal in order to ensure sufficient population growth. Such a law was almost passed as early as the sixth century B.C. During the golden age of Athens (the fifth century B.C.) a law was passed that allowed only married men to become generals or orators (our equivalent of lawyers). So Athenian men learned to carry out duty to the state, but rarely pretended that marriage was anything but such a necessity. The Greek poet Palladas must have expressed the feelings of many when he wrote:

Marriage brings a man only two happy days:
The day he takes his bride to bed, and the day he lays
*   her in her grave.*[3]

It would be interesting to know if Greek wives wasted any love on their husbands. Since they were not taught to write, we can only guess. Oppressed people sometimes have a peculiar capacity to love their masters, or at least accept their authority as beneficial. But there is some evidence that Greek wives were not always taken in. The great Greek dramatist Sophocles in his play *Antigone* has the heroine, Antigone, who buries her brother in defiance of her uncle's order, say that a brother is irreplaceable while a husband is not. It seems, furthermore, that many Greek wives remained much closer to their own families than they were to their husbands. The Greek historian Herodotus approvingly tells a story of a Persian woman who, when given the choice by a conqueror of saving the life of one person, chose her brother rather than her husband.

Whom did the Greeks love, then, if not their husbands and wives? The women that Greek men loved were prostitutes. Prostitution was widely developed, if not invented, in almost all of the first patriarchal cities. The city fathers considered it a noble solution to the problem of providing men with seductive and interesting women while ensuring that their own wives (and thus their own family lines) would remain pure. In short, they created a society of two types of women: the sexless wives and virginal daughters of the men of substance, and the women (drawn mostly from the lower class) who were trained to satisfy men's pleasures.

One of the Greek auletrides *plays the double flute as the men drink and spill wine from bowls like this one. (Master and Fellows of Corpus Christi College, Cambridge)*

GREEK PROSTITUTION:
LOVE, DEATH, AND SOCIAL DISEASE

Greek prostitution actually became quite specialized by the golden age of the fifth century B.C. There were three types of prostitutes. The common prostitutes, called *pornae,* lived in brothels marked by a large phallus on the door. They were uneducated and cheap, and they served to siphon off the sexual energy of lower-class men. Above the *pornae* in prestige were the *auletrides,* who were trained as entertainers. They were usually hired out by their teachers (who usually owned them as slaves) to play the flute, dance, and amuse men at private dinners and to spend the night with some of the guests. Both of these groups, resembling the streetwalkers and call girls of other patriarchal societies, were frowned on by men of wealth or refinement. These men recognized the necessity of such women in maintaining social order, and they might use them themselves, but they did not "love" them even when they enjoyed their company.

The love poems of the poets and the love interests of successful citizens were usually confined to the third type of prostitute—the *hetaerae.* When the word was first used in the sixth century B.C. it meant only an intimate female friend. By the fifth and fourth centuries B.C. it meant high-class courtesans. As the only well-educated and interesting women of Greece, and as women of good families who were often citizens, they ranked higher in social esteem than wives or virgins. They were trained to be not only sexually alluring but also intellectually stimulating. The *hetaerae* lived independently in their own homes, chose as few or as many lovers as they wanted, and frequently became quite prosperous and influential.

One of these courtesans, Aspasia, was probably the most influential woman of the fifth century B.C. She is said to have trained the philosopher Socrates in the skills of speaking and argument, and even to have written speeches for the greatest Athenian statesman, Pericles, who was one of her oratory students. Aspasia captivated Athenian men with her physical charms as well as her wit and sophistication. After Pericles divorced his wife he took Aspasia to his home as his exclusive mistress.

The settled, almost marital, love of Pericles and Aspasia was the exception, however. Most Greek men were interested in the excitement and bittersweet anguish of love rather than its domestication in married life. No less serious and philosophical a man than Socrates expressed this desire in his reported advice to Diotima, a courtesan renowned for her exquisite beauty:

> You will charm them best if you never surrender except when they are sharp-set. You have noticed that the daintiest fare, if served before a man wants it, is apt to seem insipid, while, if he is already sated, it even produces a feeling of nausea. Create a hunger before you bring on your banquet. . . . Seem not to wish to yield. Fly from them—and fly again, until they feel the keen pang of hunger. That is your moment. The gift is the same as when the man did not want it: but wondrous different now its value.[4]

Hetaerae were not desired for sex alone. If that were the case they would not have existed. They charged a minimum of 100 drachmas (the equivalent in our economy of hundreds of dollars) for the evening, while the average *porna* charged the equivalent of a couple of dollars. And if they were desired only for their intelligence, they would have been replaced by much cheaper teachers, or free male companionship. They were successful because they offered a tempting combination of both. A cynic might say that the courtesan offered sex without guilt. Certainly these Greeks felt the sex was less vulgar when it was so tastefully introduced. But the Greeks did not feel guilty about sexual drives in the way Christians later did. It would be more accurate to say that the *hetaerae* were sought and loved because they were complex, full-bodied human beings with whom a man could become lost in conversation, as well as in love.

In a society that had no hang-ups about sex, all women could have acquired these attributes, all could have been trained intellectually and sexually, and practiced their skills in or out of marriage. But in patriarchal society, where men felt forced to de-emphasize the sexuality of some of the women (their wives), and then in compensation to exaggerate the sexual appeal of other women (the courtesans), their relationships with these "ideal" women must have always been full of tension,

"You will charm them best if you never surrender except when they are sharp-set." One of the hetaerae *and one of the sharp set. (Hirmer Fotoarchiv)*

ambiguity, and frustration. They were interested in conversation, but talk was always a prelude. *Hetaerae* seemed to be genuinely interested in their lovers as people, but they were studiously trained to be so, and it was all for a fee. They were some of the most interesting people in Greece, but they were women—people men had consigned to inferior status. They represented what every man wanted in a companion, but the last thing in the world that he wanted from his wife.

The contradictions in this patriarchal view of women were so great that a man could not simply "love." He could feel *eros* or *agape,* rarely both. And even when he idealized his sexual passion for a courtesan and imagined her to be a noble companion, he was haunted by his unwillingness to allow the women of his own family to become so desirable.

It is no wonder then that the Greeks sensed that their deepest love, their love of these courtesans, yielded as much pain as delight, as much sickness as intoxication, and as much torment as joy. That is the way they wanted it—or rather the love that they idealized and craved could thrive only on the social illness that they created. The courtesans, all Greeks knew as well as Socrates, must tempt and frustrate in order to satisfy. Love in patriarchal society could not be love alone. In the words of the great poet Sophocles,

> Love is not love alone,
> But in her name lie many names concealed;
> For she is Death, imperishable Force,
> Desire unmixed, wild Frenzy, Lamentation.[5]

Love involved death because the ideal love of the courtesan, carried to its logical conclusion, allowed to all men and women, meant the death of the Greek patriarchal system. The poet probably did not see things that way. He was thinking of the tragically conflicting emotions of the lover. But these were tragic for Greek men precisely because the social ideals of women and love were so contradictory. The more they attempted to enforce the chastity of their wives and daughters, the more they desexualized them; the more they split the female population in two, the more they compartmentalized their own emotions. The breathless love of the courtesan that the Greeks created was possible only as long as all women were not courtesans. If all women were as exciting and intriguing as the courtesans, there would be no need or possibility of courtesan love. That was something the Greeks would not even consider.

GREEK HOMOSEXUALITY: IDEALS AND EDUCATION

Greek men always felt that there was something imperfect in loving women. The more highly they thought of love, the more foolish it seemed to waste the emotion on their inferiors. It was only natural, then, that the Greeks would develop homosexual love as an even nobler ideal than the love of the courtesan. Since, as all Greeks agreed, men were the most nearly perfect creatures, they were also the most worthy of love. But the most appealing of all, in fact the ideal love, was the love of a mature man for a youth. Some said that it could last until the boy's beard was full; others said that boys could be appealing until their late twenties.

Few Greeks were unaffected by the sight of a beautiful boy. When one entered the room, heads would turn, conversation would stop, grown men would blush or look foolish. Some men thought that it was improper to have sexual relationships with these youths, but few were untouched by their beauty. Socrates was one of these. According to his student Plato, Socrates always felt a "flame" when he looked at a handsome young man. One, Alcibiades, even tried to seduce the philosopher, but Socrates repressed his desire and treated the youth as a son. Plato (at least in his early life when he was influenced by Socrates) thought that love of a boy was useful in leading men to see the higher, ideal kinds of love—love of the ideas of beauty, virtue, and knowledge. And later Aristotle developed a philosophy of ethics that disapproved of sexual relations with young men, but insisted nevertheless that "love and friendship are found most and in their best form between men."

The avowed homosexuality of Greek philosophers and educators would shock modern educators. Far from being considered a vice or a detriment, love of the pupil was considered a necessary element of the teaching process. When Socrates went looking for students, he said he was "hunting down good-looking young fellows" because he regarded education as "a spiritual bringing to birth of beauty."

Pointing out that all Greek philosophers defined homosexuality in terms of education, H. I. Marrou writes in his *A History of Education in Antiquity:*

> For the Greeks, education—*paideia*—meant, essentially, a profound and intimate relationship, a personal union between a young man and an elder who was at once his model, his guide and his initiator—a relationship on to which the fire of passion threw warm and turbid reflections.
>
> Public opinion—and, in Sparta, the law—held the lover morally responsible for the development of his beloved. Pederasty was considered the most beautiful, the perfect, form of education. Throughout Greek history the relationship between master and pupil was to remain that between a lover and his beloved: education remained in principle not so much a form of teaching, an instruction in techniques, as an expenditure of loving effort by an elder concerned to promote the growth of a younger man who was burning with the desire to respond to this love and show himself worthy of it.[6]

Greek homosexuality may have originated, as Marrou suggests, in the military as part of the recruitment of the young, the training in physical combat, and the "comradeship of warriors." (Plato has Phaedo say in the *Symposium:* "A handful

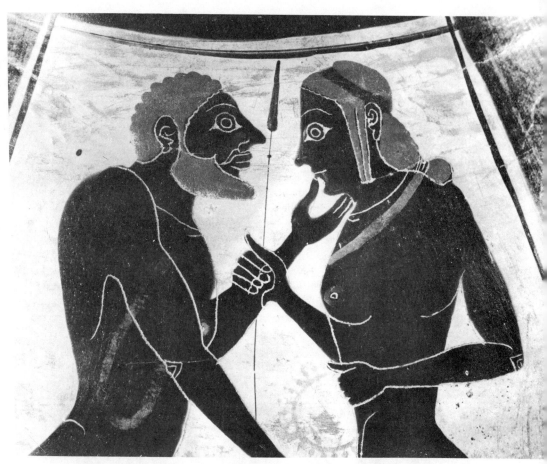

The Greek gentleman reaches beyond the arrow of love and death to grasp the virility of beardless youth. (Hirmer Fotoarchiv)

of lovers and loved ones, fighting shoulder to shoulder, could rout a whole army.") It flourished in the gymnasiums, where youths exercised and competed in the nude. Despite offical disapproval, it became an elaborate preoccupation of the educated, prosperous, and aristocratic men by the fifth century B.C. Although by no means universal, even among the well-to-do, the culture of homosexuality created rituals of flirtation and seduction that later became the repertoire of heterosexual romance as well.

GREEK ROMANCE: THE DELICIOUS DISEASE

Romance is a leisure activity. If the Greek leisure class was the first to afford the cultivation of jealousy and love because of the exclusion of women, foreigners, and slaves from its ideals, their rituals have since been opened to all. Lovers, for instance, would swear their faithfulness, allow themselves to be tested by doing foolish errands or dangerous acts. They would write long letters or poems to their beloveds, serenade them, sleep all night at their doorsteps, become speechless in their presence, or bore their friends with an endless catalog of their lovers' virtues. Almost everything that was later integrated into the romance of boy and girl was perfected in the Greek love of man and boy.

These signs of love—blushing, stammering, silly behavior—seemed so new to the Greeks that one of them, Sappho, made a long list, which was useful to physicians for hundreds of years. The Greek historian Plutarch tells the story of a young man who fell in love with his father's young wife. The doctor was called in but was as mystified as everyone else by the young man's behavior. Then the doctor noticed that every time the boy's stepmother appeared, the youth would display all of the symptoms of "love sickness" that Sappho had listed: flushed face, faltering voice, faintness, irregular violent heartbeats, darting eyes, and sweaty skin. With the aid of Sappho's list the doctor was able to diagnose the illness as the youth's love sickness for his father's new wife.

Plutarch's story is interesting because it shows how unknown the symptoms of this new "disease" must have been. Plutarch's story is instructive in another way. He goes on to tell us that when the boy's father learned of the illness he graciously gave his young wife to his son in marriage. The symptoms, we are told, vanished, but with the pain gone, the joy and ecstasy of love also evaporated. Evidently the romance that the boy found in his father's wife had a lot to do with the impossibility of ever consummating his desire. The Greeks developed romance out of very unlikely material. The love of a courtesan, or member of the same sex, or "mother figure" was not the type of love that was likely ever to become permanent. It fed on the obstacles that it created, and thrived on the social instability that it caused.

We should say one other thing about Sappho's contribution to "medical history." Sappho was a woman. Since she happened to live on the Greek island of Lesbos, and since she was sexually attracted to other women, her life is the source of our word "lesbians" today. Her study of love's symptoms, which taught the Greeks so much about the new "delicious malady," was drawn to a great extent from her own experience. And her experience was rich. She was married to a man, raised a daughter, and ran one of the few schools for girls. She fell in love with one after another of her pupils. The poems that she wrote to these girls were considered to be among the finest in Greek. Though some of her art is lost in translation, we can get some sense of her passion:

Zeus, the ruler of the Greek gods, abducts Ganymede, the most beautiful boy in the world. Zeus pleased himself with males and females, human and divine, often outwitting the plots of his wife Hera, the goddess of marriage. (Hirmer Fotoarchiv)

For should I but see thee a little moment,
  Straight is my voice hushed;
Yea, my tongue is broken, and through and through me
'Neath the flesh, impalpable fire runs tingling;
Nothing see mine eyes, and a voice of roaring
  Waves in my ear sounds;
Sweat runs down in rivers, a tremor seizes
All my limbs, and paler than grass in autumn,
Caught by pains of menacing death, I falter,
Lost in the love-trance. [7]

If the Greeks did not invent sex or friendship, they invented romantic love with all of its bittersweet moods that we know today. But the idea of passionate, romantic love that they gave us came out of relationships that were at best temporary and full of difficulty. They burned with a passion that would have been impossible in marriage, and a few Greeks seemed to care. They spoke of love as a sickness, but the "cure" was rarely as satisfying as the disease.

Romantic love hardly reached epidemic proportions in ancient Greece. Actually, it was felt deeply by only a minority of sensitive souls. Many Greeks, particularly among the upper class of citizens, had homosexual and heterosexual experiences that they might have called love. Many were infatuated with or affected by courtesans and young men, but few could afford to throw all of their time and energy into the wreckless passion that consumed Sappho and some of the poets.

The pursuit of love on such a grand romantic scale began to develop in Greece among an educated, sensitive leisure class. A system of slave labor gave a few people the opportunity to cultivate "the finer things." Since women were degraded, this new sensitivity was directed toward the rare female who magnified the magic that was denied to others and toward other men—the most worthy objects of love. The women who were not trained to excite men probably knew very little of love. A few, like Sappho, turned the tables on their masters and found deep relationships or casual sex with other women.

THE ROMAN CONTRIBUTION: LOVE AS SEX

When Roman legions marched from nowhere to take over the faded Greek cities that Alexander the Great had united briefly, they paid the Greeks the highest compliment possible—they stole their art and imitated their culture.

Returning Roman legions (like American GI's returning from France after World War II) had found sex, and they approved. Within decades after the Roman conquest of the Mediterranean empire in the second century B.C., courtesans had become popular in Rome. Even young boys were bought and sold (sometimes for the price of a nice farm), and the Romans were acclaiming the joys of "Greek love," by which they seem to have meant pederasty. The problem with the Romans was that they (like the Americans) fell in love with sex rather than love. They were not really interested in sex mixed with philosophy, and so the courtesans were never as popular or satisfying as cheaper prostitutes. Nor were the Romans interested in charming, handsome young boys for their wit and intelligence. They preferred to seduce them and leave it at that.

Romans looked to Greece in the same way that some Americans have looked to Europe. They recognized the high achievements of Greek culture, but tried to buy it or reproduce it without ever fully understanding it. Some of the better minds would write poetry or plays in the style of the Greeks or spout Greek phrases to impress other Romans with their sophistication. But when most Romans heard about Greek culture, they missed the elaborate, intricate rituals of love, and found the open attitude toward sex that lay beneath these ritualistic restraints.

When Rome consisted of just the city and some other parts of Italy, the people were repressed, or "moral," as many Americans of the 1940s and 1950s were. Marriages were valued, not for love certainly, but for the honor that children gave to the family and the prosperity that a virtuous, hardworking wife gave to the husband. But the Rome that had conquered an empire was as different from the early Rome as the American world power was different from the new republic.

FASHIONABLE ROMANS: OVID'S ART OF WAR

For the "liberated" upper-class Romans who ruled the empire, love meant sex. The fashionable society poet during the reign of the emperor Augustus (the heir and successor of Julius Caesar) was Ovid, whose popular book *The Art of Love* was simply a manual for seduction. Ovid's art had nothing to do with the Greek romantic sickness. He cautioned his readers to pretend to be incapacitated in order to manipulate the feelings of the women they desired. The tone of his advice sounds more like *Popular Mechanics* than *Modern Romance*. [8]

> *Also, the theater's curve is a very good place for your hunting,*
>   *More opportunity here, maybe, than anywhere else.*
> *Here you may find one to love, or possibly only have fun with,*
> *Someone to take for a night, someone to have and to hold.*
>   *(i, 89–92)*

> *Try to find something in common, to open the conversation;*
>   *Don't care too much what you say, just so that everyone hears. . . .*
> *Often it happens that dust may fall on the blouse of the lady.*
> *If such dust should fall, carefully brush it away.*
> *Even if there's no dust, brush off whatever there isn't.*
>   *(i, 142–143, 149–152)*

See that you promise: what harm can there be in promising freely?
  There's not a man in the world who can't be rich in that coin.
                                    (i, 443–444)

Also, make it your aim to get her husband to like you;
  If you can make him your friend, he will be useful, you'll find.
                                    (i, 581–582)

Getting really drunk is bad, but pretending to do so
  Does no harm at all, might in fact, be a gain.
Make your cunning tongue stumble and stutter a little,
  So, if you go too far, people will say, "Oh, he's drunk."
                                    (i, 596–599)

After the party breaks up, draw close to her in the confusion,
  Let your foot touch hers, finger the sleeve of her dress.
Now is the time for talk! Don't be an oaf of a farmer.
                                    (i, 603–605)

Play the role of the lover, give the impression of heartache.
                                    (i, 609)

Flattery works on the mind as the waves on the bank of a river:
  Praise her face and her hair; praise her fingers and toes.
                                    (i, 617–618)

Gods are convenient to have, so let us concede their existence. . . .
  What you are eager to be, tell her, is Only a friend.
I have seen this work, on the most unwilling of women—
Only a friend, who was found more than proficient in bed!
                                    (i, 637, 721–723)

Lying, cheating, pretending are all part of the game for Ovid. The important thing is to win. Women, any women, are the object. And nothing short of sexual conquest is acceptable to the "artist" in love. Even a little muscle is fair in love, as in war.

Once you have taken a kiss, the other things surely will follow,
  Or, if they don't, you should lose all you have taken before.
How far away is a kiss from the right true end, the completion?
  Failure the rest of the way proves you are clumsy, not shy.
Force is all right to apply, and women like you to use it;
  What they enjoy they pretend they were unwilling to give.
One who is overcome, and, suddenly, forcefully taken,
  Welcomes the wanton assault, takes it as proof of her charm.
                                    (i, 669–676)

There are times, however, when Ovid sounds like a highly civilized modern marriage counselor. Not out of sympathy for a woman's needs, but because a happy conquest is more likely to continue to make herself available, Ovid also urges a touch of tenderness.

> *Take my word for it, love is never a thing to be hurried,*
>   *Coax it along, go slow, tease it with proper delay.*
> *When you have found the place where a woman loves to be fondled,*
>   *Let no feeling of shame keep your caresses away.*
> *Then you will see in her eyes a tremulous brightness, a glitter,*
>   *Like a flash of the sun when the water is clear.*
> *She will complain, but not mean it, murmuring words of endearment,*
>   *Sigh in the sweetest way, utter appropriate cries.*
> *Neither go too fast, nor let her get there before you;*
>   *Pleasure is best when both come at one time to the goal.*
>
>   *(ii, 717–727)*

Ovid's ideal of love as mere sexual gratification was probably pretty typical of the Roman ruling class during the days of the empire. It was necessarily promiscuous. Since love was the animal passion aroused in the loins, it had nothing to do with the character or background or intelligence of the beloved. Ovid, for instance, advised his readers to imitate the person desired: the lover, like the politician, should be all things to all women. Be what they want or what they are, he instructs.

> *Use a thousand means, since there are thousands of ends.*
> *Earth brings forth varying yield: one soil is good for the olive,*
>   *One for the vine, and a third richly productive in corn. . . .*
> *If you seem coarse to a prude, or learned to some little lowbrow,*
>   *She will be filled with distrust, made to feel cheap in your eyes.*
>   *(i, 757–759, 767–768)*

Ovid is hardly interested in weighing the comparative merits of the vulgar and the prudish or the intelligent and the lowbrow. "All the stars in the sky, are less than the girls Rome can offer." The rich and poor, mistress and servant, married and unmarried, young and old, coy and aggressive, all are fish for the net. Ovid would probably have nothing but contempt for the romantic Greek ideal of love for "that special someone" with the "special something."

Like any artist, Ovid probably reflected the ideas of the upper class as much as he taught them. Some of the upstanding citizens objected to his frankness, and eventually the poet was banished by the emperor Augustus—but only after Ovid became too friendly with the emperor's granddaughter, who was beginning to follow her mother's example of taking on every man in Rome.

Adultery seemed to be the favorite indoor sport of the fashionable set. Love had nothing to do with one's own wife, but everyone else's wife was fair and exciting game. The "smart" women played the game just as eagerly as the men. It was risky in a society without motels or cars, but the risks often made it more delicious.

OLD-FASHIONED ROMANS:
PLINY LOVES CALPURNIA?

Of course, there were those who, like Augustus, found this whole "new morality" obscene and corrupt. Some voices from the past spoke of a very different kind of love, which they actually found in their relationships with their wives. One of these old-fashioned Romans, Pliny the Younger (A.D. 62–113), an author and diplomat, looked back at the sexual revolution from the perspective of the second century (when Caesar, and Augustus, and Nero were long dead), and wrote a glowing tribute to the loving marriages of imperial Rome. Pliny was convinced that there were many lovers, even in the most licentious days of the empire, who were married to each other. But almost all of Pliny's examples of loving wives were chosen because they killed themselves when their husbands died or were about to die. The emotion that Pliny called love was blind devotion and dependence.

Pliny tips his hand when he talks of his own marriage to Calpurnia, a young girl. He said that he loved her; indeed, he continually swore that he couldn't be away from her. But his letters to friends show that he barely knew the girl, and that her feeling toward him was more like that of disciple to teacher, or servant to master, than lover to lover. In a letter to his aunt he wrote:

> Her mind is keen and her tastes simple. She loves me, which proves her chastity. Besides, she likes literature, to which she was led by her affection for me. She keeps my books, reads them, and even learns passages from them off by heart. She is painfully anxious when I am to conduct a case, and delighted when I have completed it. She appoints people to tell her what applause and shouts I have received, and what the verdict was. If I am reading my work in public she sits near by, behind a curtain, and drinks in the praise of my audience with expectant ears. She also sings my verses, and even sets them to music, taught not by a musician but by love, the best master.[9]

What Pliny seemed to love most in Calpurnia, according to Jérôme Carcopino in *Daily Life in Ancient Rome,* "was her admiration for his writings." And while he missed her admiration while he was away, he was consoled by the chance to "polish the phrases" of his letters to her.

> Even when the couple were living under the same roof they were not together. They had, as we should say, their separate rooms. Even amid the peace of his Tuscan villa, Pliny's chief delight was in a solitude favourable to his meditations, and it was his secretary, not his wife, whom he was wont to summon to his bedside at dawn. His conjugal affection was for him a matter of good taste and *savoir vivre,* and we cannot avoid the conviction that, taken all around, it was gravely lacking in warmth and intimacy.[10]

On the other hand, if Roman divorce statistics are any indication, some Roman husbands and wives must have loved each other as equals. One Roman critic of

In Rome, as in Greece, love was a leisure-class activity. One needed the afternoon free and servants to set the scene and bring on the wine. (EPA; Kunsthistorisches Museum)

the high divorce rate claims that men and women were continually getting divorced to be remarried, and getting married to be divorced. Though this is an exaggeration, we know that many of the men and women in the upper class took four and five spouses, one after the other. This means two things: they frequently fell out of love with their spouses, but they also frequently married their new lovers. Again one is led to suspect that the adulterous affairs cooled off when they became legalized.

A CHRISTIAN DILEMMA

We have seen the development of two very different ideas of love in the West: the romantic love of the Greeks and the explicitly sexual love of the Romans. Neither of these ideas of love was associated with marriage. The roots of marriage were in social necessity—the needs of the community and the patriarchal family. When the word "love" became fashionable in Roman society, some people like Pliny attempted to read it into marriage. No doubt other Romans attempted to add love to their marriages or began new marriages based on love. But these were short-lived attempts for the most part, and the most passionate affairs usually lay outside the bonds of matrimony.

The Christians attempted to infuse marriage with love. But their idea of love was not Roman sexuality, not even Greek *eros*. It was the Greek ideal of *agape,* spiritual love. The Christian marriage was to be modeled on the highest type of spiritual love—the love of God. Christian love was to be romantic love, more idealized than the Greeks had ever imagined. Going way beyond the Greek tendency to romanticize the charm of a physical lover, the Christians followed Plato in the belief that all physical love was but an imperfect reflection of the ideal love. The ideal love that the Christians knew was the love for Christ. It was that love that was substituted for Plato's ideal—love of the good, of virtue, of truth, and of knowledge. All Christian love was to absorb as completely as possible the love of Christ. The effect that this belief had on Western sexuality was enormous. Imagine, for instance, what it means to love one's spouse in the same way that one loves God.

Christian love was not practiced by all, of course. No ideal ever is. But Christianity radically changed the Greek idea of love and almost abolished the Roman version. The Roman idea of love as sex revived (at least by the eighteenth century) as the influence of Christianity declined. It is perhaps one of the dominant ideas of love in today's *Playboy* culture. But the romantic idea of love is also very much with us today, sometimes in its original Greek form, but more often in the form that Christianity has made of it during the last two thousand years. Let's examine, then, what Christianity did to the romantic ideal of love that was just beginning to emerge in ancient Greece.

Educated Christians who lived in the Roman Empire were familiar with both the writings of the Greeks and the Jewish Bible, which they called the "Old Testament." From the Old Testament they inherited an un-Roman distaste for adultery, prostitution, homosexuality, and fornication. But the Jews expressed a lusty enthusiasm for sex in marriage. They felt a responsibility to their God as his chosen people to multiply, but the duty was also evidently quite pleasurable. Read the "Song of Solomon" in the Old Testament, for instance.

The attitudes of Jesus toward sex, love, and marriage are not too clear. His closest followers were twelve men, but he seems, according to some accounts, to have taken a personal interest in Mary Magdalene, a reformed prostitute. He seems to have thought highly of marriage and opposed divorce, but according to Matthew he also spoke approvingly of those "which have made themselves eunuchs for the kingdom of heaven's sake."

For most Romans, though, Jesus was a minor Jewish troublemaker in a remote corner of the empire until Paul opened the new religion to non-Jews and helped organize groups of these "Christians" throughout the empire. One of the most striking things about these communities of Christians was their obsession with sex as the source of evil. Paul went so far as to develop a whole philosophy based on the implication in the Old Testament that Eve's sin was sexual seduction and that her sin had been the cause of all human suffering ever since causing everyone to be born with this "original sin," and requiring that God purify his people by sacrificing his own son.

THE IDEAL OF CHASTITY

We can understand why some of the poorer people in Rome might have taken to the new religion. It offered the meek, humble, and dispossessed eternal salvation from exploitation, sickness, and daily misery. A loving God (even one that urged sexual abstinence) must have been very appealing to people who led loveless lives, especially women who were brutalized in the only intimate relationships they knew.

But Christianity appealed to members of all classes in ancient Rome. One of the early church historians tells us of a wealthy young Egyptian, Ammon, born into a wealthy family that employed servants, who frequented Roman theaters and games, and enjoyed fine foods and stimulating women; but Ammon decided to become a Christian. Pressured into getting married, Ammon shocked his young bride on their wedding night by reading from Paul:

> It is good for a man not to touch a woman. Nevertheless, to avoid fornication, let every man have his own wife, and let every woman have her own husband. . . . I would that all men were [chaste] even as I myself. . . . I say therefore to the unmarried and widows, it is good for them if they abide even as I. But if they cannot contain, let them marry: for it is better to marry than to burn.[11]

Ammon spoke to his young wife about the spiritual exuberation he felt by keeping his body "pure" of sexual contact, and argued that virginity brought people closer to God. Ammon's bride (probably as afraid of sex as he) pledged that she too would become a Christian and they would live together as brother and sister.

After a while the couple felt they might better serve God if they moved from the sinful city of Alexandria with all its worldly distractions, and they moved into a hut in the desert. There they ate only bread and water, often fasting for two or three days at a time. But even on such a diet they still felt an occasional prompting of the flesh, and so they moved apart to live in two separate huts. Temptation, however, did not even disappear with his wife. Ammon vowed never to remove his own clothing because "it becomes not a monk to see even his own person exposed." Once, in fact, Ammon wanted to cross a river but would have gotten his clothes so wet that he would have had to remove them. So Ammon explained his dilemma to God, who, according to the historian, immediately dispatched an angel to lift Ammon across the river dry and pure.[12]

The writings of the early Christians are full of such stories of continent marriages and ascetic behavior that other Romans must have considered bizarre. Another wealthy young man (Injuriosus in the fifth century) and his Christian wife slept in the same bed but refrained from any sexual contact. According to the story, their spiritual love was rewarded after their deaths when their two tombs miraculously came together. Tourists even today are shown the burial place of "The Two Lovers."[13]

Most of these stories were based on some event that actually happened, even if they were made more fantastic in the telling. They were self-fulfilling fantasies. They became models of proper Christian behavior. Even when a Christian could not escape from the pleadings of the body (and many certainly could not), he or she would feel guilty. Others no doubt who heard of the innumerable virgins who gave their lives rather than be forced to have sexual intercourse, or of the monks who burned their fingers or castrated themselves in order to free their minds of sex, must have tried to do the same.

LOVE AND SEX IN INDIA

If Christianity rejected sexuality and took the Greek idealization of love to its spiritual extreme, other cultures developed romance along with sex. Indian culture was one of these.

Sexuality had been an important element of Indian religion at least since the Aryan invasion around 1500 B.C. Early fertility worship centered on the large phallic stones *(lingā)* and the bowl-shaped female *yoni,* sometimes represented by lotus leaves, still seen in Indian worship today.

The intense concern for fertility in the religion of the Vedas is shocking to one brought up in the Judeo-Christian tradition. Compare, for instance, this creation story from the Brhadaranyaka Upanishad with the Hebrew account:

A painting commemorating the death of a Syrian Christian shows
some of the ascetic practices of Christian monks in the desert, where
Christian monasticism orginated. One monk, Saint Simeon Stylites of
Syria, was said to have lived on top of a column for over thirty years.
Some lived as hermits in caves. Other joined together in monasteries.
All seem to have avoided women and struggled against the
temptations of the flesh. (Musei Vaticani)

Prajapati (the Lord of Creation) thought to himself: "Let me provide a firm foundation." So he created woman. When he had created her, he honored her below. Therefore one should honor women below. He stretched out for himself that stone which projects [the *lingā*]. With that he impregnated her. Her lap is a sacrificial altar; her hairs, the sacrificial grass; her skin, the soma-press. The two lips of the *yoni* are the fire in the middle. Verily, indeed, as great as is the world of the person who performs the *Vajapeya* sacrifice [the drink of strength], just as great is the world of him who practices sexual intercourse knowing this. He takes the good deeds of women to himself. But he who practices sexual intercourse without knowing this—women take his good deeds for themselves.[14]

The Judeo-Christian Bible tended to focus on what should *not* be done, and sex was high on the list. Conversely, the emphasis in India was on attaining the goals of life, and sex was one of the four. The goals of life were *dharma* (duty, righteousness, proper behavior), *artha* (wealth, power, material well-being), *kama* (love, sex, fertility), and *moksha* (final release). The first three lead to the fourth. The path to *moksha* was usually begun with *dharma,* but there were some texts that held *kama* the more important, including this from the greatest of Indian epics, the *Mahabharata:*

One without Kama never wishes for Artha. One without Kama never wishes for Dharma. One who is destitute of Kama can never feel and wish. For this reason, Kama is the foremost of the three. . . . As nectar is extracted from flowers, so is Kama to be extracted from these two. Kama is the parent of Dharma and Artha. Kama is the soul of these two.[15]

THE *KAMA SUTRA*

The classic Indian discussion of *kama* is contained in the *Kama Sutra* by Vatsyayana. It was written between the first and fourth centuries A.D. for an Indian upper class, probably in one of the monarchial courts, just before or during the Gupta period.

Vatsyayana's "*kama* manual" presupposes an urban world where kings have harems, wealthy men have a number of wives, and many men frequent courtesans. He addresses the courtesans as well as the men, advising courtesans on how to wheedle extra money from a client, live like a wife, or get rid of a lover. Vatsyayana has counted everything. There are sixty-four arts that a woman should study, four kinds of love, but also four kinds of kissing, embracing, biting, and so forth. There are twenty-four types of men who generally have success with women, but forty-one kinds of women who are "easily gained over." There are eight kinds of go-betweens, or female messengers, and twenty-eight ways to leave a lover.

Much of this carefully cataloged advice could hardly have been news two thousand years ago. Among the twenty-eight ways to get rid of a lover, for instance, are the following: pretend to be sleepy; go out visiting; misconstrue his words; laugh without any joke; and glance at his attendants. Much more is painfully obvious: "When a courtesan is not sure how much a man will give her or spend on her, this is called a doubt about wealth."

There is much to remind us of Ovid's manipulation (unfortunately without his wit) in the *Kama Sutra*.

> When a man is endeavoring to seduce one woman, he should not attempt to seduce any other at the same time. But after he has succeeded with the first, and enjoyed her for a considerable time, he can keep her affections by giving her presents that she likes, and then commence making up to another woman.[16]

It would be a mistake, however, to see the *Kama Sutra* as merely a guide to sexual seduction. While there is considerable attention to the mechanics of sex, there is also a cultivation of romance. It is as if Vatsyayana, for all his seriousness of purpose and dull cataloging mentality, wants to teach young men gentility, charm, and romance. In a chapter on courtship, he suggests to the young man interested in winning a young woman that he entertain her with music, bring her to moonlit fairs and festivals, and give her bouquets of flowers. In another chapter on sending a go-between (or messenger) to the girl's parents, he says that the go-between should declare that the aspiring young man is going mad, and dying from his love.

Romance is hardly the central message of the *Kama Sutra,* but its presence in such an unpoetic work suggests that love was being taught in the courts of Indian society along with sex. Indeed, we do not have to look far for love stories in classical India. One of the great poetic works of Gupta culture was a love story taken from a subplot in the *Mahabharata,* the story of Shakuntala.

KALIDASA'S *SHAKUNTALA*

Kalidasa was the great poet and dramatist of Gupta India. *Shakuntala* is his best-known play. It is a richly romantic drama that centers on the love of King Dushyanta and the poor hermit-maid Shakuntala. The idea comes from a description of a meeting of the king and maid in the *Mahabharata,* that collection of legend and history that many Indians, then as now, heard over and over again. Kalidasa took a story about a contemptible king who seduced a maid and then abandoned her, and turned it into a romance. Kalidasa's play is full of the florid imagery and emotional confusions of romance. When he first sees her:

> *She seems a flower whose fragrance none has tasted,*
>   *A gem uncut by workman's tool,*
> *A branch no desecrating hands have wasted,*
>   *Fresh honey, beautifully cool.*[17]

First he is distressed that he cannot marry a woman of such low caste. Then he convinces himself that she must actually be of a similar caste to his or he would not feel so strongly toward her. They marry, but they must part temporarily. Before they reunite a curse is put on Shakuntala: King Dushyanta won't recognize her when they meet again, unless Shakuntala can produce the ring he gave her. This is fulfilled when she finally arrives at the palace with their child, but without the king's ring. The king does not remember her, and tells her to return to her real husband. Brokenhearted, she leaves. Then later the ring is found, the curse is lifted, the king remembers his love, and they live happily ever after.

INDIAN LOVE AND MARRIAGE

"Love marriage," like that of Kalidasa's King Dushyanta and Shakuntala, was not unknown in India, despite the fact that most marriages were (and still are) arranged by parents. *Gandhara* (love marriage) was one of eight recognized types of Hindu marriage: *brahma,* the giving of a daughter by her father to the groom he has chosen; *prajapatya,* the giving away of a bride by her guardian; *daiva,* the giving of a girl to a priest; *arsha,* the giving away of a daughter after the father has received a cow and a bull from the groom; *gandhara,* love marriage; *asura,* the purchase of a girl from her father; *rakshasa,* marriage by capture; and *paisacha,* the drugging and rape of a bride.[18]

That love marriage existed is perhaps less striking than its relative unimportance in a classification system that includes various forms of conquest and sale. While the plays of Kalidasa suggest what one observer calls "the romanticization of sex in the classical age,"[19] the Indian ideal remained the devoted wife. The model wife in Indian literature was Sita, not Shakuntala. Sita was the wife of Rama in the great epic *The Ramayana,* who remains faithful to her husband throughout her long captivity in the palace of the evil Ravana. When Rama, with the aid of many monkeys, rescues Sita, he is unable to accept her as his wife until she throws herself on the funeral pyre and the fire God Agni attests to her innocence by not touching her.

FOR FURTHER READING

Morton Hunt's entertaining, anecdotal *The Natural History of Love* is an engaging introduction to the subject. Other popular general histories are Reay Tannahill's *Sex in History* and Amaury de Riencourt's *Sex and Power in History.*

For specific studies of the Greco-Roman classical world, the most useful introductions are Sarah B. Pomeroy's *Goddesses, Whores, Wives, and Slaves: Women in Classical Antiquity* and Eva Cantarella's *Pandora's Daughters.* A valuable collection of short primary sources can be found in *Women's Life in Greece and Rome,* edited by Mary R. Lefkowitz and Maureen B. Fant.

There are a number of interesting studies of sexuality in classical Athens and Greece. One is *The Reign of the Phallus: Sexual Politics in Ancient Athens* by Eva Keuls. Another is K. J. Dover's *Greek Homosexuality*. Robert Flaceliere's *Love in Ancient Greece* is fascinating. W. K. Lacey's *The Family in Classical Greece* is an absorbing, relevant study. For a more general treatment of Greek social life, Emile Mireaux's *Daily Life in the Time of Homer* is superb for the archaic period, and Robert Flaceliere's *Daily Life in Greece at the Time of Pericles* is an excellent introduction to the classical period. For an intriguing interpretation of the sexuality of a Greek myth, see Erich Neumann's *Amor and Psyche*. A relevant approach to sexuality in Greece and Rome that is especially valuable on Greek homosexuality and education is H. I. Marrou's *A History of Education in Antiquity*.

There are also good studies of Roman sexuality and social life. J. P. V. D. Balsdon's *Roman Woman* is an interesting historical treatment. Otto Kiefer's *Sexual Life in Ancient Rome* is almost as readable as it was fifty years ago. E. P. Corbett's *The Roman Law of Marriage* is a solid study of legal change and complexities. There is a brilliant essay called "The Silent Women of Rome" (among others) in M. I. Finley's *Aspects of Antiquity*. Love, marriage, and sexuality are also discussed in broader interpretations of Roman social life. Jérôme Carcopino's *Daily Life in Ancient Rome* and Frederik Poulsen's *Glimpses of Roman Culture* are especially valuable.

This is one topic that can be most usefully and entertainingly approached through the rich literature of the period. The Greeks and Romans wrote frequently and vividly of love, sex, and marriage. One can approach Homer's *Iliad* and *Odyssey* (many editions) from this perspective (as does Mireaux, above). Hesiod's *Works and Days* is also full of information about archaic social life. Plato's dialogues are treasures of sexual and social attitudes for the classical period, especially the *Symposium, Phaedrus,* and *Phaedo.* Xenophon's *Symposium* and *Oeconomicus (Economics)* are also rich in detail. The plays of Aristophanes (something of an antihomosexual) are hilarious dramatizations of homosexual and heterosexual relationships, among other themes. All are available as *The Complete Plays of Aristophanes,* including his *Thesmophoriazusae* (or "Women Celebrating the Thesmophoria") and *Ecclesiazusae* (or "Women in Parliament"). But if you read only one, make it Douglass Parker's modernized translation of *Lysistrata,* about an imagined women's sex strike for peace. Other classical writings on love and sex include Plutarch's *Amatorius, Erotikos,* and *Conjugal Precepts,* Lucian's *Erotes,* and, of course, Ovid's *Art of Love.* The last is published with Ovid's *The Loves, the Art of Beauty,* and *The Remedies for Love* in an excellent translation by Rolfe Humphries called *Ovid, The Art of Love.* Humphries also has a good translation of *The Satires of Juvenal,* and there is also a good translation by Smith Palmer Bovie of *Satires and Epistles of Horace,* both of which are more general Roman works. Finally, Robert Graves's translation of *The Golden Ass of Apuleius* is a joyous classic.

An excellent introduction to the issue of religion and sexuality is *Sex in the World's Religions* by Geoffrey Parrinder. Marina Warner's *Alone of All Her Sex: The Myth and Cult of the Virgin Mary* is a thorough study, mostly of later Christian ideas, as is John Boswell's *Christianity, Social Tolerance, and Homosexuality.* As always, the *Bible* is an excellent source: the letters of Paul and the Book of Acts are particularly valuable for the attitudes of the early Christian church.

Among the sources of classical Indian ideas, there are numerous editions of the *Kama Sutra,* the *Mahabharata,* and the *Ramayana.* R. K. Narayan's short version and William Buck's longer version of the last are both excellent. There are also translations of Kalidasa's plays, including *Shakuntala.*

NOTES

1. Xenophon, *Oeconomicus*, in *Readings in Ancient History*, trans. H. G. Dakyns (Boston: Allyn & Bacon, 1912), p. 266.
2. Attributed to Demosthenes, "Against Neaera." This and much of the other material in this section is drawn from Morton Hunt, *The Natural History of Love* (New York: Knopf, 1967).
3. Quoted in Hunt, *op. cit.,* p. 26.
4. Xenophone, *Memorabilia*, III: xi, quoted in Hunt, *op. cit.,* p. 37.
5. Sophocles, Fragment 678, quoted in Hunt, *op. cit.,* p. 41.
6. H. I. Marrou, *A History of Education in Antiquity*, trans. George Lamb (New York: New American Library, 1964), p. 57.
7. Sappho, "Ode to Atthis," quoted in Hunt, *op. cit.,* p. 45.
8. This and the following selections are taken from Ovid, *The Art of Love,* trans. Rolfe Humphries (Bloomington: Indiana University Press, 1957).
9. Pliny, *Letters,* iv: 19, quoted in Otto Kiefer, *Sexual Life in Ancient Rome* (London: Routledge & Kegan Paul, 1934), and excerpted in Michael Cherniavsky and Arthur J. Slavin, *Social Textures of Western Civilization: The Lower Depths* (Waltham, Mass.: Xerox, 1972), p. 162.
10. Jérôme Carcopino, quoted in *Daily Life in Ancient Rome,* ed. Henry T. Rowell, trans. E. O. Lorimer (New Haven: Yale University Press, 1940), p. 89.
11. 1 Cor. 7: 1–9.
12. The story of Ammon is told by Socrates Scholasticus, *Ecclesiastical History* iv: 23; this version is adapted from Morton Hunt, *op. cit.,* pp. 93–95.
13. Hunt, *op. cit.,* p. 96.
14. *Kama Sutra,* I, 4:14, quoted in John W. Spellman's introduction to *The Kama Sutra of Vatsyayana* (New York: Dutton, 1962), p. 16.
15. Quoted in Spellman, *op. cit.,* p. 18.
16. *The Kama Sutra of Vatsyayana,* trans. Sir Richard F. Burton (New York: Dutton, 1962), p. 182.
17. *Shakuntala and Other Writings by Kalidasa,* trans. Arthur W. Ryder (London: J. M. Dent & Sons; New York: E. P. Dutton & Co., 1912). Quoted in William H. McNeill and Jean W. Sedlar, eds., *Classical India* (New York: Oxford University Press, 1969), p. 77.
18. A. S. Altekar, *The Position of Women in Hindu Civilization* (Delhi: Motilal Banarsidass, 1956), pp. 35–49. Cited in F. Roy Willis, *World Civilizations* (Lexington, Mass.: D.C. Heath, 1982), p. 251.
19. Richard Lannoy, *The Speaking Tree* (Oxford: Oxford University Press, 1971), p. 117.

8

War
and
Society

Empires and Armies
in Rome and China

WHAT CAUSES WAR? Are some societies more likely to engage in war than others? Is there any relationship between the size of a society and its capacity for war, or its capacity for avoiding war? Do states with large armies provide longer periods of peace than those with small armies? Are volunteer armies preferable to draft armies? Is an empire safer than a small country? Does a state provide more protection or risk? How does a war change a society?

These are some of the questions that prompt this chapter. They are important questions for us today. There are wars going on in some places in the world almost all of the time. They sometimes threaten to engulf larger areas in conflict. Another world war, especially in the age of nuclear weapons, is said to be unthinkable. But we have not devised a certain peace.

Our own country plays a significant role in the world. Some have compared the role of the United States in the twentieth century with that of the Roman Empire in the classical world. If the United States is an empire, what might we learn from the military experience of Rome and other empires? How might we avoid the problems and eventual decline of such empires?

This chapter will argue that the historical experience of Rome and other empires has much to tell us. The chapter will argue some of the following ideas. Wars are not inevitable or natural but are caused by certain kinds of warlike or aggressive societies and social situations. One of the most ancient causes of war was the tension between tribes of nomadic herders and settled, civilized states. That principal cause of war in the ancient and classical world has disappeared with the use of gunpowder and the rise of states in the last five hundred years. But another cause of war is the expansion of empires. They tend to expand to the point of resistance, resulting in conflict. Their expansion also tends to transform them internally. The society becomes militarized and socially divided. Eventually, such societies are torn apart internally or are ordered by powerful, repressive states.

There are many subsidiary arguments as well, perhaps too many to name. One is that citizen armies are better than professional ones because citizens will fight only when they have to, and they will fight for their homelands. For the same reason, draft armies are better than professional or mercenary armies. What other arguments do you see in this chapter? What is the evidence for these and other arguments? Do you find the evidence convincing? Is the United States in danger of repeating some of the mistakes of the ancient empires? Has the United States built large concentrations of economic power, like the landed estates of ancient Rome and China, that inhibit efforts for peace or defense? Or does the United States ensure the peace, as the *pax Romana* or Chinese Empire did?

FRONTIERS, SETTLERS, AND HERDERS: THE LONGEST WAR

About three thousand years ago, when the ancient Hebrews speculated about the origins of war they told a story about two brothers—Cain and Abel. To indicate their belief that war had existed a long time they made these two brothers the sons of the first parents. According to the version of the story in what we know as the Bible (Genesis, chapter 4), Eve gave birth to Cain, who became "a tiller of the ground," and then to Abel, "a keeper of sheep." "And in process of time it came to pass that Cain brought of the fruit of the ground an offering unto the Lord. And Abel, he also brought of the firstlings of his flock and of the fat thereof. And the Lord had respect unto Abel and to his offering. But unto Cain and to his offering he had not respect." Jealous that the Lord accepted Abel's animal sacrifice and rejected his agricultural offering, Cain, the farmer, killed his brother Abel, the herder.

As a symbolic account of the origins of war, the biblical tale is very instructive. Cain and Abel are symbols of the two types of life-styles before the rise of cities. Gradually, after the taming of animals by hunting tribes and the domestication of plants by the food gatherers (about ten thousand years ago), the two styles of life—farming and herding—became more and more distinct. While hunting and gathering were often practiced by the same group, often with only a sexual division of labor, farming and herding became separated ways of life. Herders required vast grasslands for their flocks. Farmers needed river valleys for irrigation or areas with higher rainfall than grasslands. Herders were always on the move in search of new grazing lands. Farmers had to stay with their crops. Herders owned little more than their animals, tents, and what they could carry. Farmers built permanent settlements—villages and eventually cities—which became centers of administration, trade, and numerous occupations.

There must have been almost inevitable tensions between farmers and herders—tensions that had not existed in more primitive hunting-gathering societies. Farming villages were able to accumulate a surplus of food and eventually luxuries that must have been the envy of the wandering herders of the grasslands. At the same time, the settled life of village communities made farmers more vulnerable as they became more "civilized" and prosperous. The herders' rough life in the open country was not far removed from the rigors of the primitive hunt. Herders valued aggression, strength, and stamina. Their tribes were something of a permanent military force, loyal to their leaders, and ready to move at a moment's notice. In short, farming communities were an easy prey and contained attractive booty for the wandering tribes of the grasslands.

Peasant farmers and nomadic herders were, as the biblical story suggests, brothers as well as enemies. Every fall when the grass of the pasture was low, and the crops of the field had been harvested, the herders must have brought their animals to feed on the stubble of the harvested grain. Cattle would be traded for the fruits of the vine and the olive trees, and the produce of the cultivated field. The nomads would also offer precious stones, axes, and decorative shells that they had acquired on their wanderings for the perishable goods and manufactured products of the civilized settlements.

The interaction of farmers and herders, settlers and nomads, villages and tribes, farm and pasture, and eventually city civilizations and barbarians—sometimes peaceful but often violent—was probably the main dynamic of world history until only a few hundred years ago. Organized, sustained warfare began in the conflict between the two groups. Nomadic herders have invaded village settlements for almost ten thousand years; city armies have fought barbarian invaders for almost five thousand years; and since the nomads learned to ride horseback habitually about three thousand years ago, the confrontations have often been brutal and frequent. If we exclude the very recent past, the last few hundred years in which the last nomadic tribes have been integrated into the laws and customs of cities and countries, the history of war has been the conflict between the settlers and the people of the frontier.

Much of ancient history can be understood in terms of that conflict. The ancient city civilizations of Mesopotamia, Egypt, and India that developed after 3000 B.C. were all overrun after 1700 B.C. by barbarian charioteers (who combined the city invention of wheeled vehicles with their own experience of domesticating horses). The descendants of these invaders had established new empires in Egypt, Mesopotamia, and China when (after 1200 B.C.) a new wave of wandering tribes with iron weapons and infantry organization proved too much for the ruling aristocracies and their few hundred chariots. These tribes (like the Dorians in Greece and the Hebrews) settled down to agriculture and city life and were, in turn, overrun by a new invasion of nomads (after 900 B.C.) whose perfection of horse riding made their cavalries too powerful for the old infantries.

Successive waves of nomads, spurred by horsemen with bow and arrow, raided and sometimes destroyed or conquered city empires from 900 B.C. until the last significant Mongol invasion in the thirteenth century A.D. Most of them came from the vast grasslands of the Eurasian steppe that stretched from Europe to China. These mounted armies were actually no more than the male members of a tribe or tribal confederacy, moving as they had always moved, but in periods of population growth or pressure from other tribes, forced to carve out new grazing lands without their women and children.

Ancient civilizations were forced to adopt their Iron Age infantries to the new cavalry warfare, hire the nomads as mercenaries to protect their flanks, or succumb to defeat. The Assyrian Empire learned the lesson the hard way: they were overrun by the nomads in 612 B.C. The Persian Empire in Iran hired the nomads as mercenaries. The rulers of the small Asian kingdom of Qin [Ch'in] were among the few who were able to adopt cavalry warfare on their own. As a result, they were not only able to stave off the nomadic invasion from central Asia, but they were also able to overwhelm rival Asian states and give the Qin [Ch'in] name to a unified China in 221 B.C. But later nomadic invasions of China proved more successful, and by the fourth century A.D. China was again a series of smaller states.

The Western Roman Empire suffered much the same fate as Han China. For almost 600 years the Romans were able to create a Mediterranean empire while keeping the Scythians and other tribal confederacies at bay. Increasingly, however, the Romans were forced to use nomads as mercenaries. Unlike the Chinese, the Roman infantry officers refused to learn the techniques of cavalry or bow and arrow. By the fifth century A.D. the Western Roman Empire had been overrun by the tribal migrations. The Eastern Romans who combined Latin and Greek culture in Constantinople (which the emperor Constantine had established separate from embattled Rome in the early fourth century A.D.) were able to survive another thousand years. The Eastern Byzantine Empire survived that long primarily because it adopted a new style of cavalry combat that had been developed in Iran to counter the threat from the steppe. Eventually that new style of cavalry— which we know as the armored knight—was to save the very tribes that overran the Western Roman Empire when they, themselves, were threatened by new nomadic invasions in the ninth century A.D.

In many ways, the most dramatic example of the potentialities of nomad warfare—the expansion of the Mongol Empire under Genghis Khan in the thirteenth century—was the last. After 1500 the widespread use of gunpowder and the complicated technology of firearms put the balance of power on the side of the more complex city-based civilizations. After 1500 these civilizations took the offensive against the nomads. While the Europeans moved to "civilize" the pastoral corners of their own continent and the "Indian" nomads of the Americas, the new Russian state conquered its own eastern frontier and brought the Bible and the law to the very heart of the Eurasian steppe.

It would not be an exaggeration, then, to say that for most of human history (at least the first forty-five hundred of the last five thousand years) the causes of war have been the disparities between settled and nomadic styles of life. The lure of city luxuries and land has exerted an irresistible pull on the ambitions of nomadic warlords and the populations of pastoral society. Perhaps there is some hope that this chief cause of war has come to an end. There are no more barbarians at the gates. Even the conflicts of the American frontier between farmers and cattle herders, or between both and Native Americans, are a hundred years past.

But neither war nor violence has disappeared from our lives. Perhaps a closer look at the Roman Empire will help explain why.

THE ROMAN PHASE OF THE LONGEST WAR: SOME QUESTIONS

In 391 B.C. a band of nomads, called Gauls, under the chieftain Brennus defeated a small army of Roman patricians (or aristocrats) and proceeded to burn the town of Rome to the ground. Eight hundred years later (in A.D. 410 to be exact) a similar tribe of Goths, led by Alaric, destroyed the city of Rome again. These dates offer convenient markers for the beginning and end of Roman history. The greatness of Rome lies in its achievements during those eight hundred years: the town became an empire, which spread its laws, its culture, and its peace from North Africa to England; the capital city of this empire was secure; meanwhile the brutal life of the nomads changed very little. The tragedy is that after eight hundred years of work, Rome was just as vulnerable as it had been before. In fact, it was more vulnerable. The defeat in 391 B.C. had been a cause for revitalization and fantastic development. The defeat in 410 was followed by the "vandalization" of the city again in 455 by another tribe (the Vandals), the murder of the emperor and his son in 476, and the final transformation of the imperial city into pasture land for the herds of any invading tribe. Rome never recovered.

Why was Rome so successful at repelling the barbarians after the defeat of 391 B.C., and so unable to recover after eight hundred years of conquering and civilizing? Why did the imperial armies of the fifth century A.D. fail to provide the security that had been won by the inhabitants of a small town eight hundred years before? Part of the answer may lie with the barbarians themselves. It is possible that the invasions of the fifth century A.D. were much more severe than those of the fourth century B.C. But that is only speculation. We know very little about the earlier nomadic tribes. They left no records, because they could not write. Therefore, most of their activity is still a mystery to us.

It seems more useful to look at what had changed on the Roman side of the equation. The barbarians were always on the frontier. The Roman armies had always responded to their threat. For eight hundred years that response was successful. Then it failed. What had happened in Rome to cause that failure?

PATRICIAN RESPONSE: REPUBLICAN CONSTITUTION AND ARMY

First, what happened after the defeat in 391 B.C.? The invasion of the Gauls convinced the surviving Romans that radical changes were necessary in their military organization. The aristocratic army of patricians was clearly no match for the barbarian tribes, in which all men were warriors. A national citizen army that included the common people (called plebeians) seemed to be the only suitable response to the warrior tribes. The plebeians had previously been excluded from the military because they were not full citizens. Without full political rights, they could hardly be expected to give their lives for the city. But these plebeians had been excluded from full citizenship because they owned little or no land. As in other ancient city-states, the Roman patricians were not willing to trust political decisions to those who had no economic stake in the country.

Only a crisis—especially a military crisis—could force the Roman patricians to bring the plebeians into the army. In order to assure the loyalty of the army, these new soldiers had to be given some political and economic power as well. The total defeat of Rome was such a crisis. The egalitarian barbarian armies forced the Romans to democratize their own armies. The creation of a more democratic army meant the democratization of the society as well.

The changes were gradual, and by no means complete. Plebeians were made full citizens. All of the land-owning *assidui,* or "settled men" (patrician or plebeians), between the ages of seventeen and sixty-five were bound to answer the summons (called *classis,* from which the later meaning of "class" came) for military service. Even the landless men (called *proletarii*) were required to back up the army, and an attempt was made to distribute conquered territory to these landless men and poor plebeians.

According to the new constitution, the popular assembly passed the laws, decided questions of war and peace, and elected the consuls (the executives who were roughly equivalent to later presidents or prime ministers). Plebeians could even become consuls. Further, the officers of the older plebeian assembly, who were called tribunes, were given the right to veto some of the decisions of the whole popular assembly or its consuls.

Despite the maintenance of classes, and despite the existence of landless *proletarii,* the constitution that emerged after 390 B.C. meant a more egalitarian society with a more representative army than had ever existed before in hundreds of years of patrician rule in Rome. "It is certain," according to one historian, "that the new organization of the citizen-body infused fresh strength into the community. The common interest now came home to the heart of each citizen: he felt himself responsible for the state and its prosperity."

Essentially the army had become the people. Since they were all mobilized when war was declared, and since they were the ones who decided when to go to war, they had created the possibility of a peaceful society—able to defend themselves to the last man in the event of an emergency. But as the case of the barbarians (whose solution they had adopted) could show, a nation of warriors might become more accustomed to the discipline of war than the leisure of peace. When the state became the army, the nation could be one of citizens who were also emergency soldiers, or a nation of soldiers who were also part-time citizens. The Romans, like the barbarians, often behaved as a nation of soldiers.

PRESERVING INEQUALITY WITH FOREIGN LAND

The primacy of the army over the state had many causes. It is unlikely that the people simply preferred war to peace. But since the patricians were not about to distribute their own land to the plebeians, military conquest was the least painful way of increasing the citizen base of the army. The poor probably recognized that their own advancement depended on the spoils of war. The more democratic army was necessarily a more imperialistic one. The alternative of genuine economic equality at home may have seemed necessary during the bleak days after the Gauls' invasion, but the patrician class must have quickly recognized the possibility of an imperialistic, military state as an alternative.

Further, despite the constitutional changes, the patrician class always remained in pretty firm control of the government. Though the popular assembly was opened to plebeians, the votes of patricians were weighted more heavily by a complicated process of voting by groups. The wealthy comprised a majority of these groups, called "centuries," and each had one vote. Even this device was usually redundant. Plebeians usually voted for patricians anyway. Whether they were used to authority, or felt more secure with the "big names," or had learned the "chain of command" in their military training, the plebeians consistently elected patricians to be consuls. This was particularly significant because the consuls became increasingly important. (A cynic might say the consuls became more important because patricians were elected.) The consuls served for only a year, but it became customary for them, after that year, to enter an advisory group for future consuls. This group was called the senate. It had a long history as a committee of noble families. It had advised ancient kings as well as the consuls of the recent republic. The reforms that followed 390 B.C. were supposed to force the senate to share some of its power with the popular assembly. Actually, the senate became more and more entrenched as the government of the Roman state. The senate changed from a traditional informal advisory body to the formal legislative body of Rome. The popular assembly voted only on bills that were offered by the consuls, and the consuls offered only bills that had been approved by the senate.

To summarize, the Roman response to the invasion of 391 B.C., reflected in the constitutional developments of the fourth century B.C., was mixed. An attempt at democratization was made in land holding and in politics, but most radically in the army. The changes, however, did not constitute a revolution. The patricians tried to integrate enough of the population into the citizenry so that the army would be popular enough to defend Rome and increase her territory. But the patrician class retained its power. Roman expansion during the next centuries was its show. There was, though, always the implicit understanding that the plebeians would go on strike from military service if they were not satisfied with their role in politics. Such a strike in fact occurred in 287 B.C. Then the plebeians won an important concession: after they agreed to let the patrician-dominated popular assembly continue to decide matters of war and peace, their exclusively plebeian assemblies were given the authority to pass laws that had the same force as the laws of the popular assembly.

A ROMAN PEACE FOR ALL OF ITALY

From their defeat at the hands of the Gauls at the beginning of the fourth century B.C. to the middle of the third century B.C., the Romans conquered most of Italy. Though their conquests were not as defensive as they insisted (whose are?), the Romans were frequently viewed as the protectors of order and city life. They usually defended the more settled towns against the more nomadic and predatory tribes. Rome was the city to organize other Italian cities and populations in part because of its central location, but also because of its superior military.

Roman soldiers submitted themselves to more rigorous drill and stricter discipline than their neighbors. The power of the commander, which was called the *imperium*, was absolute during military campaigns. Soldiers who broke ranks or slept on sentry duty were executed. When a whole unit was guilty of serious misconduct the punishment of "decimation" (executing every tenth man) was sometimes employed. Warfare was not a sport, as it was for the aristocratic armies of other cities. It was for the Romans a business that tapped the resources of the entire society.

ROMAN EXPANSION
With each expansion of Roman boundaries came new neighbors, new defenses, and new potential enemies. Long before the actual empire under Augustus, Rome was a militarized society.

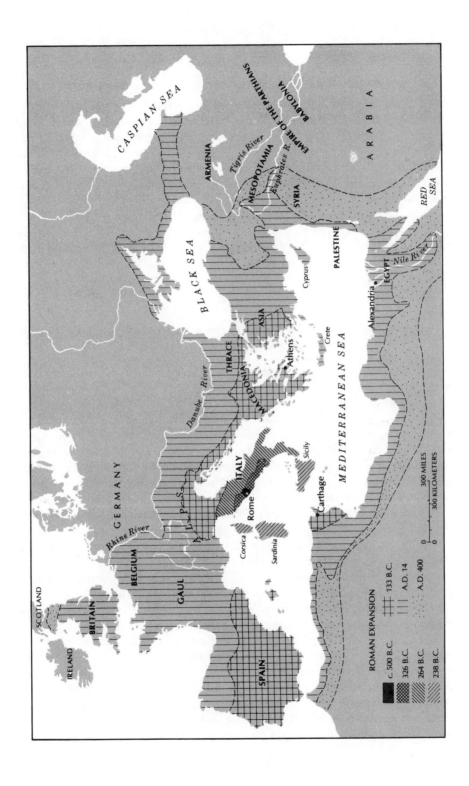

CASPIAN SEA

EMPIRE OF THE PARTHIANS

BABYLONIA

ARABIA

ARMENIA

Tigris River

MESOPOTAMIA

Euphrates R.

SYRIA

RED SEA

BLACK SEA

PALESTINE

Nile River

EGYPT

Alexandria

Cyprus

ASIA

Crete

THRACE

Athens

MACEDONIA

MEDITERRANEAN SEA

Danube River

A L P S

Sicily

ITALY

Rome

Carthage

GERMANY

Corsica

Sardinia

Rhine River

BELGIUM

GAUL

300 MILES

300 KILOMETERS

0

0

SCOTLAND

BRITAIN

IRELAND

SPAIN

ROMAN EXPANSION

c. 500 B.C.

326 B.C.

264 B.C.

238 B.C.

133 B.C.

A.D. 14

A.D. 400

Long before the Romans conquered all of Italy they had adequately secured the defense of their city. The wars after 287 B.C. (when the plebeian strike ended, giving the patricians effective authority over war and peace for sharing legislative authority with the plebeians on other matters) were increasingly directed against other empires rather than nomadic tribes. Rome's conquest of Italy was completed from 281 to 272 B.C. with the victory over the allies of the Greek Hellenistic Empire in southern Italy. But the conquest of Naples and Tarentum in southern Italy brought the Romans face to face with the Carthaginians in North Africa. Rome inherited the rivalries of the cities it conquered along with the conflict of all of southern Italy with the Carthaginians. While the Roman frontier had been a few miles from the city, it was necessary to defend the city only from the Celts, Gauls, and other tribes of central Italy. When the Roman boundaries became the Alps and the Mediterranean Sea, it seemed necessary to defend itself from Greece, Carthage, and the tribes of northern Europe.

NEW FRONTIERS MAKE NEW ENEMIES: CARTHAGE AND GREECE

From 262 to 146 B.C. Rome became occupied in continual wars with the Carthaginian and Greek empires. Later Roman historians were fond of viewing the first of these wars outside of Italy as an inevitable burden of Roman responsibility and as an essentially defensive war. The historian Polybius saw all of Roman history as the inevitable expansion of the divinely ordained Roman Empire (much as Americans later invoked "manifest destiny"—another type of divine inevitability). But Polybius and other Romans wanted it both ways: they wanted to believe that their expansion had been inevitable so that the Romans were blameless; but they also wanted to believe that their Roman ancestors had been more than passive tools of destiny. Therefore, they argued that each act of expansion was the product of "hard decisions" as well as of fate. They pointed out that each expansion brought Rome into contact with new enemies. They assumed that these new enemies had the will and the ability to conquer Rome (or a Roman province). Consequently, it was necessary—for defensive reasons—to strike first, or when the time was most propitious to Rome. Thus, these "defensive wars" were always blameless, since they merely worked the "inevitable" to the best interests of Rome, which (every Roman knew) was to the best interests of civilization.

The first war with Carthage (called the First Punic War) began in 264 B.C. because Rome had recently conquered all of Italy and was in a position to be concerned with Carthage in North Africa, Spain, and part of Sicily. According to the historian Polybius, the Romans feared that the Carthaginians were encircling Rome by threatening Sicily and "all of the coasts of Italy." Few Romans noted that Carthage had been unable to conquer all of Sicily after two hundred years, so that the likelihood of Carthage's conquering all of Italy was rather slight. A few more may have urged defensive precautions against a possible Carthaginian attack from Sicily. But the policy that won the day was an armed invasion of the island.

The war for Sicily dragged on for twenty-two years, from 262 to 241 B.C. The Romans built their first large fleet, conquered a number of Carthaginian cities in Sicily, and, intoxicated by their success, decided to end the war with one final blow. They decided to invade Carthage itself. Success in Sicily increased Roman ambitions and expanded their horizons for "preventive war." But just as success bred more war, so did failure. The Romans were not able to take Carthage, so they kept trying. At the same time, the Carthaginians realized that Rome was their implacable enemy. If the Carthaginians had never before given serious consideration to an invasion of Rome, they now had to mobilize for such a defensive war. Preparations continued after the temporary peace treaty in 241 B.C. that gave Sicily to Rome. The Carthaginian general Hamilcar increased Carthaginian control of Spain, and by 218 B.C. his son Hannibal was able to lead an army into Italy. That invasion, which lasted until 201 B.C., proved as indecisive as the Roman invasion of Carthage. It was possible to do a lot of damage to the countryside, but it was ridiculous to attempt to take the capital city. Hannibal, in fact, failed because the Roman armies harassed him, without confronting him, and the Carthaginian troops and their tribal allies were finally worn down.

The results of the two long wars with Carthage (from 264 to 201 B.C.) were that the Roman citizen army had become a well-trained professional machine, Rome had become a threat to other empires, the Roman senate had become supreme, and the people were tired. The first three results were the ones that mattered.

In 200 B.C. the senate, which had become a virtual dictatorship during the war against Hannibal, saw its chance to defeat the Greek Empire of Macedonia. The time seemed ripe because the king of Macedonia's allies were busy and the Roman war machine was so finely tuned. The fact that the centuries of the popular assembly had almost unanimously rejected the declaration of war made no difference to the senate. The tribune of the plebeians, Q. Baebius, accused the senators of "stirring up war after war to prevent the people ever tasting the fruits of peace." But the senate insisted, had the question restored to the agenda, and finally secured a favorable vote.

If earlier wars had been in any sense "defensive," the wars of the second century were unabashedly imperialistic. Macedonia (in 200 B.C. and in 146 B.C.) was not threatening Rome. There was some talk in the debate that preceded the declaration of war in 200 B.C. about defending the liberties of the smaller Greek city-states from Macedonia. But even that was a projection of a future possibility rather than an immediate threat. Rome had simply become involved in Greek affairs and wanted to prevent the rise of any strong power on its eastern flank. In a sense the wars of the previous century set the stage for further involvement. Between the first and second Punic wars, the Roman armies had pushed eastward in two Illyrian wars, which brought Roman power to the edge of Macedonia. One conquest led to another. Sometimes they would be called defensive, but after a while it did not matter.

After conquering Macedonia, Rome involved herself more and more deeply in Greek politics. For most of the first half of the second century B.C., the Romans were able to support the Macedonian upper class against lower-class movements that were both democratic and anti-Roman. Finally, a revolt of Macedonian "liberation forces" required Rome to govern the colony with her own governors and standing army—after they decisively defeated the rebels in 146 B.C. All of Greece was placed under Roman martial law, the rich commercial city of Corinth was destroyed, and its territory became the property of the Roman people.

The ancient city of Carthage was similarly destroyed in 146 B.C. without provocation. To put it differently, the best that can be said is that the rich wine, olive, and fig plantations of Carthage posed a potential economic threat to Roman landowners who were developing similar plantations in Italy. Roman historians found a sufficient explanation for the destruction of Carthage in a story they told about the leading statesman of the nationalist, landowning party returning from a trip to Carthage. Cato waved a bunch of figs at the Roman senate, recounted the improvements in Carthaginian agriculture since the last Roman-inflicted defeat in 201 B.C., and declared that the new birth of this prosperous state must be aborted.

The landowning class was in charge of the senate, and the senate was supreme. They voted the death sentence for Carthage, and sent Scipio Aemilianus, the general who had just destroyed Numantia, as executioner. Carthage was destroyed. Most of the population was massacred. The territory of Carthage became Rome's African province, and the land was leased to the wealthy landowners back home.

THE FRUITS OF EMPIRE AT HOME

In a little more than a half a century, Rome had expanded from a coalition of Italian cities into a Mediterranean empire. Her provinces included North Africa, the previous Carthaginian colonies in Spain, all of the former Greek city-states and kingdoms, and (after 133 B.C.) the Asian empire of Pergamum (Turkey today). The fever of empire had become epidemic. The riches of former empires poured into Rome. This accumulated treasure of centuries, the vast land holdings for Roman agriculture, the investment opportunities for Roman businesses, the graft for Roman governors, and the booty for Roman troops were enough to keep the Roman people occupied for another couple of hundred years. They paid for more Roman wars and more provinces. They financed an elaborate material civilization in Rome. But such wholesale banditry was inevitably shortsighted. Relations with the drained provinces deteriorated. Romans learned to rely more on booty than on innovation. War became the governor of Roman politics, and the army its kingpin. And, perhaps most significantly, the Roman people were forced to trade political participation for trinkets: the plebeians lost their farms, their leaders, their political power, their citizen army, and their concern.

It may seem at least slightly absurd to date the decline of the Roman Empire from this half-century of expansion (from 201 to 146 B.C.), since the empire did not replace the republic for another century and a half and the empire survived for four hundred years after that. But, in this brief period the events were set in motion that made both an emperor necessary and the empire inherently unstable. The empire was, after all, created in this period. Its only further extensions were into barbarian lands in northern Europe—and that cost more than it was worth. The empire was, itself, the cause of Rome's downfall. Its immediate effect in the next hundred years was internal war. Class wars, civil wars, and wars between Romans and Italians were the fruits of the empire. This violence could be controlled (and some peace restored) by the addition of actual emperors, but the root problems were never solved. Rather than dwell on the long agony, let's look at what the empire did to the Roman Republic.

We have already dropped some clues: the lack of any pretenses about "defensive war" after 200 B.C.; the rise of the landowners and the senate; Cato waving the figs. There are some other clues as to what was happening in Rome. Between 230 and 130 B.C. the population of adult male citizens rose from 270,000 to only 317,000—an insignificant increase, considering the expansion of Roman territory. (Compare American population increases in a century of similar expansion. Better yet, imagine the crack troops of something like "the army of the Swiss people" taking over all of Europe, occupying every city from London to Rome, and then looking for troops to send back to Switzerland.) Roman population did not increase at anything like the rate that would have been necessary to maintain even the semblance of a citizen army. There were simply not enough Romans to go around.

To make matters worse, the wealthy senators were not willing to open the Roman army and politics to loyal allies—even those in Italy who were citizens of non-Roman cities or tribes. As in the past, these Italian allies were expected to fight when called by the Roman government, but since they had no voice in declaring war or peace they had little direct interest in a military campaign. The Italian armies were not much more Roman than those of the Greek kingdoms that had assisted the Roman legions in their Asian campaigns.

Not only did Roman citizenship—the basis of the citizen army—increase too slowly to govern an empire, but the character of the citizenry changed as well. The poor and the plebeians were increasingly excluded. The money that poured from the conquered provinces went to those who were already wealthy. Some of it went to the generals and officers of the senatorial class. Some went to the rising business class, which had profited from military contracts. The safest investment for this new money was in buying and developing the huge tracts of land that came to the "Roman people," but were administered, leased, and sold by the officers of the senate.

Wealthy Romans were able to buy counties, even countries, of land for the reasonable prices that their friends in the senate set. The Roman treasury could, thus, turn its new possessions into the cash necessary for government, "defense," and more wars. And everyone was happy: everyone, that is, except the Roman poor, the Italian allies, and the subject foreigners.

The foreigners streamed into Rome as conquered slaves or propertyless noncitizens. Eager for work, they were a cheap source of labor for the agricultural plantations that the wealthy Roman landowners bought. Even former Roman citizens were forced to sell their small farms (which had been neglected after years of war) and become tenants on the new large estates. Others gave up their failing farms for the hope of a job in the city. They too gave up their citizenship (which had become almost worthless anyway) and their military service (which had become an intolerable burden) when they gave up their farms.

In many ways the Roman Republic of 150 B.C. looked more like the declining empire hundreds of years later than like the republic of small landholders a hundred years before. The large estates were devoted more and more to commercial crops. Foreign lands were converted to grain production, while the Romans converted their own lands to the much more profitable production of wine, olives, and figs. (This was the context of Cato's demand for the destruction of Carthage.) The change in landholding meant a change in the army. The senatorial families still provided generals who were eager for honors, governorships, and an armed following. Increasingly they recruited their armies from the poor and uprooted with the promise of booty from foreign wars. As long as they were successful, their armies belonged to them. In 88 B.C. the first of a long chain of these armies marched on Rome itself, and took over the government for its general.

RADICAL REFORM REJECTED

There were a couple of attempts to change the drift toward private armies of paid professional soldiers and the unequal land ownership that made it necessary. One radical reformer, Tiberius Gracchus, a tribune in 133 B.C. with impeccable aristocratic credentials, attempted to win some support in the senate for the idea of military reform. A slave revolt helped underline the problem of a large slave population on the estates, and it was clear to many that the citizen army had been preferable to hired troops. In an attempt to revive the citizen army Tiberius proposed a plan for distributing lands to the displaced peasants who were now tenants on the estates or city *proletarii*. He also proposed shorter military terms so that the people could remain their own soldiers without becoming too attached to war or too absent from their farms. Finally, he urged that the allies in Italy be admitted to citizenship. None of these proposals were popular in the senate. In fact they were so unpopular that Tiberius was murdered, and the senate justified the act as a suppression of a rebellion. Ten years later, Tiberius's younger brother, Gaius

Gracchus, proposed a similar plan for extending land and citizenship, with added urgency and support. This time the senate found it necessary to justify the massacre of over three thousand of the Gracchi followers as part of a "state of war." Then, to divert popular attention from the critical issues raised by the Gracchi, the senate embarked on another series of foreign wars.

The conquest of new territory in North Africa and Gaul (France) in the last quarter of the second century B.C. only intensified the problems. The senate became more venal and dictatorial. The landed ruling class increased its holdings at the expense of the poor. Businessmen, tax collectors, contractors, governors, and generals milked the provinces. The army lost any vestiges of a popular base. Everyone was out for spoils, but the plebeians and allies got the least.

In the midst of these wars, the morale of the allies and peasants who were still called for military service deteriorated to the point of mass desertions. The senate was forced to call on a popular leader, Marius, to put a final end to the myth of a citizen militia and openly to recruit a standing army from the Roman poor. Marius created his professional army with promises of pay and land. To meet these promises he attempted to revive the Gracchi program. The senate refused. Its refusal meant that the standing army they wanted would have to be paid (like everything else) on a "commission basis" through conquest. The same was true for the army of Lucius Cornelius Sulla, a general who supported the interests of the landowners.

PRIVATE ARMIES AND CIVIL WAR

When the Gracchi plans were rejected by the senate, the Italian allies declared war on Rome—first for citizenship, and then for equality. The senate sent the armies of Sulla against them. (Marius was loyal but suspect.) By 88 B.C. the three-year war had become a devastating standoff. The allies were given citizenship for laying down their arms, and Sulla's troops lost the hope of the allied lands in southern Italy. They needed land. A war with Mithradates, the Iranian king of Pontus in northern Asia Minor, loomed as their opportunity. But the popular assembly gave the campaign to Marius. Sulla marched on Rome. The ensuing century of civil wars destroyed everything that was left of the citizen republic.

Sulla, like Marius for a short time before him, brought order to Rome with a vengeance. Thousands were tortured and executed. Whole towns were leveled. Cicero later wrote that he "saw the severed heads of senators displayed in the streets of Rome."

After the deaths of Marius and Sulla the struggle continued. The soldiers of their armies were no longer farmers who needed land. They had known war too long to remember how to run a farm. There were two armies of soldiers in Rome who needed work. The only work they knew was fighting. To keep the fighting outside of Italy, they had to be sent on long campaigns into Gaul, Spain, Africa, or the East. Despite their disagreements with him, Pompey was the most loyal general the impotent senate could expect. He trusted them enough (and abhorred civil war enough) to disband his troops on entering Rome. The senate took advantage of Pompey's weakness and, forgetting its own, refused to pay his troops. In effect it asked that future generals make their own senates when they had the army to do so. Julius Caesar learned that lesson well. After a campaign in Gaul, he marched on Rome and concentrated the government in his own hands.

The senate no longer governed. By remaining a club for wealthy Roman patricians, it had lost control of the allies and the mass of Roman citizens and *proletarii*. Without the support of any of these groups it could not hope to control an army. A few senators, like Cassius and Brutus, thought they might regain senatorial initiative by killing Caesar. But Caesar had made the government so completely his own that his assassination resulted in a round of civil wars between his own followers: his lieutenant Antony and his adopted son Octavian. The fact that Caesar could designate Octavian as his heir to the government shows his contempt for the senate and its constitution. Octavian had to win his title by defeating the armies of Antony, but when he became the emperor Augustus, Caesar's contempt was justified.

EMPIRE AND EPITAPH

The imperial period of Roman history from 27 B.C. to A.D. 476 was marked by alternating rhythms of chaos and repression. The high point was the reign of the first emperor, Octavian, who was called Augustus. The previous century of civil war had been so debilitating that most Romans and allies willingly gave up freedom for order. Augustus was able to provide peace throughout most of the empire. He was even able to reduce the size of the army by half. But the army became the emperor's personal property, and he gave them land from his personal possessions (among which was Egypt). Augustus decked himself in the trappings of an oriental monarch. The class divisions that had become so great in the preceding centuries were formalized by special symbols to be worn by the senators.

Augustus was followed on his death in A.D. 14 by his stepson (in proper monarchial style) Tiberius. After a wave of violence and assassinations, Tiberius died a madman in A.D. 37, much to the relief of most of his subjects. The next six emperors from 37 to 69 all died by murder or suicide, the last four in the year 68–69 alone.

In 69 Vespasian inaugurated a new line of emperors, reigning until 96, who were not Roman but Italian. Vespasian was able to restore some of the order of Augustus without resorting to an openly military dictatorship. The "five good emperors" that followed from 96 to 180 were actually able to extend the boundaries of the empire slightly, end the worst offenses practiced in the previous century, and restore

Both the public and the underlying meanings of a Roman Empire are unintentionally presented on the top and bottom of the beautiful Gemma Augustea, which was carved in onyx about A.D. 10 to commemorate a victory of Tiberius (who descends from the chariot at the top left). The majestic top panel, where the stars of Capricorn and the goddess Roma sanction the coronation of Augustus, rests above the panel of Roman soldiers taking prisoners and erecting a trophy. Renowned works of art like the Gemma Augustea were also, in a sense, trophies of empire. (Kunsthistorisches Museum)

some confidence with continued peace. But the last of these, Marcus Aurelius, faced renewed frontier warfare that (along with plague and famine) sapped all of his strength.

The year 192, like 68–69, saw four emperors. One was the tool of the palace guard, beheaded by them when he stepped out of line; another was a wealthy senator who was the highest bidder for the crown. From then on the crown was the prize of the strongest army.

With the reign of Septimius Severus (193–211), the emperor became (without pretensions) the ruling general. "Pamper the army," he told his son, "and despise the rest." Septimius institutionalized the military changes of prior centuries. He outflanked possible Roman rivals by drawing the army from the provinces. By considerably increasing the size and pay of the army he made defense possible but aggravated the heavy tax burden. His son Caracalla (211–217) finally gave citizenship to all free persons in the empire in 212—long after citizenship had ceased to mean anything.

For the rest of the third century the empire was a shambles. From 235 to 285 a total of twenty-six emperors were put up and pulled down by plundering armies. The frontiers no longer held back the nomads. The riches of past campaigns had been exhausted. Whole provinces declared their independence. Rome itself was threatened. Aurelian (270–275) found it necessary to build a wall around the city.

Two Illyrians (the Roman province of Illyria is now Yugoslavia) postponed the inevitable. They were the emperors Diocletian (284–305) and Constantine (306–337). They divided the empire in two—the Western Empire and the Eastern Empire—and secured the more defensible eastern half for themselves. For defense against the barbarians they relied almost exclusively on barbarian armies. They further increased the bureaucracy to collect taxes and pay the army.

The Eastern Empire was able to survive. The capital city, Byzantium (Constantinople after 330), was almost impregnable. But Rome, capital of the Western Empire, was no more defensible than the barbarian frontiers. Its population was depleted, its money was debased, its treasures had been converted to huge plantations, hordes of slaves, and barbarian troops, and there was no one around who much cared if it remained. Augustine, the church father, was shocked when Alaric sacked Rome in 410, but Augustine was in North Africa, and he was much more concerned with "the city of God."

Perhaps the chief problem was that the government in Rome gave the mass of people no reason to be loyal. Hundreds of years after Romans had forgotten that the Roman Republic and its army belonged to the people, Constantine tried desperately to provide a new basis of loyalty with Christianity. But the new religion was more of an admission of the people's desperation. Its very popularity was a sign that many people felt that the "city of man" was of little importance.

After Alaric's invasion few Romans thought seriously of rebuilding their city, as the Roman citizens had eight hundred years before. The imperial city had become one of the two tax collector's offices. It symbolized the oppression as much as the majesty of the empire. Pope Leo I is said to have somehow persuaded Attila and the Huns to leave the city alone, but it is most likely that it offered much less to Attila (especially after Alaric) than the surrounding countryside. A century later the great emperor Justinian of the Eastern Empire (also an Illyrian) attempted to reorganize the remains of the Western Empire, but he found the northern Italian city of Ravenna more suitable than the ancient capital. By the time Rome was not worth ravaging (for Attila) or regaining (for Justinian), it could hardly be worth saving or rebuilding.

CHINA AND ROME

The history of China in the classical period demonstrates some striking similarities to that of Rome. The Chinese Empire was created about the same time as the Roman, the third century B.C. It was wrestled from the same nomadic barbarians of the Eurasian steppe, held about as long, and then succumbed to the barbarians about the same time, the third century A.D.

The Chinese Empire also underwent the same major internal change that the Roman Empire experienced. It too began as a society of relatively equal property holders who were soldiers but through excessive military service lost their lands to wealthy aristocrats. The results of that social transformation were also similar. Like the replacement of the early Roman Republic by the Roman Empire under Augustus, the popular Former Han dynasty was replaced by the aristocracy-dominated Later Han dynasty in the first century A.D. Both later empires had to depend increasingly on barbarian troops to police the barbarian frontier because the class of independent farmer-soldiers had virtually disappeared. How did this occur in China?

QIN CHINA

The Chinese Empire dates from the beginning of the Qin [Ch'in] dynasty, which first unified and gave its name to most of the area we know today as China. But the Qin was a brief dynasty (221–206 B.C.) and was immediately followed by the much more successful Former Han (202 B.C.–A.D. 8) and Later Han (A.D. 25–220).

Like Rome, the state of Qin expanded from a small area around its capital city in 500 B.C. to control much of China by 221 B.C. Its success over numerous rival states was due to a number of factors. Its far western location (like that of the earlier Zhou [Chou] dynasty) put it in close contact with the steppe nomads of central Asia. As a result, the Qin were particularly attentive to matters of defense and the development of a military that would be loyal to the state instead of to the numerous feudal lords that dominated the countryside in the late Zhou period. Thus, they created a class of free peasantry (farmers) who were given their own land in return for taxes and military service to the state. In conquered areas, peasants were removed from the control of aristocrats whose lands were broken up and given to the peasant-soldiers. In some respects this policy was the idea of the philosophers of legalism, Lord Shang (d. 333 B.C.) and Han Fei Zi [Han Fei Tzu] (d. 233 B.C.), who argued for the consolidation of state power over the nobility by means of taxes, laws, and the creation of a centralized bureaucracy. The Qin expansion was also made easier by the improvement of roads and communications. To give just one example, the state of Lu increased the average distance of a diplomatic mission from 112 to 454 miles between the eighth and sixth centuries. But the resemblance of the Qin policy of establishing a free landed peasantry to that of the Romans after their military crisis of the fourth century suggests broader origins. In both cases, the small states expanded by imitating the rude equality of the nomadic tribes with iron weapons and trained cavalries. The technology of iron mandated a highly motivated, well-trained army of citizens or loyal subjects.

Before the introduction into China of the mounted archer from the Central Asian steppe in the fourth century B.C., Chinese warfare had an aristocratic quality. Peasants were killed in great numbers, as always, but their infantry formations required no special training. In the Spring and Autumn period (722–481 B.C.) and the Warring States period (403–211 B.C.), when the Qin were gaining ascendancy, warfare was common and accepted but governed by elaborate rules of aristocratic politeness (very much like the later chivalry of European feudalism). The story of the battle of Zhengpu [Ch'eng-p'u] in 632 B.C., a decisive early battle for the Qin, is introduced in the historical source the *Zao Zhuan* [*Tso-chuan*] with a message from the commander of Chu to the marquis of Qin that was pure chivalry. "I request a game with your men. Your lordship may lean on the cross-board of your carriage and look on, and I too will observe." Another story describes the confrontation of the chariots of a son of the duke of Song and an opponent. The opponent swiftly fired an arrow that just missed the Duke and was drawing his bow to fire another when the duke cried out, "If you don't give me my turn to shoot, you are a base fellow." To show he was a gentleman, his opponent held his fire, and the duke shot him dead.[1]

In the fourth century B.C., two new weapons were introduced that made warfare more complicated and more expensive. They were the mounted archer and the crossbow. The mounted archer originated among the nomads. While the Qin were able to raise horses and train cavalries, at some considerable expense, they were never as adept as the nomads, who were practically born on horses. Mounted archers could move swiftly and maneuver easily, even over difficult terrain. They were far more threatening than chariots, which easily overturned if pushed too hard. The Chinese invention of the crossbow provided a match for the mobile archer. It was accurate at a longer distance but could not be shot from a moving horse or chariot. As the Qin applied these new military techniques to its process of state building and expansion, it relied increasingly on the construction of defensive walls. Crossbows directed from a protected wall could prove a match for invading horsemen. The Qin dynasty's building of territorial walls, leading eventually to the construction of the Great Wall, required conscripted labor in addition to the military service of cavalry, infantry, and crossbowmen.

As the Qin Empire expanded in the third and fourth centuries B.C., it experienced the same problems as the Roman Empire. The increasingly distant boundaries required greater and more permanent policing, and the burden fell increasingly on those who could not afford to retain their farms because of taxation, military, and labor service. These problems were aggravated in both cases by the growth of a class of wealthy merchants and landowners who could avoid taxation and service for themselves and offer jobs to the displaced. "These days," Zhao Cuo [Chao Ts'o] said early in the second century B.C.,

> a family of five peasants will have at least two persons who are liable for labour-services and conscription. . . . When the time comes that the taxes must be met, those who own something sell it off at half price; and those who own nothing borrow at doubled rates of interest. It is for this reason that some dispose of their lands and houses, and sell their children and grandchildren to redeem their debts.[2]

As in Rome, latifundia, huge estates owned by merchants and aristocrats but run by tenants or slaves, threatened to swallow up the free peasant-soldiers. According to a modern historian:

> Action thus became necessary to preserve the free peasantry as the source of the state's money and manpower. It was also desirable to weaken both the merchants, many of whom had acquired estates rather after the manner of the Italian businessmen in and after the second century B.C., and the regional aristocracy, some of whom had rebelled.[3]

In Rome this attempt at land distribution was carried out by a series of popular movements, most noticeably those of the Gracchi brothers, toward the end of the second century B.C. As we have seen, those attempts failed, so that by the first century B.C. the urban proletariat could demand only grain, having lost any hope or memory of growing their own. In China the political situation was quite different. The state was not the agency of the aristocracy or merchant class, as the Roman senate was. The Chinese emperor was an independent force, eager to curtail the powers of the regional aristocracy.

FORMER HAN DYNASTY REFORM

Thus, Emperor Wu (140–85 B.C.) of the Han dynasty took a series of drastic steps. He convicted 127 of the 197 Han princes and nobles of crimes or declared that they were without legitimate heirs and therefore confiscated their lands. He took houses, slaves, and cash from wealthy merchants, so that "most of the merchants of the middle grade and above were ruined."[4] The state became the largest landowner. Public lands were given to the poor, to those who had lost their farms, and to reward officials. "When commoners reach twenty years of age they receive land, and when they are sixty return it," the *Han History* declared, though modern historians do not think such a practice was institutionalized.[5] New taxes were imposed on the merchants. Those who violated the new laws were imprisoned. Rebellious noble families were slaughtered. State monopolies in salt, iron, and wine were established. Government bureaucrats were now selected from the lower ranks of society. A university was established to train candidates for the government entrance examinations. Finally, Emperor Wu attempted to decrease the military burden. He observed:

> In the early years of the Han dynasty, there was an increasing number of incursions into China by the four kinds of barbarians. If I had not changed this, later generations would have been helpless. If I had not sent armies out on punitive expeditions, the empire would not now be at peace. But, if one does these things, one cannot avoid putting a heavy burden on the people. If later generations repeat what I have done, they will be following in the footsteps of the ruined dynasty of Qin.[6]

If Emperor Wu had been entirely successful, we would not hear of the need to repeat his efforts in later years. In fact, however, the dispossession of the peasantry and the need for land redistribution became a constant theme in the Han dynasty. These efforts culminated with Wang Mang, the usurper who ended the Former Han dynasty. An energetic revolutionary, much like Julius Caesar, he implemented a sweeping program that reunited the forces of the old aristocracy against him. Wang's program was described in the *Han History*. Under the Qin, he said, "the accumulation of property began. Greed and vice came into being. The powerful counted their fields in thousands, while the weak had not even the space to insert the point of an awl." The Han, he continued, reduced the land tax to one-thirtieth, but that had little meaning for the peasants who had become tenants and had to pay their landlord half of their crop. The dogs and horses of the rich ate better than poor peasants, he said. What would he do?

> Henceforth, the land of the empire shall be designated 'The King's Land'. Slaves shall be styled 'private dependents'. Neither may be bought or sold. Families with less than eight male members, but with more than twelve acres of farmland each, shall divide up the surplus and give it to rural groups of nine neighboring families. Thus, in accordance with this system, those without land are now to receive it.[7]

Wang Mang's short-lived Xin [Hsin] dynasty (A.D. 9–23) was no more successful than Caesar's triumvirate. His land redistribution measure was abandoned two years after it was passed. Nor was he able to reduce the military presence on the frontiers. He waged an aggressive campaign against the Huns on the frontier with an army of over three hundred thousand men. But the diversion of manpower from the farms to the frontier was partially responsible, along with the disastrous change in the course of the Yellow River, for famine and peasant rebellions that toppled Wang Mang.

LATER HAN DYNASTY REACTION

In A.D. 25 a coalition of aristocratic families was able to return a member of the Han family as a representative of the large landowners. This later Han dynasty remained true to its founders. Local strongmen ruled as feudal lords, and those few remaining free peasant families became tenants and slaves on the large estates. The system of peasant military conscription collapsed around A.D. 46. From then on Han armies had to rely on mercenary volunteers, personal armies of local lords, released convicts, and barbarian auxiliaries. Such barbarian auxiliaries were decisive in the campaigns against the Huns in the first century A.D. and on at least one occasion, in A.D. 27, were used to quell an internal rebellion of Chinese peasants. Increasingly peasant rebellions became as threatening as barbarian incursions. The peasant uprising of the Yellow Turbans in A.D. 184 tore the country apart so that the Han dynasty ruled in name only until its final demise in A.D. 220.

THIRD-CENTURY CRISIS

Whether or not there was a renewed series of barbarian incursions in the third century A.D., the internal cohesion of the Chinese and Roman empires deteriorated rapidly. The Han Empire was replaced by three kingdoms, and the Roman Empire was divided into Eastern and Western dominions. The unity of both empires was threatened with feudalism as well as invasion. Powerful lords of rich landed estates dominated both China and Rome. A Chinese account can stand for both:

> The mansions of the great landowners stretch in rows by the hundred, their opulent domains cover the whole countryside, their slaves can be counted by the thousand, and their clients by tens of thousands. Dealers and merchants move about in their boats and carts in all directions, and the piled-up stocks of speculators fill the towns. The grandest houses are not big enough to contain all their jewels and gems; the hills and valleys are not wide enough to contain all the horses, oxen, sheep, and pigs.[8]

By the third century, the Chinese and Roman empires had become full of vast private estates with personal armies, indifferent to the central government. In earlier times an Emperor Wu or Wang or a Gaius Gracchus might have threatened to divide the great estates and redistribute the land to the poor. But that was no longer feasible. There had to be another way to secure taxes and raise an army in a world dominated by such large economic units.

CAO CAO AND DIOCLETIAN

Two soldier emperors of the third century devised similar means to prevent the fragmentation of their empires into battlefields of feudal lords and barbarians. They were Cao Cao [Ts'ao Ts'ao], the Chinese soldier-poet who founded the state of Wei while imagining himself the last Han, and the Roman emperor Diocletian, who founded the Eastern Roman Empire, which became Byzantium. Both revived the growth of their states by dominating the large estates, instead of trying to break them up.

Cao Cao instituted "state colony lands," public versions of the huge private estates, from which taxes could be collected, and "military households" from which state armies could be directed. Together, they enrolled half of the inhabitants of the state. Excessive private lands were confiscated and added to the state colonies. Private armies were ordered to become part of the military households. When a commander of a private army refused to allow his men to be enlisted in the state system, the magnate himself was conscripted.

Diocletian faced similar problems as Roman emperor from A.D. 284 to 305. Between 235 and 284 there had been no fewer than twenty Roman emperors sanctioned by the senate. Unable to govern the Roman Empire as a single entity, he divided administration in half, taking control of the Eastern half himself and appointing a coemperor for the West. He ensured continuity and coordination by appointing subordinates for each emperor. He created an imperial bureaucracy that limited the power of the great estates. Without taking them over, he practically bound people to their farms and towns, set wages and prices, and ensured the collection of taxes. He also doubled the size of the army, reorganized it, and improved the pay and promotion system.

Many historians have been critical of Diocletian. "The new Roman army was no longer a Roman army," the historian Rostovtzeff has written. "It was a special caste, maintained at the expense of the population to fight foreign enemies."[9] But, according to another historian, M. I. Finley, "the plain fact about Diocletian's reign, whether we like it or not, is that it was a success. He saved the Roman Empire so completely that in the east it lived on, much along the lines he laid down, for more than a thousand years—for Diocletian may properly be called the first Byzantine emperor. How many states in history have had a longer life?"[10]

The answer to that question is "One: China." After A.D. 280 the state of Wei was taken over by the Sima [Ssu-ma] family, which assumed the dynastic title of Jin [Chin] and reunified China. Cao Cao's system of state colonies was dismantled, but its influence continued. Land that had been "state colony land" was retained as state land and allocated for political purposes. Private land was still subject to limitations of size and higher taxes. While later historians sometimes said that the Jin land system did not work well, the failure seems to have been its large number of exemptions rather than the application of the system itself.

EMPIRES, STATES, AND LANDED ESTATES

The early Roman and Chinese empires rested on armies of peasant-soldiers. These were practicable as long as the empires were relatively small and did not require full-time policing. As long as farmers could return to planting and harvesting, or as long as they were called away only for special purposes of defense, the system worked well. Motivation was high because they were protecting their own lands, families, and neighbors. Society in the early Roman Republic and Former Han was also relatively egalitarian.

Two factors conspired to undermine the balance. One was the ever-present, but ever-changing, barbarian side of the equation. The other was the growth of large landed estates and the displacement of the class of small independent farmers. A wealthy class of merchants and aristocrats was able to use its power to avoid taxation and military service for itself and turn formerly independent farmers into tenants, clients, serfs, and slaves. Thus, military needs or ambitions undermined the older system of recruitment and led to the formation of other forms of armies: private feudal, professional mercenary, and barbarian auxiliary. These fragmented the power of the state and relinquished the edge that the state had had over the barbarians. Unchecked, the new social system led to anarchy or feudalism. Both came in the third century to Western Rome, where feudalism remained for over five hundred years. Eastern Rome and China fared differently. They were able to revive the process of state building by seizing control of the large estates and basing state power on them. As a result, they were agrarian states in which the emperor controlled the land and the army, and the nobility came to court. The aristocracies remained significant forces, especially in China, but they stayed subordinate to the emperor.

Western Rome had many more large estates than Eastern Rome. These lords were able to retain their powers in the absence of a Diocletian or Constantine, and possibly as a result of a different barbarian presence. In any case, state formation was delayed in the West until about A.D. 1000. Then when states formed, they developed on a different social base than those of Byzantium and China. They received their greatest support in the emerging cities, from the class of city dwellers rather than landed aristocrats. The result was the growth of urban, burger, or middle-class states in Western Europe that were quite different from those elsewhere.

FOR FURTHER READING

The work of Mikhail Rostovtzeff, the great social and economic historian of Rome, is now a bit dated, fifty years after first publication, but students can still do well with his *Social and Economic History of the Roman Empire* in two volumes and his shorter *Rome*. The economic emphasis of his interpretations of Roman expansion has been challenged by

Tenny Frank in *Roman Imperialism* (up to the second century B.C.) and by E. Badian in *Roman Imperialism in the Late Republic* (for the later period). M. I. Finley has challenged his anti-Soviet agenda in *Aspects of Antiquity*. Finley's *The Ancient Economy* is also a useful introduction, as is *The Economic Decline of Empires,* edited by Carlo Cipolla.

On the Roman army we have the recent *The Making of the Roman Army: From Republic to Empire* by Lawrence Keppie and (for the later period) *The Roman Imperial Army* by Graham Webster. G. R. Watson's *The Roman Soldier* is also valuable. More general studies of Roman social history are P. A. Brunt's *Social Conflicts in the Roman Republic* and Ramsay MacMullen's *Roman Social Relations: 50 B.C. to A.D. 284.*

The student who wishes to go beyond some of the issues raised in this chapter in Roman history should also be aware of the multivolume *The Cambridge Ancient History* and the earlier multivolume classics T. Mommsen's *The History of Rome* and Edward Gibbon's *The History of the Decline and Fall of the Roman Empire.* There are also some good shorter, specialized studies of Roman history: H. H. Scullard's *From the Gracchi to Nero: A History of Rome from 133 B.C. to A.D. 68,* Michael Grant's *The World of Rome,* Lily Ross Taylor's *Party Politics in the Age of Caesar,* Ronald Syme's *The Roman Revolution,* and the highly interpretive *The Romans* by R. H. Barrow.

On China, we have found Mark Elvin's *The Pattern of the Chinese Past* extremely valuable. Herrlee G. Creel's *The Origins of Statecraft in China,* vol. 1, concentrates on the Western Zhou [Chou] but has interesting things to say about later periods, including comparisons of Roman and Chinese attitudes toward the military. *Chinese Civilization and Bureaucracy* by Etienne Balazs has a number of essays relevant to this subject. A good general history is Jacques Gernet's *A History of Chinese Civilization.*

Other valuable studies that deal with the subject of this chapter are Cho-yun Hsu's *Han Agriculture: The Formation of Early Chinese Agrarian Economy,* the same author's *Ancient China in Transition,* Ying-shih Yu's *Trade and Expansion in Han China,* and N. L. Swann's *Food and Money in Ancient China.* More specialized are Pan Ku's *History of the Former Han Dynasty* and the same author's *Wang Mang: A Translation of the Official Account of His Rise to Power.* The former is also available in an abridged form as *Courtier & Commoner in Ancient China: Selections from the History of Former Han by Pan Ku,* translated by Burton Watson. Students should also be familiar with the work of the great historian of Han China Sima Qian [Ssu-ma Chien], *Records of the Grand Historian of China,* two volumes, also available as Burton Watson's *Ssu-ma Ch'ien: Grand Historian of China.*

NOTES

1. The *Zao Zhuan* is a fourth-century B.C. account based, in part, on the earlier *Spring and Summer Annals,* traditionally attributed to Confucius. These selections are from the discussion of the military in Herrlee G. Creel, *The Origins of Statecraft in China,* vol. 1 (Chicago: University of Chicago Press, 1970), pp. 258–259.
2. Cited in Mark Elvin, *The Pattern of the Chinese Past* (Stanford: Stanford University Press, 1973), p. 28.
3. *Ibid.,* pp. 28–29.
4. *Ibid.,* p. 29, quoting *Han History.*

5. *Ibid.,* p. 30.
6. *Ibid.,* pp. 29–30.
7. *Ibid.,* p. 31, adapted.
8. Cited in Etienne Balazs, *Chinese Civilization and Bureaucracy* (New Haven: Yale University Press, 1964), p. 219.
9. Mikhail Rostovtzeff, *Social and Economic History of the Roman Empire,* vol. 1 (Oxford: Oxford University Press, 1957), p. 468.
10. M. I. Finley, *Aspects of Antiquity* (New York: Viking, 1969), p. 149.

Chronological Table of
The Classical World
1000 B.C.–A.D. 500

Greece and Rome	Middle East and Africa	India	China
Trojan War c. 1200 B.C.	*Genesis* 850–500 B.C.		Zhou dynasty 1027–256 B.C.
Homer c. 700 B.C.	Zoroaster and Hebrew Prophets 650–550 B.C.	*Mahabharata* c. 600–300 B.C.	Lao Zi c. 600 B.C.
	Persian Empire of Cyrus and Darius 550–486 B.C.	Buddha c. 500 B.C.	Confucius 551–479 B.C.
Socrates 469–399 B.C.			Warring States Period c. 463–222 B.C.
Plato 427–347 B.C.			
Rome sacked by Gauls 391 B.C.			
Aristotle 384–322 B.C.			Mencius 372–298 B.C.
Alexander 356–323 B.C.	Alexandria f. 331 B.C.	Mauryan dynasty 321–183 B.C.	
First Punic War 264–241 B.C.	Parthian Empire of Persia 248 B.C.–A.D. 224	Ashoka 269–232 B.C.	Rise of Chinese state and first Chinese Empire:
Second Punic War 218–201 B.C.		Political fragmentation c. 184 B.C.–A.D. 320 and development of salvation (Mahayana) Buddhism	Qin dynasty 221–206 B.C.
			Former Han dynasty 202 B.C.–A.D. 8
Third Punic War 149–146 B.C.			

c. = circa (about)   d. = died   f. = founded   r. = ruled

Greece and Rome	Middle East and Africa	India	China
Julius Caesar 102–44 B.C.			Emperor Wu 140–86 B.C.
Augustus r. 27 B.C.–A.D. 14	Jesus c. 3 B.C.–A.D. 30		Wang Mang A.D. 9–23
Ovid 43 B.C.–A.D. 17			
Petronius d. A.D. 66			Later Han dynasty A.D. 25–220
Pliny A.D. 61–113	Romans destroy Jerusalem A.D. 70		Buddhism entered China c. A.D. 100
	Bantu migration in sub-Saharan Africa A.D. 100–500	Kanishka r. c. A.D. 90–110	Paper invented A.D. 105
Diocletian r. A.D. 284–305	Sassanid dynasty of Persia A.D. 224–651	Kushan Empire A.D. 100–240	Rise of Buddhism A.D. 300–500
Constantine r. A.D. 324–337		Gupta Empire A.D. 320–550	Huns destroy Chinese capital at Loyang A.D. 311
Alaric defeat of Rome A.D. 410			Fa Xian's pilgrimage to India A.D. 400
Augustine A.D. 354–430		Aryabhata c. A.D. 499	

c. = circa (about)   d. = died   f. = founded   r. = ruled

❧ III ❧

The Traditional World

500–1500

Preview of the Period

A.D. 500–1500

The term "traditional world" is perhaps the least awkward of a number of alternatives used for world history between 500 and 1500. Other possibilities are "the middle period," since these years are midway between the classical age and modern times, and "the medieval world," since the period in European history is often called "medieval" or the Middle Ages. European history, however, is not typical of the history of other civilizations in this era. In fact, Europe was something of a backwater throughout most of this period, especially compared with the highly developed civilizations of China and the Muslim world. Even within Europe, the eastern Byzantine Empire was for most of this period more advanced than the western Gothic barbarian kingdoms that became Western Europe. Each of the most sophisticated and powerful cities of Western Europe—Rome, Ravenna, and Venice—was, in its turn, dependent on the Byzantine capital at Constantinople during much of this period.

The World of Byzantium (500–1453). The Eastern Roman Empire withstood the barbarian invasions of the fourth and fifth centuries much better than the Western Empire did. Under the emperor Justinian (r. 527–565) many of the Western territories were reintegrated, the Latin language had still not been replaced by Greek, and a Mediterranean Roman Empire was revived. However, the seventh-century invasions of the Muslims, Slavs, Avars, and Persians put Justinian's successors on the defensive. Territories in Western Europe, North Africa, and the Middle East were lost, and Constantinople itself was threatened. Greek and Eastern influence strengthened, creating a more distinct "Byzantine civilization."

217

The important elements of Byzantine civilization were the military (an armored cavalry with stirrups and spears), the church (home of the first seven ecumenical councils, 325–789), the emperor (divinely anointed autocrat, head of church and state), and the cities (especially Constantinople) with their wealthy merchant class and sophisticated Greco-Roman culture. Monasteries and missionaries were also significant elements of the Orthodox church. As the Roman church brought Christianity to the Germans and Celts, Eastern Orthodox missionaries converted the Bulgars, Slavs, and others, bringing literacy and law as well. A series of conflicts with Western Roman churches concerning the relative power of ecumenical councils and the Roman pope culminated in the final break in 1054.

The Byzantine Empire was a highly centralized state. While it borrowed the successful Persian military armored cavalry, it supported the army with taxes and plunder rather than feudal grants of land to local lords (as the Sassanid Persians had done). This solution might have reflected an antiaristocratic bias in Christianity or the needs of a sea, rather than land, power. It emphasized the importance of the emperor over the army, clergy, and nobility, and the primacy of the city over the countryside in Byzantine civilization.

Byzantine civilization originated in one of the few successful defenses against the barbarian invasions of the fourth and fifth centuries. It was not able, however, to withstand the Mongol and Turkish invasions from the same area a thousand years later. The weakness of Constantinople had already been displayed in the conquest by Western Crusaders in 1204, but the Turkish invasion ended Byzantine civilization in 1453.

The World of Western Europe (500–1500). When the history of Western Europe in this period is told as a part of world history, it is its weakness, disorganization, and decentralization that are most striking, especially before A.D. 1000. Compared with the wealthy, powerful, and sophisticated civilizations of Asia, the kingdoms of Western Europe were "developing countries." The first wave of barbarian invasions from central Eurasia was followed in the seventh and eighth centuries by the expansion of Muslim civilization. As the armies of Allah penetrated France in the early eighth century, the Gauls of France adopted the Persian method of raising horse soldiers armed with spurs and lances. The Gauls also followed not the Byzantine example of centralized control, but the Persian example of decentralized, aristocratic control, which came to be called feudalism. Knights were given land by lords of large estates in exchange for service in war. Lowly serfs on the land supplied sufficient food and services to allow the armies of knights to wage war far afield, and without concern for work. These armies were eventually successful in keeping the Muslims out of France (at Tours in 732), and the lords of France became consolidated under a single family. The heir of that family was Charlemagne, who had himself declared emperor of the Franks and crowned by the pope in A.D. 800. His Frankish kingdom, which included parts of what is today called Germany as well as France, was divided after his death among his sons and then divided further by their sons. But for a brief moment at the beginning of the ninth century, Charlemagne ruled a larger European country than exists today and had gathered to his court some of the finest minds of Europe.

The church of Rome also underwent a change in the barbarian world of the fifth to tenth centuries. As early as the Roman bishopric of Leo I (r. 440–461) the doctrine of the supremacy of the Roman bishop emerged. Despite the superior power of Constantinople and the Byzantine church, the Roman papacy increasingly carved out a position of clerical dominance. Even the coronation of Charlemagne in 800 by the pope was thought more a compromise between powerful individuals than between ideas. By the eleventh century, however, a series of conflicts developed that pitted the secular authority against the pope. In 1076 a successor to Charlemagne, Henry IV, who deemed himself "Holy Roman Emperor," was forced to humble himself before Pope Gregory VII in the snows outside of the pope's residence at Canossa in Italy, asking for restitution after being excommunicated.

But papal acceptance allowed Henry, and future secular leaders, to carry out their own policies without church approval. Ultimately the conflict between church and state in Western European civilization separated the two powers.

The conflict between church and state was particularly European. In Byzantium, in Islam, and in most other civilizations, religious and political authority were united. The inability of European princes to dominate the church was a sign of their weakness that proved to be a strength for the entire civilization.

In other respects the Western European church was very much like that of Byzantium. In both cases, the most significant developments were in the evolution of missionary and monastic activities rather than internal organization and doctrinal development. Doctrinal changes—like the elaboration of a series of "sacraments," and the ideas of purgatory, saints, and indulgences—offered popular access to an increasingly hierarchical institution.

It appears from a global perspective that the rise of Western Europe by 1500 was due in part to its lack of a single, centralized state or orthodoxy. Since the Greeks, allegiances in Europe had been territorial (within both city-states and proto–nation-states), so the need for political and religious conformity throughout Europe was minimal.

Thus, the church-state controversy is relevant for the elbow room it provided. It encouraged the growth of towns and the development of urban autonomy. These urban centers, administered independently by a new middle class, brought a revival of trade, the spread of markets and capitalist techniques, and the Crusades. These elements of internal transformation and the external expansion of the twelfth-century Crusades gave Western Europe a dynamism that was unique.

Western Europe did not accomplish this dynamism without help. The rise of Islam was a crucial step. Nor was the development of European commerce and industry an isolated case. Islamic Spain (from the eighth to fifteenth centuries) became more technologically sophisticated than Christian Spain (perhaps until the twentieth century). Further,

Chinese economic and technological development before the Mongol invasion of the thirteenth century was even more impressive than the Western European development afterward. And Japan (which, like Western Europe, escaped the Mongol devastation) developed some similarities to Western Christendom.

The differences that Western European civilization began to show after A.D. 1000 were due in large part to changes in Western European society. Compared with peasants in most other societies, European peasants were unusually free by 1400. Many of their obligations to landlords had been converted to money rents. Many participated in the developing market economy. A few of their number became wealthy, contributing to the growth of a middle class of merchants and entrepreneurs. The authority and power of the landed aristocracy was also being reduced by monarchs who forged an alliance with the developing urban middle class. Perhaps because Europe had been more feudal, more decentralized, than other civilizations, it became more market-oriented, more middle-class or capitalist, as feudalism broke down.

The World of Islam (622–1500). The Muslim world, or the world of Islam, was not only Arabic. While it began with Muhammad (and the culture of the Arabian Peninsula), it blossomed into the world's most international and cosmopolitan civilization by 1500.

The roots of Islam were in the Judeo-Christian tradition: Muhammad was seen as the last in a line of prophets going back to Abraham, and including Moses and Jesus. The roots of the faith also sprang from the conflict between nomadic and settled societies, and in the merchant cities along the caravan routes of Saudi Arabia that linked the civilizations of Persia, India, and Byzantium.

The speed of early Muslim expansion is what was so striking. From Muhammad's flight from Mecca to Medina in 622 to his death in 632 he converted and conquered much of the Arabian Peninsula. His successors ("caliphs") Abu Bakr and Omar (634–644) conquered Egypt, the Byzantine provinces of Syria and Palestine, and most of Sassanid Persia. Under the caliphate of Omar and his successors (the Umayyad, or

Omayyad caliphate) between 661 and 750, Islam spread across northern Africa and Spain to France and across Persia to the Indus River. Under the more Persian Abbasid caliphate, which flourished from 750 to 946, continuing until 1258, Islam spread across India and down the east coast of Africa as well.

As the center of Islam shifted from a more "democratic" Arab stage at Damascus (660–750) to a more "theocratic" Persian stage at Baghdad (750–1100), it became both more sophisticated and less fervent. But the core of Islam remained an intensely felt monotheism and a commitment to an international community.

As in the other monotheistic traditions, there were deep doctrinal splits, essentially over the degree to which God the transcendent creator of the universe could be understood and represented by human beings in human institutions. The Sunnis spoke for institutional, historical, and traditional understanding and law. The Sufis (like Christian mystics) spoke for personal revelation and religious experience. The Shi'ites (like the early Protestants) spoke more militantly for a return to fundamentals, often expressed in terms that were anti-Arab. They favored a continuous hereditary succession of caliphs from the Prophet's son-in-law, Ali, rather than popular or political choices. As such, they were also more willing than the Sunnis to submit to both internal spiritual calls and external hereditary authorities.

Islam united different peoples, tongues, and societies across Europe, Africa, and Asia long after the authority of the Abbasid caliphate declined. While various smaller caliphates challenged the Abbasid, Islam remained culturally vigorous, unified, and strong. Indeed, it was the only world culture of the period.

The insistent monotheism of Islam (to be a Muslim, one had only to declare that "there is no god but God") paralleled its universalism. The centrality of the Koran, dictated by God to Muhammad, provided a law and a language that all could understand. The insistence on giving alms to the poor bred empathy, compassion, and community. The injunction to travel to Mecca, if at all possible, once in one's life made the Muslim aware of different peoples and cultures and provided a sense of a larger world.

Islam was a traveler's religion. There were always people who would understand the language, religion, and dietary needs of the faithful. The laws were everywhere expected to conform to those that the Prophet had imposed in Medina; surprises were limited. It was also an urban religion. Every city had its mosque. The visit to the holy city of Mecca was the culmination of the faith. The Prophet's establishment of the faith in the city of Medina in A.D. 622 marked the first year of the Muslim calendar. Islam was a trader's religion. Muhammad had been a merchant. Mecca lay at the intersection of major trade routes. It was a democratic religion. There were no priests, bishops, popes, or patriarchs. The prayers one made to God five times a day by kneeling on one's prayer mat and bowing toward Mecca were one's own prayers. There were no sermons. The mosque contained no seats—thus no special seats—and there was no pulpit because no one was in charge.

Because of these factors, Islamic civilization was one of the two most innovative and sophisticated in the traditional world (the other was the Chinese). The simplicity of Islam's message, its urbanity and universality, its openness to trade and foreign contacts, all made the exposure to and cultivation of new ways more likely. This was especially true of innovations in commerce and technique. Thus, the Indian zero and digital numerical system was easily adopted by Arab traders and Muslim mathematicians. Techniques of agriculture, metalwork, printing, architecture, and surgery could pass freely from one end of the Muslim world to the other, improving with cross-fertilization. While the value of Islamic culture in retaining, translating, and elaborating on classical Greco-Roman culture can hardly be overstated, Islam was more than an archive for later European development. It was the preeminent global civilization of its time.

South and Southeast Asia (500–1500). For Indian history our period falls between the decline of the Gupta rule in the fifth century and the coming of the Mughal dynasty after 1500. But for the rest of Southeast Asia, there are two great movements of the expansion of Indian culture in this period. The first is the spread of Indian classical culture (Gupta and Chola). The second is the spread of Islam after 711.

Both Indian Hinduism and Buddhism spread throughout Southeast Asia in the first half of our period. From Balinese Ramayana dances to the monuments of Borobudur in Central Java (late eighth century), the Khmer temples of Angkor Wat (twelfth century), and the Burmese temples of Pagan (1044–1287), Indian religion and culture leavened local forms.

Islam actually came to South and Southeast Asia in two waves: the first beginning in India in 711, and the second (the Mongol and Turkish conquests) after 1000, culminating in the Delhi sultanate (1206–1526) and the Mughal Empire (1526–1739). Islam forced the development of Indian traditions of reconciliation and toleration. Most notable was the fusion of Muslim Sufi and Hindu *bhakti* traditions, exemplified by the poems of Kabir (1440–1518) and Nanak (1469–1539) and the origins of the Sikhs.

East Asia (500–1500). Chinese civilization of this period was (with the possible exception of Islamic civilization taken as a whole) the most developed in the world. The reunification of China under the Sui dynasty (589–618) was as short-lived as Justinian's reunification of the Roman Empire, but the Tang dynasty (618–907) made that effort permanent. It redistributed agricultural land, developed the state examination system, and established prosperity and good government. It was in the Song [Sung] dynasty (960–1279), however, that China underwent a commercial revolution and a revolution in iron and coal industries that made its economy the most productive in the world and almost initiated an industrial revolution. This was interrupted by the Mongol invasions.

After the invasions, Chinese revival came with the Ming dynasty (1368–1644), which was far more successful in its attempt to regain and expand Chinese frontiers than it was in its efforts to revive pre-Mongol prosperity. Ming rulers sent naval expeditions as far as the Persian Gulf. Armies extracted tribute from Vietnam, Korea, and central Asia. The sudden withdrawal from overseas navigation in 1433 followed the building of a new, more northern capital at Beijing [Peking] in 1421, and increased attention to land defenses shows the continuing threat of invaders from the steppe.

The history of Japan between 500 and 1500 encompasses a number of important periods: the Late Yamato (552–710), the Nara (710–784), the Heian (794–1185), the Kamakura (1185–1333), the Ashikaga (1336–1467), and the period of warfare and reunification that preceded the Tokugawa period, which began in 1600.

Japanese history can be told with an eye to the history of Europe. Both escaped the Mongol onslaught but cultivated militaristic cultures. Both experienced feudalism but successfully encouraged the development of towns. Both struggled to gain their independence from stronger, more orthodox cultures—Confucian and Byzantine. Both created maritime fortunes and commercial capabilities that aided future industrialization.

From another perspective, Japanese history can be seen in response to China. Japan emerged from Chinese cultural dominance, while assimilating it, from the seventh century. Emulation of China included the centralized absolutism of the Nara period, modeled on the Tang dynasty. Feudal decentralization quickly followed, however.

From the Heian period (794–1185), with its rich courtly culture described in Lady Murasaki's *The Tale of Genji* (perhaps the world's first novel), until the Tokugawa shogunate (1600), Japan was a feudal society where the military values of samurai (like the European knights) and the power of the shogun prevailed.

The Afro-Eurasian World (500–1500). Perhaps the most important global development in this period is the establishment of a single intercommunicating zone from North Africa and Europe across all of Asia. Various forces were responsible for this integration. Islam forged a single civilization that, by the end of our period, was reaching out to western Africa south of the Sahara and beyond India to the spice islands that became Indonesia. The nomads of the Eurasian steppe (the Huns before 500 and the Mongols and Turks between 1200 and 1400) invaded, populated, and provided communication between Western Europe and Eastern Asia. At the end of the period Chinese fleets (until 1433) and then Portuguese, Spanish, and Dutch vessels developed trade routes through the Indian Ocean that provided another chain of links between Asia, Africa, and Europe. After 1492 that interacting zone included new continents across the Atlantic, making almost the entire world an interdependent environment.

Civilizations of Africa (500–1500). The drying up of the fertile band across northern Africa (around four to five thousand years ago) left an enormous barrier to continued intercommunication that we know as the Sahara Desert. Despite this, independent states developed along the Nile south of Egypt and in the western Sudan, south of the Sahara. Kush, south on the Nile, was the first black African kingdom, dating from the time of the Egyptian Empire. It became an Egyptian colony before briefly conquering Egypt and regaining independence in the eighth century B.C. At its height from the third to first century B.C. its capital at Meroe was a center of iron production. In A.D. 350 Kush was conquered by the neighboring kingdom of Axum under King Ezana. The king and his nobles converted to Christianity, which by the sixth century became the religion of most Axumites, who were the ancestors of the Ethiopians.

The mountainous terrain of Ethiopia made the country difficult to unify, but from the twelfth to the sixteenth century it experienced unity, military expansion, and cultural flowering. King Lalibela in the early thirteenth century had churches built out of solid rock and decorated with Christian images that showed the influence of traditional African and Islamic art as well.

In the western Sudan the Soninke pastoralists established Ghana around A.D. 300. Ghana grew rich on trade across the Sahara. It thrived from A.D. 750 until its conquest by the Berber Almoravids in 1076, at which point it became part of a larger Muslim empire from Spain to Senegal (for two hundred years).

Muslim merchants developed an extensive trade with Sub-Saharan Africa, especially after 1300. Camel caravans carried large slabs of salt mined in the Sahara to the kingdoms of the Sudan for gold, ivory, and slaves. This trade stimulated the rise of empires after Ghana in Mali (1230–1400) and Songhai (1450–1591). Kanem-Bornu grew separately in the interior from 800 to 1800.

The Mali Empire was founded by the Malinke people, whose kings *(mansas)* raised large armies of bowmen and armored cavalry. In the time of Mansa Musa (r. 1312–1337) the empire extended from the Atlantic Ocean in the west to the border of modern Nigeria in the east. In 1324 when Mansa Musa made a pilgrimage to Mecca his vast caravan brought so much gold through Cairo that the price of gold in Egypt declined 25 percent.

Between 1464 and 1528 the Songhai people built an even larger empire in the Sudan under two strong kings, Sunni Ali and Askia Muhammad. This larger Songhai Empire was also a Muslim kingdom that thrived on the trade across the Sahara. During the fifteenth century the city of Timbuktu, on the southern border of the Sahara trade, grew into an important cultural as well as trading center. Several colleges taught Islamic law, theology, and other subjects. There were so many scholars, it was said that the merchants of Timbuktu made a greater profit from books than from any other commodity.

During the thousand-year period before 1000 the Bantu-speaking peoples (originally from the high grasslands of what is now Cameroon and Nigeria) moved south and east. In the rain forests of the equator region they displaced the older inhabitants, the Pygmy communities. The migrations of these and later agriculturalists with iron tools increased the population density of the forest. Another migration from the islands of Indonesia between A.D. 300 and 800 to the island of Madagascar, off the east coast of Africa, brought rice, bananas, and the yams that became a staple of the African diet.

Some of the forest areas along the gold coast developed city-states rather than large empires. In the thirteenth cen-

227

tury the Yoruba people developed a tradition of remarkably realistic sculpture in the city of Ife. These bronze heads (probably of court officials and nobles) actually continued a tradition of clay portraiture from Iron Age Nok of the second century that was carried further by the beautiful bronze heads of the Benin people in the fifteenth century. Under King Ewuare the Great (r. 1440–1473) Benin became something of an empire, governing over two hundred towns and villages. Later a Dutch visitor remarked that the streets of Benin were wider than those of Amsterdam. Another wrote that the palace of the king *(oba)* was larger than the entire Dutch city of Haarlem.

Further south in the equatorial rain forest of what is today Zaire and Angola, the Bakongo warriors founded the kingdom of Kongo on the Congo (or Zaire) River in the middle of the fifteenth century. In 1480 the Portuguese arrived in the Kongo. In 1490 the Bakongo welcomed Portuguese missionaries. In 1506 the Christian prince Nzinga Mvemba (who took the Christian name Dom Afonso) came to the throne and ruled for nearly forty years, almost as long as Henry VIII, his contemporary in England. Soon the Kongo, like much of the rest of Africa, succumbed to the Portuguese and the European slave trade.

Other important kingdoms were formed in East Africa. In the early fifteenth century King Mutota conquered the neighboring tribes of Zimbabwe. Before 1600 Zimbabwe's Great Temple, surrounded by an elliptical wall of fifteen thousand tons of meticulously cut stone, was built. Zimbabwe was an important gold-trading center with Arab ports on the eastern coast of Africa like Kilwa and Sofala.

Civilizations of the Americas (500–1500). Geographic isolation hindered American development even more than it did African. This is because the Americans arrived even before the discovery of agriculture in Eurasia about 10,000 years ago. They seem to have discovered it independently of the Asians, starting with corn in Middle America around 4000 B.C. and then adding a rich variety of crops from the Andes to North America. Staples included corn (whose flour they made into bread tortillas), tomatoes, beans, squash, peppers, avocados, pineapples, pumpkins, and (in the Andes) potatoes. They domesticated dogs and the llama of the Andes, but they did not have horses, cattle, sheep, goats, camels, donkeys, pigs, or chickens. (The mainly hunting peoples of North America had buffalo and turkeys.) American agriculture developed without the plow, and there were no wheeled vehicles (except for children's toys). They were excellent workers in stone, jade, silver, and gold, but did not have iron.

The Middle American Olmecs developed the first urban civilization in the Americas around 1200 B.C. at San Lorenzo on the Gulf of Mexico. Another American civilization was developed by the Chavin of the Andes in Peru after 1000 B.C. Both of these faded a few centuries B.C., but they left cultural legacies to those who came later. The Olmecs left pyramid construction, corn, feathered serpent gods, a court ball game, and large stone statues.

The Mayans inherited these elements of Olmec civilization in Guatemala and the Yucatan Peninsula of Mexico, where they flourished between A.D. 300 and 900. They further developed the fairly flexible Olmec hieroglyphic writing (with phonetic elements) that is only now being deciphered. The Mayans also perfected the Olmec use of a decimal numerical system and a zero that made their mathematics superior to that of all other civilizations except India. This served as the basis for a highly precise Mayan calendar and careful astronomical observations.

The central high plateau of Mexico was the site of a series of civilizations, from the Teotihuacan (destroyed about A.D. 650) to the Toltec at Tula (770–1168) to the Aztec. The Aztecs, descended from northern invaders called the Chichimecs, destroyed the Toltec cities and ruled until the Spanish conquest (1503–1541). They ruled from the city of Tenochititlan on an island in Lake Texcoco, the site of current Mexico City. Described by the Spanish conquistadores as grander than any city in Europe, Aztec Tenochititlan also exerted a stranglehold over surrounding peoples, some of whom welcomed the Spanish as liberators.

All of these Mexican civilizations, including the Mayan,

A reconstruction of the Great Temple complex in the Aztec capital of Tenochtitlan. (The American Museum of Natural History)

were ruled brutally by the dominant class of ruler-gods and priests. They practiced regular human sacrifices of captured prisoners and conducted ritual ball games in which the winning players were sacrificed to satisfy the gods. They built monumental pyramids for ceremonial executions and as testaments to their power, and they were destroyed quickly when their powers were challenged.

After the decline of the Chavin Empire around A.D. 200, the Andean peoples lived in independent communities. Then between A.D. 600 and 1000 two cultures dominated the west coast of South America: the military Huari in the north and the Tiahuanacan south of Lake Titicaca in Chile. After another period of small independent states from about 1000 to 1370, the Chimu and then, after 1470, the Incas created a military empire that controlled most of the coast from the sea to the high Andes.

Thus, the Peruvian Inca Empire was relatively young when the Spanish arrived in 1532. Like the Aztecs, the Peruvians worshiped their ruler, the Inca, as God. While Mexican religions demanded blood sacrifices, however, the Peruvians worshiped the Inca as a benevolent representative of the sun. The Inca Empire was administered without a system of writing. An elaborate organization of runners would keep the Inca and ruling family informed; record keeping and rudimentary "writing" were accomplished by tying precisely placed knots on colored strings.

The urban civilizations in the Americas, as elsewhere, were able to control much larger populations than could be supported by hunting and gathering or by village agriculture. Often, however, the lives of villagers, when safe from the predatory empires, were less troubled. This seems to be the case in the area of North America that is currently the United States. In what is now the Southwest United States, desert dwellers practiced agriculture around 1000 B.C. Their descendants, the Anasazi (a Navaho word for "ancient people") formed villages about two thousand years ago. Around A.D. 1100 they built adobe brick structures on cliff ledges, some of which were several stories high. The remains of dense pueblo communities can still be seen at Mesa Verde, Colorado, and Chaco Canyon, New Mexico.

Pacific Peoples (500–1500). This is the period when Polynesian peoples settled many of the Pacific Ocean islands. They came originally from Southeast Asia, but had settled on Tonga and the Samoan Islands as early as 1000 B.C. Around A.D. 300 these Polynesians settled the far eastern islands, the Marquesas and the Society Islands. From there — they settled Easter Island by 400, the Hawaiian Islands by 500, New Zealand by about 800, and most of the rest of Polynesia by 1300.

The Polynesian peoples were adept at navigation and fishing. They had domesticated certain tree and root crops, chickens, and pigs. But there were also peoples in 1500 who were still hunter-gatherers without domesticated plants or animals. They existed in 1500, as some still do today, in remote areas like the Amazon basin in South America, the Kalahari Desert of southern Africa, and the Australian outback. The Australian aborigines remind us of how inventive Stone Age life could be. They know and use dozens of roots, berries, nuts, and small game for food, as well as hundreds of medicinal plants for healing. Even in the desert they are able to get water from leaves, roots, and hidden springs. As in more urban or civilized cultures, their songs and stories give their lives meaning and direction. ∿

✖ 9 ✖

Violence
and
Vengeance

Religion and
the State

WHAT MAKES SOME SOCIETIES more violent than others? What makes some people less violent than others? Does religion reduce violence? Did violence decline with the rise of the state, government, and law? Is violence increasing, or decreasing, in the world? Are people more, or less, violent than they were a thousand years ago?

To understand what makes societies violent, and whether violence is increasing or decreasing, we must take a broad look at the past. We will select examples from a number of different societies that existed in the world between A.D. 500 and 1200. These societies will show us different causes and functions of violence and aggressive action. The examples should enable us to understand better the role of violence in human history.

None of these investigations will give us anything like mathematical certainty. History is not like that. Humans are too complex, and we cannot go back and interview the dead. Frequently, people in the past did not even bother to keep the records we would like from them. Statistics were virtually nonexistent. Most peoples did not write. In general, they did not question the same things we do.

We can, however, get a sense of who some of these peoples were and what they were like.

As you read about these societies, you might ask yourself how they are similar to, or different from, your own. In what ways were these societies of the traditional world more violent, in what ways less violent than your own? What in their societies made them violent or peaceful? Do any of these causes still exist in your own society? What, if anything, do these examples suggest about the control of violence in your own society? What, if anything, do they suggest to us about making our societies more peaceful?

CHILDREN OF ATTILA: THE BARBARIANS

Many Europeans and Americans are descended in part from the barbarian tribes that swept over the Roman Empire from the steppes of Asia around A.D. 500. These ancestors were a pretty unruly bunch. The Roman gentleman Sidonius Apollinaris boasted that he would rather "have braved destitution, fire, sword and pestilence" than submitted to the Visigoths or Gauls. But when these tribes moved into Italy, he resigned himself to rub shoulders with their unkempt chieftains, whose hair smelled of rancid butter and whose mouths emitted odors of onion and garlic and strange Germanic sounds.

One of the best of these chiefs, according to their own storytellers, was "good king Guntramn," a leader of the Franks (who settled in what is now France). Guntramn could be as jovial and lustful as the next guy, but "when he was with his bishops he conducted himself like one of them." In fact he was made a saint by the early church. The only thing you might say against Guntramn is that he had a taste for murder. Among his many victims were two physicians who were unable to heal his wife.

The Lombard king Alboin, who brought the tribe from the Danube into Italy, killed the king of the Gepids and married his daughter. He might have created a unified Lombard state in northern Italy (in the sixth century) if he had been more sensitive. Paul the Deacon tells a story of Alboin's offering his wife some wine in a goblet that was made from her father's skull. It seems she didn't get the joke. Paul tells us that the "silly woman" had the old jokester assassinated.

It is possible that Guntramn and Alboin were not unusual. One seventh-century historian of the tribal invasions has a mother of a barbarian king advise her son: "If you want to accomplish something and make a name for yourself, destroy everything that others have built and massacre everyone that you have conquered; for you are not able to build better monuments than those constructed by your predecessors and there is no more noble accomplishment for you to make your name." Whether or not any mother's son ever heard those words, they certainly express a part of the barbarian consciousness. The leaders of nomadic tribes were particularly sensitive to the issue of proving their abilities in war: courage, strength,

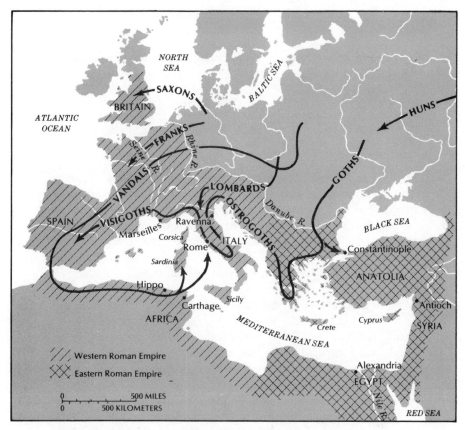

*THE BARBARIAN INVASIONS OF EUROPE, FOURTH TO SIXTH
CENTURIES A.D.*
*Successive waves of barbarian nomads were pushed out of the
Eurasian grasslands and northern Europe by the Huns. Some, like the
Goths and Vandals, migrated throughout Europe: The Ostrogoths
settled in Italy, the Visigoths in Spain, and the Vandals throughout the
Mediterranean.*

and even cruelty must have ranked high among tribal values. The fortunes of these
tribes, especially in hard times, were often a direct product of their capacities for
destroying and taking. And throughout their lives they were trained to hunt, to
wield a sword, to carry out lightning invasions on horseback, and to bring booty
and slaves back to camp.

The tribes that penetrated deepest into the Roman Empire were probably less
fierce than those that were pushing them from the steppes. (The earliest invaders
closest to Rome were actually often semicivilized tribes "retreating" across the
Alps.) Even the barbarians told stories about the greater cruelty of other tribes
further away from civilization. The Huns, according to Ammien Marcellin, were
the least civilized and the most feared:

Their ferocity knew no bounds. They branded their own children's cheeks so that they grew old beardless. These stocky, thick-necked creatures cooked no food, but gorged themselves on wild roots and the raw flesh of the first animal they saw. They had no shelters, no burials, and only rat skin clothing that they wore until it disintegrated. It was said that they were nailed to their horses. They did not dismount to eat or drink. Often they stayed mounted to sleep and dream.[1]

These tribal ancestors were certainly "barbarians." The word is appropriate. They were barbarians in the sense that the Greeks and Romans used the word: they spoke strange "bar bar"–like sounds. But, more significantly, they were barbarians in the two modern senses of the word: they were both violent and primitive (or, more precisely, at a preurban state of development). The brutality of their lives and their lack of the tools, knowledge, arts, or comforts of more advanced city societies are enough to warrant the description "barbarian."

We do not use the word "barbarian" in order to make moral judgments about these people. Some of the early Christians and Romans did. It was enough for some of the educated witnesses to the invasions to point out that the tribes were pagans or Germanic: that was just like saying that the invaders were morally inhuman. This attitude was particularly common in the Roman aristocracy and among the bishops of the church. But at least one monk in Marseilles around the year 440, who called himself Salvien, gives us a different view.

It is true, Salvien wrote in a book that has somehow survived, that the Saxon people are cruel, the Franks untrustworthy, and the Huns immodest. "But," he asks rhetorically, "are their vices any more sinful than our own? Is the lewdness of the Huns more criminal than ours? Is the treachery of the Franks to be blamed more than our own? Is the drunken German more reprehensible than a drunken Christian? Is a greedy barbarian worse than a greedy Christian? Is the deceit of a Hun or of a Gepid so extraordinary?"

The barbarians, Salvien reminds us, had no monopoly on brutality or sin. In fact, they were not much different from the Roman authorities that they displaced. Their invasion was successful because Roman society had become as violent and insecure as nomadic society. From the perspective of the poor in Roman society the barbarians were sometimes preferable masters:

> The castaway Roman poor, the grieving widows, the orphans under foot, even many of the well-born and educated Romans took refuge among their enemies. They sought Roman humanity among the barbarians so that they would not perish from barbarian inhumanity among the Romans. They were different from the barbarians in their manners, their language, and the smell of their clothes, but these differences were preferable to injustice and cruelty. They went to live among the barbarians on all sides, and never regretted it. They preferred to live free under the appearance of slavery, than to be slaves under

the guise of liberty. Roman citizenship, once highly esteemed and bought at a high price, is today not only worthless, but despised. Those who did not flee were forced to become barbarians by the persecution of Roman law or the anarchy of Roman lawlessness. We call them rebels and lost men, but it is we who have forced them to become criminals.[2]

Salvien says a lot. Rome had become as violent as the barbarian world. The invasions were accompanied by the revolt of the Roman oppressed and dispossessed. The Roman Empire wasn't assassinated. It committed suicide. At least (since civilizations are not mortal), the owners of Rome allowed their possession to be mangled beyond repair.

Europe was born in this marriage of settled barbarian and barbarized Roman poor. The barbarian had learned that you get from life only what you take from others. The Roman poor had learned that there is no peace or security when a few wealthy families take everything from everyone else. Neither the barbarian nor the Roman knew anything of freedom or the peaceful life. The only world they were allowed to have was chaotic and violent—and even that had to be taken by force.

Life meant very little in early European society. Few writers were concerned with the hardships of the common people, but a few examples taken at random give us an idea of what it must have been like in the first few centuries after the barbarian migration.

One writer, Gregory of Tours, tells a story about the people of Orléans and Blois looting and burning the houses of Chateaudun and Chartres, massacring many of the people, and then receiving the same treatment from the survivors. Another, Gregory I, writes of the tyranny of the tax collectors forcing the inhabitants of Corsica to sell their children and seek refuge among the "unspeakable Lombards." Another, the Venerable Bede, describes how after three years of drought and famine one group of forty or fifty people "exhausted by hunger, went to a cliff top above the sea and flung themselves over, holding hands."

The neutral language of the law codes expresses the cheapness of life: "the fine for cutting off someone's hand, foot, eye, or nose is 100 sous; but only 63 if the hand is still hanging; for cutting off a thumb 50 sous, but only 30 if it is still hanging; for cutting off an index finger the fine is 35 sous; two fingers together is 35 sous; three fingers together is 50 sous."

Written law (like the excerpt from the Salic code above) had little meaning if you fell into the hands of the enemies. When Saint Leger, the bishop of Autun, was captured by an enemy palace mayor in 677, they cut out his tongue; then they forced him to walk barefoot in a pool of sharpened rocks that cut like spikes; then they pierced his eyes. The stories are endless. Another tells of some unfortunate soul being tortured for three days and then tied to the rear of a vicious horse who was whipped until it bolted. Others were killed by being "drawn and quartered": attached to two horses who ran in opposite directions. Cruelty was limitless.

THE BARBARIANS CIVILIZE THEMSELVES

One thing that is indisputable is that the chaos of the barbarian invasions gradually abated. By the sixth and seventh centuries, the number of invasions declined and most of the nomadic tribes had settled down to an agricultural life. The Goths who had terrorized Roman legions had produced a fairly elaborate culture by the sixth century. One of them, Jordanes, a historian, could boast that the Goths had a king who was a philosopher and scientist and that they had enough professors of philosophy to rival ancient Greece. He exaggerates, of course, but these are not exaggerations that would please a real barbarian.

By the eighth century the sudden terror of barbarian life had given way to the stable regularity of farming, collecting taxes, and making laws. The Franks had established a kingdom with relatively fixed boundaries and laws that was healthy enough to ward off an invading Muslim army from Spain. By 800 Charlemagne had himself crowned by the pope as "Emperor of the Romans," and this was not a completely foolish analogy: his empire included all of France and a good part of current Germany, Austria, and Italy (including Rome). Though he himself could not write, he gathered many of the leading European intellectuals (monks) to his court. One of them, Alcuin, could tell Charlemagne: "If your intentions are carried out, it may be that a new Athens will rise in Frankland."

A new series of invasions from the north (which we'll turn to soon) were to cut short the Carolingian summer of high culture and established law. But stability and prosperity had conditioned even the common peasant to demand "justice" where an ancestor may have needed "blood." The customs of the people were no longer those of barbarians.

Barbarian morality had been based on the need for vengeance. Tribal families were often ripped apart by feuds that continued indefinitely. When an affront was committed against one's family or tribe, honor required that it be avenged. It was impossible to sleep until the wrong had been righted with blood. Gradually, settled barbarian chiefs (and later, kings) were able to insist on a legal settlement of tribal disputes. Money or something of value became a symbolic substitute for blood vengeance. The excerpt from the Salic code (which we quoted disparagingly before) was actually a step toward a less-violent society. "An eye for an eye" satisfied the basest human passions for vengeance, but (as the Christian monks taught) the motives of an assailant were also important. What was the point of blinding another merely to even the score? One life could not be brought back by the loss of another, and (as the tribal elder, king, or administrator well knew) the score was never even: the feud or vendetta meant continual warfare and prevented the rise of an orderly state.

Thus, the vendetta was gradually replaced by a system of "blood prices" for various kinds of mutilation and murder. These fines depended on the extent of the damage and the "blood worth" of the victim. The result, as the Lombard king Rothbari explained at the end of his own list of fines, was that "for all of the above-mentioned wounds we have provided a higher compensation than our forebears, so that when such compensation is paid, all hostility will cease."

The blood price should be judged a step beyond barbarism, since it made family feuds less frequent as they became more expensive. But even the notion of a blood price was barbaric from the perspective of the Christian church. It limited violence but withheld blame. As long as the price was paid, the matter was settled. The church welcomed the substitution of the blood price for the vendetta but still insisted that a moral issue was involved. Churchmen compiled books of God's punishments for acts of violence. These acts were seen as sins, not just temporary imbalances in the social order. Eventually, the Lombards and other tribes viewed the spilling of blood and taking of life as moral wrongs that should not be committed—even if compensation were possible. This more "moral" attitude toward violence was still not based on any modern humane faith in the sacredness of life. It was based only on the fear of God's punishment. Gradually, the barbarian indifference to death was replaced by a feeling of "shame" for committing antisocial acts. In turn, shame, which was produced only by social pressure, was eventually transformed into Christian feelings of personal guilt. The history of the human conscience has not yet been (and may never be) written, but it seems quite likely that as barbarians became settled, civilized, and Christian, they developed greater capacities for shame and then guilt. Even guilt became increasingly internalized. In medieval Europe guilt was little more than the verdict rendered by the Christian king or his judge. In modern society guilt is still the verdict of the jury, but it is much more: it is the massive internal regulator that responds to so much of what we do.

From indifference to shame to guilt, from vendetta to blood price to responsibility, as barbarian society became more settled, as the individual became more responsible for his or her behavior, as laws and procedure replaced the gut need for vengeance, European society became less violent.

The change has sometimes been agonizingly slow, however. The family feud was a way of life in Appalachian America only decades ago. The vendetta is still common in Italy, Eastern Europe, and other poor regions of the developed world. Banditry, secret societies (like the Mafia), and vigilantes are still more important than the law and the justices of the peace in some relatively "modern" areas. And besides these remnants of the old world in the new, the newest, most developed countries (like the United States) often display a considerable appetite for violence.

The remnants of old world barbarism are easier to understand. The Sicilian home of the Mafia has not changed all that much in the last thousand years, neither has the climate of Latin American revolutions and Indian massacres, nor has the culture of social oppression and natural catastrophe in much of the developing world. These examples remind us that this sort of violence—even in the barbarian period—was the natural life of "hardship society."

Charlemagne's empire was never able to overcome hardship. Its thriving culture and law were only a hint of what was possible. That possibility was shattered by a new series of invasions: Hungarian nomads from the steppes, Muslim cavalry from the south, and Viking pirates from the north.

ISLAM AND THE MUSLIMS

If you had to dream up a name for a people who were to conquer most of the territory of two major world empires in little more than a generation, you would probably not call them the "Surrenderers" or the "Submitters." But that is the meaning of the Arabic *slm,* which, with added vowels, becomes Islam (for the religion) and Muslim, or Moslem (for the followers). The apparent contradiction between their name and their activity can be resolved easily. They thought of themselves as those who submitted completely to the will of God, and they believed that God wanted them to spread his word to the ends of the earth.

God's word came in a book called the Koran (or, again with different vowels and emphasis, the Qur'an). According to tradition, the Koran was dictated in ringing classical Arabic to the illiterate prophet Muhammad in the mountains overlooking the trading town of Mecca in Saudi Arabia beginning around the year 610.

The religion of the people of Mecca at the time was mixed. There were some Jews, Christians, and Persian Zoroastrians, but most Meccans worshiped the natural spirits called *jinn* and some more important tribal gods, usually associated with a particular tree, grove, stone, or other natural spot. Many of the surrounding tribes came on pilgrimages (and accompanying merchant fairs) to shrines like the Ka'bah building in Mecca, where sacred objects were kept. The pilgrimages and trading fairs were held during four sacred truces each year. The Quraysh tribe and one of their more abstract gods, Allah the creator, presided over the truce.

At some point, Muhammad found the monotheistic religions more appealing than the tribal deities and practices of his birth. Zoroastrianism, Judaism, and Christianity were highly moralistic faiths. They enrolled their adherents in personal struggles on behalf of Ahura Mazda the force of light, Yahweh the God of Abraham, and the God of Christ, respectively.

As we shall see, it is not always clear whether the moralistic religions end up killing fewer people than other religions. The morality of tribal religions might seem limited. There is much bargaining with the gods for favors. The morality enshrined in Bedouin life centered on "individual and group pride and point of honour—pride in birth, pride in one's wealth or prowess, pride which led, when crossed to an unremitting, pitiless vengefulness; to a passionate and heedless (if sometimes magnificent) pursuit of self-centered, inherently trivial ends."[3] While the tribal religions of the Arabian Peninsula made practical accommodations with their enemies in order to carry on trade, Irano–Semitic monotheism sought to create justice. The victory of justice in history required the activity of God's community of the faithful. It was an imposing responsibility.

Not all monotheistic moralisms sought the same kind of justice. The moralism of the Iranian prophet Zoroaster reflected the power of the landed Persian aristocracy: its sense of justice had much to do with obedience and order. The Abrahamic moralism of Judaism and Christianity reflected more of the experience of the merchants' class than that of the landed aristocracy. Its sense of justice had less to do with obedience and more to do with human interaction, honesty, fairness, and equality.

Muhammad's justice was based on the merchant's equality before God, and the market. But it retained some important elements of Zoroastrianism: the eternal struggle between good and evil, lightness and darkness, and the expectation of the imminent end of the world.

> When the sun shall be darkened, when the stars shall be thrown down, when the mountains shall be set moving, when the pregnant camels shall be untended, when the savage beasts shall be stampeded, when the seas shall be set boiling, when the souls shall be coupled, when the buried infant shall be asked for what sin she was killed, when the scrolls shall be unrolled, when the skies shall be stripped off, when Hell shall be set blazing, when Paradise shall be brought near—a soul shall know what it has produced.

Passages like this from the Koran (81: 1–14) do not so much introduce new moral ideas (except, here, that female infanticide was wrong). The very word for moral behavior in the Koran was "the known." What the Koran demanded was a moral commitment. It commanded the faithful to do what was right, without hovering halfway, before God the creator.

Muhammad's calling to speak for one transcendent God and one righteous community did not please all the gods of Mecca. For the ruling Quraysh tribe, the pilgrimages constituted a profitable magnet of tourism and business. When Muhammad denounced what he called their idol worship, he was run out of town. In the middle of the night, he escaped with a few trusted supporters to the town of Medina, an oasis further up the mountain chain that stretched along the Red Sea.

That escape in A.D. 622 (since called the *hegira,* or journey) marks the year 1 of the Muslim calendar because in Medina, Muhammad was able to create the righteous community. What, we might ask, did he do?

He elaborated a set of rules that, much like those of Christian Europe, prohibited some of the most violent behavior of tribal society. Arbitration replaced blood feud. Infanticide (as we have seen) was condemned. Provision was made for the care of orphans, widows, and the poor. Drinking, gambling, and the charging of interest on loans were prohibited. Nevertheless, the rugged warrior caste of desert nomadic society was not eliminated. In fact, in some ways it was encouraged.

An early event sets the problem clearly. Raiding was a common activity among the tribes of Arabia. It was the way small tribes got larger. Muhammad condoned raids by his followers, especially if the raids might humiliate the Quraysh. The first successful raid occurred at Nakhlah, near Mecca. A small group attacked a caravan of the Quraysh during truce month and brought home the booty. One man was killed. It is not clear if Muhammad sanctioned the raid during truce month, but he allowed the booty to be accepted. The people of Medina were outraged until they read in the Koran that while violation of the truce was wrong, it was justified by the persecution of the faith.

Here we see, on a limited scale, the conflict between the practical morality of tribal religion and the demands of monotheism. The truce was a symbol of the success of Meccan tribal religion, but it was accepted by Jews, Christians, and Zoroastrians as well. It was not a superstitious custom, and neither Muhammad nor his followers had ever questioned it. Thus, the raid at Nakhlah was an outright betrayal, which created an irreparable breach between the holy community (the *Ummah*) of Islam and the customs of the surrounding Arab and Berber tribes. But for Muhammad to accept the truce would have been to accept the moral jurisdiction of the entire community, including the Quraysh and other tribes. Instead he chose to seize the opportunity to declare the moral independence of Islam.

Muhammad also found it necessary at an early stage in Medina to differentiate his community from that of other monotheists. Medina was chosen for the first community because there were a large number of Jews, who were presumed to be sympathetic. Many of Muhammad's early converts were Jews and Christians. Muhammad was seen as the last of a line of biblical prophets that included Abraham, Moses, and even Jesus. Initially, the Muslims of Medina prostrated themselves five times a day facing Jerusalem. Muhammad expected the Jews of Medina to be won over. But they were not. They could not accept Muhammad's abstract universalism or his different accounts of biblical stories. As a result, Muhammad decided to expell the Banu Qaynuqa tribe of Jews from Medina. He made fewer attempts to convert other monotheists. He reinterpreted his relationship to Judaism. His monotheism stemmed directly from Abraham, rather than the later Moses, he said. Similarly, he replaced Jerusalem with Mecca as the point of orientation for daily prayers. Muhammad also turned his attention to the religious needs of the Bedouin and Arab tribes. The Ka'bah at Mecca, formerly the object of tribal pilgrimage, now became identified with Abraham and the destination of a yearly Muslim pilgrimage, the *hajj*. As Islam took on its own identity, the Islamic community offered its own rituals. The month of Ramadan, when Muhammad was said to have received the Koran, was set aside for fasting and prayer during daylight hours. An "alms" or charity tax for the poor was instituted. A new attitude toward war and force developed.

THE *JIHAD* AND THE GROWTH OF ISLAM

War had been endemic among the Bedouin tribes of the Arabian Peninsula. Muhammad was able to suppress it and turn it outward to win conquests for the faith. After 629, when he entered Mecca unopposed, he was able to draw from the leadership of the Meccan tribes as well as those of Medina to lead his armies. In 630 he led an army against Byzantine colonies in the northern half of the peninsula and supported attacks on the Persian Empire in the east. By the time of his death in 632, his troops had conquered almost the entire peninsula. "Fight in the cause of God against those who fight against you," the Koran commanded. Those who die in the cause of a *jihad,* a holy war, are not really dead.

> Indeed, they are living in the presence of their Lord and are provided for. They are jubilant over that which God has bestowed upon them of His bounty, and because on them shall come no fear, nor shall they grieve.
>
> (3:169)

The dramatic explosion of Arab armies out of the Arabian Peninsula in the years after the death of Muhammad in 632 is astonishing. Abu Bakr (r. 632–634) consolidated and extended control of the peninsula. His successor, Omar (r. 634–644), conquered Damascus in 635, Jerusalem, Syria, and Palestine by 638, and the Persian Empire as far as India in the east and the Byzantine territory of Egypt and North Africa by the time of his death.

SUCCESSION, SECTARIANISM, AND THE BLOOD OF MARTYRS

If tribal conflict could be channeled into the *jihad,* conflict did not disappear entirely. The very stature of Muhammad as the Prophet of Islam, and the important role he played in the governance of the Islamic community, left the question of succession unresolved. Abu Bakr, the first successor ("caliph"), was elected because he was one of Muhammad's earliest followers. Omar, too, was elected, but when he was killed in 644 the electors were divided between two members of Muhammad's clan. The vote went to Othman, who had married two of the Prophet's daughters, rather than Ali, Muhammad's cousin, who had also married a daughter. When Othman proved unpopular he was murdered. This led to a civil war (656–661) between the party of Ali (who was recognized by some as the successor) and that of Othman's relative Muawiya. Arbitrators were called to decide who should be caliph. Some of the fundamentalists among the arbitrators withdrew (and were therefore called Kharijites, or Seceders) because they believed that arbitration

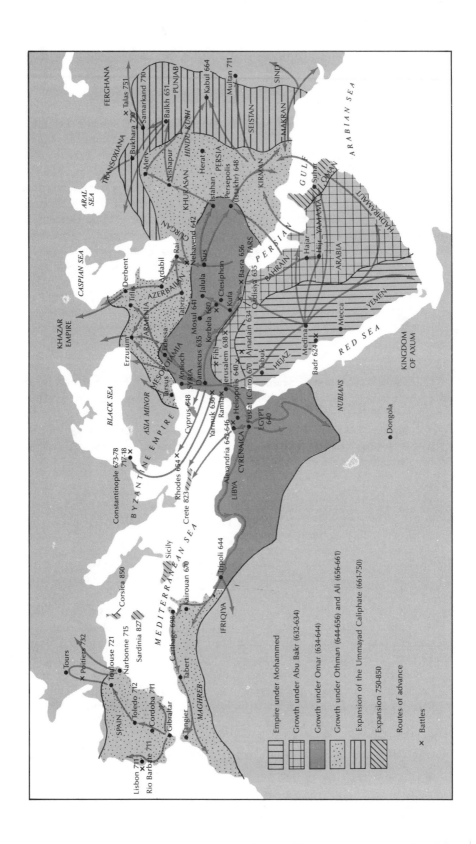

FERGHANA

× Talas 751
Samarkand 710
Bukhara 730 · Balkh 651 · Kabul 664
TRANSOXIANA   PUNJAB · Multan 711
· Merv   Nishapur   HINDU KUSH SEISTAN MAKRAN SIND
ARAL SEA   · Herat PERSIA
KHURASAN   · Isfahan Persepolis
· Rai   Susa · · Istakhr 648
CASPIAN SEA · Derbent   KIRMAN
Ardabil × Nehavend 642
Tiflis AZERBAIJAN · Tabriz Jalula FARS
ARMENIA   · Ctesiphon · Basra 656 PERSIAN GULF
KHAZAR EMPIRE   Erzurum Mosul 641 Kerbela 680 × Kufa × Qadisiya 635 BAHRAIN · Hajar ARABIA Suhar OMAN
Edessa   × Ajnadain 634 · Medina × Badr 624
MESOPOTAMIA Antioch × Fihl × Jerusalem 638 Tabuk HEJAZ YEMEN
BLACK SEA Tarsus Damascus 635   HADHRAMAUT YAMAMA
ASIA MINOR × Yarmuk 636 · Ramla × RED SEA
BYZANTINE EMPIRE Cyprus 648 Heliopolis 640 · Mecca
Constantinople 673-78 × Rhodes 644 Fustat (Cairo) 670 KINGDOM OF AXUM
× 717-18   EGYPT 640
SYRIA   × Alexandria 642-646
Crete 823 CYRENAICA · Dongola
Sicily LIBYA   NUBIANS
Corsica 850 Tripoli 644
Sardinia 827 MEDITERRANEAN SEA
Tours Carthage 698 Kairouan 670 IFRIQIYA
× Poitiers 732 · Tabert
Toulouse 721 Narbonne 715 MAGHREB
SPAIN Toledo 712 · Tangier
Lisbon 711 × Cordoba 711
Rio Barbate 711 × Gibraltar

Empire under Mohammed

Growth under Abu Bakr (632-634)

Growth under Omar (634-644)

Growth under Othman (644-656) and Ali (656-661)

Expansion of the Ummayad Caliphate (661-750)

Expansion 750-850

Routes of advance

× Battles

was a compromise. Ali had them massacred for their refusal to arbitrate. Finally, in 661, Ali was killed by a Kharijite, and Muawiya became caliph. Muawiya inaugurated the Ummayad dynasty (661–750), thus institutionalizing the succession. But the conflict over legitimacy did not end. Those who had supported Ali continued to support his descendants. These partisans of Ali (Shi'at Ali, or Shi'a, or Shi'ites) supported Ali's son Husayn (Muhammad's grandson) in a revolt against Muawiya that was brutally defeated by the Ummayad army. The murders of Ali and Husayn became central events in the formation of Shi'a sectarianism. It appeared to them that Ali's blood tie to his cousin Muhammad combined with his marriage to the Prophet's daughter made Ali the designated successor. From this Shi'a perspective, the martyrdoms of Ali and Husayn proved that every true *imam* (religious leader) was destined to be excluded by corrupt governments until a *mahdi* (especially inspired *imam*) would appear and bring about the final struggle, victory, and last judgment. The imagery of bloodshed, the faith in violence, and the call to martyrdom in this Shi'a tradition made it generally uncomfortable to established governments. It was more frequently a voice of protest than an official orthodoxy. Some of the more militant Shi'ites (like the Ishmailis, who believed that a sixth-generation *imam* in Muhammad's family named Ishmail was the *mahdi*) formed secret brotherhoods that condoned terrorist attacks against corrupt rulers. "Brothers," one Ishmaili poet wrote, "when the time of triumph comes, with good fortune from both worlds as our companion, then by one single warrior on foot a king may be stricken with terror, though he own more than a hundred thousand horsemen."[4] One group of Ishmaili Shi'ites in Iran and Syria trained their devotees to kill enemy rulers with daggers on what were virtually suicide missions. Their name, the Assassins, has come to stand for all political and public murder.

Most Iranians were members of a more moderate Shi'a sect called the Twelvers (because they accepted a twelfth-generation *imam* as *mahdi*). But all Shi'a sects were particularly strong in Iran, possibly because of the importance of righteous struggle in the Older Persian Zoroastrian tradition. Iran became a Shi'a state after 1500 and again after 1979.

Other Muslim sectarians waged militant campaigns against worldly governments, infidels, and backsliders. Some, like the Kharijites who were descendants of the Seceders of the first civil war, refused to cooperate with any governments or accept any secular or religious leaders. They also took an uncompromising position

---

THE EXPANSION OF ISLAM, A.D. 632–936
The spread of Islam beyond the Arabian peninsula began almost immediately after the Prophet's death in 632. By 711 Arab armies were about to extend the faith to northeastern India and Spain at the same time. By 750 when the Abbasids ousted the Ummayad Caliphate, Islam was the major civilization west of China.

on who could be a Muslim, eliminating from the *Ummah* anyone who had ever committed a major sin.

SUNNI CENTRISM

Most Muslims were not Shi'ites or sectarian purists. The Muslim mainstream is called Sunni because it accepts the Sunna, or tradition established by the Prophet, the Koran, and the history of the Muslim community. Sunnis tend to include everyone in the *Ummah* instead of separating themselves from others. For them, the *Ummah* is not an invisible brotherhood but a visible theocratic state under the guidance of the Koran and the consensus of the Muslim community. The Sunnis accept the caliphs, good and bad, but as rulers who protect the Muslim state, not as authorities in matters of faith. For the Sunnis, everyone who declares that "there is no god, but God, and Muhammad is His Messenger" should be accepted as a Muslim because "only God knows what is in the heart."

Mainstream, or Sunni, Islam was no more violent than Christianity or Persian Zoroastrianism; in fact, it was probably less so. Muslim conquest was greeted in some parts of the Byzantine and Persian empires as liberation. After an initial disastrous occupation of the Persian capital, Muslim soldiers and officials lived openly and mixed freely in garrison towns. Koran reciters were sent as advance missionaries with the troops. Mosques were built along with military garrisons in every conquered town of any consequence. There all Muslims came as brothers to perform public worship, especially Friday midday, each individual reciting the Koran. Tribal tensions and social distinctions did not disappear in the administration of the Ummayad caliphate. Arabs were chosen as governors of provinces over local ethnic leaders. Sometimes, in fact, Arab Christians were included among the most trusted. Muawiya's Syrian Arab army at the capital in Damascus included Syrian Christians as well as Muslims. One of the greatest poets at the court in Damascus was al-Akhtal (640–710), a Christian Arab.

Non-Muslims were sometimes plundered when conquered and always taxed when governed. In general, however, non-Muslims were left alone to abide by their own laws and customs, as long as these laws and customs did not conflict with Muslim law or the administrative needs of a Muslim governor. Many subjects converted to Islam and, except for some Arabs, were treated equally with other Muslims. Christians and Jews were respected as comonotheists and "people of the Book," the Bible.

Perhaps all monotheistic societies were likely to persecute the faithless, but the political enforcement of religious doctrine varied. The Muslim state, unlike the Christian or Persian, was a theocracy: political and religious authority were united; the state was the fulfillment of God's plan for a just society. But despite this, or possibly because of it, Muslim caliphs and political governors left religious matters to the people. The religious persecution of pagans, nonbelievers, and heretics might have been greater in Christendom than in the *Dar al-Islam* (lands under Muslim rule).

NOMADS AND KNIGHTS: TWO WAYS OF WARFARE

The classical civilizations that had prospered in the cities of the great seas and river valleys of Eurasia—in China, India, Persia, and the Mediterranean region—were invaded from north and south. From the south came the Arabs. From the north came Huns, Goths, Turks, Vikings, and Mongols. Between A.D. 200 and 1200 barely a century passed without the appearance of a new threat from the horsemen of the Eurasian grasslands or the southern deserts.

There were important differences between the first invasions of the Goths and Huns beginning in the third century and that of the Arabs of the seventh century. The Arabs who led the Muslim invasions were partially urbanized. In some cases they were products of sophisticated market towns and cities. But many of the converts who made up the armies of invading Muslim horsemen were drawn from the Arab, Bedouin, and Berber nomads of Arabia and North Africa. In that respect they were similar to the nomadic horsemen of the great Eurasian steppe. To the farmers and city people of China, Persia, Byzantium, and western Rome, invaders were invaders. Rapidly moving horsemen, with swords or bows and arrows, were a fearsome sight.

The effect of these invasions was similar from the Mediterranean to the East China Sea. As we have already seen, the invasions aided the process of political decay and decentralization. Empires were broken up into more defensible private domains, run by powerful nobles or clans. Cities were less safe. Castles were built and life closed in behind the walls. There is one notable exception to this: Constantinople, which remained a vital city throughout. But in China, India, Persia, Western Rome, and much of the Byzantine Empire outside of Constantinople, city life diminished, and political power became less centralized and more feudal. In some cases the invaders established a new political order. The Arabs are the best examples of this. But the response of the old civilizations to the invasions is also significant because it affects us even today. They developed the armored knight that is still such an important part of our folklore.

In most cases knighthood was a product of a manorial economy, in which serfs or tenant farmers provided the lord of the manor with part of their produce, labor, and military service in return for his protection. It was also usually the product of a feudal society, in which personal pledges of protection between lords and their subordinate vassals replaced the official trappings of the state: office, law, administration, and professional or citizen armies. In short, these were usually societies dominated by large agricultural estates rather than central governments. Even in the case of strong centralized states, however, the armored cavalry was the best answer to the invading horsemen. Thus in the Chinese Sui (589–618) and Tang

(618–907) dynasties, feudalism ended and the empire was reunited, but manorialism remained the dominant economic institution, and the armored cavalry the best defense. Similarly in Byzantium, since it fended off tendencies toward feudalism, the state ensured that the large estates would produce the horses necessary for the military corps of armored warriors.

Thus, there were two types of military societies that emerged across Eurasia in the first millennium A.D., one based on the nomadic horsemen and the other on the armored knights. One encouraged speed, individual agility, and the success of the lightning strike. The other required vast organization and elaborate rules, and was more useful as a defense. The one could attack at will. The other could hold.

STATE LANDS AND ARMIES: CHINA AND BYZANTIUM

In the case of China and Byzantium, where state formation was relatively well advanced by the seventh century, the heavily armed cavalries were based on the cultivation of government land rather than on feudal lords. In China, the founder of the Sui dynasty, Emperor Wen-di [Wen-ti] (589–605), instituted a formal combination of farming and fighting that had first been suggested as "state colonies" by Cao Cao around 196 and had actually been furthered by the Toba barbarians who ruled northern China as the Northern Wei dynasty (386–534). In 590 Wen-di settled soldiers as small farmers on state-owned land, some of which was new land opened up near the frontiers and some of which had been confiscated from the aristocracy. This "equitable fields system" undermined the separate authority of large landowners and supplied an independent class of farmer-soldiers at one stroke. Military leaders were selected for special training by a "divisional militia" system, also inaugurated by Wen-di. One strong young man was selected from every six families of middle rank and higher. He was exempted from taxation in return for extensive military training and service, supported partially by the state and partially by the other five families. While this system did not survive intact into the Tang dynasty, the practice of providing tax exemption for military service did. Further, the equitable fields system was retained by the Tang. These military farming lands offered economic independence in return for continued military training. "For three out of four seasons they worked at farming and plowing," a ninth century writer observed. "For one season they perfected themselves in the military skills of riding, swordsmanship, and archery."[5]

A similar state-supported system developed in Byzantium. It was called the "theme system" because it substituted military districts, or "themes," for the "provinces" that had been established by Diocletian. Themes were permanent military organizations of society, in which military officials governed instead of landed aristocrats. Each theme was responsible for providing imperial troops. Those who served were, as in China, small landholders who were farmer-soldiers, excused from taxation in return for military service. The themes probably originated in the Byzantine conquest of Persian territories under the emperor Heraclius (610–641) and increased in importance with the crisis of the Muslim invasions. The themes served the same purpose as the divisional militias in China. They gave the emperor control over the provincial nobility, who, in both civilizations, deprived the state of soldiers and taxpayers at the same time. But while the Chinese state became increasingly dominant after the Sui, the Byzantine state was weakened. The theme structure of the Byzantine Empire was discontinued by Alexius I after 1081. New invasions (by Seljuk Turks), central government weakness, and the revival of provincial nobles caused its demise. An ominously feudal institution called *pronoia* gave rural magnates large grants of land in return for military service. These grants often included immunity from taxation and the right to administer justice. Eventually they included exemption from military service as well.

Byzantium survived until 1453 because Constantinople survived, and Constantinople survived because of the Byzantine navy more than the army. For most of its history the Byzantine navy controlled access to its shores. On the occasion when the port of Constantinople was blockaded by the Muslims (674–678), a recently invented weapon called "Greek fire," a chemical mixture that ignited even on contact with water, proved decisive. The impact of such a weapon on the Rus (Russians) in 941 is recounted in the *Russian Primary Chronicle:*

> Theophanes [the Byzantine commander] pursued them in boats with Greek fire, and dropped it through pipes upon the Russian ships, so that a strange miracle was offered to view. Upon seeing the flames, the Rus cast themselves into the sea water, being anxious to escape. . . .[6]

"Some," according to the Byzantine account, "weighted down by their breastplates and helmets sank to the bottom of the sea. . . . Others were burned as they swam on the waves."[7]

If Greek fire was the Byzantine "lightning from heaven" (as the Russians called it), their heavily armored cavalry was their secret weapon on earth. The heavily armored cavalry of Byzantium depended on a couple of military innovations that originated in the Persian Parthian Empire of the second century and were continued by the Persian Sassanid Empire after 226. These were big horses and stirrups. Larger horses than the ponies of the steppe nomads were necessary to carry men in heavy armor. The breeding and raising of such horses required rich grasslands and considerable wealth, probably more of both than most nomadic tribes commanded. The stirrup gave the horseman greater control over his mount and cushioned the blow of a heavy lance. Arrows could be shot with a bow at full gallop by well-trained horsemen who needed not fear falling off the horse. Lances required stirrups.

Most peasants in Byzantium (as elsewhere) fought in the infantry, but the heavy cavalry was the elite force of the imperial army. In Byzantium and China the heavy

"Greek fire" gave the Byzantine navy an effective weapon against Muslims and Russians after 675. (The Bettmann Archive)

cavalry was rigorously trained to respond in unison to horn, drum, and flag signals. The Byzantine "cataphracts" (as the armed cavalry was called) formed a wedge shape that gave the shock force of a battering ram in a cavalry charge. Their attack on the vaunted Russian axe-wielding infantry in 971, according to a Byzantine historian, suggests their value:

> In the earlier clashes, neither side prevailed. The Russians felt it to be unendurable that they, who held among their neighbors a record of unbroken victory, should now lose it shamefully to the Byzantines, and they fought with desperate courage. But the Byzantines, for their part, thought it a foul disgrace if, hitherto successful against all opposition, they should now be worsted in a struggle against a foot-soldiering nation who couldn't even ride. . . . The evening star was already sinking when the Emperor John launched his final cavalry-charge on the Russians with devastating effect: "You are Romans!" he cried; "Now show your valor in your deeds!" Thus heartened, the cavalry burst out with irresistible ardor. The bugles sounded the charge. The Byzantine battle-cry rang out. The Russians wavered and fled. Their losses were enormous.[8]

EUROPEAN KNIGHTHOOD AND FEUDALISM

The first sign of an armored cavalry in Western Europe came in response to the invasion of the Muslims in the eighth century. In order to defeat the invading Muslim horsemen, the Franks borrowed the Byzantine model of heavily armored warriors on large horses and the stirrup. The Franks disdained use of the bow and arrow, which was more popular in Byzantium and the main weapon of the Chinese.

Charlemagne (768–814) united the Germanic tribes of central Europe in a series of military campaigns of foot soldiers and cavalry that he conducted almost every year that he was king of the Franks. He extended his realm as far north as Scandinavia, as far east as the Avars in Hungary, as far south as the Lombard kingdom of Italy, and as far west as to push the Muslim across the Pyrenees into Spain. These conquests encouraged him to challenge Constantinople by having the pope crown him "Emperor of the Romans" on Christmas Day in the year 800.

Charlemagne's empire did not last much beyond his own lifetime. The threat of foreign invasion lessened, but imperial political power disintegrated. Knights, who were used to plunder, rape, and domination in an ever-expanding empire, turned inward to exploit the peasants.

> Now they no longer joined forces with the king in one great army; instead, they sallied forth from a thousand lairs, from those castles dotting the country-side that had been built to ward off the invading foe. At first they did battle against the enemy, defending the homeland. But when in the tenth century the intervals between the waves of invasion grew longer, instead of laying down their arms they continued their rapine. Only the prey was different. What they still took now and then from the pagans they began to demand now from the "plebs," from the "unarmed people." After the year 1000, in the Frankish kingdom, the populace became the sole object of their pillaging, which went on with still greater impunity than before in view of the king's inability henceforth to check their violence and rapacity.[9]

In response to the rise of internal violence and oppression in the Frankish dominions, there arose a *"peace* movement, which grew inexorably around the year 1000."[10] A society increasingly distinguished not between lords and commoners, but between knights and farmers, sword bearers and unarmed men, called for a code governing the use of weapons. The church enjoined the poor to take cover under its cloak. Churchmen insisted that "all who are horsemen and bear secular arms" take an oath. The oath proposed by the Frankish bishops in 1024 was the same oath to respect order and refrain from violence against the poor that Charlemagne had required of all his subjects. Now it was demanded only of the horsemen. The rest of society had become so poor and oppressed that "it would have been inconceivable for such a people to have continued to pledge their faith by sworn oath,"[11] according to the historian Georges Duby.

By the middle of the eleventh century in Europe, three "orders" of society had distinguished themselves: those who fought, those who worked, and those who prayed. Knights, peasants, and clergy led three different lives. The knights, however, were clearly becoming the dominant power in the society. They adopted the church's oath, with its religious sanction, to their own affairs, instituting an elaborate process of sanctifying knights, and swearing mutual loyalties. As knighthood became endowed with religious sanction, the clergy looked to redirect its activities to holier goals than the rape and plunder of Christians.

> Rekindling the memory of Charlemagne, the Church dreamed of the halcyon days when pillage afflicted not peasants but pagans; it envisaged turning armed marauders into heroes of the righteous cause, soldiers of evil into knights of Christ.[12]

But before Europeans could organize a holy crusade against the Muslims, they had to meet an internal threat from the north.

TRADING AND RAIDING: THE VIKINGS

The Vikings are one of the most colorful "warrior societies" of European history. Between the eighth and eleventh centuries Viking ships and soldiers terrorized village settlements from Ireland to Russia, fought and traded in the cities of the Byzantine and Muslim empires, and established European outposts across the Atlantic Ocean. Not too much was known about the origins of these Norse when they first struck out from Scandinavia to conquer the English island of Lindisfarne in 793. Their ancestors may have been the "German" tribe that the Roman historian Tacitus called the Suiones in the first century. Tacitus remarks that the Suiones "are strong not only in arms and men but also in their fleets," that their curious ships have "a prow at both ends" but no sail, and that they can be found with their slaves along the ocean and rivers in search of wealth. Apparently, the Suiones were more settled than the nomadic tribes that Tacitus described. We hear no mention of them after Tacitus until the sixth century, when the Gothic historian Jordanes reports that the inhabitants of Scandinavia are unusually ferocious and tall. It was not until the end of the eighth century that the European tribes and descendants of the Romans had firsthand experience with the Norse. By that time the Scandinavians had improved their ships, added sails, and realized the potential plunder to be gained from a more settled Europe.

"Out of the north an evil shall break forth." The warning of the prophet Jeremiah must have rung in the ears of the Christian monks at Lindisfarne when the Norse sailed into history in 793. The English scholar Alcuin, who was staying in France at the court of Charlemagne, expressed the shock of European Christians at the sudden "pagan" attack. "Never before had such a terror appeared in Britain," he wrote, as the invasion of Lindisfarne by the Vikings. The Church of St. Cuthbert was robbed of its treasures and "spattered with the blood of the priests of God."

In a matter of decades the Vikings had conquered much of England, Scotland, and Ireland. They came usually as pirates. They murdered unarmed monks, looted sanctuaries, plundered the libraries that had preserved the literary heritage of the ancient world, and burned what they could not carry away. The booty they sought

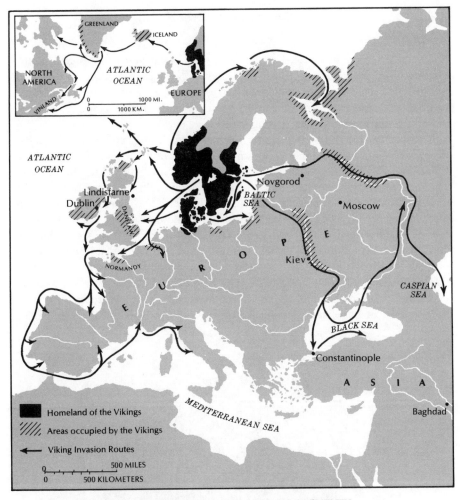

THE EXPANSION OF THE VIKINGS, EIGHTH TO ELEVENTH
CENTURIES A.D.
The Vikings (or Norse) spread eastward from Sweden to Russia and
Constantinople, and westward from Norway to North America and the
Mediterranean.

was more precious than the literary achievements of Charlemagne's civilization.
They took gold and jewels, valuable objects that they might trade, and they raped
and enslaved the wives and daughters of their victims. Sailing first from Norway,
and then from Denmark and Sweden, these pirates terrorized the inhabitants of the
British Isles especially throughout the ninth century.

In time, the terror of the Norse became modified or institutionalized. In 865 the
English began paying a yearly ransom to their Scandinavian overlords, which was
kind of a "protection" payment called the *Danegeld* (money for the Danes). Much

of central England was placed under the Danish king and administered as the *Danelaw*. Scandinavians established their own villages (like Dublin) in occupied territory or set up colonies in existing towns. These settlements were sometimes fortified encampments used for further pirate expeditions, but gradually became more like administrative and trading centers.

Perhaps there has always been a hazy line between raiding and trading, or maybe the sons of raiders are the ones who can afford to trade. Whatever the case, there is evidence for both continual piracy mixed with trading in Viking history and a gradually increasing emphasis on trade instead of raids. Piracy certainly continued throughout the Viking age, but the raids of the tenth and eleventh centuries up the rivers of France, along the coast of Spain, and into the Mediterranean Sea often became trading missions. This was especially true when the Vikings established fairly permanent colonies, as in Normandy in northern France and on the island of Sicily in the Mediterranean. It's safer to pillage distant ports than to plunder a neighbor.

Viking expansion was not all piracy and business, even in Western Europe, as the examples of colonization indicate. But colonization was usually a secondary

Head of a Viking ship, probably eighth century. (Granger)

activity in populated Western Europe. It was the major type of Scandinavian expansion in the east along the long rivers of Russia and in the west beyond the edge of the world.

Russia is, of course, the land of the Rus. The Rus were the Swedish colonists who began settling on the river trade routes between Scandinavia and the Byzantine capital at Constantinople in the ninth century. There the Swedes met some of the older inhabitants, Slavs (whose name reminds us that the Vikings took them as slaves) and Asians. The meetings must have often been violent, but eventually the Swedish towns at Novgorod and Kiev lost their Viking flavor and became the trading centers of the emerging Russian state. From these towns the Rus learned of the magnificence of the Byzantine Empire. The Rus were too weak to pose a serious threat to Constantinople, but Viking courage and military ability were famous enough for the Byzantine emperors to recruit these Rus for a special palace guard and as mercenaries in the Byzantine army. Meanwhile the Rus traded northern furs, honey, amber, wax, and captured slaves in exchange for the fine textiles, spices, wines, and luxuries of the Byzantine Empire at Constantinople and the Muslim Empire at Baghdad. According to a Muslim visitor, the Rus merchants would pray: "O Lord, I have come from distant parts with so many girls, so many sable furs. . . . Please send me a merchant who has many *dinars* and *dirhems,* and who will trade favorably with me without too much bartering."

While the Swedish Vikings turned piracy into colonization, and colonization into commercial activity in the vast eastern lands that were to be known as Russia, the Vikings of Norway explored the Atlantic Ocean. Since Viking society condoned piracy, its criminals and outcasts were not admitted to such a "respectable" calling. They were forced instead, like Erik the Red, to explore and settle in relatively unpopulated areas. Erik the Red had to leave Norway in a hurry "because of some killings" in the late 970s. He went to Iceland, which Vikings had taken from Irish priests about a hundred years before. He got into trouble there also, and was outlawed around 980. With another Icelander he set sail westward, arriving finally at a bleak mountainous land that he called Greenland. He ran into more trouble on his return to Iceland, so he was forced to make Greenland his permanent home. Soon a colonial settlement had been established on Erik's farm, a haven, probably, for the outcasts of "polite" Viking society.

Bjarni Herjolfsson discovered America about 985. Of course, Asians had arrived there by way of the Bering Sea over a thousand years before. It is also quite possible that the Irish priests who settled Iceland also "discovered" America before Bjarni. In any case, it was an accident (though less accidental than Columbus's later voyage). After a visit to Norway, Bjarni returned to his home in Iceland to find that his parents had left for Erik the Red's colony in Greenland. Bjarni set out to follow them. After a longer trip than expected, Bjarni and his crew finally saw land, but it lacked the mountains of Greenland.

Realizing they had gone too far, Bjarni and his crew did not land but sailed back until they found Greenland and Erik's colony. When they told the colonists of their discovery, Erik's sons Leif and Thorvald gathered a crew to explore the new land. They named part of it *Helluland,* and part of it they called *Vinland,* presumably because of its vine foliage. It is also reported that Thorvald lived there for two years until he was killed by the local inhabitants. The only certain Viking site that has been unearthed so far is at the northern tip of Newfoundland, but it is quite likely that further archeological exploration will yield other sites.

The important thing, of course, is that the colony did not last. That fact tells more about Viking society than the fact of discovery. Viking society was capable of vast oceanic explorations, but it possessed neither the will nor the capability to maintain all of these far-flung colonies for long. The Vikings did not even remain in Greenland. They stayed in Iceland because its climate and vegetation and animal life were much more inviting, and also because it was within relatively easy supply distance of Norway. They remained in Russia because their settlements were prosperous trading centers close to the junction of three thriving cultures: the Byzantine, the Muslim, and the European Christian. Perhaps Viking culture was always more attuned to raiding and trading than to isolated, peaceful settlement.

The causes of Viking failure, as well as success, lie in the character of its militaristic culture. It was a culture in which aggressiveness was channeled into long-distance trade and profit seeking or war. Its long-term success was in the revival of trade and the development of both feudal and capitalistic institutions in Europe. The warrior element in Viking society that was not "civilized" into economic aggression was defeated in battle. The usual closing date is 1066, since that was the year that Harald the Hard Ruler, king of Norway, was killed by the English. The death of King Harald is a fitting symbolic end to Viking ascendancy. He represented Viking expansiveness at its zenith. As a boy he had fled from Norway to Kiev. To win back his father's Norwegian crown he prepared himself as a member, and then as the commander, of the Byzantine emperor's palace guard. He fought for the Greeks in Asia Minor, the Caucasus Mountains, and Jerusalem. He returned to Kiev as a seasoned victor, married a Russian princess, and lived to rule Norway, explore the Atlantic, and reconquer England. This "Thunderbolt of the North," the ultimate Viking ruler, was defeated, almost by chance, by Earl Harold Godwinson on September 25, 1066. The Vikings lost England, and gradually thereafter much more of their overseas empire.

The death of a universal Viking king like Harald was the proper symbol for the end of the Viking age. Except for the fortuitousness of his actual defeat, the event had all of the drama of final tragedy—almost the final Twilight of the Gods imagined in Viking legend. But despite the hopes of heroic culture, the death of a single individual never means the end of an age. Actually, Godwinson was killed a few days later by William of Normandy, a descendant of the Vikings who had conquered northern France. In a sense, 1066 marks the final victory, rather than defeat, of Viking culture. At the same time, Scandinavia became disorganized, European armies became better able to cope with pirate raids, and within a couple of hundred years new military techniques and gunpowder made Viking military tactics obsolete.

As a military culture, the Vikings were doomed to fail when their victims learned how to defend themselves. The weakness of Viking culture was that it remained largely militaristic. Only those elements of the raid that could be channeled into trade survived. Much of Viking beliefs and behavior could not. The trading outposts in Normandy, France, made it possible for Vikings' sons to conquer England and parts of Italy. By the twelfth century they were engaged in a phase of European expansion called the Crusades.

PRAYING AND PREYING: THE CRUSADES

Like any civilization, that of Western European Christendom was propelled by conflicting tensions. Like other civilizations emerging from tribal or barbarian experience, it was torn between personal and public loyalties. Like other expansive civilizations, it vacillated between raiding and trading. Like other monotheistic civilizations, it was torn between a sense of human brotherhood and a desire to enforce conformity to God's will. Its attitudes toward war and violence were polarized by these tensions. Tribal, and then feudal, moral codes demanded vengeance; states substituted laws. Trading bred partners and predators. Christianity tamed barbarian aggressiveness, but it also recruited soldiers for Christ. The Crusades were the successful attempt of the church to take over and use the feudal structure and armies for its own purposes. Documents from the eleventh century in the West reveal a sharp increase in the number of prayers for victory. In the same century we see the first records of sword blessing. Progressively, the knight was expected to live according to the religious standards of the church. Paul's phrase "fighting for Christ" (by which he had meant, and the Byzantine church still meant, a spiritual fight with "the weapons of Christ"—or no weapons at all) had become identified in the West with the service of the knights.

The first Crusade began, ironically enough, after a series of attempts by the pope and his councils to institute a "Truce of God" over rival feudal barons and their armies. Pope Urban II included in his list of reasons for a Crusade the hope that Christian knights would "fight righteous wars instead of iniquitous combats" among fellow Christians. Urban detailed other reasons for a holy war in his speech to the Council of Clermont on November 27, 1095: the Byzantine emperor had asked for help against the Arab Muslims; the Muslims not only threatened Constantinople but also occupied Jerusalem and the Holy Land; a Christian conquest of the Muslims might restore Christian rule of Jerusalem and possibly even reunite the Eastern and Roman churches, which had been separate since 1054.

It may have been true that the Byzantine emperor Alexius asked the pope for assistance against the Muslims. But if he made such a request, he was clearly

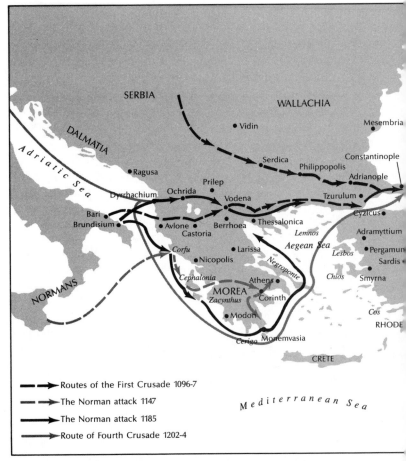

THE CRUSADES AND THE WEAKENING OF BYZANTIUM, 1096–1204
*The Crusades established European outposts in the Middle East
without seriously challenging Islam. At the same time they hastened
the end of the rival Christian civilization in Byzantium.*

thinking of the usefulness of an aristocratic army of knights. The knights (especially
the Norman and Frankish second sons, who would not inherit the family lands)
formed fairly disciplined armies. They hoped to do holy work at the same time
that they might win their fortunes from Muslim infidels (or even Byzantine
heretics).

Pope Urban's call struck a responsive chord at the other extreme of the scale
of European society as well. As the pope's message was popularized by wandering,
barefoot preachers like Peter the Hermit, hordes of poor people hurried out of

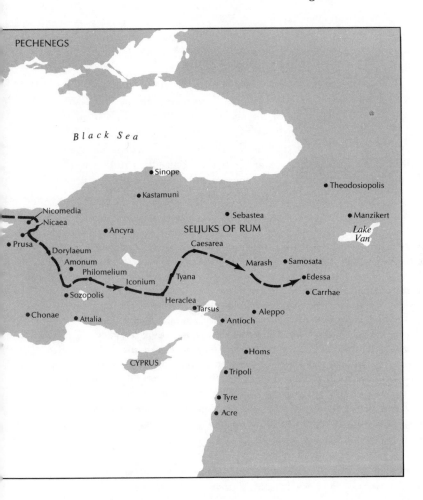

overcrowded areas to make their lives meaningful in holy war. Untrained and undisciplined "people's crusades" joined the armies of knights in the march across Europe to Constantinople. Before they left to exterminate "the sons of whores, the race of Cain," as they called the Muslims, the vagabond armies seized their own European towns for Christ. The Crusades began with the first large-scale massacre of Jews. "We have set out to march a long way to fight the enemies of the East," one of the Crusaders declared, "and behold, before our very eyes are his worst foes, the Jews. They must be dealt with first." In France, where Jewish communities had gathered for centuries under the protection of Christian bishops, the mobs demanded the conversion or extermination of the Jews. In May and June of 1096 alone, between four and eight thousand Jews were massacred.

The massacre of Jews was only practice for the real business at hand. The vagabond armies that survived the long walk to Constantinople horrified the Byzantine emperor and the inhabitants of the ancient city. They had no plan or organization, and they could just as readily sack Constantinople as Jerusalem. With a little luck and a good deal of diplomatic skill, the Byzantine ruling class managed to redirect the armies of the dispossessed toward Jerusalem. Since the Muslims were disorganized and did not expect an attack as ferocious and determined as had been executed, the Crusaders were able to take the ancient city where Jesus had lived and died. The city was captured in 1099.

> The fall of Jerusalem was followed by a holocaust; except for the governor and his bodyguard, who managed to buy their lives and were escorted from the city, every Moslem—man, woman and child—was killed. In and around the Temple of Solomon "the horses waded in blood up to their knees, nay up to the bridle. It was a just and wonderful judgement of God that the same place should receive the blood of those whose blasphemies it had so long carried up to God." As for the Jews of Jerusalem, when they took refuge in their chief synagogue the building was set fire and they were all burnt alive. Weeping with joy and singing songs of praise the crusaders marched in procession to the Church of the Holy Sepulchre. "O new day, new day and exultation, new and everlasting gladness. . . . That day, famed through all centuries to come, turned all our suffering and hardships into joy and exultation; that day, the confirmation of Christianity, the annihilation of paganism, the renewal of our faith!"[13]

European sources estimate that ten thousand Muslims were massacred in the wake of that first capture of Jerusalem. Muslim sources put the figure at a hundred thousand killed. Whatever the numbers, the bloodbath taught the Muslim (and the Byzantines) to hate the West as they never had before. "The west stands for war and exploitation," a Byzantine diplomat concluded. "West Rome . . . is the mother of all wickedness." The Muslims mourned their losses at the hands of these "Christian dogs," and vowed to fight fire with fire. The Arab poet Mosaffer Allah Werdis poignantly expressed the pain and bitterness of the Muslims:

> *We have mingled our blood and our tears.*
> *None of us remains who has strength enough to beat*
> *off these oppressors.*
> *The sight of our weapons only brings sorrow to us*
> *who must weep while the swords of war spark off*
> *the all-consuming flames.*

Ah, sons of Muhammad, what battles still await you,
  how many heroic heads must lie under the horses'
  feet!
Yet all your longing is only for an old age lapped in
  safety and well-being, for a sweet smiling life, like
  the flowers of the field.
Oh that so much blood had to flow, that so many women were
  left with nothing save their bare hands to protect
  their modesty!
Amid the fearful clashing swords and lances, the faces of
  the children grow white with horror.[14]

By the end of the eleventh century Islamic society was more stable and civilized than Europe. It produced philosophers, mathematicians, astronomers, doctors, and artists with the same urgency with which Western Europe produced soldiers. The desert horsemen had brought an agricultural technology to Spain that made the land blossom more luxuriously than ever before, more (perhaps) than today. The descendants of horsemen became doctors who staffed the first faculties of European medical schools. Their philosophers taught the West Plato and Aristotle. Their merchants and mariners taught Europeans mathematics, bookkeeping, and maritime travel. In short, the Muslim civilization that was destroyed by the Crusaders at Jerusalem was considerably more sophisticated and peaceful than that of its conquerors.

Some Christian Franks who ruled Jerusalem from 1099 to 1185 realized that the Muslims were more tolerant than themselves. They were aware that Christians had for centuries held high positions in the Muslim courts of the Middle East. They found Syrian Christians who were physicians, astronomers, and officials of Muslim princes. They told stories of Muslim generosity, even in battle. One Christian, Oliverus Scholasticus, told of Sultan al-Malik-al-Kamil, who defeated one of the later invading armies of Crusaders and then gave the survivors food: "Who could doubt that such goodness, friendship and charity came from God? Men whose parents, sons and daughters, brothers and sisters had died in agony at our hands, whose lands we took, whom we drove naked from their homes, revived us with their own food when we were dying of hunger, and showered us with kindness even while we were in their power." Some Christians, like Arnold of Lubeck, even understood that the Muslim idea of brotherhood was more tolerant than the Christian view of Jews and Muslims as Antichrists. Arnold put the following words in the mouth of a Muslim: "It is certain, even if our beliefs are different, that we have the same Creator and Father, and that we must then be brothers, not according to our faith but as men. Let us then remember our common Father and feed our brothers."

As tolerant as the Muslims had been, however, they could not be expected to lie back after the Christian massacre of Jerusalem. They had been disorganized at

O armes a graunt cupdïne   p ref te euer Wic

This thirteenth-century battle scene shows mounted knights, possibly Crusaders, in combat. (University Library, Cambridge)

the time of the Christian conquest, but they were able to recapture Jerusalem by 1187, under the leadership of the Syrian sultan Saladin, who had unified Syria and Egypt. Although the Christians had launched a second Crusade from 1147 to 1149 (which began with another massacre of European Jews), Saladin treated the de-

uuc sef paa E ii cuntre fu en une lande

scendants of the first Crusaders in Jerusalem with remarkable charity. Those who could afford to buy their freedom were allowed to do so. The poor were freed without payment. Later, Saladin actually bequeathed his wealth to Muslim, Jewish, and Christian poor alike.

Europe's answer was a third Crusade. This time the pope induced three of Christendom's greatest kings to lead armies against the Muslims: Frederick Barbarossa, Holy Roman emperor; Philip Augustus of France; and Richard I (the Lion Hearted) of England. They brought their personal quarrels and national conflicts with them. Only Richard (who relished war) actually made it to the Holy Land to confront Saladin. He captured Acre (just north of Jerusalem) and established a Christian outpost that was to last another hundred years (1189–1291), but he was unable to take Jerusalem. Negotiations with Saladin dragged on too long for Richard's spirited temper. To show his determination he ordered the massacre of two to three thousand of his Muslim prisoners. Then he had their bodies cut open and searched for gold, which some had swallowed. Last, but not least, he had their bodies burned so that the ashes could be sifted for any gold that might have been missed. Such atrocities soured Muslim toleration for some time.

If Muslims needed the third Crusade to learn the militant character of Western civilization, the Byzantine Greeks may have needed the fourth. Pope Innocent III asked the kings of Europe in 1202 to capture Jerusalem for the last time. However, Philip Augustus and John of England (Richard had been kidnapped for ransom in Germany) were too busy fighting each other. Lesser lords pleaded poverty, but Innocent prevailed upon them, and the city of Venice offered transportation for a percentage of the take. Once the Crusaders had set sail, the Venetian merchants and businessmen were in control. The Doge (or leader) of the city convinced the Crusaders to make a stop at Zara (which he declared had been taken from Venice by the Hungarian king). The Crusaders proceeded to loot, sack, and destroy this perfectly good Christian city. Innocent was horrified. He excommunicated the whole army, then reconsidered. Finally, he lifted the ban so that they could continue on to Jerusalem.

Tempted by a claimant to the Byzantine throne who offered the Crusaders enough to pay the Venetians if their armies would help him take Constantinople, they stopped again. Resistance was minimal, and the Crusaders were successful. But the pretender was slow in paying, or the Venetians cornered most of it. The enraged armies then conquered Constantinople for themselves. The city, which had withstood the invasions of barbarians, Hungarians, and Turks, fell in 1204 (almost a thousand years after the collapse of Rome) to a motley army of Westerners. The wars for Christ ended in the destruction of the greatest Christian city in the world. Shrines and churches were looted. Priceless art objects were melted down for metal. Altars were broken up and carried away. Mosaics were destroyed for their jewels. Manuscripts of the church and the ancient world were lost forever.

The destruction of Constantinople put an end to the Crusade for the Holy Land. The armies never left for Jerusalem. The crusading spirit, though, became a way of life. Pope Innocent himself sought to organize another Crusade in 1215. But for the most part the Crusades turned inward. They were launched against the elaborate Muslim civilization in Spain, against Roman Christian heretics in southern France, against foreign nationalities, and (as always) against the Jews. By the end of the thirteenth century, the Crusade had a lot to do with national glory, profit, and extermination, and very little to do with prayer. The goals of Christianity had no doubt been perverted, but the shift from praying to preying had been natural and lasting.

FOR FURTHER READING

On barbarian Europe, one of the better, brief introductions is J. M. Wallace-Hadrill's *The Barbarian West*. His more recent *The Long-Haired Kings* is also valuable. The classical studies (written about fifty years ago) are J. B. Bury's *The Invasion of Europe by the Barbarians*, Samuel Dill's *Roman Society in the Last Century of the Western Empire*, and Ferdinand Lot's *The End of the Ancient World and the Beginning of the Middle Ages*. All are still worth reading. One of the more interesting recent studies is P. R. L. Brown's *The End of Antiquity*. *The Dark Ages*, edited by D. Talbot Rice, brings together excellent articles. For firsthand accounts of the barbarians, the student can also take advantage of two excellent primary sources: Tacitus's *On Britain and Germany* and Gregory of Tours's *History of the Franks*.

The best study of Islam is Marshall G. S. Hodgson's *The Venture of Islam*, but its length (three volumes) and sophisticated analysis are demanding. More accessible introductions are Caesar E. Farah's *Islam*, Hugh Kennedy's *The Prophet and the Age of the Caliphates*, J. J. Saunders's *A History of Medieval Islam*, W. Montgomery Watt's *The Majesty That Was Islam*, and B. Lewis's *The Arabs in History*. For introductions to Muhammad, see W. Montgomery Watt's *Muhammad, Prophet and Statesman* and Maxime Rodinson's *Mohammed*.

Given the centrality of the *Koran* to Islam, students should take advantage of the many editions now available. A useful guide is Fazlur Rahman's *Major Themes of the Qur'an*. There is also an excellent collection of primary source materials in Bernard Lewis's two-volume *Islam* and in *Islam from Within*, edited by Kenneth Cragg and R. Marston Speight.

Among the general introductions to China, Mark Elvin's *The Pattern of the Chinese Past* is especially useful for economic history. F. A. Kierman, Jr., and J. K. Fairbank have edited a valuable collection of articles in *Chinese Ways in Warfare*. C. O. Hucker's *China's Imperial Past* is an excellent overview. For the period of unification, Arthur F. Wright's *The Sui Dynasty* is a useful introduction. *Sui and Tang China, 589–906*, edited by D. Twitchett, is a thorough collection of articles.

For Byzantium, D. A. Miller's *The Byzantine Tradition* is a good brief introduction. René Guerdan's *Byzantium* is a bit more thorough. D. A. Miller's *Imperial Constantinople* is a good introduction to the city. There is also an excellent collection of primary source materials in *Byzantium: Church, Society, and Civilization Seen through Contemporary Eyes*, edited by Deno John Geanakoplos.

On Western Europe, we have found the work of Georges Duby, especially *The Three Orders: Feudal Society Imagined* and *The Early Growth of the European Economy*, extremely helpful. On the peace movement see his *L'An Mil*. The work of Jacques Le Goff is also extremely insightful. See, for instance, his *Time, Work, & Culture in the Middle Ages*. Philippe Contamine's *War in the Middle Ages* is a comprehensive account of combatants and weapons.

For general histories of medieval Europe, perhaps the best place to start is with Henri Pirenne's *A History of Europe,* vol. 1, a book written without the aid of libraries by the Belgian scholar while in a German prison camp during World War I. Another classic French study is Marc Bloch's *Feudal Society.* One of the more interesting of the modern approaches is Robert Lopez's *The Birth of Europe.* Norman Cantor's *Medieval History* is also strongly interpretive, and particularly useful on the medieval church. Among other histories, C. Warren Hollister's *Medieval Europe: A Short History,* Denys Hay's short *The Medieval Centuries,* and Joseph R. Strayer's *Western Europe in the Middle Ages* are fairly easy. *The Making of Europe,* by Christopher Dawson, and *Early Medieval Society,* edited by Sylvia L. Thrupp, are more sophisticated. Hugh Trevor-Roper's *The Rise of Christian Europe* and Jacques Boussard's *The Civilization of Charlemagne* are particularly well illustrated.

A few other books are especially valuable for judging the tenor of violence in medieval Europe. T. S. R. Boase's well-illustrated *Death in the Middle Ages* is rich and disturbing. J. Huizinga's classic *The Waning of the Middle Ages* is indispensable. Lynn White, Jr.'s *Medieval Technology and Social Change* is a classic account of the relationship of medieval technology and the warrior society of chivalry. For the richness of contemporary detail there is none better than John Froissart's *The Chronicles of England, France and Spain,* which was completed in 1400.

On the Vikings, there is a well-illustrated introduction in David Wilson's *The Vikings and Their Origins: Scandinavia in the First Millennium* and a very good history of their culture from 800 to 1100 in Johannes Brondsted's *The Vikings.* Other useful recent titles are P. G. Foote and D. M. Wilson's *The Viking Achievement,* G. Jones's *A History of the Vikings,* and P. Sawyer's *The Age of the Vikings.* On the Atlantic voyages, see Gwyn Jones, *The Norse Atlantic Saga.*

On the Crusades, various interpretations are brought together in J. A. Brundage's *The Crusades: Motives and Achievements.* Eyewitness accounts are available in F. T. Marzialis's *Memoirs of the Crusades.* Arab versions are presented in *Arab Historians of the Crusades,* edited by Francesco Gabrieli, and Amin Maalouf's *The Crusades through Arab Eyes.* The standard multivolume histories are K. M. Setton's *History of the Crusades* and the older work by Steven Runciman, *A History of the Crusades.* R. A. Newhall's *The Crusades* is a brief, introductory account. The warfare of the period is described in R. C. Smail's *Crusading Warfare, 1097–1193.* Finally, Norman Cohn's superb *The Pursuit of the Millennium* puts the Crusades into a broader perspective of medieval religious hysteria and relates their popular psychological dimension to modern totalitarianism.

NOTES

1. Adapted and translated from Jacques Le Goff's *La Civilisation de L'Occident Medieval* (Paris: Arthaud, 1964), pp. 31–32.
2. Salvien, adapted and translated from Le Goff, *op. cit.,* p. 36.
3. Marshall G. S. Hodgson, *The Venture of Islam,* vol. 1 (Chicago: University of Chicago Press, 1974), pp. 173–174.
4. W. Ivanow, "An Ismaili Poem in Praise of Fidawis," *Journal of the Bombay Branch of the Royal Asiatic Society,* 14 (1938), p. 71. Quoted in Bernard Lewis, *The Assassins* (New York: Basic Books, 1968), p. 130.

5. Adapted from Mark Elvin, *The Pattern of the Chinese Past* (Stanford: Stanford University Press, 1973), p. 56.

6. Translated by S. Cross and O. Sherbowitz, *Russian Primary Chronicle* (Cambridge, Mass.: Medieval Academy of America, 1953), p. 72.

7. Liudprand, *Antapodosis,* trans. in Deno John Geanakoplos, *Byzantium: Church, Society and Civilization Seen through Contemporary Eyes* (Chicago: University of Chicago Press, 1984), p. 113.

8. Trans. by R. Jenkins, from Leo Diaconus, *Historia,* in P. Whiting, *Byzantium: An Introduction* (New York: New York University Press, 1971), p. 76.

9. Georges Duby, *The Three Orders: Feudal Society Imagined* (Chicago: University of Chicago Press, 1980), p. 151.

10. Jacques Le Goff, *Time, Work, and Culture in the Middle Ages,* trans. Arthur Goldhammer (Chicago: University of Chicago Press, 1980), p. 267.

11. *Ibid.,* p. 138.

12. Duby, *op. cit.,* p. 157.

13. Norman Cohn, *The Pursuit of the Millennium* (New York: Harper & Row, 1961), pp. 48–49.

14. Friedrich Heer, *The Medieval World* (New York: New American Library, 1961), pp. 135–136.

❧ 10 ❧

Love
and
Devotion

Chivalry and
Sexuality

HAVE YOU EVER WANTED TO FALL IN LOVE? Have you ever felt guilty about sex? Then there's a good chance that you have been raised in a culture descended from medieval Christian Europe.

We live in a society in which people expect marriages to be based on love. Hardly anyone thinks an arranged marriage is a good idea. We learn as children to begin the process of choosing a mate in an elaborate agenda of dating and self-examination. We learn to distinguish between infatuation, liking, loving, falling in love, being in love, and numerous other expressions. We have more phrases for love than Eskimos have for snow.

Our society makes a religion of romantic love. Romance is the daily bread of popular magazines, novels, television, and films. Popular music consists almost entirely of love songs. A movie without a love story is a formula for empty theaters.

People expect a lot from romance. They expect it to heal all wounds, mount all obstacles, save all marriages. Our society places pretty heavy demands on the emotional involvement of two people in love.

We call it love, but we mean some very specific, and some very extraordinary, ideas, most of which developed in the codes of chivalry in the European Middle Ages. We mean romantic love. If we were to lay out its principles, which we never do, they would look something like the following. Love is entirely involuntary. It just happens, usually when we are least prepared, as if by magic. It can be triggered by a first glance, the sound of a voice, a smell. When it occurs, it transforms us, as if we swallowed a magic potion. It is chemical. We are never the same. Love is the communication of two hearts. It is immediate and intense, but vulnerable to the conventions and deceits of the world. The world is against it, continually placing obstacles in the way. True love can be recognized by its ability to overcome these obstacles. The deepest loves prove themselves in the continual struggle against obstacles. Often the obstacles are so great that the lovers die. Love is too perfect for an imperfect world. True love ends in death.

We have all known people (ourselves excluded, of course) who have acted according to these principles: people who have preferred the passion, the struggle, and the obstacles; people who seemed always to choose the wrong person and persist in the struggle almost for its own sake; people who prefer the quest to the attainment of love; people who prefer the magic to the reality.

When we wonder about the high rate of divorce in our society, we might ask about the high expectations for marriage based on romantic love. Romantic love may be a pretty fleeting emotional base for an institution as serious and permanent as marriage. Do we desire incompatible ends when we ask for both deeply personal emotional experience and long-term institutional stability too? Can the kind of love we have learned serve our institutions as well as ourselves?

In order to answer some of these questions, we will explore the origins of our idea of romantic love. Where did the idea of romantic love come from? How did it develop? Perhaps the first question is this: What, after all, was the idea of romantic love doing in Christian Europe?

THE ARABS AND GREEK PHILOSOPHY

How was it that Christian culture, uneasy with sex and often hostile to women, developed the idea of romantic love that still seduces us? A classic, still compelling answer to that question was provided fifty years ago by Denis de Rougemont in *Love in the Western World*. He argued that the roots of romantic love were in Greek philosophical idealism channeled into Islamic mysticism, especially the tradition called Sufism, as learned and adapted by Christian heretics in southern France at the beginning of the twelfth century. Now, what does all of that mean?

Long after Christians lost touch with Greek culture, the Arabs retained an interest in and knowledge of the Greek classics. They were familiar with the tradition of idealism that had been cultivated by Plato and the Platonists. Some found the ideas of Platonic idealism particularly useful in understanding and spreading the new Islamic religion.

For Plato, the world was an illusion, a shadow play formed by a source of light too bright for human eyes. We exist, Plato said, as if in a cave, taking the flickering shadows in our cave as the ultimate reality, unaware that the real world begins outside. We spend all of our time absorbed in the reflections of things, and we never realize it.

Islamic thinkers found this Platonic idealism a rich source of ideas to suggest the power of God and the nature of the religious experience. Islam was, more than anything else, an extreme, uncompromising monotheism. "There is no god but God," the Muslim says over and over again. "God will bar Paradise to anyone who associates anything with God," the Koran says (V:72). Christian ideas of Jesus as the son of God, of the trinity, and of saints were thought by many Muslims to smack of pagan polytheism. Muslim tradition opposed pictures of God out of concern that the ignorant would worship the image rather than the reality of God. Platonic philosophy provided metaphors for this radical monotheism, especially among the cultivated upper class.

In extreme form it led to a philosophy called gnosticism. The Gnostics were religious mystics. They accepted Plato's sense of philosophic wisdom as illumination, *gnosis*. They believed that the soul could be liberated from the darkness and falsehood of the material body by an act of illumination. The world, they believed, was like Plato's cave. Truth lay behind the appearances and in the enlightened soul.

Sects like the Gnostics existed throughout the Mediterranean and Byzantine world, especially in the third to sixth centuries A.D., influencing the development of Christianity and Islam. Persian Manichaeanism was a similar movement that affected those religions.

THE LOVE OF THE MUSLIM SUFI

The Muslims most influenced by gnosticism, more influential than numerous, were called Sufis. As did other religious mystics, they sought an intimate personal experience of God. This was a desire necessarily full of difficulty. Extreme monotheism emphasized the distance between God and human beings, making it seem more difficult for humans to understand or communicate with God. But the feeling of extreme separation from God also led some sensitive souls to strive even harder for contact with God.

One of the earliest of these Sufis was a woman named Rabi'a (d. 801) of Basra. We have only fragments of her poetry, but there are a number of stories told about her that capture the Sufi idea of love. According to one story, she once ran through the streets carrying a torch in one hand and a jug of water in the other. When asked why, she said she was going to burn the gardens of paradise and douse the flames of hell so that no one again would worship God out of fear of hell or desire for paradise, but only for the love of God himself. Another story was told that when a number of devout Muslims asked for her hand in marriage, she declined, saying "the contract of marriage is for those who have a worldly existence. But in my case, I have ceased to exist in this world. I exist only in God and am altogether His. I live in the shadow of His command. The marriage contract must be asked for from Him, not from me."

This sense of extreme closeness to God got some devout Sufis in deep trouble with orthodox authorities. Some orthodox Muslims held that it was not even possible for the believer to "love" God because finite creatures can love only other finite creatures, and God is infinite.

But Sufis were mystics: they sought to lose themselves in God. Bayazid Bistami (d. 874) explained this experience in the following way: "I gazed upon God with the eye of truth and said to Him: 'Who is this?' He said: 'This is neither I nor other than I. There is no god but I.' Then He changed me out of my identity into His Selfhood. I communed with Him with the tongue of His Grace. And he said: 'I am thine through thee; there is no god but Thou.' "[1]

This kind of dramatic reversal of Islamic creed sprung from sincere religious piety, to be sure. But it was heresy nonetheless. Not only did it deify man instead of God, but it led to personal emotional excesses and a disregard for the *shari'ah,* or sacred law of the Muslim community.

Some Sufis were able to avoid public scandal, but others eagerly threw themselves into controversy. One of the most famous Sufis, al-Hallaj (d. 922), wandered throughout the Islamic world telling the common people to open themselves to the love of God. The immediacy of God's love, al-Hallaj taught, was infinitely preferable to rituals and formal obedience to the *shari'ah.* Even prayer, al-Hallaj wrote, "is Unbelief Once one knows." When he began to attract followers in high places at Baghdad, the seat of the Abbasid caliphate, he was imprisoned as a heretic and brutally executed in 922.

MASKING LOVE OF GOD

In order to avoid the fate of al-Hallaj and other Sufi martyrs, Sufi poets adopted various strategies to disguise their deep feelings of longing and love for God. They pretended to address their declarations of love to other people, rather than to God. They used conventional names for lovers or actual names of friends, in order to disguise their love affairs with God. They spoke of the intoxication of wine when they meant union with God. In many different ways they masked the source of their passion. As de Rougemont explained it:

> Arab mystics all insist that the *secret* of divine Love must be kept. They constantly complain of prying persons who want to find out about the mysteries, but not to take part in them with a whole-hearted faith. To somebody's hasty question: "What is Sufism?" al-Hallaj replies: "Do not turn

on Us: see our finger which has already been stained with the blood of lovers."[2]

According to de Rougemont, the poetry of the Sufi mystics attracted Christian heretics in southern France, called Cathars, who had been raised on Sufism, gnosticism, and Manichaeanism. It appealed to a number of Cathar (or Albigensian) beliefs: that the spirit was incorruptible, but the body corrupt; that marriage was a worldly compromise that true love disdained; and that the purest love was utter and abject devotion. These beliefs, according to de Rougemont, account for the linking of love and death in the Arab and European traditions. "Whoever does not die of his love," the poet Ibn al Faridh wrote, "is unable to live by it."[3]

LOVING MASKS OF GOD

If the world of appearances is a mask of God, one can worship God by loving the appearances as certainly as one can by attempting to transcend them. In a classical account of the loves, ideas, and mythologies of appearances, called *The Masks of God,* Joseph Campbell takes issue with de Rougemont's *Love in the Western World.* The courtly love poems of the European troubadors and minstrels were not products of gnostic denial, according to Campbell. They were, rather, affirmations of life, experience, sensuality, and nature. Campbell writes that while

> according to the Gnostic view, . . . nature is corrupt and the lure of the senses [is] to be repudiated, in the poetry of the troubadours . . . nature in its noblest moment—the realization of love—is an end and glory in itself; and the senses, ennobled and refined by courtesy and art, temperance, loyalty and courage, are the guides to this realization.[4]

While the religious mystic attempted to lose the self in the divinity, romantic love was an assertion of personal choice, Campbell argues. While the mystics celebrated a communal, indiscriminate love feast *(agape)* in which they "loved" all mankind, the troubadours sang the personal love *(amor)* of the individual's eye and heart. Campbell gives an example from one of the great troubadours, Guiraut de Borneilh (c. 1138–1200):

> *So, through the eyes love attains the heart:*
> *For the eyes are the scouts of the heart,*
> *And the eyes go reconnoitering*
> *For what it would please the heart to possess.*
> *And when they are in full accord*
> *And firm, all three, in the one resolve,*

At that time, perfect love is born
From what the eyes have made welcome to the heart.[5]

This too had already been developed in Arabic culture. It was called *adab*.

ADAB AND *THE DOVE'S NECKLACE*

"The senses, ennobled and refined by courtesy and art"—Campbell's description of troubadour love can stand as a definition of Arabic *adab*. Marshall Hodgson, the historian of Islam, called *adab* "the worldly culture of the polite classes."

> While the Muslim courtier, administrator, or intelligent landowner paid due honor to the aspirations of the professional Muslims, most of their efforts were devoted to living out a very different pattern from what the latter approved. Their etiquette, their conversation and fine arts and literature, their ways of using poetry and music and even religion, and their whole social pattern of position and privilege, with its economic and political institutions and its politics, formed a distinct set of genteel standards, prevailing among Muslims and non-Muslims of wealth and position. These standards, this adab, spread from one end of the Islamic domains to the other; fashions would most commonly be created in Baghdad, the most important seat of government, and would be eagerly adopted everywhere else.[6]

In the Abbasid court at Baghdad, in the courts of Egypt, North Africa, and Spain, the culture of *adab* provided new "genteel standards" for life and love. These cities and courts throughout Islam provided a leisure class that had the time and inclination to develop romantic love.

One of the great exponents of, and commentators on, this culture of *adab* was Ibn Hazm (994–1064), Spanish scholar and vizier (financial chief and head of the government) to the caliphs in Valencia and his native Córdoba. His greatest work was a massive study of comparative religion that examined the contradictions of Judaism, Christianity, and Islam from a simple monotheistic, commonsensical perspective. His most popular work, however, is a study of "love and lovers" called *The Dove's Necklace,* which shows us the roots of European courtly love. He reveals to us a world in which "falling in love" has become a fine, but popular, art.

> Love has certain signs which the intelligent man quickly detects and the shrewd man readily recognizes. Of these the first is the brooding gaze: the eye is the wide gateway of the soul, the scrutinizer of its secrets, conveying its most private thoughts and giving expression to its deepest-hid feelings. You will see the lover gazing at the beloved unblinkingly; his eyes follow the loved one's every moment, withdrawing as he withdraws, inclining as he inclines, just as the chameleon's stare shifts with the shifting of the sun. . . .
> Love for a thing renders you blind and deaf. If the lover could so contrive

that in the place where he happens to be there should be no talk of anything but his beloved, he would never leave that spot for any other in the whole world. . . . Weeping is a well-known sign of love, except that men differ very greatly from one another in this particular. Some are ready weepers; their tear-ducts are always overflowing, and their eyes respond immediately to their emotions, the tears rolling down at a moment's notice. Others are dry-eyed and barren of tears; to this category I myself belong. . . . I indeed marvel profoundly at all those who pretend to fall in love at first sight; I cannot easily prevail upon myself to believe their claims, and prefer to consider such love as merely a kind of lust. . . .

Know now—may God exalt you!—that love exercises an effective authority, a decisive sovereignty over the soul; its commands cannot be opposed; its ordinances may not be flouted; its rule is not to be transgressed; it demands unwavering obedience, and against its dominion there is no appeal. Love untwists the firmest plaits and looses the tightest strands; it dissolves that which is most solid, undoes that which is most firm; it penetrates the deepest recesses of the heart, and makes lawful things most strictly forbidden.[7]

Many of the elements that later became the subject of troubadour poetry are present in Arab *adab:* the importance of eye and heart that Campbell alludes to, the authority of love and submission to it, irrational behavior, and love at first sight. One of the differences, you might have noticed from the above, is that the Arab cultivation of love was not gender-specific. It focused men's eyes on young boys as well as on girls. This was especially true of the sophisticated cities of Spain. (Córdoba was the largest city in Western Europe in the ninth and tenth centuries.) This was a world where kings, like al-Mutamid, the eleventh-century king of Seville, wrote love poems to their male subjects: "I made him my slave, but the coyness of his glance has made me his prisoner. . . ."[8]

TROUBADOURS AND LADIES

Islam was a man's world, even though it had roots in the matriarchal clans of Medina. *Adab* was an urban, an urbane, style. Occitania (today's southern half of France) was a rural world in which women were able to inherit property and hold fiefs of land; at the beginning of the tenth century women held the counties of Auvergne, Beziers, Carcassonne, Limousin, Montpellier, Nimes, Perigord, and Toulouse. Often women were the effective rulers of a lord's vassals, serfs, and tenants when the lord was away, as in the period of the Crusades.

The Crusades not only acquainted Europeans with a more sophisticated urban culture (some of which had already been discovered in the settlers from Spain), they also frequently put returning knights in a position of questionable utility, dependent on a woman.

The poetry of courtly love began in Occitania in the early twelfth century, in the years immediately following the first Crusade. The first troubadour was Guilhem de Poitou, who began to write in 1102, just after returning from the Crusade. Although himself the seventh count of Poitiers and the ninth duke of Aquitaine, he sounded a note of subservience to women that struck a chord among his listeners and reached a crescendo in following years.

Ibn Hazm had written a chapter called "The Submissiveness the Lover Owes His Lady," but this became one of the main themes in the poetry of Guilhem. "No man has ever had the cunning to imagine what it is like," Guilhem wrote of obedience to a lady. "Such joy cannot find its like." He imagined homage to a lady as a source of mystic joy.[9]

One historian has a simple explanation for this dramatic role reversal:

> Most of the troubadours who followed Guilhem IX were men of modest or even humble origins. Many of them . . . depended for their living on the generosity of wealthy patrons. They were court poets, responsible for entertaining the large crowds that frequented the homes of Occitania's elite.
>
> The model for their lady—the object of their eternal, abject passions—was the wife of their employer. . . . The wife of the *senhor* was rich and powerful. If her husband was away on military escapades or on Crusade, she was his replacement; even when he was at home it was often she who made cultural decisions.[10]

The lady of the manor was both means and inspiration for knights aspiring to court. Service to the lady was both method and metaphor for the knight's elevation.

> *Good lady, I ask you for nothing*
> *but to take me for your servant,*
> *for I will serve you as my lord,*
> *whatever wages come my way.*[11]

This is an odd combination of the economic and emotional, practical and flirtatious, to the modern ear. For one thing, the medieval world made fewer distinctions between such categories. For another, the identity of the "lady" was deliberately ambiguous. The troubadour's song was a performance at court that might tantalize many lords and ladies with its secrets and suggestions. Indeed, like any successful art form, the songs of the troubadours could be exploited to suggest many meanings. The feudal hierarchy could be reinforced with the singer's homage to his lord's lady; the order could be dramatically challenged with the suggestion of less than a "pure love" between lordly lady and lowly knight. Lyrics might suggest adultery or worship of the Virgin Mary, a specific or general love that was real or imagined. "There never was a man so pleasing in a chamber and so savage and excellent in armor," Peire Vidal sang. "Each day I am a better man and purer, for I serve the noblest lady in the world," Arnaut Daniel wrote, more typically.[12]

IN THE SERVICE OF WOMAN

In the twelfth century the courtly love tradition of the troubadours traveled north into France and Germany, and it became a guide to behavior for many young knights.

We are lucky to have the autobiography of one of these romantic knights, a minor noble who was born in Austria about 1200. His name was Ulrich von Lichtenstein, and he called his autobiography, appropriately enough, *In the Service of Woman.*

At an early age Ulrich learned that the greatest honor and happiness for a knight lay in the service of a beautiful and noble woman. He seems to have realized, at least subconsciously, that true love had to be full of obstacles and frustrations in order to be spiritually ennobling. So at the age of twelve Ulrich chose as the love of his life a princess. She was a perfect choice: far above him socially, she was also older than Ulrich and already married. Ulrich managed to become a page in her court so that he could see her and touch the same things that she touched. Sometimes he was even able to steal away to his room with the very water that she had just washed her hands in, and he would secretly drink it.

By the age of seventeen Ulrich had become a knight and took to the countryside to joust in tournaments wearing the lady's colors. Finally after a number of victories, Ulrich gained the courage to ask his niece to call on the lady and tell her that he wanted to be a distant, respectful admirer. The princess would have none of it. She told Ulrich's niece that she was repulsed by Ulrich's mere presence, that he was low class and ugly—especially with that harelip of his. On hearing her reply Ulrich was overjoyed that she had noticed him. He went to have his harelip removed, recuperated for six weeks, and wrote a song to the princess. When the lady heard of this she finally consented to let Ulrich attend a riding party she was having, suggesting even that he might exchange a word with her if the opportunity arose. Ulrich had his chance. He was next to her horse as she was about to dismount, but he was so tongue-tied that he couldn't say a word. The princess thought him such a boor that she pulled out a lock of his hair as she got off her horse.

Ulrich returned to the field for the next three years. Finally the lady allowed him to joust in her name, but she wouldn't part with as much as a ribbon for him to carry. He sent her passionate letters and songs that he had composed. She answered with insults and derision. In one letter the princess derided Ulrich for implying that he had lost a finger while fighting for her when he had actually only wounded it slightly. Ulrich responded by having a friend hack off the finger and send it to the lady in a green velvet case. The princess was evidently so impressed with the power that she had over Ulrich that she sent back a message that she would look at it every day—a message that Ulrich received as he had the others, "on his knees, with bowed head and folded hands."

More determined than ever to win his lady's love, Ulrich devised a plan for a spectacular series of jousts, in which he challenged all comers on a five-week trip. He broke eight lances a day in the service of his princess. After such a showing, the princess sent word that Ulrich might at last visit her, but that he was to come disguised as a leper and sit with the other lepers who would be there begging. The princess passed him, said nothing, and let him sleep that night out in the rain. The following day she sent a message to Ulrich that he could climb a rope to her bedroom window. There she told him that she would grant no favors until he waded across the lake; then she dropped the rope so that he fell into the stinking moat.

Finally, after all of this, the princess said that she would grant Ulrich her love if he went on a Crusade in her name. When she learned that he was making preparations to go, she called it off and offered her love. After almost fifteen years Ulrich had proved himself to the princess.

What was the love that she offered? Ulrich doesn't say, but it probably consisted of kisses, an embrace, and possibly even a certain amount of fondling. Possibly more, but probably not. That was not the point. Ulrich had not spent fifteen years for sex. In fact, Ulrich had not spent fifteen years to win. The quest is what kept him going. His real reward was in the suffering and yearning. Within two years Ulrich was after another perfect lady.

Oh yes. We forgot one thing. Ulrich mentions that in the middle of his spectacular five-week joust, he stopped off for three days to visit the wife and kids. He was married? He was married. He speaks of his wife with a certain amount of affection. She was evidently quite good at managing the estate and bringing up the children. But what were these mundane talents next to the raptures of serving the ideal woman? Love was certainly not a part of the "details of crops, and cattle, fleas and fireplaces, serfs and swamp drainage." In fact, Ulrich might expect that his wife would be proud of him if she knew what he was up to. The love of the princess should make Ulrich so much more noble and esteemed in his wife's eyes.[13]

COURTLY LOVE

The behavior of Ulrich von Lichtenstein reflected in exaggerated form a new idea of love in the West. Historians have called it "courtly love" because it developed in the courts of Europe, where noble ladies and knights of "quality" came together. For the first time since the Greeks a man could idealize a woman, but only if he minimized her sexuality. The evidence is overwhelming that these spiritual affairs would ideally never be consummated.

It is difficult for us to understand how these mature lords and ladies could torture themselves with passionate oaths, feats of endurance, fainting spells when they

This painting from about the year 1300 contains all the elements of love and chivalry: horses, knights, and admiring ladies. (Universitatsbibliothek, Heidelberg)

heard their lover's name or voice, in short the whole repertoire of romance, and then refrain from actually consummating that love. Why did they insist on an ideal of "pure love" that allowed even naked embraces but drew the line at intercourse, which they called "false love"? No doubt the Christian antipathy for sex was part of the problem. Earlier Christian monks had practiced a similar type of *agape,* Christianity had always taught that there was a world of difference between love and lust. The tendency of these Christian men to think of their ladies as replicas of the Virgin Mother also made sex inappropriate, if not outright incestuous.

But these lords and ladies were also making a statement about their "class" or good breeding. They were saying (as did Sigmund Freud almost a thousand years later) that civilized people repress their animal lust. They were distinguishing themselves from the crude peasants and soldiers around them who knew only fornication and whoring and raping. They were cultivating their emotions and their sensitivity, and priding themselves on their self-control. They were privileged (as members of the upper class) to know that human beings were capable of loyalty and love and enjoying beauty without behaving like animals. They were telling each other that they were refined, that they had "class."

The statement that they were making was evidently so new that they suffered unendurable frustration to make it. They adapted to the frustration by savoring the tension and the agony. The more they repressed their natural instincts, the more "civilized" they felt. "They put on finer clothing, started to use handkerchiefs, and began to bathe more often; they practiced genteel discourse and sophisticated argumentation."[14] Sexual repression became part of a whole new style of life: a life of manners.

In contrast to the Greeks, they could afford to let women into their polite, sophisticated, elite company at a level higher than that of paid help. But only a few women could join them, and even these could participate in the game only if they remained perched on pedestals. Men could treat them as living, breathing, thinking human beings, but it was still necessary to idealize them so that both could remain a privileged minority.

Further, despite the new romanticized view of the woman (maybe because of it), wives were just as excluded as they had always been. Noble, uplifting love, genuine romantic love, could not be felt for someone who swept the floor any more than it could be felt *by* someone whose life was preoccupied with such trivia. The lords and one of their special ladies, Marie, the countess of Champagne, issued the following declaration in 1174:

> We declare and we hold as firmly established that love cannot exert its power between two people who are married to each other. For lovers give each other everything freely, under no compulsion of necessity, but married people are in duty bound to give in to each other's desires and deny themselves to each other in nothing.[15]

THE COURT OF LOVE

This proclamation was one of many that were made by the "courts of love" that these lords and ladies established in order to settle lovers' quarrels—and to decide for themselves the specifics of the new morality. Some of these trials are summarized by Andreas Capellanus, one of the most famous "judges" of love, in France, in the twelfth century.

One typical case was brought to the court by a knight whose lady found another lover but promised the knight, her first love, that she would return to him if she ever lost her new lover. Accepting this standby role, the knight was asking the court of love to declare that she had lost her lover because she had just married the man.

The queen of France judged this case. She decided in favor of the knight. It was obvious, she said, that the lady had lost her lover when she married him, since it was impossible for love to continue in marriage. The lady, according to the queen, should now love the knight as she had promised.

No court, of course, had the power to legislate feelings; certainly not this voluntary, aristocratic "people's court." But by hearing so many cases, the noble ladies and gentlemen were able to devise rules of behavior that made love more polite than the open warfare that Ovid preached, and the crude brutality that most men practiced.

No one did more to formulate these rules than Andreas Capellanus. Andreas not only summarized the numerous cases that came before the court, but he used these decisions to write a manual of polite, courtly love. He called his influential book *A Treatise on Love and Its Remedy,* a title that indicated his debt to Sappho and the Greek romantic idea of love as a sickness. Andreas, however, did not think that he was advocating a "romantic" idea of love. The word was not even used in his day. He considered himself to be a modern twelfth-century Ovid—merely updating the Roman's *Art of Love.* He called himself Andreas the Lover and, like Ovid, considered himself an expert on all aspects of love.

But Andreas only used the same word as Ovid. The similarity ended there. The "aspects" of love that Andreas taught concerned the loyalty of the lovers, courteous behavior, the spiritual benefits of "pure love," the importance of gentleness, the subservience of the man to his lover, and the duties of courtship. There is none of Ovid's preoccupation with the techniques of seduction. Andreas is not talking about sex. In fact, he clearly advises against consummating the relationship.

Ovid made fun of infatuation and silly emotional behavior, but urged his readers to imitate such sickness in order to get the woman in bed. Andreas valued the passionate emotional attachment that Ovid mocked. Sincerity and honesty were too important to Andreas to dream of trickery, deceit, or pretense. Love, for Andreas, was too noble an emotion, too worthy a pursuit, to be put on like a mask. In short, the Roman had been after sexual gratification; the Christian wanted to refine lives and cleanse souls. They both called it love, but Andreas never seemed to realize that they were not talking the same language.

COURTING AND CAVORTING

Courtly love was not an absolute disaster for Western men and women. It taught men for the first time to concern themselves with the feelings of at least some women. Among Andreas's thirty-one basic rules of courtly love we find such new ideas as the following:

> *That which a lover takes against the will of his beloved has no*
> *relish. . . .*
> *A true lover considers nothing good except what he thinks will please*
> *his beloved.*[16]

In comparison with Ovid's idea of love as sexual conquest, there is a lot to admire here: concern for human feelings, emotional empathy for others, an honest presentation of the self, a distaste for using other people or treating them as sexual objects.

On the other hand, romantic love was an idealized love. The lovers never permitted themselves to really know each other. They fell in love with ideals, not living, breathing human beings. They created myths to feed their passion; these exaggerated images of each other could be maintained only at a distance. They could not allow themselves to come close enough to see the warts or stay long enough to learn the longings and fears of real people. And so they gloried in everything that kept them apart. They chose impossible love objects, demanded impossible loyalties, and preoccupied themselves in the quest. They cut themselves off from other people by convincing themselves there was only one ideal. But more importantly they cut themselves off from the realities of their relationship and the needs of their own bodies. They could work up a degree of feeling, an emotional intensity, that no other people had known—but that passion was based on repression. They could yearn so deeply only because they could not have what they yearned for. The game of passion could be played only under rules of "civilized" politeness, which were repressive enough to insure that their passions would not be abated. In search of the exaltation of the spirit, they renounced the demands of the flesh.

THE TRIUMPH OF ROMANCE

The romantic idea of courtly love spread rapidly throughout the royal courts of Europe after the twelfth century. All of the young gentlemen of the fashionable set learned to view women as objects of honor and esteem. Romances (or romantic stories) were invented of ideal love affairs between knights and ladies. According to one, King Arthur's loyal knight Lancelot falls hopelessly in love with the king's bride, Guinevere. His love for Guinevere so overwhelms him that he is unable to refuse any of the lady's foolish or demeaning requests: he shows his obedience by falling off his horse for her, and spends all of his energy distinguishing his illicit love, arranging secret meetings, rescuing her from everything, overcoming one obstacle after another.

In another famous romance, a young knight, Tristan, is instructed to bring the lady Iseult to be the bride of his king. Iseult, however, falls madly in love with Tristan when she drinks a love potion by mistake. The rest of the romance describes the feverish attempts of the couple to get together to consummate a love that can end only in death. The romance of Romeo and Juliet, of course, reaches the same conclusion: true love is the complete sacrifice of the self; its passion and ecstasy are too much for this world; its perfection is death.

The romantic story has become one of the most popular types of literature in the modern Western world since the twelfth century. Many of the same old stories have been revived or updated. But even when the names and situations are changed, the same romantic themes have survived intact. Modern romances still describe "ideal" loves that must overcome impossible obstacles. Lovers are still supposed to be attracted "at first sight," as if they had just swallowed a magical potion. They still are expected to surrender all reason to the "irresistible force" of their love. The fullness of their love is still measured by the extent to which they sacrifice themselves. The most "perfect" loves are still thought to involve passions so intense that they lead the lovers irreversibly to their deaths.

We have all been raised on the same ideas of romance that developed around the twelfth century. We idealize our lovers. We look for the "one and only," expecting some day we will suddenly without warning meet the one person who is best for us. We are sure that we will know when we are in love because we will have "that special feeling" whenever we are near the "special someone." Besides the sweaty palms and quickened heartbeat and other symptoms of love sickness that Sappho described, we are trained to hope that bells will ring and psychedelic lights will flash when we kiss or consummate the love. Love is still for us a world of magic and mystery. And we want to keep it that way. We prefer to romanticize the experience and idealize the beloved, rather than analyze or realistically evaluate either. The fantasies of love still excite us more than the realities of human relationships.

What about sex, someone might ask. If we have kept the "romance" of courtly love, haven't we at least made that romance more sexual than it was in the twelfth century? The answer is probably yes and no.

We still live in a predominantly Christian culture. That means that men still tend to see women as either seductive, corrupting, but exciting Eves or pure, sexless Virgin Mothers, and they feel guilty about loving the first type and childlike in their love of the second type. It is true that Christian men over the last thousand years have concentrated more on Mary than on Eve. They have elevated the status of women—almost to the point where they view them as equals. But because sex was such an evil to Christians, they have usually elevated women by making them less sexual. We have seen that in the early stages of courtly love the knight or poet could most easily idealize the particular woman who was sexually unattainable or "pure." This tendency continued during the European Renaissance (fourteenth to sixteenth centuries). Poets like Dante and Petrarch wrote endless lines to women they loved obsessively, but from afar. Both made their love-ideals, Dante's Beatrice and Petrarch's Laura, the all-encompassing focus of their lives. Dante's love for Beatrice became the model for educated Europeans (including Petrarch) for hundreds of years. The poet never spoke to her, nor did he want to. Rather, he was uplifted by the depth of feeling that her presence gave him. Since he probably had never experienced comparable feelings, he thought of Beatrice as a source of spiritual guidance to the love of God. His feelings for Beatrice (which he called love) were considerably greater than anything he felt for his wife or any of his mistresses. Similarly, Petrarch permitted Laura to enrich his soul with her mere image. He never hoped for anything more from his ideal; Laura had eleven children by her husband, and Petrarch had at least two sons by his mistress.

In other societies these lives may have been strange models for people to follow, but in Christian Europe they made some sense. Another Italian of the Renaissance, Castiglione, summarized the new Platonic view of love in a book called *The Courtier,* written around 1500. The lady was loved, according to Castiglione, for her moral virtue as well as her beauty—both of which led the lover to contemplate the divine. Love of the ideal woman was a force that tamed the wild souls of men. "Pure love" could "civilize" men only because it forced them to repress their sexual needs.

In one sense, all that has happened in the last few hundred years is that the ideas of a few upper-class poets in the fourteenth century have become the ideas of almost everyone in the twentieth century. The great American middle class has accepted the earlier aristocratic idea that women are worthy of men's protection and love. Americans no longer feel so close to barbarism that they must repress every physical desire, but women are still expected to be less sexual than men, less experienced and aggressive. Men no longer expect the beauty of a woman to lead their minds to understand the beauty of human nature or knowledge of God, but they still see women as spiritual healers, pacifiers, or peacemakers. The romantic idea of love, then, even in some of its antisexual, spiritual forms, is still a part of us.

While any cultural idea of love, besides the romantic one we have inherited, might harmonize with our sexual needs—as our bodies tell us that we can "love" anyone—our romantic culture insists that there is only one love for each of us. Our bodies are satisfied by sensual gratification, but our romantic culture finds the deepest ecstasy in passion that cannot be satisfied, or in the love of the most idealized, abstract sort. The conflict between the Romans and Christians rages even now, but in each one of us.

A MEDIEVAL INDIAN ALTERNATIVE:
MYSTICAL EROTICISM

Sometimes the best way to understand our own traditions is to study those of a different culture. It is difficult, for instance, for us to see Christian sexual morality as unusual because it has shaped our culture to such a great extent.

There have been alternatives, however. One of the most remarkable was the Indian ecstatic religion of the Middle Ages. Here the erotic played a central role, not as temptation to be shunned but as a source of salvation. Most medieval temple sculpture was erotic.[17] The temples at Khajuraho and Orissa are full of sexual imagery: sensuous nudes and embracing couples. The temple architecture itself suggests fertility and reproduction. The temple sculptures, like the popular story *Gita Govinda* of the twelfth century, tell of the loves of the god Krishna. He is shown scandalizing young women, dancing deliriously, and bathing with scores of admirers. Krishna's erotic appeal is a testament to his charisma. He is "divine in proportion to his superiority as a great lover."

> Worshippers were encouraged to commit excesses during festivals as the surest way to achieve . . . ecstasy, the purging climax of the orgiastic feast, the surmounting of duality.[18]

Among the most popular forms of medieval Hindu worship were the *bhakti* cults, which originated in devotion to Krishna in the *Bhagavad Gita*. *Bhakti* cults underline the difference between Indian and European devotion. While the Christian church discouraged spiritual love that might easily lead to "carnal love," the Indian *bhakti* sects encouraged rituals of ecstasy and sensual love precisely because they obliterated moral distinctions. The ecstatic union with the divine Krishna, Vishnu, or Shiva enabled the worshiper to transcend the limitations of self and confining definitions of good and evil.

Thus, Indian ecstatic religion sought sexual expression as a path to spiritual fulfillment. It is interesting that the word *bhakti* meant sex as well as worship, while we use the word "devotion" to mean worship and love. Hindu eroticism had nothing to do with the private expression of romantic love. In fact, it was the opposite. While romantic love depended on the development of the individual personality and the cultivation of individual feelings, *bhakti* depended on the loss of self in the sexual act.

Bhakti cults differed from the European courtly love tradition in one other important respect. They were not expressions of upper-class control. They were popular expressions of religious feeling. In essence they were directed against the dominating *brahman* and *kshatriya* castes because they challenged the importance of caste distinctions altogether. The ecstatic communion with the deity that they

Krishna playing his flute for a group of admiring women. (Werner Forman Archive)

preached was open to all, regardless of caste. They appealed even to women and untouchables, as well as to farmers and artisans.

As Christianity did in Europe, popular Hinduism of the Middle Ages replaced a classical formal tradition with a spiritual passion. Ovid's *Art of Love* and the *Kama*

Sutra were mechanical, passionless exercises for tired ruling classes. Both India and Europe turned to more emotionally intense religious experiences in the Middle Ages. Perhaps the classical ideals seemed sterile after the spread of salvation religions like Christianity, Buddhism, and revived Hinduism. The similarity between Christian and Hindu emotionalism may be a product of uncertain times, barbarian threats, and diseases that stalked the Eurasian continent. But the differences between Christian courtly love and *bhakti* cults were also profound. In India, sexual passion was an avenue to spiritual salvation. In Christian Europe sexual passion was at best a dead end, and at worst a road to hell.

POLYGAMY, SEXUALITY, AND STYLE:
A JAPANESE ALTERNATIVE

At the same time that feudal Europe was developing a code of chivalry that romanticized love and almost desexualized marriage, the aristocracy of feudal Japan was evolving a code of polygamous sexuality without chivalry and almost without passion. We know about the sexual lives of Japanese aristocrats between 950 and 1050—the apex of the Heian period—through a series of remarkable novels and diaries, almost all of which were written by women. These first classics of Japanese literature, like *The Tale of Genji* and *The Pillow Book,* were written by women because Japanese men were still writing the "more important" but less-informative laws and theological studies in Chinese (just as Europeans still wrote in a Latin that was very different from the everyday spoken language).

When well-born Japanese in the Heian court spoke of "the world" they were referring to a love affair, and the novels that aristocratic women like Murasaki Shikibu or Sei Shonagon had time to compose in the spoken language were full of stories of "the world."

In *The World of the Shining Prince* Ivan Morris distinguishes three types of sexual relationships between men and women of the Heian aristocracy. (Homosexuality among the court ladies was "probably quite common," he writes, "as in any society where women were obliged to live in continuous and close proximity," but male homosexuality among "warriors, priests and actors" probably became prevalent in later centuries.) The first type of heterosexual relationship was between the male aristocrat and his "principal wife." She was often several years older than her boy-husband and frequently served more as a guardian than as a bride. She was always chosen for her social standing, usually to cement a political alliance between ruling families. Although the match must frequently have been loveless, her status was inviolate; it was strictly forbidden, for instance, for a prince to exalt a secondary wife to principal wife. Upon marriage the principal wife would normally continue to live with her family, visited by her husband at night, until he became the head of his own household on the death or retirement of his father. Then the principal wife would be installed with all of her servants and aides as the head of the north wing of her husband's residence. An aristocratic woman (but never a peasant woman) might also become a secondary wife or official concubine. If she were officially recognized as such (much to the pleasure of her family), she might be moved into another wing of the official residence (leading to inevitable conflicts with the principal wife and other past and future secondary wives), or she might be set up in her own house. The arrangements were virtually limitless. The third and most frequent type of sexual relationship between men and women was the simple (or complex) affair—with a lady at court, another man's wife or concubine, but usually with a woman of a far lower class than the man. Ivan Morris writes of this kind of relationship:

> Few cultured societies in history can have been as tolerant about sexual relations as was the world of *The Tale of Genji*. Whether or not a gentleman was married, it redounded to his prestige to have as many affairs as possible; and the palaces and great mansions were full of ladies who were only too ready to accommodate him if approached in the proper style. From reading the *Pillow Book* we can tell how extremely commonplace these casual affairs had

Lady Murasaki Shikibu (978–c.1025), author of The Tale of Genji. *(Granger)*

become in court circles, the man usually visiting the girl at night behind her screen of state and leaving her at the crack of dawn.[19]

That emphasis on "the proper style" is what distinguishes the sexuality of medieval Japan from that of ancient Rome, and reminds us of the medieval European's display of form—the aristocracy's mark of "class." Perhaps because the sexuality of the Heian aristocracy was potentially more explosive than the repressed rituals of European chivalry, style was that much more important. Polygamous sexuality could be practiced without tearing the society apart (and destroying aristocratic dominance in the process) only if every attention were given to style. Listen, for instance, to what the lady of *The Pillow Book* expected from a good lover:

> A good lover will behave as elegantly at dawn as at any other time. He drags himself out of bed with a look of dismay on his face. The lady urges him on: "Come, my friend, it's getting light. You don't want anyone to find you here." He gives a deep sigh, as if to say that the night has not been nearly long enough and that it is agony to leave. Once up, he does not instantly pull on his trousers. Instead he comes close to the lady and whispers whatever was left unsaid during the night. Even when he is dressed, he still lingers, vaguely pretending to be fastening his sash.
>
> Presently he raises the lattice, and the two lovers stand together by the side door while he tells her how he dreads the coming day, which will keep them apart; then he slips away. The lady watches him go, and this moment of parting will remain among her most charming memories.
>
> Indeed, one's attachment to a man depends largely on the elegance of his leave-taking. When he jumps out of bed, scurries about the room, tightly fastens his trouser-sash, rolls up the sleeves of his Court cloak, over-robe, or hunting costume, stuffs his belongings into the breast of his robe and then briskly secures the outer sash—one really begins to hate him.[20]

The stylistic elegance of the lover's departure was one of the principal themes of Heian literature. Perhaps no situation better expressed the mood of the Japanese word *aware* (a word that was used over a thousand times in *The Tale of Genji*), which meant the poignant or the stylishly, even artistically, sorrowful—a style of elegant resignation. The word also suggests the mood of "the lady in waiting" and even the underlying anguish and jealousy of a precariously polygamous existence for the women consorts and writers of the Japanese feudal age. The ladies of the court were trained in calligraphy, poetry, and music; they were dressed in elaborate, colorful silks, painted with white faces and black teeth, and rewarded by sexual attention that always had to be justified by its cultured style.

The rigid rituals of courtship and marriage were highly stylized. The gentleman interested in a lady writes her a thirty-one-syllable poem. The lady responds with a similar effort, which is examined meticulously by the gentleman for signs of good breeding: the calligraphy and poetic skill are sure signs of her character. If he is pleased, he arranges for a "secret" night meeting (which the lady's parents or attendants pretend to ignore). The gentleman conventionally keeps the lady awake all night, comments on the rooster's crow with appropriate expressions of dismay, and drags himself away at dawn. On his arrival home he immediately composes his "next-morning" letter, which laments his long hours away from the lady and concludes with a love poem that usually includes an image of flowers covered with dew. Everything about the letter expresses the appropriate sentiment: the color of the paper, the type of incense, the style of calligraphy, even the choice of the messenger—who is regaled by the lady's family with abundant presents. If the lady is interested she gives an equally appropriate letter (following the "rule of taste") with the same imagery to the same messenger. The same series of events is followed on the following night.

A third-night repetition, with the addition of rice cakes left by the parents for the gentleman, could seal the relationship in marriage. This time the gentleman remains with his new wife in the morning behind her curtain of state. That evening a feast is held in which the groom meets the bride's family officially, the Shinto priest recites a simple ceremony, and the couple perform the three-times-three exchange of wine cups. The couple are officially married. The groom may visit his bride's house at any time, or even install her in his own home according to her status as principal or secondary wife.[21]

Aristocracies have behaved in similar ways throughout the world, and throughout history. They demonstrate their "class" or "good breeding" with elaborate rituals that differentiate their world from the ordinary. But the example of aristocratic Heian Japan a thousand years ago points to some of the differences between Eastern and Christian culture. The Japanese developed rituals of courtship and seduction for the leisured few that were sexually satisfying and posed no threat to marriage. They were rituals that showed artistic refinement rather than sexual "purity" or chastity. They could be sexual because Japanese culture did not disparage sexuality. Rather it disparaged lack of "taste." The affair did not threaten marriage because the culture did not insist on monogamy. The new sexual interest could be carried on outside or inside the polygamous estate of the Japanese aristocrat. Perhaps the main difference, then, is that the Japanese aristocrat invented stylized sex rather than romantic love.

FOR FURTHER READING

Denis de Rougemont's *Love in the Western World* is dated but still worth reading. It offers little help on the Arab or Islamic background to European courtly love, however. The relevant parts of Joseph Campbell's *The Masks of God* are more helpful, though this is only one among many of his subjects. The best introduction to Islamic history and culture is Marshall G. S. Hodgson's *The Venture of Islam*. On the background to European courtly love see Peter Dronke's *Medieval Latin and the Rise of European Love-Lyric*. On the troubadours see Robert Briffault's still valuable *The Troubadours*, Frederick Goldin's anthology *Lyrics of the Troubadours and Trouveres*, and Meg Bogin's *The Women Troubadours*. C. Steven Jaeger's *The Origins of Courtliness: Civilizing Trends and the Formation of Courtly Ideals, 939–1210* is an erudite study focusing on Germany.

Morton Hunt's *The Natural History of Love* is a highly readable source of anecdote and example. On chivalry, Maurice Keens's *Chivalry* is a rich recent survey. Georges Duby's *The Chivalrous Society* offers a collection of his articles. Richard Barber's *The Knight and Chivalry* is still useful, as is Norbert Elias's *The Court Society*. Marina Warner's *Alone of All Her Sex: The Myth and Cult of the Virgin Mary* is an engaging, exhaustive study of changing perceptions of Mary. Georges Duby has two valuable studies of medieval marriage. His *Medieval Marriage* is a short account of two models from twelfth-century France; *The Knight, the Lady and the Priest* shows how indissoluble marriage developed. David Herlihy's *Medieval Households* finds the roots of modern family life. Eileen Power's *Medieval Women* is a brief introduction. Margaret Wade Labarge's *Women in Medieval Life* is a charming, readable, well-illustrated introduction. *Women in the Middle Ages* by Frances and Joseph Gies is also readable and thorough. For a richly absorbing view of sexuality, marriage, and love among the peasantry, see Emmanuel Le Roy Ladurie's *Montaillou* on the Cathars. On homosexuality see John Boswell's *Christianity, Social Tolerance, and Homosexuality*, covering the period up to the fourteenth century. There are also abundant primary sources that provide entree to this topic and period. Among the most accessible are *The Romance of Tristan and Iseult* and *The Letters of Abelard and Heloise*. Two of the great guides, Castiglione's *The Book of the Courtier* and Andreas Capellanus's *Art of Courtly Love*, also are quite accessible.

On India in this period we have relied on Richard Lannoy's marvelous *The Speaking Tree: A Study of Indian Culture and Society*. Histories of India and primary sources recommended in earlier chapters are also useful here. Additional approaches are taken up by Nirad C. Chaudhuri in *The Continent of Circe*, Arthur Koestler in *The Lotus and the Robot*, Alan Watts in *Nature, Man, and Woman*, and Max Weber in *The Religion of India*.

On Japan in the Heian period *The World of the Shining Prince* by Ivan Morris is a superb introduction. There also are excellent translations of Murasaki Shikibu's *The Tale of Genji* available, a recent one by E. Seidensticker and an older one by Arthur Waley. Morris and Waley each has also translated *The Pillow Book* of Sei Shonagon.

NOTES

1. Adapted from Marshall G. S. Hodgson, *The Venture of Islam*, vol. 1 (Chicago: University of Chicago Press, 1974), p. 404.
2. Denis de Rougemont, *Love in the Western World*, trans. Montgomery Belgion (New York: Harper & Row, 1956), p. 105.
3. *Ibid.*
4. Joseph Campbell, *The Masks of God: Creative Mythology* (New York: Viking Press, 1968), p. 176.
5. *Ibid.*, p. 177.
6. Hodgson, *op. cit.*, p. 239.
7. Ibn Hazm, *Ali ibn Ahmad. The Ring of the Dove: A Treatise on the Art and Practice of*

Arab Love, trans. A. J. Arberry (New York: AMS Press, 1953). Excerpted in *Anthology of Islamic Literature: From the Rise of Islam to Modern Times,* ed. James Kritzeck (New York: New American Library, 1975), pp. 124–130 *passim.*

8. Quoted in John Boswell, *Christianity, Social Tolerance, and Homosexuality* (Chicago: University of Chicago Press, 1980), p. 196.
9. Cited in Meg Bogin, *The Women Troubadours* (New York: Norton, 1980), p. 38.
10. *Ibid.,* p. 49.
11. Bernart de Ventadorn, trans. in Bogin, *op. cit.,* p. 52.
12. Bogin, *op. cit.,* pp. 52 and 9, respectively.
13. The story of Ulrich von Lichtenstein is paraphrased from Morton Hunt, *The Natural History of Love* (New York: Knopf, 1959), pp. 132–139. Quotation marks indicate Mr. Hunt's words.
14. Quoted in Hunt, *op. cit.,* p. 141.
15. Quoted by Andreas in *Tractatus de Amore,* bk. 1, ch. 6, Seventh Dialogue; quoted in Hunt, *op. cit.,* pp. 143–144.
16. Andreas Capellanus, *The Art of Courtly Love,* trans. John Jay Parry (New York: Frederick Ungar Publishing, 1957), pp. 42–43.
17. Richard Lannoy, *The Speaking Tree: A Study of Indian Culture and Society* (Oxford: Oxford University Press, 1971), p. 64.
18. *Ibid.*
19. Ivan Morris, *The World of the Shining Prince: Court Life in Ancient Japan* (Baltimore: Penguin Books, 1964, 1969), p. 237.
20. *The Pillow Book of Sei Shonagon,* trans. and ed. Ivan Morris (Baltimore: Penguin Books, 1967, 1971), pp. 49–50.
21. Morris, *op. cit.,* pp. 226–228.

❧ 11 ❧

Citizens
and
Subjects

City and
State

WHAT IS THE MEANING OF CITIZENSHIP? How do you get it? Where does it come from? What good is it? How do you lose it? These are some of the questions that prompt this chapter.

We examine an argument, first enunciated by the great German sociologist Max Weber almost a hundred years ago, that citizenship was the product of the medieval European city. It resulted, according to this view, from the political demand of a rising middle class of merchants, craftspeople, and professionals that they be able to control their own environment.

In order to explore this idea, we begin by looking at two other societies for the purposes of comparison. We focus first on the Chinese city. Chinese capital cities of the period 700–1300 were the largest and most powerful in the world. Did they offer citizenship? Did they have a middle class of merchants, craftspeople, and professionals? Was there an urban class that was different from the people of the country? Was there an interest in urban autonomy, independence, or self-government? If not, why not? If not, did the Chinese city offer a different sort of political participation? These are some of the questions we ask.

We then turn briefly to the second great world civilization of this period, Islam.

How autonomous were Muslim cities? Who were the real powers in the Muslim city? Did Muslim cities encourage citizenship? If not, why not?

Finally, we look at the development of the city in Europe. Here we see the import of Weber's thesis. How was the European city different from the cities of China and Islam? What were the causes of these differences? What were the advantages and disadvantages of European cities? What has happened to citizenship and community since?

CITY AND COUNTRY: CHINA AND EUROPE

Today the great cities of the world look increasingly alike. The international style of high concrete and glass boxes creates the same skyline from Chicago to Canton. But that was not always the case. Even ten years ago, one could enter Beijing, the capital of China, without knowing it. Suburban countryside faded imperceptibly into city streets. There was no dramatic increase in the height of the buildings, no sudden end of parks and gardens, not even a visible increase in population density. One who is used to seeing the protruding skyline of an American city from a distance could easily miss the distinction between city and countryside in China. After miles of similar architecture on the road to Beijing, you turned a corner and suddenly you were in Tian An Men Square, the center of the city, in front of the Imperial Palaces.

Traditional Chinese architecture favored the horizontal plain and the lay of the land. In city and country, natural building materials—stamped earth, baked brick, plaster, wood, and tile—were preferred for the living. Concrete and stone were thought more appropriate for the construction of more "permanent" structures—tombs, roads, or fireproof warehouses. According to Joseph Needham:

> Chinese architecture was always with, not against nature; it did not spring suddenly out of the ground as if aiming to pierce the sky like European "Gothic" building. . . .[1]

But the different look of Chinese and European cities is more than an aesthetic difference. The absence of buildings like Gothic cathedrals in China suggests much about the difference between the two cultures. Not only was Chinese architectural space more horizontal than vertical, the materials more natural than permanent, and the size on more of a human scale. Chinese religion was different from European. Chinese religious buildings did not have to reach up to the skies because Chinese ancestral spirits walked the earth. Ancestor worship, emperor worship, even Buddhist and Daoist reverence for nature, were more "immanent" than "transcendent" religious traditions: God was not in the sky.

Chinese religion was also not primarily urban. Christians called the unconverted "country people" (pagans). Muslims required a mosque in every city. The Chinese often built finer temples in the country than in the city. Chinese religion was also nonhierarchical. There were no equivalents of bishops, archbishops, or popes in Chinese religions. A cathedral in Europe was a "bishop's church," situated at his principal city.

There is perhaps a more important reason why city and country were so sharply distinguished in Europe and barely separated in China. Socially and politically, as well as aesthetically and architecturally, the Chinese city was not a different place from the countryside.

Max Weber (1864–1920) alluded to this difference at the beginning of this century:

> In contrast to the West, the cities in China and throughout the East lacked political autonomy. The Eastern city was not a "polis" in the sense of Antiquity, and it knew nothing of the "city law" of the Middle Ages, for it was not a "commune" with political privileges of its own. Nor was there a citizenry in the sense of a self-equipped military estate such as existed in Western Antiquity.[2]

A contemporary historian of China, Frederick W. Mote, agrees with Max Weber's observation:

> The Chinese city . . . had no "citizens," nor any corporate identity, and the authority under which it was directly administrated extended beyond the city to include the surrounding countryside. It had therefore no need of a town hall as a monument to urban pride and urban group identity, or as a place of assembly where citizens could exercise political rights. Not even the defense of the Chinese city was a responsibility of the urban entity; its defenses were constituted and maintained by the central government to which all alike were subservient, and as part of its nation-wide defense installation.[3]

The Chinese city was a city of subjects rather than of citizens. We can see this in many cities in China's long history.

CHANGAN: SUBJECTS AND CITIZENS

The emperor Wen-di, founder of the Sui dynasty (589–618), chose the site for Changan very carefully. It was close enough to the imperial cities of the Han dynasty to remind people of past glories, but it was distant enough to be distinct. The city was built from scratch. Laid out in a grid plan with the streets running exactly north-south and east-west (see the map), it was the fitting center of the world for this Son of Heaven. At its fullest development under the Tang (618–907) the city contained about one million inhabitants inside the walls and another one million outside. Its life and its inhabitants were as varied as any city in the world.

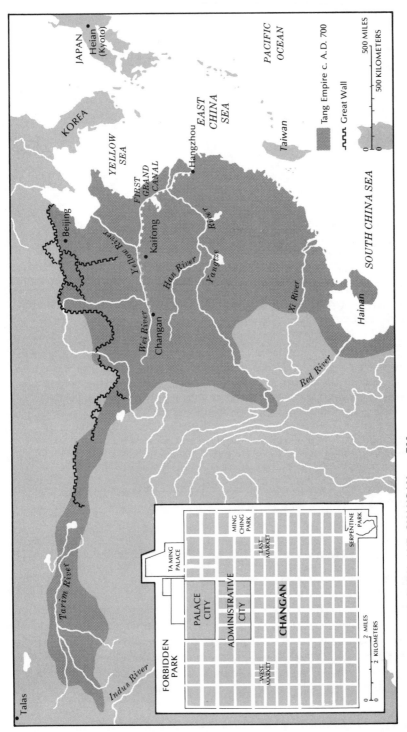

TANG CHINA AND CHANGAN A.D. 700
Changan was the imperial ideal of a city, laid out to pay homage to the Son of Heaven. It was the capital of the vast Tang dynasty.

But everything—even the business of the poorest street sweeper or most foreign merchant—was directed toward the pleasure of the emperor and his court.

> No buildings in Changan were built from what we call "civic pride." Building and rebuilding were first of all at the initiative of the imperial family, which commanded the resources and could confiscate and relocate property at will. . . . Officials in their public role would frequently petition for funds to build or remodel a particular bureau or to dig a canal. But they argued for these projects in terms of improving the efficiency of imperial administration, not in terms of civic pride or "civic improvement." Although we read much of the parks and pleasances of the great, of their ball-fields and archery halls, there is no mention of any such facilities for the populace. Philanthropy expressed itself through the Buddhist temples with their charitable functions, but the "bread and circuses" of Rome and Constantinople are not to be found. Nor is there anything comparable to the forums, public baths and arcades built by the Roman emperors for the pleasure and convenience of the citizenry. The residents of the city were not "citizens" but the emperor's subjects. This is reflected in the layout of the city, in its administration and in its functioning. . . . There was neither mayor nor city council, and there was no charter. The city and its populace were controlled by the throne through officials of the imperial bureaucracy.[4]

Instead of neighborhoods, there were districts administered by an imperial appointee. Laws forbade the construction of housing facing the main avenues. The gates of each district were closed at sundown, and no one was allowed out on the avenues until the drums were beaten in the morning. Any commoner who crossed the wall of a district or entered an official compound without authorization was to be punished with seventy lashes. The large east and west market areas were also strictly regulated: opened at noon, closed at sundown; activity, transactions, and prices checked and regulated.

The Chinese imperial city was to be treated, according to at least one edict at Changan, as the "Mansion of the Emperor." Not only the palaces and imperial offices and gardens, but the whole city was the emperor's preserve. "Long ago, among the flowers and willows," Li Bo [Li Po] (701–762) recalled, "we sat drinking together at Changan."

> *In the arts and graces of life we could hold our own*
> *With any dandy in the town—*
> *In the days when there was youth in your cheeks*
> *And I was still not old. . . .*
>
> *We thought, you and I, that it would be always like this.*
> *How should we know the grasses would stir and dust rise on the wind?*
> *Suddenly foreign horsemen were at the Hsien-Ku Pass*
> *Just when the blossom at the palace of Ch'in was opening on the sunny boughs. . . .*[5]

The poet's Changan was overrun in a rebellion aided by Turkic horsemen under An Lushan (755–763). The emperor Xuan-Zong [Hsüan-tsung] (r. 713–756) was forced to flee to Sichuan [Szechwan]. While Changan and the dynasty continued for another two hundred years, it did so on a much smaller and more feeble scale.

KAIFENG: COMMERCE AND CIVIL SERVANTS

The Song [Sung] reunified China in 960, establishing their first capital at Kaifeng. Near the juncture of the Yellow River and the start of the Grand Canal to the southeastern coast, Kaifeng was an existing merchant city. It did not have the classic grid outline of Changan. It lacked the geometrical order and spaciousness of the earlier capital. But its disorder and congestion may have been appropriate, since the Northern Song Empire crammed twice the population of the Tang into shrinking frontiers. Like other merchant cities, Kaifeng was originally unwalled. When walls were constructed during the Tang dynasty they were erected rather haphazardly, and the Song never properly realigned them. The palace compound of the Song emperor was neither central nor spacious. It measured less than half the size of the palace grounds at Changan. The main difference between Kaifeng and early capitals, however, is conveyed by a single event in the beginning of the dynasty. With a view toward enlarging his quarters for his large retinue, Emperor Tai-zong [T'ai-tsung] commissioned a survey of the city in 986. But when he discovered that his plans would inconvenience too many of his neighbors, he canceled them. Founded by soldiers, the Song dynasty rejected the military expansion of the Tang for prosperity in a smaller home.

The existence of a large artisan and merchant class in early Kaifeng of Tang times made it less necessary for the Song royal family and court to import retainers for all of their needs, a practice that had been common in capitals designed from scratch. Nevertheless, the population increased from about a half-million registered inhabitants within the walls (and twice that, counting the suburbs) in 1021 to over a million in the 1120s (probably two million including those unregistered and beyond the walls).

Wealthy merchants were not the only influential class in Kaifeng. The capital of the Northern Song also made extensive use of the civil service examinations in order to fill appointments at court. The exams were used more regularly and widely than in any dynasty before or since. They became in Song Kaifeng the principal means of filling high government offices.[6] In a sense, the civil service examinations were a commercial society's challenge to the domination of the government by the sons of landed aristocrats. Success could now be measured and was less dependent on family connections. But since examinations measured only what was already learned, a national university was established in the capital by Wang Anshi [Wang An-Shih] (1021–1086), chief minister of emperor Shen-zong [Shen-tsung] (r. 1068–1086). As long as it was well funded (during the Song dynasty), its doors

A busy bridge in Kaifeng in the twelfth century. (Werner Forman Archive)

were open to capable poor students as well as the heirs of the wealthy, and education shaped the exam instead of vice versa.[7]

Kaifeng shows us the beginning of a new kind of Chinese city, especially a new kind of imperial capital. The palace is not the absolute center. Order is not the only value. A new class of people that can only be called urban appears: actors, singers, prostitutes, fortune-tellers, and jugglers. The Tang curfew is ignored. Night markets are allowed.

We are fortunate in having lively contemporary descriptions of daily life in

Northern Song Kaifeng and the later Southern Song capital at Hangzhou, but, as Etienne Balazs reminds us, these are not typical of the enormous body of Song literature.

> It is both interesting and revealing to note that it is precisely works such as these that . . . were written not by scholar-officials but by private individuals with no official function who remained unknown or anonymous. This is not fortuitous. The professional honor of a scholar or an official—in short, of a gentleman—would never have permitted him to take an interest in such frivolities, and the authors could only have come from bourgeois, plebeian, nonofficial circles. Their social origin is in fact clearly revealed by the obvious affection and even pride with which they describe every detail of the streets, shops, traveling shows, pleasure grounds, inns, and taverns.[8]

HANGZHOU: MIGRANTS, MERCHANTS, AND MANDARINS

Kaifeng was sacked by invasions from the steppe in 1127, and the Song dynasty gave up the northern third of China, retreating to the Yangtze Valley, where it established a new capital at Hangzhou [Hangchow]. At first thought to be a temporary home until the north could be reconquered, it eventually became accepted as the permanent capital of the Southern Song dynasty (1127–1279). New invasions by the Mongols in the north not only made reconquest of Kaifeng impossible, but also eventually conquered Hangzhou and ended the Song dynasty.

While the northern Yellow River Valley had been the traditional home of Chinese civilization and the site of all imperial capitals before 1127, large numbers of Chinese had migrated south to the Yangtze Valley since the Sui dynasty. In the year 606 only 23 percent of the registered households were in the south. By 742 the southern population had grown to 43 percent of the empire. By 1078 a decisive 65 percent of the Chinese population were in the south. Initially, this migration had been fueled by the availability of fertile lands in the south, but increasingly in the Tang-Song period migrants came south as refugees from invasion and war.

One result of this enormous migration was the rapid development of new cities in the Yangtze Valley. These were economic, trading centers rather than political, administrative cities and were therefore left to develop in terms of local needs, which were largely commercial. In contrast to imperial capitals, each city did not have to be self-sufficient. Each was allowed to develop regional specializations and to engage in trade with the other cities. As a consequence, a far-flung regional economy developed along the Yangtze and the Grand Canal.

While Hangzhou was designed almost from scratch by the emperor, it is important to note that its location at the terminus of the Grand Canal made it a natural center of trade and communications, which it remained long after it ceased to be the capital. As did the other cities of the Lower Yangtze Valley, Hangzhou

This Chinese painting of Hangzhou as seen from the West Lake shows only a small part of the city, but it captures the accent on pleasure and the beauty of the tamed natural environment.
(Freer Gallery of Art)

had uncontrolled markets, merchant and craft guilds, and a growing " 'city bourgeoisie' that created their own new culture."[9]

> The Southern Song was a "financial" state in a way the northern dynasty could never have been; wealthy city-dwellers came powerfully close to establishing a distinctive urban class, and social leadership in the countryside was lodged firmly in the hands of men whose only common characteristic was their wealth.[10]

By the end of the Song dynasty, Hangzhou was probably the largest city in the world. Estimates of its population (including suburbs) range from 1.5 to 5 million. Marco Polo visited Hangzhou in 1275, the year before Kublai Khan moved to incorporate the Song capital into his expanding northern empire. The visitor from Venice wrote that Hangzhou "is the greatest city which may be found in the world, where so many pleasures may be found that one fancies himself to be in Paradise."

Hangzhou offered lowly officials, foreign merchants, and native working people a variety of recreational facilities and amusements that had been unavailable in more circumspect Changan. There were many specialized restaurants: some served everything ice cold, including fish and soups; some specialized in silkworm or shrimp pies and plum wine; even teahouses offered sumptuous decor, dancing girls, and musical lessons of all kinds. On the lake there were hundreds of boats, many of which could be rented, according to Marco Polo, "for parties of pleasure."

> These will hold ten, fifteen, twenty or more persons, and are from fifteen to twenty paces in length. . . . Anyone who desires to go a-pleasuring with the women or with a party of his own sex, hires one of these barges, which are always to be found completely furnished with tables and chairs and all other apparatus for a feast. The roof forms a level deck, on which the crew stand, and pole the boat along whithersoever may be desired, for the Lake is not more than two paces in depth. The inside of this roof and the rest of the interior is covered with ornamental painting in gay colours, with windows all round that can be shut or opened, so that the party at table can enjoy all the beauty and variety of the prospects on both sides as they pass along. And truly a trip on this Lake is a much more charming recreation than can be enjoyed on land. For on the one side lies the city in its entire length, so that the spectators in the barges, from the distance at which they stand, take in the whole prospect in its full beauty and grandeur, with its numberless palaces, temples, monasteries, and gardens, full of lofty trees, sloping to the shore. And the Lake is never without a number of such boats, laden with pleasure parties; for it is a great delight . . . to pass the afternoon in enjoyment with the ladies or their families, or perhaps with others less reputable, either in these barges or in driving about the city in carriages.[11]

Even the soldiers and poor had their "pleasure grounds"—almost two dozen in all. Each was a large fairground with markets, plays, musical groups, instrumental and dance lessons, ballet performances, jugglers, acrobats, storytellers, performing fish, archery displays and lessons, snake charmers, boxing matches, conjurers, chess players, magicians, imitators of street cries, imitators of village talk, and specialists in painting chrysanthemums, telling obscene stories, posing riddles, and flying kites. Gambling, drinking, and prostitution were also part of the scene here as elsewhere in the city.

Market areas were equally a source of entertainment and business. Marco Polo saw so much fish in a single market that he could not imagine it would ever be eaten, but it was all sold in a couple of hours. There were markets devoted to specialized goods and crafts that could hardly be found in the rest of China. Fortunately, one "guidebook" has survived, which tells us where we can get the best rhinoceros skins, ivory combs, turbans, wicker cages, painted fans, philosophy books, or lotus-pink rice.

The invention of movable type in the tenth century (five hundred years ahead of its invention in Europe) may not have actually increased the number of books available because there were over seven thousand Chinese characters (compared with the European twenty-six letters) and hand printing had become a work of art that was appreciated in itself. Nevertheless, the resident of Hangzhou could find books (hand or mechanically printed) on a fantastic variety of subjects: curious rocks, jades, coins, bamboo, plum trees, special aspects of printing and painting, foreign lands, poetry, philosophy, Confucius, and mushrooms, and there were encyclopedias on everything.

Marco Polo, of course, did not know Changan, but he tells a couple of stories that suggest that the imperial capital at Hangzhou, for all of its luxury and variety, was not entirely different from the ancient capital of the Tang.

> And again this king did another thing; that when he rides by any road in the city . . . and it happened that he found two beautiful great houses and between them might be a small one . . . then the king asks why that house is so small. . . . And one told him that that small house belongs to a poor man who has not the power to make it larger like the others. Then the king commands that the little house may be made as beautiful and as high as were those two others

The Diamond Sutra *(868) is the earliest known printed book. It is a Chinese translation of an Indian story of the Buddha. Each of the six "pages" of the scroll was printed with a separate wooden block. The tenth-century invention of movable type permitted each Chinese character to be printed separately, but there were too many characters for movable type to replace block printing. (Granger)*

which were beside it, and he paid the cost. And if it happened that the little house belonged to a rich man, then he commanded him immediately to cause it to be taken away. And by his command there was not in his capital in the realms of . . . Hangchow any house which was not both beautiful and great, besides the great palaces and the great mansions of which there were great plenty about the city.[12]

Hangzhou, like Changan, was the emperor's city. And the emperor and his scholar-officials (mandarins) were aware of everything:

> There is another thing I must tell you. It is the custom for every burgess in this city, and in fact for every description of person in it, to write over his door his own name, the name of his wife, and those of his children, his slaves, and all the inmates of his house, and also of the number of animals that he keeps. And if anyone dies in the house then the name of that person is erased, and if any child is born its name is added. So in this way the sovereign is able to know exactly the population of the city.[13]

Perhaps Max Weber was right, after all. The inhabitants of Hangzhou seemed to be more subjects than citizens. Ultimately, it was the emperor's city. Ultimately, perhaps, the mandarins were more important than the merchants. A Song magistrate wrote,

> Those who are not capable of being Confucian scholars may make their living without disgracing their ancestors by working as spirit-mediums, doctors, Buddhists, Taoists, farmers, merchants or experts of some sort. It is the greatest disgrace to the ancestors if sons or younger brothers degenerate into beggars or thieves.[14]

Better to be a merchant than a thief. Those who can do, teach; others must find an occupation that won't disgrace the ancestors. These are traditional Chinese attitudes.

But this is not just a matter of merchants versus mandarins, though there undoubtedly were conflicts. Weber's point is that merchants were more likely than mandarins to seek self-government, political autonomy, or citizenship. As we shall see, that is what happened in Europe.

We may ask, however, if the Chinese did not find other ways to participate politically. Was not the civil service examination system, with its emphasis on education and its role in staffing the bureaucracy, an alternate route to political participation? Might not civil service be an equivalent of citizenship? Is it possible that the Chinese emphasis on learning created better-informed subjects than did European cities of citizens? Is it possible that the openness of the examination system to talent and learning, regardless of wealth or birth, made for greater social mobility in China than was true in European cities of citizens? These are questions to consider.

ISLAM AND CITIES

If Chinese cities were the largest in the world, Chinese culture remained predominantly agrarian. This was not true of the second great civilization of the traditional world, Islam. The culture of Islam was distinctly urban.

It might seem odd that a religion that originated among desert nomads "has been able to multiply cities almost at will,"[15] but one does not have to look far for reasons. Even the nomads required temporary settlements, oases, caravan stops, and trading centers. Islam needed the city to realize its religious and social ideals. Its history began in the *hegira* from one town, Mecca, to another, Medina. One of the five pillars of Islam was the *hajj* to the holy city of Mecca. Another was the participation five times a day in community prayer. A third was the fasting of

The Muslim city of Timbuktu in Northwest Africa. Islam thrived on cities, especially the important oasis cities, which made possible the desert trade of North Africa. (Granger)

Ramadan; a fourth, the giving of alms. All of these made more sense in an urban community. Only the other pillar, the declaration of belief in God, might be as potent in solitude as in a community. Islamic legends abounded about pious Muslims who founded towns. To found a town was to build a mosque, and every mosque meant the spread of Islam. Perhaps with a sneer for the nomadic world of makeshift camps and portable gods, some strict Muslims held that a Friday prayer was effective only when offered in a permanent, completely built mosque.

ISLAMIC CITIES AND AFRO-EURASIAN UNITY
A single zone of trade and communication was established by the fifteenth century, principally by the merchants and travellers of Islam but also by Chinese, Mongols, and Europeans, which brought a common material culture to the inhabitants of the cities of much of the Afro-Eurasian land mass.

The city was the setting for Islam. The city was "the pillar of the faith and a framework within which to live the good life," according to one modern scholar. And yet he writes, echoing Max Weber, there was an absence of municipal life.

> And yet these Islamic cities are strangely lacking in cohesion. This is the fundamental difference which separates them as much from the cities of antiquity as from the medieval cities of Europe. The Roman city rested at the

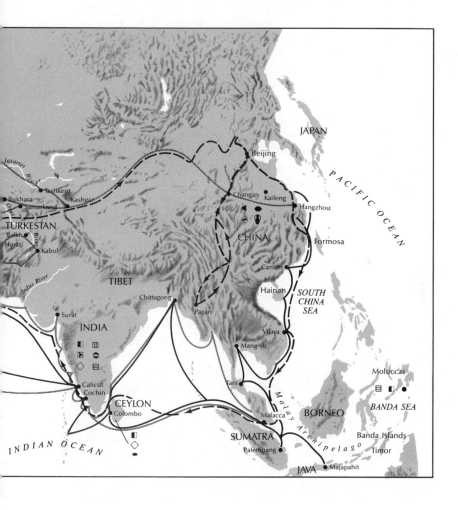

center of a territory which belonged to the city; the medieval town in the western world was a refuge, usually cut off from the neighboring countryside. In both cases there were a lively feeling of solidarity, a notable pride in the city, and many close forms of understanding and co-operation among the citizens. There is nothing of the sort in an Islamic city. It has no separate municipal life. No privilege of exception, no special freedom of action, attaches to citizenship.[16]

The cities of Islam did not have municipal governments. They were run by governors, emirs (military commanders), and market inspectors appointed by the state. Like the Chinese capitals controlled by the emperor, most Islamic cities were too important to the caliph, sultan, or other lord to be allowed independence. In most cases there was no urban party that desired independence anyway. In fact, there was usually no unified political view at all, and rarely an occasion or place to express it. Muslim cities were highly segmented. Each district of the city contained its own homogeneous community—clan, tribe, or Muslim sect—and its own market. Each group walled itself in, sometimes closing in alleyways that crossed its boundaries and sometimes taking extra space from the street, in either case leaving a tight winding maze with little public space. This was probably just as well: debated space could easily become a battlefield when divisions required walls.

The great caliphal cities, Damascus of the Umayyads (661–750) and Baghdad of the Abbasids (750–932), were tightly controlled by the caliph, just as the Chinese imperial capitals were by the emperor. Most early Arab conquests were treated as military garrison towns, with the Arab armies remaining outside. Damascus, on the other hand, was an old city in which Arabs and non-Arabs settled, each group in its district. In Damascus, it was not possible to treat Arabs as an occupying military force and non-Arabs as a subject population. Nevertheless, the successful revolt of the Abbasids gained strength not only from Shi'ites but also from many who resented Arab dominance.

The move of the Abbasids further east to Baghdad, on the Tigris, was a revival of the Persian monarchial court in Islamic dress. Here caliphs like Harun al-Rashid (786–809) and Ma'mun (813–833) ruled with a show of force and splendor that has become legendary in such tales as *The Arabian Nights*. The Abbasids relied on non-Arab troops from the eastern province of Khurasan (northern Iran and Afghanistan) who increased the distance between ruler and ruled. Beginning in the ninth century they enlisted Turkish forces from the northern steppes who were slave-soldiers (*mamluks*, literally "owned"). As a personal army these mamluks were controlled by means of lavish rewards and considerable power. Their domination further alienated the population.

In 945 Baghdad was conquered by the Buyids, who already controlled the western Iranian highlands. The Buyids (932–1062) ruled less oppressively and less completely than the Abbasids. The administration of a frontier town might be relatively innocuous. One that has been studied, Qazvin (a mountain fortress just south of the Caspian Sea), had an emir who played little role in the governance of the town. The maintenance of law and order seems to have been the province of a local militia. Even taxes were collected by local leaders rather than by a government tax collector. "For the man in Qazvin bazaar," one historian writes, "the real and effective government must have been in local officials" while "the comings and goings of *amirs* [emirs] and their retinues were probably marginal to the day to day administration."[17]

A later incident in Iran, however, suggests the limitedness of a local militia's autonomy. The Buyids were challenged by Mahmud of Ghanza (998–1030) throughout Iran. The militias of two towns, Rayy (south of the Caspian and just east of Qazvin) and Balkh (further east on the Oxus River), supported Mahmud against the Buyids. Both militias were able on their own initiative to stave off enemy attacks and deliver their towns to Mahmud. His response was not what you might expect. Rather than thank them, he severely reprimanded those responsible. They should have submitted to his enemies, Mahmud said, and waited for him to save them. Mahmud well recognized that a victorious urban militia would be an independent force and a possible alternative to his own power. And this was not a case, it should be pointed out, of the city militia's attempting to rule on its own. This militia merely wanted to choose its outside master. Despite an occasional exception (Tripoli in Syria for a time), a city was to depend on the armies of an emir to keep ultimate order.

Muslim city administration varied widely. There were both tolerant officials and absolutists who oversaw every detail of city life. Sometimes absolutism was combined in the same person with an extreme commitment to social justice. Such a ruler was al-Hakim (996–1021), Fatimid dynasty caliph of Cairo. A devoted *imam* in an Ishmaili Shi'ite dynasty, he had a passion for social justice that spelled brutality to the rich or corrupt. He renounced personal comforts and rode around Cairo on a donkey. As caliph he felt responsible to impose justice on fellow Muslims. Thus, he had the vineyards of Cairo destroyed and forbade women to leave their homes. Once he insisted that the shops of Cairo be open at night, when he preferred to be active, forcing the entire city to find time during the day to sleep. On another occasion he is said to have offered a lottery in which some people would win undreamed of wealth and others would suffer sudden death. But even his most bizarre whims had a religious purpose. His reversal of day and night showed the rigor of his justice, even at night, and his lottery served as a reminder of the unpredictability of the hand of providence. His intense concern for justice for the common people was remembered long after he disappeared forever into the desert, and the wealthy returned to their luxuries, but his eventual return is one of the central expectations of the Druzes of Syria and Lebanon.

Even when Muslim cities were under the occupation of foreign forces (as long as they were also Muslim) there was usually no united opposition by the inhabitants. During the Mamluk period (1260–1517) when the Turkish slave soldiers occupied Egypt and Syria, the inhabitants of cities like Cairo, Damascus, and Aleppo did not unite among themselves. The "Mamluk rulers and *emirs,* many of whom never learned to speak Arabic, depended on the tacit co-operation of Arabic notables and middle classes in the towns."[18] Both the merchants and the religious leaders *(ulema)* found it in their best interests to legitimate the rule of the foreigners in order to protect private property and avoid anarchy.

Ironically, the Christian and Jewish quarters in these cities were often granted greater autonomy than the Muslim because the Muslim authorities could not presume to speak for them. The Christians in Mamluk Damascus had two patriarchs, one for each of the Christian denominations (Melchites and Jacobites), and each was responsible to the governor of the province. These patriarchs were selected by their communities, with the approval of the sultan. They, and the head of the Jewish community, along with their assistants, were expected to settle disputes of law, serve as the final authority in matters of religion, and report matters of concern to the community to a state-appointed supervisor of religious communities. "This system of granting some sort of autonomy to the various religious communities solved a number of administrative problems and enabled such communities to develop their own societies," according to one historian.[19]

For Muslims, there were some organizations that spanned the separate city segments of the city. Craft guilds, neighborhood groups, fraternities, Sufi lodges, and schools of law linked city inhabitants to a larger world.

> Yet these regional associations extending outside the city walls serve to remind us once more that Islamic cities did not develop legal and military autonomy and consequently did not create a tradition of independent guilds and voluntary city-wide associations which were typical of European burgher culture. The very word *madina* [used for city] meant an administrative center within the state structure rather than "city" in the European sense. An Islamic city was first and foremost a place where government business was carried out.[20]

Why, then, was this the case? Why did the Islamic city fail to develop its own identity and autonomy? Why were there no municipal governments in Islam? Why was there no tradition of urban citizenship and civic pride? A simple answer is because the "burgher," or middle class, was not in control. Another is that cities remained under the control of landed aristocrats and their armies. A third is that the rulers considered the cities too important to allow them independence. But these are only partial answers, perhaps because we have asked only one side of the question. We have asked what European characteristics the Muslim culture lacked. We might just as well ask what characteristics of Muslim culture made urban independence unnecessary or undesirable. What did Islam gain by not seeking urban autonomy? The answer is obvious once we ask the question. Islam abolished provincialism in favor of universalism. Muslims gained world citizenship instead of city citizenship.

Perhaps Islam was too cosmopolitan to create special privileges for residents of particular cities. In a truly universal brotherhood, why should a visiting Muslim merchant or stranger have fewer rights than a resident? Muslims were proud of their hospitality. They were world travelers, generous hosts, and accomplished guests. A culture of merchants and militant monotheists could hardly be expected to prefer local pride to membership in the *Dar al-Islam*.

> Under Islam, with its cosmopolitan outlook, such parochial rights and duties were not judicially recognized. A person was not a citizen of a particular town, with local rights and responsibilities determined by his local citizenship; as a free Muslim he was a "citizen" of the whole Dar al-Islam, with responsibilities determined by his presence before God alone.[21]

THE REVIVAL OF CITIES IN THE WEST: THE COMMUNE

It may have been the very destructiveness of the barbarian invasions in the West that made regeneration of Rome or any imperial city impossible. City life virtually disappeared, if not completely with the fall of Rome, at least with the rise of Islam in the seventh century. By then there was no one with the power of a Wen-di to reorganize the empire, or there was little to reorganize. Justinian, the Byzantine emperor (527–565), codified Roman law and attempted to reorganize the Western Empire of the Caesars, but it was hopelessly fragmented. For almost the next thousand years, the West lagged far behind the prodigious accomplishments that continuity gave Chinese civilization, but the West enjoyed the rare luxury of a fresh start. The village again became the center of Western life. The lessons of village community could be relearned. Town and city life could mature gradually and autonomously (we might almost say organically) from the soil of village institutions. There was no emperor around to lay out the grid plan of a new metropolis and then proceed to fill it with subjects. After Charlemagne there were Holy Roman emperors who were sometimes able to actually govern the peasants of a small German state. But none of these feudal lords had the resources of a Wen-di. And there were other kings to reckon with, too many to name. There were minor princes and barons, each in charge of miles of field and a few villages. And, of course, there was the pope. The medieval Western towns profited from the feuding of the feudal lords, and took the initiative in carving out their own jurisdictions.

Increasingly after the tenth century old towns won from feudal lords grants of independence and self-government that were often put in written, charter form. Towns won the right to hold a regular market, to coin money, to regulate weights and measures, to try their citizens in their own courts, to write their own law, and to protect their cities with their own militia. In return the burghers (inhabitants of the burg, or town) offered the feudal lord the services of the militia in case of invasion. The town also provided a variety of crafts, manufactured goods, even foreign luxury commerce that could enhance the lord's style of life on the manor. In many cases the lords founded new towns for these advantages as well as the rent revenue of the land they owned. In short, the lords often gave the towns political freedom in return for military help, economic prosperity, a larger population, and cultural resources that the greatest castle could not afford.

The history of the rise of the medieval town is full of stories of conflict between lord and citizen; towns often demanded rights that threatened even far-seeing feudal lords; and the military and economic power of towns eventually proved more deadly than gunpowder to the feudal regime. But the conflict was often over particulars; many lords built and nourished new towns, and it was the very weakness, poverty, and decentralization of the feudal regime that made free towns possible: the lords, after all, had little to grant but land and rights.

Freedom was in the city air. The serf who remained in the city for a year and a day was legally free. The citizen was free of feudal dues and services. Citizenship itself meant freedom of association, freedom of movement, freedom to own, make, spend, and marry without the lord's permission or dues. Citizenship replaced the ancient ties of blood and soil, family and feudal allegiances. The citizens became autonomous individuals who freely gathered together to establish their own governments and laws, united in a corporate effort, allied in common associations, for the good of the commune.

The medieval city was a "commune" from the beginning, Weber said. He meant that it was a corporate or collective association of equals that did not have to be based on ties of family, clan, or tribe. "Commune" was a good word to express common citizenship. A city would call itself, for example, "The Commune of Florence" (or Pisa or Milan or whatever). It is interesting that we in modern America think of the commune as the antithesis of the urban settlement. Our cities seem so impersonal and competitive that we cannot imagine commune or community away from the countryside. It is also interesting that when American sociologists asked Weber at a meeting in Saint Louis early in this century to speak about "rural community" he replied that the phrase was a contradiction in terms. Weber had studied the history of the city well enough to know that it was the only place that had made genuine community possible.

LATE MEDIEVAL AND RENAISSANCE CITIES: PAGEANTRY AND PARTICIPATION

Late medieval and Renaissance towns and cities created a new corporate life that rivaled the best of the ancient city-states. The acropolis returned in the form of the parish church, built by the townspeople, not by imperial decree. Many villages or city parishes of fewer than a hundred families had their own church. The churches were often named for local saints (whose tombs they frequently were). Their construction and maintenance were a source of civic pride and common work. The village church or the bishop's cathedral offered opportunities for charitable care, refuge, meditation, sociability, and festivity. Hospitals, poor houses, homes for the aged, sanitariums, previously available only to the wealthy or in the monastery, became typical features of the new urban landscape—often forming common neighborhoods with chapel, gardens, and fountains. "All that the territorial state now seeks to do on a wholesale scale was first done," Lewis Mumford points out, "in a more intimate way, often probably with more feeling for the human occasion, in the medieval town."[22]

In one important respect the medieval towns and Renaissance city-states were more genuine communities than had existed ever before—even in ancient Athens. The majority of the inhabitants were free citizens, working side by side, without an underlying slave population. Christianity had made work more respectable than it had ever been before. "To labor is to pray," was the way the Benedictine monastic order expressed the Christian attitude. Working associations were as important as religious associations. The first guilds were actually religious fraternities. They never lost their religious coloring. Merchant and producer guilds served the interests of their members and consumers in insuring the quality of work, just prices, and the economic prosperity of the town. But they were equally engaged in planning and performing religious plays for fellow townspeople; building schools, chapels, and meeting halls for citizens; and providing their members with insurance, feasts, and festivals.

Festivity and pageantry were the drama and elixir of communal city life. Religious holy days, celebrations of peace, guild-sponsored dances, the completion of the harvest, and the safe return of a ship were all occasions for collective rejoicing. The drama, the pageant, the sports contest, and even the parade were participatory, not spectator, activities. The painter Albrecht Dürer tells us about a parade in sixteenth-century Antwerp:

> On Sunday after Our Dear Lady's Assumption, I saw the Great Procession from the Church of Our Lady at Antwerp, when the whole town of every craft and rank were assembled, each dressed in his best according to his rank. And all ranks and guilds had their signs, by which they might be known. In the intervals, great costly pole-candles were borne, and three long old Frankish trumpets of silver. There were also in the German fashion many pipers and drummers. All the instruments were loudly and noisily blown and beaten.
>
> I saw the Procession pass along the street, the people being arranged in rows, each man some distance from his neighbor, but the rows close behind the other. There were the Goldsmiths, the Painters, the Masons, the Broderers, the Sculptors, the Joiners, the Carpenters, the Sailors, the Fishermen, the Butchers, the Leatherers, the Clothmakers, the Bakers, the Tailors, the Cordwainers— indeed, workmen of all kinds, and many craftsmen and dealers who work for their livelihood. Likewise the shopkeepers and merchants and their assistants

of all kinds were there. After these came the shooters with guns, bows, and crossbows, and the horsemen and foot-soldiers also. Then followed the watch of the Lord Magistrates. Then came a fine troop all in red, nobly and splendidly clad. Before them, however, went all the religious orders and the members of some foundations, very devoutly, all in their different robes.

A very large company of widows also took part in the procession. . . . Wagons were drawn along with masques upon ships and other structures. Behind them came the Company of the Prophets in their order, and scenes from the New Testament. . . . From the beginning to end, the Procession lasted more than two hours before it was gone past our house.[23]

Like the parade, "singing, acting, dancing were still 'do-it-yourself' activities." Music was composed primarily for the voice, that is, for the singers rather than the listeners. Guilds had their own choral groups. Even the wealthy insisted that an ability to join a family sing—and hold a part—was a prime requirement for a young serving maid.

It would seem as if the city commune were designed for social interaction. Actually, however, the sociability of the commune was due as much to the absence of large-scale planning as it was to the creation of piazzas, plazas, courts, parks, and open space. These meeting and walking areas were not laid out to magnify the power of a prince or to expedite the flow of traffic (as was the case in the later baroque cities). They were instead piecemeal clearings by the citizens that enhanced rather than abolished neighborhoods. Even the winding medieval streets served to unite neighbors and freshen the view at every turn.

According to the author of a fourteenth-century work in praise of the city of Pavia (a new popular literary style that shows the extent of civic pride), the fifty thousand inhabitants of this Italian city "know each other so well that if anybody inquires for an address he will be told it at once, even if the person he asks lives in a quite distant part of the city; this is because they all gather twice a day, either in the 'court' of the commune or in the (adjoining) cathedral piazza."[24]

In some cities (usually smaller than Pavia) the citizens came together in a general assembly to make the laws, very much the way the Athenian citizens had at the Ecclesia. More often, though, in cities of over twenty thousand inhabitants, the citizens would elect representatives to serve (usually for no more than six months or a year) as a legislative council. Sometimes the members of a guild or neighborhood would each choose one of their number (by election or lot) to serve or elect others to serve. The processes of selection varied enormously, as did the size of the councils. Italian city-states, for instance, often had a "great council" of four hundred or a thousand (Modena had sixteen hundred), and an inner council normally closer to forty. The meetings of the great councils were not limited to formalities, nor were they necessarily passive rubber-stamping affairs. A council of about six hundred members met in Genoa in 1292 to discuss deteriorating relations with France; over a hundred councillors gave speeches in seven days of sessions.

The piazza of Italian Renaissance cities was a public meeting place, a focus of civic pride, or (in darker days) the sight of an execution. In this case the people of Florence put their former monastic leader Savonarola to the stake in 1498. (Alinari)

The degree of political participation must have surpassed that of ancient Athens, considering the commune's larger citizen body and the relative absence of slaves. It has been estimated that Florence drew over two thousand of its ninety thousand inhabitants each year for official positions. Smaller cities no doubt required a larger percentage to serve in public office. A budget for the city of Siena in 1257 mentions 860 public offices including 171 night watchmen and others we might call "police," but excluding military—and this in a city whose adult male population could not have been more than five thousand.

But the unpaid citizens, giving speeches in the council and voting on every imaginable question of public interest, are a better clue to the vitality of communal life than are the paid officers. It is difficult for us to imagine how these citizens could take time out from their busy lives to deal with all of the vexing questions of public policy. The answer is that the life of the commune was a very important

THE STATES OF ITALY, 1494

*On the eve of the French invasion of Italy in 1494, a few Italian states
had already conquered much of Italy. Milan, Venice, Florence, the
Papal States, and the Kingdom of the two Sicilies continued their
expansion in the early 1500s.*

part of their business; the give-and-take of debate and the burdens of decision making were all of the civic training that they needed.

Since the city-state was itself both a city and an independent state (with surrounding countryside and possibly allied or subordinate villages and towns), questions of war and peace were most crucial. But the records of council debates (carefully recorded by one of the dozens, sometimes hundreds, of the cities' "notaries") show a phenomenal range of interest and legislation. Hygiene and sanitation was perhaps the second most important concern. No one could build without permission in Siena in 1309. At Cremona "no man is to demolish his house except for the purpose of building a better one."[25] Most communes had ordinances requiring the regular cleaning of streets, forbidding the careless disposal of wastes and fouling of the rivers, and preventing the dryers or tanners from contaminating public water sources and hanging their cloths and hides over the street.

On the assumption that the rich man's wasteful expenditure was the people's loss, there were also often ordinances against gluttonous eating in taverns or the wearing of ostentatious crowns of pearls. When class divisions became extreme *and* when the people's parties outvoted the nobles, there were even attempts to use legislation to counterbalance the economic power of the wealthy. Thus, on the assumption that the rich could always find a way to buy their freedom, the popular party made the fines of the wealthy double or triple the fines for poorer citizens convicted of the same offense.

THE RENAISSANCE CITY: A SCHOOL OF ART

The commune was an education in more than politics, government, and social relations. It was also a school of art. The beauty of the city was part of the "job" of the citizen. The citizens of Florence voted to decide the type of column that was to be used on their cathedral. A responsibility like that certainly did not turn all Florentines into art critics, but it must have lifted the minds and aesthetic feelings of many. The city of Leonardo da Vinci and Michelangelo could have easily called on "experts," but the city that turns all questions of taste into questions of expertise and hires professionals as decision makers ends up with a pretty apathetic public.

Cities like Florence hired artists—the way our cities hire engineers. The great Renaissance painter Giotto, called by many today the founder of the modern style of painting, was hired by Florence as architect for many churches, walls, and bridges. He implemented the desires of the public and also broadened their education. Florence could rely on native craftsmen and artists to serve as chapel architects or overseers of public buildings. The artist was another of many craftspeople who was expected, like other citizens, to devote some of his efforts to communal needs. In a city like Orvieto that had to hire outside artists for such work, the citizens would sometimes welcome the newcomer with five or fifteen years of tax exemption—the way our cities attract businesses.

Florence in 1490, a quarter of the city-state, surrounded by its wall and nurtured by its river and its citizens. (Granger)

Even the most business-oriented city-states, like Florence and Venice, were works of art. The leading merchants or bankers (like the Medici family of Florence) might direct the finances of distant kings and nations, but the beauty of the public spaces and buildings of their own cities was often more important than their commercial possibilities. With the dedication of a modern city administration that has been sold a bill of goods on a downtown parking lot, office tower, or shopping center, the council of Siena would decide to have a public meadow in the city because

> among those matters to which the men who undertake the city's government should turn their attention, its beauty is the most important. One of the chief beauties of a pleasant city is the possession of a meadow or open place for the delight and joy of both citizens and strangers.[26]

And beauty was as necessary for the homes of the officials as it was for public space, according to the council of Siena:

> It is a matter of great honor to the various communes that the officials occupy beautiful and honorable dwellings, both for the sake of the commune and because foreigners often go to their houses upon affairs. This is of great importance for the commune [of Siena] according to its quality.[27]

Siena and Florence show us that small, independent city-states could retain the community and democracy of the village without necessarily succumbing to the tedium and creative stagnation that is all too often typical of village life. Culturally, artistically, and intellectually, Siena and Florence were more dynamic and creative than most cities of any size before or since. Community does not necessarily mean conformity.

The remarkable thing is not only that a Siena or Florence produced giants—Giotto, Dante, Petrarch, Boccaccio, Botticelli, Machiavelli, Leonardo da Vinci, Michelangelo, to name a few—but that it created an environment in which genius was almost institutionalized and expected. The public service required of the artist, and the personal encouragement of artists and philosophers by the Medici family in the fifteenth century, made art and intellect an inspiration to all. Schools (probably half of the male population in Florence had attended), libraries (among them the first public library), Verrocchio's art institute–workshop (where the young Leonardo learned mechanics, mathematics, and music, as well as architecture, bronze casting, goldsmithing, painting, and sculpture), Lorenzo Medici's finishing school for sculptors (where Michelangelo studied), and the city itself were living lessons of a new ideal: beauty and creative expression as the goal of human life and the commune.

Creativity is still possible in a communal city when culture is as important as business. What about larger cities? Are neighborhood communities and a human scale of life impossible in large cities?

THE RENAISSANCE CITY: THE LESSONS OF VENICE

At least one Renaissance city-state, and perhaps the most beautiful one, still says no. Out of necessity as much as foresight, the Republic of Venice found a way to preserve the human dimensions of the neighborhood in a large and most prosperous city. The islands that make up the city of Venice are separated by canals and lagoon waters. Each of the island neighborhoods has its own parish, its square, its school, and its guildhall—for each was originally the site of one of the city's six guilds. As Venetian population and prosperity grew, it was impossible to abolish the original neighborhoods by filling in the waters that divided them. Consequently, the Venetians had the good sense to allow each island to perform the function that it did best. One became a shipbuilding center that built the Venetian merchant and warships with a new canal "conveyor belt" system that startled visitors. The Arsenal, as it was called, housed the workers in the shipyard, their magistrates (or elected officials), and their own class of wealthy citizens. On another island, Murano, the Venetian glass industry was established, by an act of the Grand Council, by 1255. It was settled by the workers, merchants, and artists active in the industry. Again, they had their own neighborhood organizations, markets, and facilities. In this way the central business and administrative district did not become overly congested and eventually suffocated. This district, the area of the largest island, around Saint Mark's church, became the center for international merchants, specialized shops and restaurants, hotels, tourism, and city wide politics. The larger square in front of Saint Mark's and the administrative Ducal Palace also became the scene of citywide festivals. It could be enjoyed by the whole population, but they did not have to "commute" there daily to work or shop. Finally, other island neighborhoods were clustered around the separate concerns of religion (the convent of San Giorgio), burial (the cemetery of Torcello), and later, in the nineteenth century, a beach (the Lido).

The great modern architect Corbusier called Venice "an object lesson for town planners." It shows, even today, how neighborhood communities can be retained, how functional zoning can organize the separate concerns of the city, how major thoroughfares can be separated from local streets, and how a large urban area can avoid high-density sprawl. Venice's population has rarely risen beyond the Renaissance peak of one hundred and ninety thousand. There are still no cars permitted beyond the entrance to the city. The Venetian or tourist can take a fast public *vaporetto* up the Grand Canal or out to one of the smaller islands, or hire a gondola to wander. On the island he or she can walk. Nothing is very far from the water's equivalent of a subway, bus, or taxi stop. Places to walk and places to ride: the sea has forced Venetians to distinguish between getting there and being there. As a result, each "place to be" has retained its particular identity, its neighborhood, and its community.

The model, but not the necessity, is there for any large city to follow. With modern high-speed public transit, even with our socially expensive expressways, the Venetian model might suit a city of ten or twenty times the size. Today we have the capacity to design our cities to achieve what came to Venice naturally. Large parks, woodlands, lakes, or rivers (instead of the canals and the lagoon) could provide relief from mass sprawl and the refuge of the neighborhood. Separate functions could be separated by location without, at the same time, forcing people to commute long distances to work. Spaces could be designed for social interaction, public activity, and walking and wandering. Instead, we turn every alley into a street, every street into a thoroughfare, and every neighborhood into a block. We forget how to walk, we don't know who our neighbors are, and we find our way by counting the numbered streets. Every part of the city looks the same, and the monotony continues for miles. The city has lost its human scale, and it is not ours.

THE CITY SINCE COMMUNITY: THE BAROQUE AND THE BROKEN

Two things have happened to the city-state community in the last few hundred years. It has lost its independence, and the new rulers from outside have broken it up with streets, avenues, and boulevards for easy entry, control, and exit. The two developments are obviously related. Independence went down the avenue.

There are still a few city-states left. At least places like Monaco, Liechtenstein, and Andorra have preserved much of the independence of city-states. Many of the Swiss cities are also relatively free and self-governing. In general, however, the city-state has been consumed, and replaced, by the nation-state. Cities have come to be governed from outside—first by the princes and kings who welded them together as capitals or subjects of the new nation-states, then by national governments, and more recently by national and international corporations. The "corporate community" now refers to something very different from the assembly of citizens in the town council. The new corporate community may run many cities, but has no particular allegiance to any.

The communal city was defeated, however, long before the rise of corporate capitalism or the industrial revolution. It was first sacrificed to the baroque quest for power and opulence by the monarchs and ministers of the nation-state. In some ways the city-states defeated themselves. Like the Greek city-states, they experimented with alliances and confederations. Some such larger organization of cities seemed necessary. In half of Italy in 1300 there were more self-governing states than could be counted in the whole world in 1933. Their rivalries often led to war, but even in good times they were frequently unable to keep the peace in the countryside or agree on uniform laws, coinage, or standard weights and measures. The independence of cities was particularly frustrating to the rising class of national and international merchants: the number of tolls that merchants had to pay feudal lords and municipalities along the Rhine River, for instance, increased from nineteen at the end of the twelfth century to sixty-four at the end of the fourteenth.

Confederation was not impossible. In fact, it worked pretty well in Switzerland and Holland. It was not a viable alternative where there was already a strong monarchy, as in England. But even in Italy, where the alternative to civic independence was alliance with a German emperor or a French king, the Italians often chose the foreign monarch. The reason for such a choice probably had a lot to do with divisions within the Italian city-states themselves. Class and economic differences tended to increase during the Renaissance, forcing a noble, merchant, or popular party of "outs" to bargain for foreign intervention. Venice, one of the most stable but least democratic of the Italian city-republics, remained independent until conquered by Napoleon in 1797.

In some cities the merchants and national manufacturers and bankers formed alliances with kings to make the national economy more efficient. In Germany, Scandinavia, and England (but not in Switzerland or the British colonies in America) the Protestant Reformation served the national interest of kings and princes at the expense of city independence. But the most centralized nation-states to be organized in the sixteenth to eighteenth centuries were probably in Catholic France, Spain, and Austria, and in Russia. In any case, the king's capital replaced the commune as the nation-state became the dominant form of political organization. By commanding the main routes of trade, the bureaucracy, and professional armies, the capital city was able to unify the state. The capitals and their subsidiaries (where the king's court ruled) virtually monopolized the population increases of the sixteenth to eighteenth centuries. The capitals' populations reached the hundreds of thousands (London and Paris almost a million), while older cities languished and very few new ones (outside the colonies) were built.

Old cities were transformed and new cities were created often by a single monarch: Henry IV's Paris, Louis XIV's Versailles, Ivan III's Moscow, Peter the Great's Saint Petersburg, Philip II's Madrid, Manuel's Lisbon. Magnificent palaces were built or redesigned or enlarged in line with baroque style and ambitions: opulence, majesty, extravagance, order, and power—to tame the nobility and intimidate the populace. Gathered around the palace in the center of the city were the new town house mansions of the aristocracy (under the king's watchful eye), the official bureaucratic buildings, and the army citadel. Everything was purposely designed on a scale larger than life. These were monumental buildings, which were not to be approached by ordinary mortals. Their uniformity of arches, columns, and endless walls and windows is still a forbidding or awe-inspiring sight. The monotony, impersonality, and anonymity of modern city or bureaucratic life is neither accidental nor inevitable. Peter the Great asked that the twelve large office buildings of Saint Petersburg look exactly alike. Henry IV advised his minister in charge of the construction of a street in Paris to make the fronts of the houses alike, "for it would be a fine ornament to see this street with a uniform facade from the end of the bridge." The king's view was what mattered, and his tastes ran from the uniform–regular to the uniform–extra-large.

Baroque city building was like theatrical stage design. Indeed, many of the new planners got their start by designing stage scenery and props. The monarch's city was to be, as one said, "like a single building," and that, presumably, the theater. Everything was done for effect. Broad vistas of unbroken columns moved the eye to the distant focal point of the palace. The ideal street plan for baroque tastes was radial (a plan Aristophanes had proposed almost two thousand years before as a joke, thinking that the idea of bringing all traffic crashing together at the same spot was a sufficiently obvious satire on the megalomania of ancient planners). Broad avenues converging on the palace, the citadel, or a monumental arch was a theatrical way of attracting attention to the monarch's power, but it was also a very practical way of maintaining that power. Troops could be marched from the central precinct in any direction, for a parade—or for an attack. The architect Alberti distinguished between secondary streets and avenues; the latter he called *viae militares.* Another architect urged that all streets be wide enough so "that there be no place in them where armies may not easily march."

The broad avenue also served the purpose of breaking up the medieval tangle of streets that might be barricaded by the last holdouts of urban liberty. As Mumford remarked, "soldiers cannot fire around corners, nor can they protect themselves from bricks heaved from chimney tops immediately overhead: they need space to maneuver in."[28]

If the baroque style of cities reminds us of the ancient imperial capitals, it is because their rulers sought to emulate the pharaohs, Ptolemies, and Caesars. Louis XIV styled himself *Le Roi Soleil* ("the Sun King"). Like lesser monarchs of the period he got his theoreticians and writers to work out new theories of absolute sovereignty and "divine right," ideas that no European since the Caesars had dared to propose. Although some medieval communes had gotten along without any explicit sovereign (or final power) and many others had assumed that the only sovereign was the people or the law, the new theorists, like Jean Bodin, argued that a true state exists only when there is a sovereign and that *he* (or she) must exercise "supreme power over citizens and subjects, unrestrained by law."

As an artistic style the baroque has been dead about three hundred years. The age of absolute monarchy has been replaced by parliaments, congresses, presidents, and prime ministers in the last couple of hundred years. Few presidents these days think they are above the law. But most of our cities are direct descendants of the baroque capitals. The sovereign state is often as absolute as absolute monarchs. City life still means subjection to outsiders.

> The baroque cult of power has been even more tenacious than the medieval ideology: it remained in being and extended its hold on other departments of

life, creating Napoleons not merely in statecraft but in business and finance. . . . Armies, governments, capitalistic enterprises took the characteristic animus and form of this order, in all its inflated dimensions. . . . Right on into the twentieth century urban planning itself, at least in the great metropolises, meant chiefly baroque planning: from Tokyo and New Delhi to San Francisco.[29]

The baroque city has always been one of the ways the ruler displayed his power. For the absolute monarchs it was the main theater for such display. Perhaps the new rulers, the sovereign national state and the international corporation, no longer need the city as showplace. Like Louis XIV, corporations can build their own Versailles in the suburbs. They and the government can advertise well enough on television. Perhaps television and suburban cultural facilities can even provide the wealthy with the "civilization" that previously depended on cities. Perhaps.

FOR FURTHER READING

Among general approaches, Max Weber's *The City* is the classic, if somewhat difficult, starting point. Richard Sennett has edited Weber and a number of other sociological interpretations of the city in *Classic Essays on the Culture of Cities*. Gideon Sjoberg surveys *The Preindustrial City* from the perspective of modern historical sociology. Lewis Mumford's *The City in History* is still the most stimulating, interpretive history of the Western city. *Cities of Destiny*, edited by Arnold Toynbee, offers beautifully illustrated essays on some of the great cities of world history by noted specialists. Fernand Braudel's magnificent *Capitalism and Material Life 1400–1800* concludes with a fascinating chapter on the world's towns. F. Roy Willis offers an urban-centered world civilization text in his two-volume *World Civilizations*.

On the Chinese city, Joseph Needham's *Science and Civilization*, volume 4, part 3, discusses city planning. Paul Wheatley's *The Pivot of the Four Quarters, A Preliminary Enquiry into the Origins and Character of the Ancient Chinese City* discusses the symbolism. G. William Skinner's *The City in Late Imperial China* is a useful survey.

On Changan see Arthur F. Wright's "Changan" in Toynbee's *Cities of Destiny*. Edward H. Shafer's *The Golden Peaches of Samarkand* also deals with the city. On Song Kaifeng see "Sung Kaifeng" by Edward Kracke, Jr., in John W. Haeger's *Crisis and Prosperity in Sung China* and Lawrence Ma's *Commercial Development and Urban Change in Sung China*. On Hangzhou see Jacques Gernet's magnificent *Daily Life in China: On the Eve of the Mongol Invasion, 1250–1276. The Travels* of Marco Polo is also quite readable.

On the Islamic city, Xavier de Planhol provides a valuable geographical introduction in *The World of Islam*. Bryan Turner's *Weber and Islam* discusses many of the theoretical issues. *Muslim Cities in the Later Middle Ages* by Ira Lapidus concentrates on Egypt and Syria. Marshall G. S. Hodgson's *The Venture of Islam*, in three volumes, is full of insight and information. A series of short introductions to historical cities published by the University of Oklahoma Press includes Nicola A. Ziadeh's *Damascus under the Mamluks*, Roger Le Tourneau's *Fez in the Age of the Marinides*, and A. J. Arberry's *Shiraz*. There is also Gaston Wiet's *Baghdad: Metropolis of the Abbasid Caliphate*.

For the European city, some of the classics are still the best introductions: Max Weber's *The City*, Lewis Mumford's *The City in History*, and Henri Pirenne's *Medieval Cities* are all well worth reading. Some of the classic interpretations are gathered in John F. Benton's *Town Origins.* Other useful introductions include Maurice Beresford's *New Towns of the Middle Ages,* M. V. Clark's *The Medieval City-State,* and J. H. Mundy and Peter Riessenberg's *The Medieval Town.*

On English medieval towns see Susan Reynolds, *An Introduction to the History of English Medieval Towns,* and on London, Christopher N. L. Brooke's *London: 800–1216,* Gwyn A. Williams's *Medieval London from Commune to Capital,* Timothy Baker's *Medieval London,* or Sylvia Thrupp's *The Merchant Class of Medieval London.* For Germany see Fritz Rorig's *The Medieval Town* or Paul Strait's *Cologne in the Twelfth Century.*

On medieval Italy, Chris Wickham's *Early Medieval Italy: Central Power and Local Society, 400–1000* and J. K. Hyde's *Society and Politics in Medieval Italy: The Evolution of the Civil Life, 1000–1350* are both valuable. Robert Brentano's *Rome Before Avignon: A Social History of Thirteenth Century Rome* shows the expansion of a noncommercial city, and William H. McNeill's *Venice, the Hinge of Europe, 1081–1797,* a preeminently commercial one.

The best introductions to the city in Renaissance Italy are *Power and Imagination: City-States in Renaissance Italy* by Lauro Martines and *The Italian City-Republics* by Daniel Waley. For the impact of the computer and the social sciences on recent histories of the Renaissance, see Gene Brucker's "Tale of Two Cities: Florence and Venice in the Renaissance," *American Historical Review,* 88 (1983), pp. 599–616.

For studies of specific Italian cities see D. Herilhy's *Pisa in the Early Renaissance: A Study of Urban Growth,* William Bowsky's *The Finance of the Commune of Siena,* and J. K. Hyde's *Padua in the Age of Dante.*

There are libraries on Florence. One might begin with the works of two who were there: Francesco Guicciardini's *History of Italy* and *History of Florence,* and Niccolo Machiavelli's *History of Florence and the Affairs of Italy.* Among the better modern introductions are Gene Bruker's *Renaissance Florence,* J. Lucas-Dubreton's *Daily Life in Florence in the Time of the Medici,* John Gage's *Life in Italy at the Time of the Medici,* Marvin B. Becker's *Florence in Transition,* and Cecilia M. Ady's *Lorenzo de Medici and Renaissance Italy.* J. R. Hale's *Florence and the Medici: The Pattern of Control* and Gene Brucker's *Florentine Politics and Society 1343–1378* are excellent analyses of political power. Raymond De Roover's *Rise and Decline of the Medici Bank* provides important economic background, and Donald Weinstein's brilliant *Savonarola and Florence: Prophecy and Patriotism in the Renaissance* shows the conflict between religious piety and patriotism.

NOTES

1. Joseph Needham and Ling Wang, "Civil Engineering and Nautics," in *Science and Civilization in China,* vol. 1 (Cambridge: Cambridge University Press, 1970), p. 61.
2. Max Weber, *The Religion of China,* trans. Hans H. Gerth (New York: Free Press, 1951), p. 13.
3. Frederick W. Mote, "The City in Traditional Chinese Civilization," in *Traditional China,* ed. James T. C. Liu and Wei-ming Tu (Englewood Cliffs, N.J.: Prentice-Hall, 1970), pp. 42–43.
4. Arthur F. Wright, "Changan," in *Cities of Destiny,* ed. Arnold Toynbee (New York: McGraw-Hill, 1967), p. 146.

5. Arthur Waley, *The Poetry and Career of Li Po* (New York: Macmillan, 1950), pp. 87–88. Pin yin equivalents are "Xian Gu Pass" and the "palace of Qin."

6. Diana Gregory, "Sung K'aifeng: Some New Ideas," an unpublished paper brought to my attention by Lynda Shaffer, Tufts University.

7. Ichisada Miyazaki, *China's Examination Hell,* trans. Conrad Schirokauer (New Haven: Yale University Press, 1976), pp. 116–117.

8. Etienne Balazs, "Chinese Towns," in *Chinese Civilization and Bureaucracy,* trans. H. M. Wright (New Haven: Yale University Press, 1964), p. 71.

9. Yoshinobu Shiba, "Urbanization and the Development of Markets in the Lower Yangtze Valley," in *Crisis and Prosperity in Sung China,* ed. John Winthrop Haeger (Tucson: University of Arizona Press, 1975), p. 42.

10. Haeger, *op. cit.,* p. 11.

11. *The Book of Ser Marco Polo concerning the Kingdom and Marvels of the East,* Vol. I, trans. and ed. Sir Henry Yule, 3rd edition revised by Henri Cordier, 2 vols., (London: J. Murray, 1926), p. 205. Cited in Jacques Gernet, *Daily Life in China: On the Eve of the Mongol Invasion, 1250–1276* (Stanford: Stanford University Press, 1970), pp. 53–54.

12. *Marco Polo, The Description of the World,* ed. A. C. Moule and Paul Pelliot (London: George Routledge & Sons, Ltd., 1938), vol. I, pp. 312–313. Cited in Gernet, *op. cit.,* pp. 31–32.

13. *The Book of Ser Marco Polo . . . ,* vol. I, p. 192. Cited in Gernet, pp. 28–29.

14. Yuan Ts'ai, "Yuan-shih shif-fan," in Shiba, *op. cit.,* p. 46.

15. Xavier de Planhol, *The World of Islam* (Ithaca: Cornell University Press, 1959), p. 2

16. *Ibid.,* p. 7.

17. Hugh Kennedy, *The Prophet and the Age of the Caliphates* (London: Longman, 1986), pp. 248–249. The study referred to is R. Mottahedeh, "Administration in Buyid Qazwin," in *Islamic Civilization 950–1150,* ed. D. S. Richards (Oxford: Oxford University Press, 1975), pp. 33–45.

18. Bryan S. Turner, *Weber and Islam: A Critical Study* (London: Routledge & Kegan Paul, 1978), p. 99.

19. Nicola A. Ziadeh, *Damascus Under the Mamlūks* (Norman: University of Oklahoma Press, 1964), p. 87.

20. Bryan S. Turner, *op. cit.,* p. 102.

21. Marshall G. S. Hodgson, *The Venture of Islam,* vol. 2 (Chicago: University of Chicago Press, 1974), p. 108.

22. Lewis Mumford, *The City in History* (New York: Harcourt Brace Jovanovich, 1961), p. 268.

23. *Ibid.,* pp. 279–280.

24. Cited in Daniel Waley, *The Italian City-Republics* (New York: McGraw-Hill, 1969), p. 53.

25. *Ibid.,* p. 99.

26. *Ibid.,* pp. 147–148.

27. Cited in Helene Wieruszowski, "Art and the Commune in the Time of Dante," *Speculum,* 19, no. 1 (January 1944), p. 31.

28. Mumford, *op. cit.,* p. 369.

29. *Ibid.,* pp. 399–401.

❧ 12 ❧

Ecology
and
Theology

Religion
and Science

ECOLOGY IS A PROBLEM that we normally identify with modern industrial society. We are not used to associating ecology with theology, or with medieval history. But this chapter makes that association to suggest that our ecological problems lie very deep. Although we may have "discovered" an environmental crisis only recently, its causes go back at least as far as the Western industrial revolution of the last few centuries. The point of this chapter is that the industrial revolution itself, and the transformation of the human relationship to nature that it entailed, had even earlier causes in Western thought and action. Why, after all, was it Western Europe, of all places, that initiated the industrial revolution? This chapter will explore some of the cultural traditions that might have prepared the way.

Specifically, we will examine two Western cultural traditions that have been linked by some scholars to our ecological and environmental problems. They are the Western religious, or Judeo-Christian, tradition, and the development of science. Christianity and modern science might almost be called the hallmarks of Western culture. Although much of Western history is contained in the struggle between these two cultural forms, they also have much in common. We will examine the continuity between Christianity and science in order to explore the roots of Western predominance over nature and the world.

We are therefore raising a number of issues that should be kept in mind. We are asking about the relationship between religion and science, and specifically between Christianity and the development of modern science. We are asking about the validity of tracing such a modern issue as ecology back to the Middle Ages when ecological issues were minimal or nonexistent. We are asking about the different "ideas of nature" that are found in different religious traditions. And we are asking to what extent such ideas matter in people's daily confrontations with the natural environment.

We will proceed by first examining the argument that the Judeo-Christian religious tradition shaped Western ideas of nature in a way that made the natural world more exploitable. Then we will ask if religious ideas really matter all that much by examining some of the inconsistencies between religion and practice in other religious traditions. Then we will survey the link between Western religion and science and examine some of the assumptions about nature that were implicit in the Western scientific revolution.

THE RESPONSIBILITY OF THE JUDEO-CHRISTIAN TRADITION

Those scholars who have argued that the roots of our ecological problems lie with the Judeo-Christian attitude toward nature emphasize the uniqueness of Judeo-Christian monotheism compared with more "primitive" polytheistic, animistic, and "nature" religions.

Arnold Toynbee put the case this way:

> The thesis . . . is that some of the major maladies of the present-day world—for instance the recklessly extravagant consumption of nature's irreplaceable treasures, and the pollution of those of them that man has not already devoured— can be traced back in the last analysis to a religious cause, and that this cause is the rise of monotheism.[1]

Why monotheism? What does the ancient Hebrew insistence that there is only one God have to do with our modern ecological problems? Toynbee's answer is to remind us that the monotheism of the Hebrew Bible was an injunction against older forms of nature worship, and that once monotheism was fully accepted in Judeo-Christian culture, nature could be exploited instead of worshiped. "For premonotheistic man," Toynbee points out,

> nature was not just a treasure trove of "natural resources." Nature was, for him, a goddess, "Mother Earth," and the vegetation that sprang from the Earth, the animals that roamed, like man himself, over the Earth's surface, and the minerals hiding in the Earth's bowels, all partook of nature's divinity.[2]

The Bible not only deprived nature of its ancient sacred awe in order to acclaim a higher creator God. It also specifically counseled mankind to subdue the natural world. Here Toynbee and others point to the injunction in Genesis 1:28:

> And God blessed them: and God said unto them, Be fruitful, and multiply, and replenish the earth, and subdue it; and have dominion over the fish of the sea, and over the birds of the heavens, and over every living thing that moveth upon the earth.

It is difficult to know what to make of a logical connection between monotheism and the desacralization of nature, or of any specific statements in the Bible. One wants to know if Jews and Christians actually behaved more arrogantly toward nature because of these ideas. In this regard, the work of Lynn White, Jr., a historian of medieval Christianity, technology, and science, makes a more formidable case for the responsibility of the Judeo-Christian tradition.

White's essay "The Historical Roots of Our Ecologic Crisis" has become a classic, reprinted many times since its first publication in *Science* in 1967. It was prompted, he tells us elsewhere, by watching Buddhists in Ceylon build a road.

> Noting cones of earth left undisturbed upon the intended roadbed, he discovered that these were the nests of snakes. The Buddhists would not destroy the cones until the snakes departed of their own accord from the scene of activity. Among other things, White could not help reflecting that had the road builders been Christian, the snakes would have suffered a different fate.[3]

White's essay begins with two points worth repeating:

> One thing is so certain that it seems stupid to verbalize it: both modern technology and modern science are distinctively *Occidental.* Our technology has absorbed elements from all over the world, notably from China; yet everywhere today, whether in Japan or in Nigeria, successful technology is Western. . . .
>
> A second pair of facts is less well recognized because they result from quite recent historical scholarship. The leadership of the West, both in technology and in science, is far older than the so-called Scientific Revolution of the 17th century or the so-called Industrial Revolution of the 18th century.[4]

Lynn White himself has contributed much to the view that Western technological inventiveness and dominance can be traced back to the Middle Ages. His book *Medieval Technology and Social Change* shows (among other things) the revolutionary effects of such an apparently simple invention as the stirrup for medieval society. Others (see Lewis Mumford, for instance) have found the origins of modern ideas and methods of work in the medieval monastery. In this essay, however, White draws our attention to the transformation of agriculture in Christian Europe about the time of Charlemagne (whose coronation was in A.D.

800). In this period, White relates, the peasants of northern Europe began to use a plow that turned over the land more violently than anything known before. Previous plows only scratched the surface of the soil. These new plows not only cut into the soil with a vertical knife, but they also cut underneath with a horizontal knife and turned the land completely over with a moldboard (a curved attachment that twisted the freshly cut sod). This system of plowing (which is still the method of modern tractors) caused so much friction with the soil that it required eight oxen instead of the usual two.

The new plow brought with it a much more aggressive attitude toward nature because of the kind of society that it required.

> In the days of the scratch plow, fields were distributed generally in units capable of supporting a single family. Subsistence farming was the presupposition. But no peasant owned eight oxen: to use the new and more efficient plow, peasants pooled their oxen to form large plow teams, originally receiving (it would appear) plowed strips in proportion to their contribution. Thus, distribution of land was based no longer on the needs of a family but, rather, on the capacity of a power machine to till the earth. Man's relation to the soil was profoundly changed. Formerly, man had been part of nature; now he was the exploiter of nature. Nowhere else in the world did farmers develop any analogous agricultural implement. Is it coincidence that modern technology, with its ruthlessness toward nature, has so largely been produced by descendants of these peasants of northern Europe?
>
> This same exploitive attitude appears slightly before 830 in Western illustrated calendars. In older calendars the months were shown as passive personifications. The new Frankish calendars, which set the style for the Middle Ages are very different: they show men coercing the world around them—plowing, harvesting, chopping trees, butchering pigs. Man and nature are two things, and man is master.[5]

The separation of man and nature that White notices in medieval calendars was certainly not completed by the ninth century, even in the most Christian sections of Europe. The peasant idea of a living nature persisted, we shall see shortly, as an obstacle to the scientific revolution well after 1500. Indeed, even today Greek peasants sing of their mother fields and daughter olive trees. But the question that White poses is whether Judeo-Christian monotheism has been playing a role in creating that separation. To answer this, let us look at some of the alternate visions of nature in polytheism and Eastern religions.

ALTERNATE VISIONS: POLYTHEISM AND ANIMISM

To say that the Judeo-Christian victory over polytheism was an unmitigated environmental disaster is to say too much. Polytheistic religions could also encour-

In this French calendar scene of March from the early fifteenth century, we see the coercion of nature that Lynn White, Jr., refers to. Peasants are clearing the brush, planting, and plowing (with an early moldboard plow that requires only two oxen). Above, the signs of the zodiac suggest much older, naturalistic images of the months. (From Les trés riches heures du duc de Berry, *Giraudon, Musée de Condé)*

age environmental exploitation. Roman polytheists mined mountains and exploited natural resources more than early Christians did. Polytheism is literally the belief in many gods. We must ask who those gods were, and what they protected. Romans worshiped civic and imperial gods who were easily disposed to exploitation, as well as nature gods who were not. Most polytheists, however, were animists: they believed that the natural world was full of *anima* (spirits or souls). That was a belief that could offer considerable protection to the natural environment.

Most tribal societies were animistic and polytheistic. But these are the categories of the missionaries and anthropologists, and so they are sometimes sources of confusion. Most African and Native American peoples, for instance, were polytheists. But they were also monotheists. Missionaries, not Africans, had to classify people into monotheists and polytheists. Two scholars of African culture put it this way:

> All African religions are monotheistic in the sense that there is a single High God, who is said to be the creator of the world and of mankind, and a central source of order and of whatever sense is to be found. Many African religions are also polytheistic in that either pantheons of gods or large numbers of spirits or ancestors or some other kind of divinities may stand between man and the ultimate God.[6]

Traditional African religions are called "animist" to designate their awareness of the living force in nature. Animism is not the "nature worship" that missionaries imagined. It is rather a sense of commonality with, or participation in, nature, and a belief that cooperation with nature is essential. This belief is suggested by a traditional prayer by the official "keeper of the community woods and forests" among the Didinga people of the Sudan:

> O Earth, wherever it be my people dig, be kindly to them. Be fertile when they give the little seeds to your keeping. Let your generous warmth nourish them and your abundant moisture germinate them. Let them swell and sprout, drawing life from you, and burgeon under your fostering care. . . .
>
> . . .
>
> O rivers and streams, where the woodman has laid bare the earth, where he has hewn away the little bushes and torn out encumbering grass, there let your waters overflow. Bring down the leafy mould from the forest and the fertilizing silt from the mountains. When the rains swell your banks, spread out your waters and lay your rich treasures on our gardens.
>
> . . .
>
> Conspire together, O earth and rivers: conspire together, O earth and rivers and forests. Be gentle and give us plenty from your teeming plenty. For it is I, Lomingamoi of the clan of Idots, who speaks, Keeper of the clan lands, Warden of the Forest, Master of the clan.[7]

NATIVE AMERICAN ENVIRONMENTAL RELIGIONS

The polytheism of Native Americans is perhaps more extensive than that of African societies. At least the monotheistic belief in a creator God is not universal among them, as it is among Africans.[8] More common is the belief in an earth goddess or mother goddess. She is found in North and South America, in cities as well as farming villages, and even among hunting-gathering peoples. As an example of the last, there is the testimony of Smohalla, charismatic chief of the Shahaptin peoples of the state of Washington in the 1880s. When pressured by the military to give up hunting and learn farming, he replied:

> You ask me to plow the ground. Shall I take a knife and tear my mother's bosom? Then when I die she will not take me to her bosom to rest. You ask me to dig for stone. Shall I dig under her skin for her bones? Then when I die I cannot enter her body to be born again. You ask me to cut grass and make hay and sell it, and be rich like white men. But how dare I cut off my mother's hair?[9]

Native American religion has been called an "environmental religion"[10] because of the centrality of concerns like these. The relationship of humans and nature was almost a preoccupation. Nature was the source of life. It gave birth to humans and fed them. But hunters had to kill the animals, and farmers had to cut the ground. It was a relationship that required constant attention. Thus, hunters apologized to animals for having killed them.

> Ethics included rules against boasting about hunting prowess. . . . They included the idea that humans could not kill animals at improper times, such as bears when they hibernated, or any animal when a member of the immediate family was expecting the gift of life.[11]

Such rules could not always be observed, and people had to eat. But even the taking of animal life was part of a religious context of mutual obligation between humans and animals. When a Wintu hunter was unable to kill a deer, it was because "deer don't want to die for me." Hunters would charm their prey to die for them. The culture hero of the Ojibwa was always trying to outwit the animals so that he could control them. The hunters were not always successful. But when they failed, there had to be a reason, and the reason might just as readily lie with the animals as with themselves. When the compact between humans and animals broke down, "humans fell into dis-ease from nature."[12] According to a common myth, when humans began to kill too many animals, the animals retaliated by creating diseases; but the plants took pity on the humans and offered a cure. Epidemic disease might, in fact, have provided a reason or excuse for the Eastern Algonkin to participate in the international fur trade as retaliation against the animals that were thought responsible for the epidemic.[13] Thus, the relationship often produced frustration, guilt, and anger toward the animals. But even then, it was a relationship.

ALTERNATE VISIONS: EASTERN RELIGIONS

The term "animism" was first used by the anthropologist Edward Tylor to refer to the religious beliefs of some of the Indians of Asia (and then later applied to the "Indians" of the New World). Respect for nature was certainly an important concern of Hinduism, and especially of Buddhism and Jainism.

The Jains, followers of Mahavira, who was a contemporary of the Buddha, were the most unrelenting on this point. The following is from the Jain *Book of Sermons:*

> *Earth and water, fire and wind,*
> *Grass, trees, and plants, and all creatures that move,*
> *Born of the egg, born of the womb,*
> *Born of dung, born of water—*
> *These are the classes of living beings.*
> *Know that they all seek happiness.*
> *In hurting them men hurt themselves,*
> *And will be born again among them.*[14]

Indian Hinduism in the period after the classical age became more devotional. *Brahmans* had learned that the mass of people preferred devotion *(bhakti)* to a personal God over ritual and sacrifice. They translated the Upanishads and composed popular songs in local languages, and they joined in the singing of their praises to Shiva and Vishnu. Devotion to a personal God, even a Creator God, did not exclude nature, however, anymore than it did in the Upanishads. A song by Shankaradeva (1449–1568) shows how the creator God could still be identified with nature:

> Thou art the Author of the World. Thou art the Oversoul and the sole Lord of the world, and nothing else exists besides Thee. Thou art the cause and effect, the universe of the static and the moving, even as an ear ornament is inseparable from the gold of which it is made. Thou art the animals and the birds, the gods and the demons, the trees and the shrubs. Only the ignorant taketh Thee as different [from the universe].[15]

Both Chinese Daoism and Buddhism expressed reverential attitudes toward nature. The "Dao" was the way of nature. "Let there be no action contrary to the Dao," the *Dao De Jing* [*Tao Te Ching*] advised, "and nothing will go unregulated." A common Daoist belief held that "even insects and crawling things, herbs and trees, may not be injured." Schools of Buddhism in traditional China varied on matters of doctrine, but they shared a reverence for nature only slightly less central.

This is a typical example of the popular Chinese art of landscape painting. As is usually the case in this art form, human beings are barely noticeable. The artist is much more interested in the towering beauty of the natural world. Even when the Chinese artist painted a city (like Hangzhou in the previous chapter) nature is predominant. Compare our views of Florence. (Freer Gallery of Art)

IDEALS VERSUS BEHAVIOR?

One should not assume that all Chinese (even all Daoists or Buddhists) approached nature with such concern, however. The student of traditional China reads of official inspectors of the mountains and forests, prohibitions against cutting trees except at certain times, and other enforced conservation practices. But one also hears why such rules were necessary. Reports of deforestation, soil erosion, and flooding are common. After the tenth century, Chinese manufacturing had so depleted the timber reserves that it became increasingly necessary to substitute coal for wood.

From the Tang dynasty to the late Southern Song, China experienced a technological and economic boom that almost became an industrial revolution, like that which transformed Europe five hundred years later. Iron production reached per capita amounts that were not equaled until the British industrial revolution in the eighteenth century. Paper, paper money, printing, and publishing fueled an intellectual and financial revolution not equaled by the European Renaissance. New agricultural techniques—especially in wet rice cultivation, new seeds and fertilizers, iron plows with moldboards, doubling cropping that enabled two harvests a year—aided by widespread distribution of published work on the new techniques gave China "probably the most sophisticated agriculture in the world, India being the only conceivable rival"[16] by the thirteenth century. With the invention of gunpowder, iron bombs, and the gun by the Chinese and the invading nomadic Jin [Chin] in the 1220s, warfare entered the modern age. With the mariner's compass, star charts, and navigator's manuals, Chinese ships sailed from Japan to Arabia and East Africa between 1405 and 1433. Chinese ships were the travel choice of foreigners during the Song and early Ming dynasties.

Much of this economic prosperity was reversed by the Mongol invasions and the Mongol Yüan (1279–1368) dynasty and the following Chinese Ming (1368–1644). But the dynamism of Chinese society—its expansion throughout the southeast and the Yangtze Valley, its systematic technological innovation, and its economic, industrial, and intellectual productivity—raises a number of questions. Why was China so expansive? How did such dynamism occur in a Buddhist or Daoist culture?

Perhaps the expansion of Song China occurred despite Buddhist and Daoist ideas. Perhaps it should be seen as the culmination of other traditions, notably Confucianism, which regained favor under the Song. The revival of Confucianism, often called neo-Confucianism in the West, was an effective counter to the spiritualism and social indifference of many Buddhist and Daoist thinkers. Confucian values motivated reformers like Fan Zhongyan [Fan Chung-yen] (989–1052), who said a true Confucian was "one who is first in worrying about the world's problems and last in enjoying his own pleasures," and Wang Anshi (1021–2086), who played a key role in developing a national money economy. The Confucian revival called for a renewed attention to matters of state and invested heavily in education. One of the elite schools, the White Deer Grotto Academy, was run for a time by Zhu Xi [Chu Hsi] (1130–1200), the Song's preeminent Confucian philosopher. The expansion of China during the Song was in keeping with Confucian human and material values rather than Buddhist or Daoist spiritualism.

Chinese ecological ideals must also be reconciled with the building of such gigantic cities as Changan and Hangzhou. Villages and rural roads were usually laid out according to the principles of *fengshui:* a preference for following the lay of the land, the natural hills and curves, and a distaste for straight lines, geometrical grids, or structures that seemed to dominate nature. But *fengshui* was virtually ignored in the construction of Changan. The astronomers who laid out the thirty-one-square-mile site sought conformance to the heavens rather than the earth. They carefully measured the shadow of the noon sun and the position of the north star in order to align the city of the Son of Heaven, its walls and gates, with the four directions. In the process, villages were leveled and (according to legend) all of the trees, except the old locust that shaded the chief architect, were uprooted.[17]

If Changan, with its broad straight avenues, conformed to an astronomer's idea of nature, Hangzhou was constructed according to the ideals of a romantic artist. Nature was not followed. It was reconstructed. The many parks and gardens were all carefully constructed, planted, and groomed. Even the West Lake was an artificial construction. The illusion of a natural setting had to be rigorously maintained in the thirteenth century by peasants recruited to clear and enlarge the lake, and by military patrols empowered to enforce the various prohibitions against throwing rubbish or planting lotuses or water chestnuts.[18]

What is one to make of examples, such as these, of a disregard of nature in traditional China? The author who has suggested them, Yi-Fu Tuan, calls them "discrepancies between environmental attitude and behavior." They are that, certainly. But the inference that attitudes are one thing, and behavior is something else (or, more generally, that people never live up to their ideals) skirts a number of issues. If the behavior of the builders of Changan and Hangzhou did not conform to the attitudes of Buddhism or Daoism, might it have conformed to the attitudes of some other tradition? We have already suggested that interpretation by writing of Confucianism, and of astronomers' and artists' attitudes toward nature. That still leaves the construction of such cities within the Chinese religious tradition, but it extends the behavioral possibilities of that tradition. Yi-Fu Tuan himself uses the traditional Chinese distinction between the *yin* (passive, natural, female) and the *yang* (active, artificial, male) to see city building as assertions of traditional *yang* attitudes, ideas, and ideals. If Buddhism and Daoism are *yin* religious traditions, then emperor worship, ancestor worship, Confucianism, perhaps even astronomy and military rituals can be seen as *yang* religious traditions. In that vein, there is no "discrepancy" between the *yang* religion of emperor worship and the act of moving mountains or digging lakes to build the emperor's city.

Chinese emperor worship may have played a role similar to European Christianity in sanctioning the exploitation of nature. Astronomical and artistic interpretations of Buddhism and Daoism could also serve the cause of redesigning nature. No intellectual tradition is purely naturalistic or entirely hostile to nature. But, on balance, the Chinese seem to have been more attuned to the natural world (in thought and action) than were their European contemporaries. It is difficult, for instance, to imagine the Western equivalent of the Chinese Tang dynasty emperor "who went off in the springtime with his court musicians to gladden the flowers with soft music."[19]

It is impossible to imagine the Western equivalent of an inscription in a Japanese monastery that praises the beautiful blossoms of a particular plum tree and warns: "Whoever cuts a single branch of this tree shall forfeit a finger therefor."[20] The Eastern equation of the human and the natural could redound to the disadvantage of humans as well as to the advantage of nature.

Medieval Christianity was not entirely lacking in equivalents of Eastern holy men. But the story of one, who appeared around 1200, shows more, perhaps, about the differences than the similarities of the East and West. Like a Christian Buddha, Saint Francis of Assisi led a group of monks who not only humbled themselves by giving up their possessions to live with the poor, but attempted to humble humanity by rejecting human control over nature. Legend describes Saint Francis preaching to the birds and persuading a wolf not to attack an Italian town. Saint Francis believed that animals also had souls. To him all of nature was sacred. He

*Saint Francis of Assisi preaches to the birds. The Christian tradition
approaches the Chinese. But even here the great florentine artist
Giotto places humans in the foreground, and the birds (like the
viewers of the painting) are placed at the eye level of the saint. One
suspects that a Chinese artist of the period would have preferred the
top half of the painting, but with the birds back in the air and trees.
(Granger)*

spoke of Brother Ant and Sister Fire and urged his listeners to glorify all of God's
creations. He may even have believed in reincarnation; some Christians and Jews
in southern France did at this time.

The challenge that Saint Francis and these others made to the Judeo-Christian tradition of dominating nature was so radical that it could not succeed. The group in southern France was suppressed violently. Pope Innocent III was able to bring Saint Francis and his disciples into the church (despite a dream that they might be able to take over) and defuse their message. In the end Francis died, the Franciscans were given a lot of money, and they became the caretakers, rather than the comrades, of the poor and the animals.

That was about as close as Christianity came to nature worship. Saint Francis could never have been a Buddha because Christianity did not even give him the vocabulary for such an extreme. It was a big step for Saint Francis to argue that animals had souls. That had never been an issue for the Hindus. They assumed all along that animals were just as divine as humans. The Buddha had been beyond that point when he struggled with the question of reincarnation. Saint Francis shows us the limits of Christianity in two ways: his views were much more moderate than those of Eastern holy men; and there was never much of a chance that he would change the direction of Christian culture. He was much too extreme for the church.

In stressing the different philosophical orientations of the East and the West, we do not mean to ignore the question of behavior. Lynn White's argument, in fact, depends on a difference between the ecological behavior of the West and that of the East. We have observed examples of ecological damage or avoidance in traditional China. Do such examples refute White's argument?

We think not. First, the damage does not seem that severe. Second, White is not arguing that monotheism is the only cause of environmentally harmful behavior; emperor worship may have had a similar effect. But most importantly, White is arguing that the Judeo-Christian separation of man and nature gave rise to a particular kind of science that has transformed the world. We must turn, then, to the rise of Western science.

THE RESPONSIBILITY OF THE WESTERN SCIENTIFIC REVOLUTION

Science certainly existed long before Christianity. In fact it took the Christians over a thousand years to recover the highly advanced science of the ancient Greeks. This knowledge had been kept relatively intact by the scholars of the Byzantine Empire in Eastern Europe and the Arab scientists in North Africa and Spain. But when, after 1200, the Christians of Europe finally regained Greek science and translated it into Latin, they approached it very differently from the way the Greeks of Byzantium and the Muslims of the Arab world did. The Byzantine Greeks saw science as symbolic communication from God. They viewed the ant as God's message to the lazy. Fire, to them, was God's way of showing the Christian how to rise to heaven. The rainbow was a symbol of hope—the sign that God sent to Noah after the forty days of rain and flood.

However, in the Latin West by the early thirteenth century natural theology was following a very different bent. It was ceasing to be the decoding of the physical symbols of God's communication with man and was becoming the effort to understand God's mind by discovering how his creation operates. The rainbow was no longer simply a symbol of hope first sent to Noah after the Deluge: Robert Grosseteste, Friar Robert Bacon, and Theodoric of Frieberg produced startling sophisticated work on the optics of the rainbows, but they did it as a venture in religious understanding. From the thirteenth century onward, up to and including Leibnitz and Newton, every major scientist, in effect, explained his motivations in religious terms. Indeed, if Galileo had not been so expert an amateur theologian he would have gotten into far less trouble: the professionals resented his intrusion. And Newton seems to have regarded himself more as a theologian than as a scientist. It was not until the late eighteenth century that the hypotheses of God became unnecessary to many scientists.[21]

Thus, modern science began as an attempt by very religious philosophers to understand the natural world that God had created and given them. They believed that God had revealed his intentions in a number of ways. He had revealed his word in the Bible—the teachings of the Old Testament and of Jesus—and he had shown his handiwork in the planets and natural environment that he had created for human use.

The first scientific thought was motivated by the hope of understanding God rather than conquering nature. Saint Thomas Aquinas, for instance, declared:

> The Creatures upon earth were not all made, no not the most of them, for man's eating and drinking; but for his glorifying the Wisdom, Goodness and Power of his Creator in the contemplation of them.[22]

By the seventeenth century, however, the work of the first modern scientists— people like Copernicus, Galileo, Sir Francis Bacon, Descartes, and Sir Isaac Newton—had led in two ways to conclusions that Saint Thomas Aquinas and the other theologians of the Middle Ages would not have been able to accept. First, the study of nature led to an increased awareness of the difference between the natural world and human beings. Second, the Europeans who became conscious of that difference became aware of the possibilities of exploiting or controlling nature.

It may seem strange to us that people did not always realize that nature was separate from man. We are so convinced that the grass or the moon or a wooden table is apart from us that it is difficult to imagine how people could think otherwise. The fact remains, nevertheless, that we in the modern Western world make a sharper distinction between people and things, man and nature, ourselves and the things around us, than did anyone before us. It is almost as if our skins have toughened in the last couple of hundred years. They haven't of course, but we have developed a sense of ourselves as separate individuals, operating in a world full of things, that is very recent.

Perhaps modern science has done more than anything else to separate our bodies from nature. We have already seen how earlier traditions have emphasized the community of the human and animal world. Certainly, the religion of the Jews and Christians aided the separation of the human individual from the animal world. But the scientists of the fifteenth to eighteenth centuries carried this idea of separation a lot further. Even when they were religious they thought of themselves as *observers* of a separate reality. Previously—that is, before the last five, six, or seven hundred years—almost all people imagined themselves as *participants* in, rather than observers of, nature.

The feeling of participating in, rather than looking at, nature was particularly common among the lower classes in the Middle Ages. The farming peasants, serfs, and tradespeople were usually unaware of the Christian doctrines that insisted on the separation of the human and the animal world. They were more likely to think as Saint Francis did, or they were so involved in the work of farming that they still accepted much older, Neolithic ideas about the similarity of soil and human mothers, and they personalized the rain, wind, and harvest.

Even the best-educated Christians of the Middle Ages believed that the basic elements of nature—air, earth, fire, and water—were found in varying proportions in human beings just as in the natural world. Just as a high amount of earth would account for the stability of a mountain or a chair, it would also be identified as the cause of human melancholy or laziness. The same thing that made the clouds float—an overdose of air—was thought responsible for making some people giddy or flighty. Fire might ignite the human spirit just as readily as it would a bale of hay. The same elements were found in man and beast, and even in stones and plows.

The Christians of the Middle Ages also accepted the assumptions of an astrology that may have originated locally or traveled from ancient India. The lives of human beings were thought to be just as determined by the moon and other "stars" as the seasons and the droughts and the quality of the crops.

In short, the people of medieval Europe were almost as sure of nature's power in human life as people had always been. And like earlier civilizations, they imagined that the things of the world lived very much as people did. Stones fell because they wanted to; they were attracted to the earth, or they "desired" to be reunited with other stones. The world was full of magic, and everything (including people) participated.

THE WORLD AS GARMENT OR STAGE: GALILEO

We can almost see how revolutionary modern science must have been to these people if, instead of reading the new scientific books, we look at their paintings of themselves. The paintings of the Middle Ages have no three-dimensional per-

The appeal and meaning of modern science: the eyes have it. To see is to measure and possess. How high? How far? How deep? How much? Why are none of these men looking at the woman in the tower, or at each other, or at any living thing? Were the trees cut down because they obstructed the view? Are those lines of vision latent rifle shots? No, it is only the gentlemen of the new scientific age celebrating the power of sextant, quadrant, telescope, and compass. (Deutches Museum)

spective. Crowds of people are painted on top of each other as if they occupy the same space. Angels and devils are just as real as people. Halos are just as real as heads. Suddenly, beginning in the 1300s in Italy, and later elsewhere, the artists show people and buildings in three dimensions. They seem suddenly aware that things are placed in space, that people in the foreground appear larger than people in the background because they are separated by distance. Even the rectangular shape of paintings (which we take for granted) became increasingly standardized about this time: a painting was to become like a window on the world. What had happened is that the artist had begun to view the world as an observer. He had detached himself from his surroundings and attempted to duplicate what he saw. This is exactly what the first modern scientists attempted to do. They stepped back to look at the world—the stars or butterflies—as detached observers rather than as participants. They measured things instead of vibrating with them—and that was a revolution. By the 1600s the world had become, in Shakespeare's words, a stage; it was no longer a piece of clothing one would wrap around oneself, but a spectacle that one would observe.

All of the "discoveries" of modern science had helped bring this about. Perhaps they were not discoveries as much as they were "creations," or new ways of seeing things. To put it another way, we might say that the discoveries of individual scientists were not nearly as important as the new attitude toward the world that led them to these discoveries. The attitude of this new science—the assumption that men and nature were fundamentally different—had enormous ecological implications.

Galileo (1564–1642) is usually credited with improving the telescope, turning it on the heavens, and supporting the theory of Copernicus (1473–1543) that the earth revolved around the sun, rather than vice versa. All of this is true. But the reason that Galileo wanted to use the telescope in the first place was that he believed the planets were not living sources of light (as most of his contemporaries believed), but were instead dead balls of matter like the earth and moon.

The great achievement of European physical science (from about 1500) was that it developed a method of describing the separate physical world in terms that could not be refuted. This was because scientists such as Galileo turned their attention from all of the "subjective" features of the world to its "objective," or measurable, qualities. Instead of asking about such subjective qualities as the "hopefulness" of rain, they measured the rainfall. Instead of asking about the taste or sound or smell of an object, they asked about its size, shape, or rate of motion. They focused, in short, on those qualities of an object that could be measured because measurements were not open to interpretation. Anyone could disagree about the "meaning" of a falling object. There might even be different interpretations about the sound that such an object made as it struck the ground. But no one could disagree about its rate of motion, once that had been computed. The value of science was that its results were indisputable.

The problem with science (from an ecological point of view) was that the human, or "subjective," element had to be overlooked so that the objective qualities could be understood. The result of the scientific approach was to see the objects of the natural world as if they were dead. See how Galileo explains his method:

> As soon as I form a conception of an object, I immediately feel the necessity of seeing that it has boundaries of some shape or other; that relative to others it is great or small; that it is in this or that place, in this or that time; that it is in motion or at rest; that it touches, or does not touch, another body. . . . But I do not find myself absolutely compelled to determine if it is white or red, bitter or sweet, sonorous or silent, smelling sweetly or disagreeably. . . . Therefore I think that these tastes, smells, colors, etc., with regard to the

object in which they appear to reside, are nothing more than mere names. They exist only in the observer. . . . I do not believe that there exists anything in external bodies for exciting tastes, smells, and sounds, etc., except size, shape, quantity, and motion.[23]

In our terms, Galileo had concluded that only the "primary qualities" (those which could be measured) existed. The secondary qualities, which could not easily be measured, did not exist. This has been a tendency in modern science ever since. The scientist is concerned with providing exact information. In attempting to be exact, he or she singles out the impersonal, "objective," or quantitative qualities of the object under investigation. That is the only way that measurement is possible. But it means divorcing these measurable qualities from the total organic context of the object.

Let us take the case of butterflies. We can appreciate butterflies for their beauty, their colors, or their grace—or we can attempt to understand them. The job of science is understanding. The process of understanding something like butterflies requires that we ask questions that can be answered: How large do they come, what different types are there, how fast do they fly, and how do they stay aloft? These are all questions that can be answered objectively because they require only that we make certain measurements and computations. We do not ask which butterflies are beautiful because there is no way of measuring that, no way of getting an objective answer.

The job of the scientist can be very useful—even ecologically. We might, for instance, want to know about the different types of butterflies in order to replenish an endangered species. The problem is that the more we become preoccupied with measuring and counting, the less we see natural objects in their totality. We are speaking only of a tendency in science—but the tendency is very real. One tendency of science is to isolate and abstract the qualities of an object that can be measured—to treat such qualities as if they were divorced from the total object. But these are not only the conditions of orderly scientific research, they are also the conditions under which organisms die. Try to weigh and measure a live butterfly.

Modern science has enabled us to understand our world because it has simplified complex organic processes so that they conform to mechanical laws. Galileo and Newton were able to tell us much about the acceleration of bodies by treating moving things as "bodies," whether they be people or animals or balls or meteorites. When you are studying movement, everything that moves is equal. The scientists of the seventeenth and eighteenth centuries could tell us so much about the motion of the planets and the objects of the earth by imagining that both behaved as so many Ping-Pong or billiard balls. This was a way of simplifying problems of weight, mass, and matter. The answers that science has gained are of invaluable assistance. Such answers were impossible with the medieval assumption that even planets and rocks behaved of their own will or inclination. No science was possible as long as people treated the rocks and planets as if they acted by whim. Science appropriated the whim and the will of natural forces with its mechanical laws, and those laws were used in Christian culture to give "dominion over the fish of the sea, and over the birds of the heavens, and over every living thing that moveth upon the earth."

SCIENCE, SCIENCE, EVERYWHERE

The scientific revolution that occurred in Western Europe between 1300 and 1700 has since transformed the world. It is the root of the science taught in all of the schools and universities of the world. There is no other. There is no Chinese as opposed to Muslim or Christian science. This is because all scientists are involved in the same enterprise of explaining how the natural world works. All are involved in the scientific process of observation, experimentation, and the development and evaluation of explanatory theories. They may sometimes champion different theories; but when they do, the process of science itself helps resolve their differences. This is the value of science, and the reason there is only one. It works. Ultimately the scientific method and the community of scientists can resolve any differences and come to a generally accepted conclusion because the overarching commitment of science is to "the truth" about the natural world.

We have seen that the truth that is obtained by science is the truth about a separate reality—that is, a reality separate from the human observer. The scientific revolution that we have discussed depended on a conceptual revolution that allowed people to observe nature as a separate reality. We have argued that that conceptual revolution occurred first in the West because the Judeo-Christian tradition provided the necessary framework. Judaic monotheism posited a creator God separate from his creation. Judaism also said that God gave humans the natural world to exploit. Perhaps more significant, however, was the way in which Christianity changed Judaism. By making its appeal universal, rather than tribal, it made belief more important than membership. Christianity was, and is, a very theological religion. It is rich in doctrines, dogmas, and beliefs, as well as in a history of heretics. You can be born a Jew, but you have to believe to be a Christian. It is that combination of monotheism and the stress on theology, beliefs, explanations, or "truth" that made the conceptual breakthrough to modern science a Christian event, rather than, say, a Muslim one.

Muslim scientific knowledge was considerably greater than the Christian in the period between 900 and 1400. Ibn al-Haytham (965–1030) of Basra made major contributions in optics, astronomy, and mathematics that would not be improved on in Europe for seven centuries. Muslim medicine was renowned. Muhammad al-Razi (860–940) wrote a medical encyclopedia that was used in Europe into the fifteenth century. He identified smallpox and measles, and was the first to use alcohol as an antiseptic and mercury as a purgative. Ibn Sina (Avicenna in Latin,

980–1037) read entire libraries and wrote on virtually every subject. His medical encyclopedia constituted half the medical curriculum at European universities through the fifteenth century. That Islam did not initiate the breakthrough to modern science, despite these achievements and despite its insistent monotheism, is puzzling. What Islam lacked, according to one modern Muslim scholar,[24] was Christianity's obsession with theology, finding out, beliefs. It was, perhaps, that obsession that made the conceptual revolution of modern science (as well as later secularization) easier. Islamic literature concentrated not so much on attempting to understand, but on experiencing and loving God.

Chinese thought was directed more to understanding. During the Song dynasty, Chinese painting was vividly naturalistic, almost scientific in detail; Confucian philosophers like Zhu Xi had urged "seeking for principle in everything." Neo-Confucianism, like Confucianism, was more interested in the human realm than in a separate world of nature, and while it was not monotheistic it was also not religious.

After the Mongol invasion and during the Ming dynasty (1368–1644) the confident, socially responsible, neo-Confucianism of the Song declined with a general drop in productivity, innovation, and expansion. Buddhist and Daoist thinkers seemed to have more to say in uncertain times. The sixteenth-century alternative to neo-Confucianism was, perhaps, the moral intuitionism of Wang Yangming. According to Wang, nature was only a part of human consciousness. It had no other existence. "Outside the mind," he said, "there are no principles. Outside the mind there are no phenomena."[25]

This turn inward, away from the natural world, occurred also in Chinese painting of the period. The earlier naturalistic style of the Song was abandoned in the Ming by subjective and introspective images. "The new emphasis on Mind," the historian Mark Elvin has written, "devalued the philosophical significance of scientific research by draining the reality from the world of sensory experience."[26] Instead of developing mechanical and quantitative models in order to understand an outside reality, Chinese philosophers and scientists sought an intuitive communion with the mind.

It is instructive to compare the deductions of one of the great Chinese scientists of the seventeenth century with those of one of the great Europeans. Fang Yizhi [Fang I-Chih] (1611–1671) was a leader of the Chinese encyclopedic tradition. A neo-Confucian scholar and official, Fang Yizhi was swept up in the chaos of the seventeenth-century peasant uprisings, the Manchu invasion and bandit raids, and the collapse of the Ming. Like many intellectuals of his age, he sought solace in Buddhism and took refuge as a monk after 1650. His *Brief Record of the Principles of Things* (1664) dealt with such topics as astronomy, anatomy, botany, zoology, and physics. He was critical of his predecessors, asked questions about scientific method, and conducted experiments. He debated the Jesuit missionaries in China while accepting many of their insights. He understood the circulation of blood and the nature of eclipses.

On the central issue of Chinese intellectuals, the investigation of things, Fang Yizhi was more of a materialist than many of his contemporaries. Contrary to Wang Yangming, Fang urged his readers to accept the existence of things, to know specific things in detail, and to learn to manipulate things for human benefit.[27] But, perhaps especially after his Buddhist withdrawal in 1650, Fang Yizhi was more concerned with "general principles" than with specifics, and he thought that these general principles could be gained intuitively rather than through analytical, quantitative, or experimental method. The problem with Western science, Fang wrote (on the basis of his contacts with the Jesuits), was that they "use a variety of techniques for their swift computations, but they are still out of touch with general principles."[28] General principles were spiritual. They existed in the mind, not in the material world, according to Fang. Ultimately for Fang the specific things, the empirical reality, the objects of scientific study in the West, were unknowable. "Since it is only the mind which knows and perceives," he wrote, "everything is shadows and echoes."[29]

In a famous formulation of much the same problem, but one that led to a radically different conclusion, René Descartes (1596–1650) wrote in his *Discourse on Method* (1637), "I think, therefore I am." For Descartes the existence of mind was proof not that everything is shadows and echoes but that the material things of the world exist. The French philosopher said he tried to doubt everything but that even by doing so he had to admit his own existence as the doubter or thinker. Then, he concluded, since he could not doubt his own existence, he could also not doubt that there was something greater than himself. He, after all, was imperfect because he doubted. He did not know everything.

Descartes was both a Christian theologian and a scientist, both medieval and modern. Ultimately, his reason for accepting the reality of the world as more than a figment of his imagination is that God would not deceive him by giving him ideas that had no relation to reality. For the Christian the separate reality exists, and God has given humans the reason with which to understand it. The Buddhist belief that the world is fundamentally shadows and echoes was not an option.

SCIENCE AND ECOLOGY

We are led then to a difficult question. Can we have Christian science and Buddhist ecology too? Are the achievements of science necessarily destructive to the environment? Are the goals of science and ecology necessarily at odds? Do we have to choose between scientific progress and environmental well-being?

Perhaps our only response can be to try to have the best of both worlds. We know that science can be an effective instrument, as Fang Yizhi said for human welfare. Science is our problem-solving tool. Science can be applied to environmental problems as easily as to any others. We have also learned, however, that the process of distancing, distinguishing, abstracting, and analyzing that is part of science can obscure deeper organic connections—perhaps what Fang Yizhi meant by general principles. It would seem wise, then, to keep in mind both tendencies of science (alienating and liberating) so that we can use it most effectively and for the greatest good.

FOR FURTHER READING

Lynn White's "The Historical Roots of Our Ecologic Crisis" is reprinted in *Ecology and Religion in History,* edited by David and Eileen Spring, in Robert Detweiler's *Environmental Decay in Its Historical Context,* and in *Western Man and Environmental Ethics,* edited by Ian Barbour, all of which have other good articles. The contrast between Christian and Eastern attitudes toward nature is discussed both more theoretically and more popularly in Alan W. Watts's *Nature, Man and Woman.* But the grand interpretive synthesis on the Christian background of Western technology is Lewis Mumford's marvelous history *Technics and Civilization.*

To understand the medieval Christian attitudes toward nature, one normally thinks of histories of science and of philosophy. There are many good books on each. Perhaps the best history of science is Stephen Toulmin and June Goodfield's *The Fabric of the Heavens* on astronomy, their *Architecture of Matter* on physics, and their *The Discovery of Time* on history and geology. For more attention to medieval science, there is A. C. Crombie's *Medieval and Early Modern Science,* Charles Singer's *From Magic to Science,* and M. Clagett's *The Science of Mechanics in the Middle Ages.* Similarly for medieval philosophy, there is E. Gilson's *History of Christian Philosophy in the Middle Ages,* Gordon Leff's *Medieval Thought,* H. O. Taylor's *The Medieval Mind,* Maurice De Wulf's *Philosophy and Civilization in the Middle Ages,* F. B. Artz's *The Mind of the Middle Ages,* and F. C. Copleston's *Medieval Philosophy.*

Almost all of these books, however, concentrate on the discoveries and innovations of intellectuals, leaving the attitudes of most people and even the unchanging assumptions of the intellectuals between the lines. Thus, the tenor of the medieval attitude toward nature might be better understood with a book like C. S. Lewis's *Discarded Image* or (equally superb and unconventional) Owen Barfield's *Saving the Appearances.* Another is Arthur O. Lovejoy's classic *The Great Chain of Being,* or E. M. W. Tillyard's *The Elizabethan World Picture* for a slightly later period. Equally useful is the first chapter of William J. Brandt's *The Shape of Medieval History: Studies in Modes of Perception.* Two other previously mentioned classics should also be indicated in this regard. They are J. Huizinga's *The Waning of the Middle Ages* and Lynn White, Jr.'s *Medieval Technology and Social Change.*

For those interested in the comparison with Asian civilization, the same advice is in order. Joseph Needham's multivolume *Science and Civilization in China* is a compendium of insight and information. It is invaluable for comparisons with Western civilization. But the introductory student might better understand the Asian attitude toward nature with Joseph Campbell's *The Masks of God: Oriental Mythology,* Frederick W. Mote's *Intellectual Foundations of China,* or even Hermann Hesse's *Siddhartha. The Book of Mencius* is a classic that includes references to wastefulness in energy use, conservation, food storage, and flood control. Leon E. Stover's *The Control Ecology of Chinese Civilization: Peasants and Elites in the Last of the Agrarian States* is a demanding modern account.

Among the more readable introductions to the conceptual revolution of modern science are Herbert Butterfield's *The Origins of Modern Science,* Arthur Koestler's *The Sleepwalkers,* and the Toulmin and Goodfield volumes mentioned above. More theoretical and challenging approaches are E. A. Burtt's *The Metaphysical Foundations of Modern Science* and Thomas S. Kuhn's *The Structure of Scientific Revolutions.* For a more thorough history there is Charles C. Gillispie's *The Edge of Objectivity* and A. R. Hall's *The Scientific Revolution, 1500–1800.*

There are, of course, many other ways of approaching the subject of ecology—even in the time period we have chosen. Sometimes, in fact, the most innovative and interesting books are those that ignore traditional chronological, geographical, and even topical boundaries. One thinks first of Fernand Braudel's *The Mediterranean and the Mediterranean World in the Age of Philip II.* The first half of the first volume of this masterpiece discusses the role of the environment in ways that might serve as a model for future works on other areas and other times. Another monumental starting point for the history of ecology is Emmanuel Le Roy Ladurie's *Times of Feast, Times of Famine: A History of Climate Since the Year 1000.* The subject of ecology can also be approached from the perspective of the single world ecological system that has been emerging in the last five hundred years. *The Columbian Exchange: Biological and Cultural Consequences of 1492* by Alfred W. Crosby, Jr., begins this study in a most engaging and readable way. Finally, for a very tentative overview of human ecology throughout human history we should note the introductory *Man and Nature: An Anthropological Essay in Human Ecology* by Richard A. Watson and Patty Jo Watson, and Edward Hyams's *Soil and Civilization.*

NOTES

1. Arnold Toynbee, "The Religious Background of the Present Environmental Crisis," *International Journal of Environmental Studies* 3 (1972), pp. 141–146. Reprinted in *Ecology and Religion in History,* eds. David and Eileen Spring (New York: Harper & Row, 1974), p. 146.
2. *Ibid.,* pp. 142–143.
3. Spring, *op. cit.,* pp. 4–5. Lynn White's account is in "Continuing the Conversation," in *Western Man and Environmental Ethics,* ed. Ian Barbour (Reading, Mass.: Addison Wesley, 1973), p. 55.
4. Lynn White, Jr., "The Historical Roots of Our Ecologic Crisis," in Spring, *op. cit.,* pp. 19–20.
5. *Ibid.,* pp. 22–23.
6. Paul Bohannan and Philip Curtin, *Africa and the Africans,* rev. ed. (New York: Natural History Press, 1971), p. 173.
7. Quoted in John S. Mbiti, "African Religion and Its Contribution to World Order," *Whole Earth Papers,* n.d. no. 16, p. 31.
8. Ake Hultkrantz, *The Religions of the American Indians,* trans. Monica Setterwall (Berkeley: University of California Press, 1979), p. 15.
9. J. Mooney, "The Ghost-Dance Religion and the Sioux Outbreak of 1890," *Annual Report of the Bureau of American Ethnology,* 1896, 14, no. 2, p. 721. Quoted in Hultkrantz, *op. cit.,* p. 54.
10. Christopher Vecsey, "American Indian Environmental Religions," in *American Indian*

Environments: Ecological Issues in Native American History, eds. Christopher Vecsey and Robert W. Venables (Syracuse: Syracuse University Press, 1980), pp. 8–37.

11. *Ibid.,* p. 21.
12. *Ibid.*
13. This argument is made by Calvin Martin in *Keepers of the Game: Indian-Animal Relationships and the Fur Trade* (Berkeley: University of California Press, 1978).
14. From *Sutrakratanga,* I:1–3. Adapted from *Sources of Indian Tradition,* vol 11., ed. William Theodore de Bary (New York: Columbia University Press, 1958), p. 57.
15. Adapted from de Bary, *op. cit.,* p. 359.
16. Mark Elvin, *The Pattern of the Chinese Past* (Stanford: Stanford University Press, 1973), p. 129.
17. Quoted in Yi-Fu Tuan, "Discrepancies Between Environmental Attitude and Behaviour: Examples from Europe and China," *Canadian Geographer,* 12, no. 3 (1968). Quoted in Spring, *op. cit.,* p. 107.
18. *Ibid.,* p. 93.
19. Kakuzo Okakura, *The Book of Tea* (New York: Dover, 1964), p. 54. Okakura's charming little introduction to the Orient was first published in 1906.
20. *Ibid.*
21. Quoted in Spring, *op. cit.,* pp. 26–27.
22. Quoted in Ernest L. Tuveson, *Millennium and Utopia* (Berkeley: University of California Press, 1949), p. 84.
23. Adapted from Lewis Mumford, *Technics and Civilization* (New York: Harcourt Brace Jovanovich, 1962), p. 49.
24. Fazlur Rahman, *Islam and Modernity* (Chicago: University of Chicago Press, 1982).
25. Quoted in Elvin, *op. cit.,* p. 226.
26. *Ibid.,* pp. 226–227.
27. Willard J. Peterson, "Fang I-Chih: Western Learning and the 'Investigation of Things'," in *The Unfolding of Neo-Confucianism,* ed. William Theodore de Bary (New York: Columbia University Press, 1970), p. 379.
28. Quoted in Elvin, *op. cit.,* p. 231.
29. *Ibid.,* p. 232.

Chronological Table of
The Traditional World

500–1500

Europe	Middle East and Africa	China	Japan
Barbarian invasions 300–600			
Constantinople counters barbarians with heavy cavalry 300–600			
Justinian 527–565			Late Yamato period 552–710
Byzantine "theme system" under Heraclius 610–641	Muhammad 570–632	Sui dynasty 589–618	Importation of Buddhism and Chinese civilization 550–800
Development of cavalry in West 600–900	Hegira 622	Tang dynasty 618–907	
Battle of Tours, Muslims contained to Spain 733	Muslim expansion 632–738 Umayyad Caliphate 661–750	Height of Changan Eighth century	
Coronation of Charlemagne 800		Li Bo ˋ 701–762	Nara period 710–784
	Abbasid Caliphate 750–932		Heian period at Kyōto 794–1185
Viking invasions 793–1066	Buyids replace Abbasids 932–1062		

c. = circa (about)   d. = died   f. = founded   r. = ruled

(continued)

Europe	Middle East and Africa	China	Japan
	Ibn Sina 980–1037 Ibn Hazm 994–1064	Northern Song dynasty at Kaifeng 960–1127	Dominance of Fujiwara clan 866–1160
Height of feudalism 1000–1200		Printing Tenth century Wang Anshi 1021–1086	*Tale of Genji* and *Pillow Book* c. 1000
Cult of Virgin, chivalry, and courtly love 1050–1350			
Final schism with Rome 1054			
First Crusade 1096–1099	Berber Almoravids conquer Ghana 1076		
Second Crusade 1147–1149	Saladin 1138–1193	Southern Song at Hangzhou 1127–1279 Zhu Xi 1130–1200	Kamakura 1185–1333
Third Crusade 1189–1192			
Fourth Crusade 1202–1204			Feudalism After 1185
Constantinople sacked 1204		Chinggis Khan 1162–1227	Age of military lords (shogun), warriors (samurai), and Zen Buddhism 1200–1500
Ulrich von Lichtenstein 1204	Delhi Sultanate 1206–1526	Kublai Khan 1260–1290	
Saint Francis of Assisi 1182–1226	Mali Empire 1230–1400	Marco Polo visits Hangzhou 1275	Mongols attack Japan 1274, 1281

c. = circa (about)   *d. = died*   *f. = founded*   *r. = ruled*

Europe	Middle East and Africa	China	Japan
Saint Thomas Aquinas 1225–1274			
Roger Bacon 1214–1294			
Dante 1265–1321			
Giotto 1276–1337		Mongol Yüan dynasty 1279–1368	Height of feudalism 1300–1600
Petrarch 1304–1374	Mansa Musa r. 1312–1337		
Black Death 1348–1350		Ming dynasty 1368–1644	Ashikaga 1336–1467
Printing press 1450	King Ewuare of Benin r. 1440–1473	Ming maritime expeditions 1405–1433	
Leonardo 1452–1519			
Capture of Constantinople by Turks 1453	Songhai Empire 1450–1591		
Dürer 1471–1528			
Michelangelo 1475–1564		Wang Yangming 1472–1529	
Copernicus 1473–1543			
Sir Francis Bacon 1561–1627			
Galileo 1564–1642			
Descartes 1596–1650		Fang Yizhi 1611–1671	

c. = circa (about)   *d. = died*   *f. = founded*   *r. = ruled*

❀ Credits ❀

TEXT

13, 20 Excerpts from Frances Dahlberg, ed., *Women the Gatherer,* reprinted by permission of Yale University Press. Copyright © 1981. The excerpt on page 20 is from "Mbuti Womanhood" by Colin Turnbull, reprinted in Dahlberg, *op. cit.* **20, 21** Turnbull quotes are from *The Forest People,* copyright 1961 by Colin M. Turnbull. Reprinted by permission of Simon & Schuster, Inc. **28, 39, 138, 139, 141, 144, 145, 315–316, 325–326** Mumford quotes are from *The City in History,* 1961. Reprinted by permission of Harcourt Brace Jovanovich. **37** Free verse translation from the Laws of Manu appears in *The Wonder That Was India* by A. L. Basham. Reprinted by permission of Sidgewick & Jackson Ltd. **44** Quote from Aristophanes' *The Acharnians* reprinted with the permission of New American Library and William Arrowsmith and Douglass Parker. **112** Excerpt from *The Iliad* by Homer, trans. Andrew Lang, Walter Leaf, and Ernest Myers, reprinted with permission of *The World's Great Classics,* © 1969, Grolier Inc. **114** Excerpt from *A World History,* Third Edition, by William H. McNeill. Copyright © Oxford University Press, Inc. 1967, 1971, 1979. Reprinted by permission. **118** From *The Satyricon* by Petronius, translated by William Arrowsmith. Copyright © 1959 by William Arrowsmith. Reprinted by arrangement with NAL Penguin Inc., New York, New York. **121–122, 124** Buddhist story and aphorism excerpted from *Sources of Indian Tradition,* William Theodore de Bary, ed. Copyright © 1958 Columbia University Press. Used by permission. **137, 299**   Toynbee quotes are from *Cities of Destiny,* Arnold Toynbee, ed., 1967. Reprinted by permission of Thames and Hudson Ltd. Selections from "Changan" by Arthur F. Wright and "Alexander Under the Ptolemies" by Claire Preaux are reprinted by permission of Thames and Hudson Ltd. **146, 147, 148, 149**   Thapar quotes are from *A History of India,* vol. I, by Romila Thapar, 1966. Reproduced by permission of Penguin Books Ltd., London. **160, 161, 163, 165, 170, 178, 279–280, 282**   Quotes and paraphrased text from Morton Hunt's *The Natural History of Love,* 1959, 1987, are reprinted by permission of Morton Hunt. Copyright 1987 by Morton Hunt. **226–228**   Passages from Ovid's *The Art of Love,* trans. Rolfe Humphries, are reprinted by permission of Indiana University Press. **262–263**   Muslim poem appears in *The Medieval World* by Friedrich Heer. Reprinted by permission of Harper & Row, Publishers, Inc. **278**   Troubadour poem and lyrics are from *The Women Troubadours* by Meg Bogin, 1976. Reprinted by permission of Meg Bogin. **299**   Li Po poem appears in *The Poetry and Career of Li Po,* trans. Arthur Waley. Reprinted by permission of Macmillan. **331, 332**   Quotes from "The Historical Roots of Our Ecologic Crisis" by Lynn White, Jr., which originally appeared in *Science,* 155 (10 March 1967), are reprinted by permission of *Science.* Copyright 1967 by the American Association for the Advancement of Science. **336**   Jain poem and Hindu song are from *Sources of Indian Tradition,* William Theodore de Bary, ed. Copyright © 1958 Columbia University Press. Used by permission.

MAPS

4–5, 100–101, 237, 260–261, 308–309   Centers of Domestication, The Spread of Religions, The Barbarian Invasions of Europe: Fourth to Sixth Centuries, The Crusades: 1096–1204, and Islamic Cities and Afro-Eurasian Unity. Adapted from the *Times Concise Atlas of World History,* ed. Geoffrey Barraclough, Times Books Ltd., London, 1982, 1986, pp. 7, 26–27, 40–41, 43, 58–59. **57, 59**   Sumerian Ur: The Walled City and Opened Life, and Egyptian Akhetaton: Open Spaces and Imperial Order. Maps taken from *History of Mankind: Cultural and Scientific Developments, Volume I: Prehistory and the Beginning of Civilization,* Part I by Jacquetta Hawkes and Sir Leonard Wooley, George Allen & Unwin, 1963. UNESCO 1963. Reproduced by permission of UNESCO. **129, 140**   Athens, *c.* Fifth Century B.C., and Imperial Rome. Redrawn by permission of Macmillan Publishing Co., Inc., from *The Western Heritage,* Volume I by Donald Kagan, Frank M. Turner, and Steven E. Ozment. Copyright © 1979 Macmillan Publishing Co., Inc. **134**   Alexandria Under the Ptolemies. From *Cities of Destiny,* edited by Arnold Toynbee. © 1967 Thames and Hudson Ltd. **298**   Tang China and Changan A.D. 700. From Hilda Hookham's *A Short History of China.* Copyright © 1969, 1970 The Longman Group Ltd. By permission of the Longman Group Limited. The Changan map is used by permission of the British Library.

Index